TELLING OUR STORIES

ORAL AND FAMILY HISTORY

A Bibliography

5TH EDITION

Mary M. Flekke

HERITAGE BOOKS
2011

HERITAGE BOOKS
AN IMPRINT OF HERITAGE BOOKS, INC.

Books, CDs, and more—Worldwide

For our listing of thousands of titles see our website
at
www.HeritageBooks.com

Published 2011 by
HERITAGE BOOKS, INC.
Publishing Division
100 Railroad Ave. #104
Westminster, Maryland 21157

Copyright © 2011 Mary M. Flekke

All rights reserved. No part of this book may be reproduced or transmitted in any form or by any means, electronic or mechanical, including photocopying, recording or by any information storage and retrieval system without written permission from the author, except for the inclusion of brief quotations in a review.

International Standard Book Numbers
Paperbound: 978-0-7884-5340-3
Clothbound: 978-0-7884-8820-7

Table of Contents

Acknowledgements	iii
Oral History	1
Quick Tips for Oral History	7
Oral History Books	9
Heritage Photography	38
Heritage Photography Books	40
Tracing Your Family Tree: Beginning Genealogy	53
Genealogy Tips	57
Genealogy Books	59
Genealogical Resource Books	106
Localized Genealogical Resource Books	161
United States & Canada	161
International	225
Legal Resource Books	264
Writing Your Story	268
Writing, Bookmaking and Publishing Books	271
Preservation Books	291
Odds and Ends	301
Journals	317
Oral History	317
Archive, Family History, Preservation	317
Genealogy	318

Archival, Genealogical and Oral History Organizations	321
Archival, Family History, and Genealogy Publishers	345
Archival and Genealogical Supply Sources	349
Photograph Copying and Restoration Services	353
Scrapbooking Resources	354
Archives, Genealogical Societies, Libraries, Vital Records	356
United States Agencies	356
International Agencies	445
Archives General Interest	502
Genealogy/Oral History Sites Web Sites	502
Preservation, Family Albums, and Scrapbooking	510
Genealogical Software	512
Microforms & Miscellaneous Information Sources	516
Genealogical Services	519
Form Services	520
Archives and Genealogical Listservs	520

Acknowledgements

A number of people have been of great assistance during this project with faith, help and devotion. I would especially like to thank my mother, Muriel Flekke for her belief in my abilities; without her strength and perseverance I would not be where I am today. I would also like to thank Carl and Patty Kaltreider, Carol Durham, Kristen Storms and Jennifer Gardner for their assistance at the local libraries when I needed an extra pair of hands, Nora Galbraith for assistance with Inter-Library loan (ILL), Eridan Thompson, and everyone else who has been there for me. I would especially like to thank the Venice, Selby, Tampa, Orlando, and Jacksonville Public Libraries and Polk County Genealogical and Historical Library of Florida and the Minneapolis Public Library System of Minnesota for the use of their collections which saved me waiting for many items to come via the ILL process and their kindnesses in helping us to locate difficult to find items on the shelves. I would also like to thank my editors, the Rev. Carl F. Kaltreider and the Rev. Carol A. Solovitz.

Oral History

Oral history began as oral tradition, the passing down of information from generation to generation. Today, we commit nearly everything to "paper." However, there are places in the world where the passing of history is still truly an oral tradition. Within our own families, oral tradition is the main way most of us retain our favorite family stories. Unfortunately, by not recording these stories, they frequently undergo changes as they pass from parent to child, also, with the advent of technology and the decline of the extended family, these family stories are rapidly being lost.

From its inception, oral history is the term for the generation of significant historical data from interviews with men and women who have unique or firsthand knowledge as participants or observers of historical events.[1] The chartering of your organization, the building of your church building, a family celebration or other major events may be tucked in the memories of some of the older members of an organization or family. Reminiscences serve to fill in gaps that paper documents do not cover. Many people are just waiting to be asked for their memories, and get excited when asked to participate in an oral history project. I talked to one of our older church members and he remembers the move from the old building to our present facility which took place in 1956. He started spouting information and there I stood without paper and pencil, much less a tape recorder! All it takes is the right question and you hit a gold mine. Always have paper and pencils handy when talking to people you intend to interview, information may escape in idle conversation. People interviewed about the same event may also come up with conflicting stories. If this happens, try to get at least three sources for your story. This should provide at least a "majority" slant on the story.

Stone tablets and chisel, papyrus and stylus, paper and pencil, reel-to-reel tapes, cassette tapes, and video tape have all been used in the recording of oral history, and CD-ROM, DVD, and the Internet are becoming more popular, though the qualifications and legalities of the Internet are currently being debated. Two formats that we have most commonly available to us are audio and video tapes.

Audiotape is probably the easiest format for most people, as not everyone has access to video cameras, and video editing facilities. Tape recording

---

[1] Donald Ritchie, Doing Oral History (Twayne Publishers, 1995).

equipment has changed drastically in recent years! The two that are the most common are the cassette recorder and the mini or micro cassette recorder. Even with these, transcription is much easier if you have a transcribing machine or a Dictaphone. If you have to do your own transcription, a cassette recorder with its larger buttons is easier to work with. For storage purposes, the micro cassettes are wonderful, they take up very little space and even with paper transcriptions, and the tape should be retained.

Many people are microphone shy. If they are, the micro cassette is probably your best friend. It usually has a built in microphone, so that you do not have that extra piece of equipment staring the interviewee in the face. Though most books and many professional interviewers still recommend the 'detached' microphone as giving better sound quality, improvements in technology have made the micro cassette recorder a much improved instrument.

Videotape provides an attractive product if you have access to the equipment and editing facilities. You get not only the interview, but a record of what the interviewee looked like. If you have access to a college campus, or know someone who runs a photo shop with video capabilities, they may be willing to help you edit the film into a cleaner, less choppy version. If you are not a professional interviewer, the experience will be somewhat "choppy."

The interview itself is basically a three step process. Arranging for the interview with the person to be interviewed; researching and preparing for the interview; and then actually conducting the interview.

When arranging for interviews, you first have to decide who you want to interview, and the purpose of the interview. The purpose will drive who you select to be interviewed. If you are looking to fill in the history of your church congregation, you would probably want to identify its oldest members, those who have been there the longest. If you are aware of medical or health problems, you might want to make those people a priority.

Personal contact with people is important. Advertising in a newsletter will only bring out a few of the most interested persons. As with most of us, people tend to be flattered when you seek them out on an individual basis to ask for their assistance. Pursue them in the manner in which you are most comfortable, a letter explaining the project might be sent with a note that you will be phoning shortly to set up an interview time, or a make a phone call to set up a time. You will find that as soon as you start discussing the project, the memories will start to flow. Be sure to have a paper and pencil handy to take notes; this will help you in developing questions for the interview.

If your family, church, or organization has done a written history for a prior anniversary celebration, read these, they will help you to generate questions for the interview. Old minutes, committee reports, directories, photos, worship bulletins, scrapbooks, and special mailings, will all provide materials from which to construct a basic questionnaire. Check with other family members, the secretary, the pastor, or the archivist if you have one in a church or organization, to see about looking at the old files.

Be sure you keep a pen and paper handy during the interview, questions will occur stemming from a random comment and you will probably want to come back to them later. Do not try to rely on your memory, a really interesting interviewee will probably make you forget half of what you intended to ask if it is not written down.

If the interviewee is intimidated by the tape recorder or video camera, chat a while with the recording equipment running until they forget about it or seem comfortable in its presence. If using a cassette tape, keep the machine close enough so that you can see when your tape is running low, there is nothing worse than getting to a real interesting story, only to realize that you ran out of tape three minutes ago. If you have a microphone independent from the machine itself, *do not* play with it, this will create extraneous noise on the tape. Cushion it on a piece of foam or soft cloth so table noises are not picked up by the microphone.

Before starting the actual interview, record your name, the interviewee's name, the place and time of the interview on the tape. If you feel self-conscious doing this, do it before the interviewee arrives. Simply say at the beginning of the tape, my name is ....and I will be interviewing ....and get them to give their own name. Then identify the place and time.

Remember, you are mainly a listener, not part of the story. The interviewer must try to keep the interviewee on track, and try to avoid tangents unless they are related to the topic at hand, though sometimes they do generate potential questions. Avoid getting into conversations such as comparing experiences. This is the interviewee's history, not yours! Keep comments other than direct questions to a minimum.

Do not try to interview too many people at one time. One is optimum, but if they come as a couple, do not let them talk at the same time! If necessary, explain to them prior to the interview that they "should please, not talk at the same time!" Trying to transcribe more than one person talking at a time is almost impossible! Also, carefully select the environment; find a quiet place for the interview. Places with interruptions, traffic going by, or doors creaking, do NOT work. Extraneous sounds are all magnified on tape. **DO NOT, ABSOLUTELY DO NOT,** tap your pencil. If you do not do your own transcription, your transcriber will kill you!

Each interview will be unique. The traditional question routine is always safe - Who, What, Where, When and How - but make sure you ask open ended questions to elicit a full response. Questions with only yes and no answers lead to frustrating, unproductive interviews. Try to get them to tell you a story. Avoid generalities, stick with specifics. If you are using photographs as a conversation piece, try to verbally identify the photo in some way or make a note on a piece of paper to be kept with the tape describing the content of the photo. Show the interviewee you are interested in what they are saying; interject remarks that will draw out more information without taking over the conversation.

Use props when possible or necessary - photos, documents, scrapbooks, letters, etc. - to generate conversation. Photos are especially good at bringing back memories. But as was mentioned before, be sure to note the item discussed so that it may be identified later during the transcription process.

Do not turn off your recorder prematurely. If you have tape left, let it run until the interviewee leaves. It seems like as soon as you shut it off, the interviewee all of a sudden launches into another story, probably the best one of the afternoon! If the tape runs out, stop the conversation to turn it over. (60 minute tapes are recommended, the tape is more durable. 90 to 120 minute tapes are thinner and can "bleed" through if stored too long.) Try not to go longer than an hour or so, with one person. Talking for too long can be tiring, especially for older persons. A second session can be scheduled if you don't get finished, and a review of the first hour's interview may generate further questions. A good idea, when using audio tape, is to take a photo of the person interviewed, that way if the oral history is going to be used for publication later, you will have a picture to put with the text.

There are a couple of ways in which to process your interview. One is to index the tape by topic. This gives the user a basic outline of what the interview was about. If your recorder has a number counter, you can list the location on the tape where each topic occurs. (Not all recorders are identical, so the numbers may be off slightly if the same machine is not used for playback each time.)

The most popular form of transcription is the verbatim, word for word copy. This usually takes about five hours per one hour of tape if you are an experienced transcriber. Getting someone with a Dictaphone to transcribe is helpful, however, you still need to go through and listen and read what is transcribed. A transcriber who was not there for the interview may have trouble hearing exactly what was said. If difficult names are mentioned during the interview, note them and ask the interviewee for the spelling, this will save both you and the transcriber time later. It is also a nice gesture, and some interviewees may request it, to send them a copy of the transcript for review. They might want to revise or add something in a further interview.

There are several different directions you can go with your interviews once you have them in hand. You can do special interest articles for a newsletter, or a genealogical publication if you happen to be a member of such a society in your area, you can flesh out a family, church or organization's history with personal accounts of the family or membership, or you could write a book. Probably the major difficulty in putting together a historical document from interviews will be the fact that people remember events differently or interpret them differently, and some of their memories may differ accordingly, making the actual writing of a history somewhat difficult. The final products of oral history interviews are limited only by your imagination.

One of the things that you must be careful of when doing oral histories is copyright. Technically, each person owns her/his own history. Just because they taped it at your institution does not necessarily mean you can do anything you want with it. In effect, you have a wealth of information, but it can't really be used. Common sense tells us that a narration cannot be altered in such a way as to change the meaning of what was said, even with permission to publish. It is VERY important to have the interviewee sign a release form allowing you or the receiving institution the freedom to utilize the information you have just received. Numbers of books about oral history methodology include sample legal consent or sample deed of gift forms that can be utilized for obtaining permission to use the interviews. Some are very detailed and some quite general. Try to envision what your end product might be so as to cover all contingencies when asking your interviewee to sign a release form.

The following annotated bibliography provides a list of many of the books published on how to do oral histories, genealogies, and how to write up the end product, several by authors who are very prominent in this field. While this list is by no means complete, it provides information on books that are relatively easy to use and easy to access. In addition to instructions on how to make the most of your genealogical searching, most of the genealogy books also list many more addresses and contacts for source information than could be included here. Many of these are held by libraries and archival societies across the country. Each year oral history and genealogy become more and more popular as families, individuals, and organizations realize they are losing touch with their history and heritages. As a result, several of the books on the list are being revised and new guides and resources are being published in quantity. Another resource to consider when looking for guidance is the local history society. Many of these publish in-house guides to assist local amateur historians in researching family histories and in preserving their family treasures.

Reprinted with permission from Bob Thaves.

Oral History Tips:

1. Determine the purpose of and topic of the discussion.
2. Determine the person(s) to be interviewed.
3. Make arrangements for the interview and obtain the cooperation of the interviewee.
4. Research the background of the person (and topic) you are interviewing.
5. Compile a list of questions; *do not ask "yes/no" questions.*
    - Who, What, Where, When, Why and How
    - pursue anecdotes, descriptions
    - Remain neutral, do not argue with the interviewee.
6. Know how to operate your equipment - tape recorders or video cameras.
    - Use 60 minute cassette or microcassette tapes
    - Make sure completed tapes are labeled
7. Allow your subject to become comfortable with the equipment with a few 'easy' questions before getting too in-depth.
8. Do your interviewing in a quiet environment.
    - Try to restrict the interview to one person at a time if possible.
    - Do not tap pencils or fingers while listening to the interviewee.
    - Do not interrupt unless the person is getting off on a non-essential tangent.
9. Take notes of ideas that come up during the interview that you might want to pursue later.
    - Make a note of unfamiliar names/words so you can check spelling.
10. Do not tire your interviewee, you can always schedule a second or third interview later.

11. Take photos or other memorabilia to the interview as a memory stimulant.
    - Be sure to describe the photo, etc. for the tape; it cannot see what you are looking at!
12. Get a signed release form at the first interview.
13. Transcribe tapes.
14. Review the transcription, arrange for the narrator to review the transcription also.
15. Deposit corrected transcripts, tapes, and release forms in the appropriate library, archives or historical society.

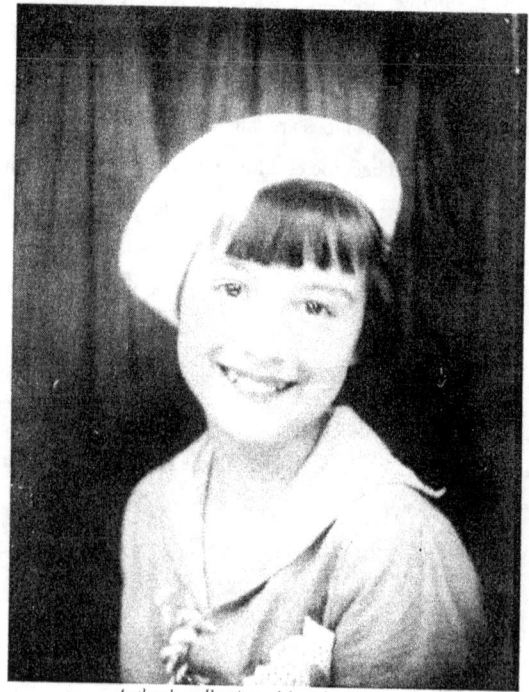

Author's collection: Muriel - circa mid-1930s

Oral History Books

Akeret, Robert U. *Family Tales, Family Wisdom: How to Gather the Stories of a Lifetime and Share Them with Your Family.* New York: Henry Holt and Company, 1991.

Family gatherings are a time not only of joyous gathering and community, but an opportunity to gather treasured memories and stories of one's past. Dr. Akeret explains the process of using memory effectively by utilizing triggers such as old photos, letters, passports, ticket stubs, and other memorabilia collected throughout a lifetime. He provides ten possible scenarios for different family story telling sessions as ways to organize your family's memories. He also discusses his 'Elder Tale Program' for about half the book using examples of family stories of his own.

Alessi, Jean and Jan Miller. *Once Upon a Memory: Your Family Tales and Treasures.* White Hall, VA: Betterway Publications, 1987.

Alessi and Miller present techniques to help recall and discover long-past memories. Structured as a series of "memories and tips," the memories list questions to assist in garnering information and the tips suggest various activities to assist in the practical aspects of family research such as how to obtain records and vital statistics. The memory questions can be easily used for putting together an oral history interview.

Allen, Barbara and William L. Montell. *From Memory to History: Using Oral Sources in Local Historical Research.* Nashville, TN: American Association for State and Local History, 1981.

The goal of this publication is to take the oral histories you have taped and guide you through the evaluation and writing process. It deals with using local history, to evaluate oral histories, testing for validity, recognizing folkloristic elements, personal and group bias, corroboration from written sources, physical artifacts, identifying attitudes about the past, community values and beliefs embodied in nonfactual accounts and suggestions for incorporating oral histories into written manuscripts.

Arthur, Stephen and Julia Arthur. *Your Life and Times: How to Put a Life Story on Tape: An Oral History Handbook.* 5th printing. Baltimore, MD: Genealogical Publishing, 1986, 1997.

This work is basically an outline for taping an oral history of a person's life. It offers a step by step guide in the introduction and follows up with sample questions on almost any aspect of a person's life. The appendix offers a helpful list for those doing further research into family histories.

Atkinson, Robert. *The Life Story Interview.* Thousand Oaks, CA: Sage Publications, Inc., 1998, 2000.

Prior to discussing interview techniques, Atkinson talks about the classic functions of stories, the research uses, the generation of data, and the art and science of life story interviewing. He examines the potential benefits of pursuing oral history and sharing your stories with your descendents, as well as discussing the interview process, getting the information you wish, the questions to ask, and the transcription process and interpreting of the information received in the interview when you are finished.

Baum, Willa K. *Oral History for the Local Historical Society.* Nashville, TN: American Association for State and Local History, 1995.

Revised many times, this text has become the "bible" for the oral historian. Giving step-by-step instructions on every facet of the oral interview process, this work is a must read for the budding oral historian. Beginning with an introduction explaining oral history, it goes on to describe in detail how to start an oral history program, choose equipment, how to do the interview process, who should interview, tips for interviewers, indexing, transcription, agreements on use, ethics, preservation of interviews, use of materials, and developing expertise.

---. *Transcribing and Editing Oral History.* Walnut Creek, CA: AltaMira Press, 1991.

Intended for nonprofessionals, this covers the four basic steps of oral history: creating, processing, curating, and using. Dealing with the processing end, Baum contends that non-transcribed tapes have little scholarly value, she discusses the process of transcribing and editing recorded interviews, and touches briefly on the other three stages as they apply.

Beck, Jane C. and Gregory Sharrow. *Recording Words: Collecting Oral History and the Art of Interviewing: "I'm a Storyteller. I'm Not a Writer."* Middlebury, VT: Vermont Folklife Center, 1994.

Oral history is in a sense, the writer putting the storyteller's words down on paper. Many people can tell stories, but they cannot always write them down, an oral historian is needed to take these stories and make them available. Beck and Sharrow present a brief, logical methodology for gathering oral history. Choosing a topic, person, equipment, developing interview skills, gathering background materials, setting up an interview and the interview process are all discussed. Hints for developing the interview, what to do with it when it is completed, and a sample interview are included. Discussions of transcription techniques are included as are sample release forms, questions, and a list of oral history organizations.

Biagi, Shirley. *Interviews That Work: A Practical Guide for Journalists.* 2nd ed. Belmont, CA: Wadsworth Publishing Co., 1992.

Though geared toward journalists, this book offers suggestions on finding the best sources and preparing for the interview. It also describes the best way to take notes, how to get answers from reluctant interviewees, how to deal with ethical problems and how to handle 'off-the-record-material.' Biagi interviewed forty-six expert journalists for their expertise in the interview process.

Bi-Folkal Productions. *A Time Machine Called Memory.* Videocassette. Madison, WI: Bifolkal Productions, Inc., 1992.

A Time Machine Called Memory is the introduction to a series of kits structured to trigger the memories of senior citizens. Each kit contains a media presentation, a programming guide, artifacts, music, and questions geared to trigger memories of the past. The kits may be used in senior centers, classrooms, by adults, children, or anyone interested in finding the memories of their parents or friends. Materials included in the kits are planned to recreate memories and include anyone who might be present for the program. These kits may be used to generate oral histories or family histories for those looking for family history and genealogical information. Individual video and kit topics include such events as birthdays, family picnics, Christmas, New Years, 4th of July and many other topically oriented videos.

Brady, John. *The Craft of Interviewing.* New York: Vintage Books, 1977.

This is a readable book on how to do interviews. Chapters are organized to provide a step-by-step process for the reader, Getting Interviews, Doing Research, Face to Face, Popping the Questions, Getting Tough, Off the Record, Notes on Note taking, Tape Recording,

Hazardous Zones, Written and Phone Interviews, It's Over, and Pasting it Together. Within the table of contents, each of the chapters has a brief description that tells what that chapter discusses.

Brecher, Jeremy. *History from Below: How to Uncover and Tell the Story of Your Community, Association, or Union.* New Haven, CT: Commonwork Pamphlets/Advocate Press, 1986, 1995.

This is a how-to guide for people who are not professional historians, but who want to explore the history of their own community, workplace, or local organization. It will assist one in designing a project with the time and resources that are available to the average person, how to collect documents, and how to do interviews. It also discusses how to put together the materials gathered and how to present them.

Brown, Cynthia S. *Like It Was: A Complete Guide to Writing Oral History.* New York: Teachers & Writers Collaborative, 1988.

Written for anyone age twelve and up, this is a how-to guide written by a teacher who works with oral history. It gives clear, specific advice on using a tape recorder, conducting the interview, transcribing, editing, writing short pieces, writing full biography, writing from multiple narratives, and publishing the results. Easily read and not overly long.

Burley-Allen, Madelyn. *Listening, The Forgotten Skill: A Self-Teaching Guide.* New York: John Wiley & Sons, Inc., 1995, 2007.

Discussing listening skills, this book includes tips on not only how to be an effective listener, but on how to ask the kind of questions that elicit useful responses. This is also available as of 2007 as an online or recorded book publication.

Capturing the Past: How to Prepare and Conduct an Oral History Interview. (Video or DVD) Provo, UT: Brigham Young University, 1997, 2007.

Narrated by two Brigham Young students, this 31 minute tape discusses techniques and tips for doing oral history. Showing examples of oral history, and with an enclosed brochure summarizing the tape, this is an easy to understand demonstration of what you will be doing. This video was mastered to DVD in 2007.

Case, Patricia Ann. *How to Write Your Autobiography: Preserving Your Family Heritage.* Santa Barbara, CA: Woodbridge Press, 1977, 1995.

    While this book is primarily geared toward writing an autobiography, it also presents a good base for the person putting together an interview to do an oral history. Most of the writing tips given make smooth transitions to a spoken format. Especially valuable are the extensive lists of questions which can be tailored easily to an oral history.

Caudill, Orley B. *The Spoken Word: A Manual for Oral Historians.* Hattiesburg, MS: Caudill, 1975.

    Beginning with a rather extensive and technical history of oral history and how to design an oral history program, Caudill moves into legal aspects and sample forms for not only obtaining the rights to the interview, but also letters involving the etiquette of setting up and concluding the interview process. Dr. Caudill includes suggestions for the interviewer, the transcriber and for the interviewee. A couple of sample interviews are included. The first three chapters are fairly technical, but the last chapters are easy to follow and very practical for oral history instruction.

Caunce, Stephen. *Oral History and the Local Historian.* London, UK: Longman Group UK, Ltd., 1994.

    This book was not designed to be a manual for oral history, but rather a menu from which you can pick what you need to assist in your oral history project. Oral history means slightly different things to different people, and each has his own methods, it is primarily a means of filling historical gaps. Mr. Caunce discusses the definition of oral history and how it relates to people, places, lifestyles, language, alternative histories and contemporary themes. He also goes over the basics of how to do an oral history, and the gathering of materials and doing transcription. Suggestions for how to use oral histories are also a part of his work as are listings of further readings in the field.

Chapin, Alice Zillman. *Reaching Back: A Workbook for Recording Your Life's Most Meaningful Moments to Share With Future Generations.* Cincinnati, OH: Betterway Books, 1996.

    Writing *Reaching Back* from a sense of loss in realizing that there were many things her mother shared that she could no longer remember and could no longer ask, Chapin presents a book of questions that form an automatic oral history project that one can pick up and do with their family. Beginning with a series of interview tips, the rest of the book is pages of questions that span a lifetime of experiences with room for clippings or photos, to make this an heirloom for your family.

Charlton, Thomas L., Lois E. Myers, and Rebecca Sharpless, eds. *Handbook of Oral History.* Lanham, MD: AltaMira Press, 2006, 2008.

The *Handbook of Oral History* is a combination of practical and theoretical guidance to the discipline of oral history written by leaders in the discipline. Chapters cover the history of oral history; oral history as evidence; research design and strategies; legal and ethical issues; interview development; oral history and archives; transcribing and editing; memory theory; aging, the life course, African American narratives of struggle, social change and decline; analytical approach to interviewing; woman's oral history; narrative theory; publishing oral history; biography and oral history; oral history based performance; and sound and moving image documentation. The goal of the authors is to provide a manual of benefit to both professional oral historians and members of the general public who have an interest in oral history. Each chapter also includes notes and further references and there is a complete list of references at the end.

Croom, Emily A.. *Unpuzzling Your Past: A Basic Guide to Genealogy.* 4th ed. Cincinnati, OH: Betterway Books, 2001.

Included in *Unpuzzling Your Past* is a chapter on the basic techniques of oral history. Other chapters also include information that is useful in collecting and identifying questions to ask in discovering your past history, as well as helpful questions.

Curtiss, Richard D., et. al., eds. *A Guide for Oral History Programs.* Fullerton, CA: California State University Oral History Program and Southern California Local History Council, 1973.

The choice and use of equipment, researching the interview, interviewing techniques, and legal considerations are discussed in this publication.

Cutting-Baker, Holly, et. al. *Family Folklore Interviewing Guide and Questionnaire.* Washington, DC: U.S. Government Printing Office, 1978, 1990.

This is a basic guideline on how to conduct an oral history interview. An extended pamphlet, it has text and photos that guide one through the interview process. Questions and topics are suggested at the end. The pamphlet was written to accompany a traveling Smithsonian exhibition.

Davis, Cullom, et. al. *Oral History: From Tape to Type*. Chicago: American Library Association, 1977.

Covering all aspects of oral history, the final chapter entitled "Managing Oral History," is recommended as the most useful. This book functions as a workbook as well as a guide, with each chapter containing exercises that are intended to help the reader gain the necessary experience. A glossary of oral history terminology and 'rules of style' should be helpful in transcribing raw tapes.

Deering, Mary Jo and Barbara Pomeroy. *Transcribing Without Tears: A Guide to Transcribing and Editing Oral History Interviews*. Washington, D. C.: George Washington University Library, 1976.

This is a practical guide to direct someone through the transcription process. The book discusses various strategies for transcription and editing, i.e. verbatim as opposed to actually editing the text and gives samples of various interviews and their preliminary and final forms. Methods, policies, styles, accountability, final texts, and final product are all discussed. Guidelines and sample formats are included.

Douglas, Louise, Alan Roberts and Ruth Thompson. *Oral History: A Handbook*. Boston: Allen & Unwin, 1988.

While written from an Australian viewpoint, Douglas examines the development of oral history and the debate surrounding the uses of oral history. She also helps to guide the reader in the choice of recording equipment, the administration of oral history projects, and advice on interviewing techniques. She also demonstrates some uses for oral history and includes some forms for usage in documenting the histories.

Dunaway, David and Willa K. Baum, eds. *Oral History: An Interdisciplinary Anthology*. 2nd ed. Walnut Creek, CA: Alta Mira Press, 1996.

This anthology is comprised of articles collected from journals which cover various aspects of oral history research. Each article has a full bibliography which provides a key to all the writings on oral history up to 1995.

Epstein, Ellen Robinson and Rona Mendelsohn. *Record and Remember: Tracing Your Roots Through Oral History.* Washington, D. C.: Center for Oral History, 1978. Revised ed. 1994.

> The authors have provided a complete guide to all phases of preparing for, and conducting, an oral history. Topics include: the value of oral history, researching background information, conducting the interview, and using the cassette tape recorder and accessories (equipment has been improved immensely since this was published in 1978!) Interviews the authors have conducted are quoted throughout.

Ericson, Stacy. *A Field Notebook for Oral History.* 4th ed. Boise, ID: Idaho Oral History Center, Idaho State Historical Society, 2001.

> Published in a notebook in simple outline form, this guide presents basic information about the oral history process. Adapted from oral history workshops, it attempts to provide a step-by-step guide to procedures, techniques, problems, and organizational methods which have proved most useful to the workshop presenters. The notebook is intended to be used as a beginning guide to an oral history project, and should work well for the beginner or someone working alone. Arranged in three parts, it provides a simplified methodology to the Interview process, the Project, and the possible end uses for the project.

Everett, Stephen E. *Oral History: Techniques and Procedures.* Washington, DC: Center of Military History, 1992.

> Defined from the military point of view, Everett reviews the basics of oral history and presents a concise, easy to follow guide for conducting an oral history interview. While he covers some aspects that will not be applicable in a non-military setting, he covers all the usual procedures of preparation, interview, and transcription and use. He deals both with audio and video taping. Questions are suggested for the military background, and equipment is discussed.

Farber, Barry. *Making People Talk [Sound Recording].* Studio City, CA: Dove/William Morrow Books on Tape, 1987, 1994. (Also published as a book.)

> Talk show host Barry Farber shares professional anecdotes and offers advice on how to get people to talk and ask questions that reveal "what's special about them." Tips include: researching a person before a meeting if possible, asking for advice (everyone likes to give it,) and the importance of good listening. This book reads much like a novel, so is recommended for preliminary reading in oral history.

Finnegan, Ruth. *Oral Traditions and Verbal Arts: A Guide to Research Practices.* New York: Routledge, 1992.

>Finnegan takes an in-depth look at the nature of oral tradition and the methods used to record it.

--- and Michael Drake, eds. *Studying Family and Community History: 19th and 20th Centuries, Volume 1: From Family Tree to Family History.* Cambridge: Cambridge University Press, 1994.

>This four volume series is aimed at stimulating the development of personal research in family and community history. Volume one moves from a focus on individual families to the broader patterns of population, household structures, domestic economies, family relationships, and family myths. It has a brief section discussing oral history. Other volumes in the series include: *From Family History to Community, Communities and Families,* and *Sources and Methods for Family and Community Historians: A Handbook.*

Fletcher, William P. *Recording Your Family History: A Guide to Preserving Oral History With Videotape, Audiotape, Suggested Topics, and Questions, and Interview Techniques.* Berkeley, CA: Ten Speed Press, 1989.

>This is a step-by-step guide to creating an oral history of your family. It takes the interviewer through each stage of a person's life and provides sample questions to use or tailor to the interviewer's personal taste. The last chapters provide questions for ethnic groups and the introduction provides an overview on equipment and interview techniques.

---. *Talking Your Roots: A Family Guide to Tape Recording and Videotaping Oral History.* Washington, DC: Talking Your Roots, 1983.

>Though already several years old, this guide to creating a family oral biography, provides hundreds of pages of questions on a wide variety of subjects. In addition, it gives basic guidelines on the conduct of an oral history interview. Using this extensive list of questions, one could tailor a list to meet almost any family member's background and experience.

Frisch-Ripley, Karen. *Unlocking the Secrets in Old Photographs.* Salt Lake City, UT: Ancestry, 1990.

>In her straight-forward, personable book, Karen Frisch-Ripley illustrates the methods of detection that go into finding names to go

with the unidentified faces in your mother's photo album. She discusses the identification of photographs, the keeping of accurate records, utilizing public sources of information, recognizing the different types of photographs, the care and preservation of photographs, and how to locate family photos. Using her own family and photos as her subject, she sprinkles tips and 'how-tos' liberally throughout her text. Photos can be useful as conversation starters and triggers in oral history interviews.

Greene, Bob and D. G. Fulford. *To Our Children's Children: Preserving Family Histories for Generations to Come.* New York: Doubleday, 1993.

> This is a guidebook of questions that makes recording a personal history as easy as writing a letter. After a brief introduction the rest of the book consists of chapters of engaging questions designed to open the doors of memory.

— and —. *To Our Children's Children: Journal of Family Memories.* New York, Doubleday, 1995.

> This continuation of *To Our Children's Children*, contains 365 thought provoking questions, one for each day of the year, to assist families or individuals to build their life history stories.

Grele, Ronald J., ed. *Envelopes of Sound: Six Practitioners Discuss the Method, Theory, and Practice of Oral History and Oral Testimony.* Chicago: Precedent Pub., 1975.

> The purpose of this work is to introduce the reader to the methods and problems of oral history, and to discuss the larger and more theoretical issues of the practice, and to increase the reader's understanding of the nature of oral testimony and its use. It includes actual verbatim transcripts of interviews.

---, ed. *Envelopes of Sound: The Art of Oral History.* Revised ed. Westport, CT: Meckler, 1985,1991.

> A revised edition of Grele's work which introduces the reader to the methods and problems of oral history, and discusses the larger and more theoretical issues of the practice, and increases the reader's understanding of the nature of oral testimony and its use. It includes actual verbatim transcripts of interviews.

Guberman, Jayne K., ed. *In Our Own Voices: A Guide to Conducting Life History Interviews with American Jewish Women.* Brookline, MA: Jewish Women's Archive, 2005.

> The guide is laid out around 10 frameworks of topics – family, education, work, community service Jewish identities, home and place, leisure and culture, health and sexuality, women's identities, and history and world events. The guides function as the areas which are usually central to a woman's life. The first chapter of the work discusses how to get ready for and to conduct an oral history interview, discussing the choice of narrators, questions, choosing equipment, and doing research as well as other interview tips. Sample forms encompassing a pre-interview questionnaire, a preliminary release form, a final release form, an interview log and a proper word form are included in the appendices.

Gubrium, Jaber F. and James A. Holstein. *Handbook of Interview Research: Context & Method.* Thousand Oaks, CA: Sage Publications, 2002.

> An expensive book, more for professional interviewers than amateur, this book discusses several questions pertaining to the interview process. Some of these include how the interviewer and respondent view each other and how that affects the interview process, where do the questions and answers come from, how does the institutional auspices under which the interview is conducted affect the shape of the interview data, and others. Leading experts in the field of interviewing have contributed chapters examining the interview process in the age of information technology. Their articles provide information on the conceptual and methodological issues surrounding the interview process in relation to forms of interviewing, new technology, diverse data gathering and analytic strategies, and the various ways of interviewing in relation to diverse respondents. The forty-four chapters in this text discuss such topics as the history of the interview; the life story interview; interviewing children and adolescents, men and women; interviewing older people; interviewing the ill; interviewing in education; Internet interviewing; transcription quality; analysis of personal narratives; analytic strategies for oral history interviews; and elicitation techniques as well as many other interview related subjects.

Harris, Ramon I., et. al. *The Practice of Oral History: A Handbook.* Glen Rock, NJ: Microfilming Corp. Of America, 1975.

>This is a small, rather intense, how-to-do-it text on oral history. There is a good list at the back of helpful hints, and some good examples of release forms and interview record forms. Somewhat dated in discussion of equipment being already 23 years old, but the basic information on interviewing and research methods is sound.

Hart, Elisa. *Getting Started in Oral Traditions Research. Occasional Papers of the Prince of Wales Northern Heritage Centre, No. 4.* Yellowknife, NT: Government of the Northwest Territories, 1995.

>A manual written to teach video equipment skills and how to record interviews on video for people who wants to do their own research and interviewing but don't know how to get started. It outlines how to get started and suggestions for the finished project. This guide may be purchased from the Training Director at Inuit Broadcasting Corporation, Box 700, Iqaluit, NT, XOA 0H0, Fax (819)979-5853.

Hartley, William G. *The Everything Family Tree Book: Finding, Charting, and Preserving Your Family History.* 2nd ed. Holbrook, MA: Adams Media Corporation, 2006.

>Hartley's *Everything Family Tree Book*, is a comprehensive and easy to follow guide to putting together a family history; not just the family tree, but an entire history. Chapter five is a well written instruction on how to do an oral history, complete with a few sample questions, and information on equipment and the pros and cons of audio versus video interviews. Also included is a sample legal form, information on transcription and editing, and suggestions for the possible uses of the oral history.

---. *Preparing a Personal History.* Salt Lake City: Primer Publications, 1976.

>Hartley offers advice on the reasons for doing a personal history, types of history that can be created, how to file the information gathered, where and how to search for information, how to create a balanced history, what finishing touches you can add to make a difference in the final product and how to update a finished product. He also lists "memory triggers" for those who claim they have nothing to write about.

Havlice, Patricia P. *Oral History: A Reference Guide and Annotated Bibliography.* Jefferson, NC: McFarland, 1985.

> This volume is an annotated listing of both how-to and oral history books and journal articles. These works appeared in print from 1950 to late 1983.

Heffler, Ira. *How to Create a Video Biography: A Legacy for Your Family.* Lake Arrowhead, CA: Arrowhead Publishing, 1999.

> Most of us have seen photos of our grandparents, great-grandparents, and other relatives that we have never known personally, stories of them have been handed down from our parents, but many of us have never actually been able to talk to or hear their own stories. In his work *How to Create a Video Biography*, Heffler provides instructions and scripting for creating a video to pass down to our descendants. Videos are more personal and are able to convey more actual information than a scrapbook or photo album. A video reveals not only what the person looks like but what they sound like, it makes history truly alive. Heffler discusses the equipment, lighting, audio, how to create a good video, pre-tape hints, advice on what to wear, how to put the subject at ease, what to do in the pre-interview before taping, creating a profile sheet, how to direct the action, the actual taping process, the editing process, scripting for both adults and children, and the finished product. The scripts suggested by Heffler also provide numerous questions which would be useful for other oral history situations.

Henige, David P. *Oral Historiography.* New York: Longman, 1982.

> Geared more to those gathering oral history in Third World countries, this book nevertheless, discusses the methodological aspects of gathering and interpreting oral data. Chapter six focuses on issues such as validity, triviality, memory and confidentiality that oral historians must take into consideration. This is a book for the very serious researcher, who likes to do in-depth reading.

Hoopes, James. *Oral History: An Introduction for Students.* Chapel Hill: University of North Carolina Press, 1979.

> This 'how to' book was developed especially for students. It is a thorough guide for courses devoted entirely to oral history. Chapters tell how to conduct interviews, legal aspects of oral interviews and how to write up the interview later.

Howarth, Ken. *Oral History: A Handbook.* Gloucestershire, UK: Sutton Publishing, Ltd., 1998.

>The intent of this handbook is to provide a solid introduction to the principles of oral history. The concept of oral history has been around for many years, and has sometimes been done well, and sometimes not so well. Howarth's book is seeking to provide a more formal basis for a practice that has frequently been approached less than formally or professionally. In addition, he offers commentary on how it has been used in the various environments he discusses. Howarth discusses the definition of oral history; its value for the archive, library and museum; oral history for business, management and environmental planning; oral history in the community and classroom; the planning, interview, storage, cataloguing, and retrieval of oral history; oral history on video; and using oral history.

Huberman, Rob and Laura Janis. *Video Family Portraits: The User Friendly Guide to Video Taping Your Family History and More.* Bowie, MD: Heritage Books, Inc., 1987.

>*Video Family Portraits* provides interviewing and video tips, a family history question guide, a section on copying home movies onto video, and a guide to videotaping special occasions. Helpful hints and tips assist the amateur and professional video taper in the techniques best suited to dealing with family histories.

Ives, Edward D. *A General Interview Guide.* Orono, ME: Northeast Archives of Folklore and Oral History, 1987.

>Accompanying material for the video recording: *An Oral Historian's Work*. This guide offers questions on various settings for interviewing people. Questions were developed around the topics of communications and trade, the community, nature, time, entertainment, sports, pastimes, historical tradition, personal comments, medicine, human life, and livelihood and household support.

---. *An Oral Historian's Work.* (Video) Orono, ME: Northeast Archives of Folklore and Oral History, 1987.

>Professor Ives explains and demonstrates the procedure of oral history through a series of tape-recorded interviews with woodsmen and river drivers who worked in the Maine woods in the 1920s. During the course of this video he explains the evaluation of equipment, conducting pre-interview research, making contact with informants, how to get the most out of an interview, preparing the transcripts, and preserving the work for future use. VHS Video.

---. *The Tape-Recorded Interview: A Manual for Field Workers in Folklore and Oral History.* 2nd ed. Knoxville: University of Tennessee Press, 1995.

> Ives discusses a step by step introduction to the interview process and the preservation of collected materials. Finding and evaluating interviewees, establishing contact and maintaining rapport, making advance preparations, interviewing, equipment needs, controlling the interview, eliciting information, obtaining a release, on-site interviews, photographs, and post-interview recommendations are all covered in this work. The appendix contains examples of letters, archival forms, catalogs and transcripts.

Jenkins, Sara. *Past, Present: Recording Life Stories of Older People.* Washington, DC: National Council on Aging, 1978.

> Methods and forms are presented from a "listening" project initiated in a senior citizens' center in which a group of older volunteers developed a program for informal life history interviews.

Jolly, Brad. *Videotaping Local History.* Nashville, TN: American Association for State and Local History, 1982.

> Photographers and historians have been using film to capture historical events and stories since photography was invented. Matthew Brady chronicled the Civil War in still photos well over 100 years ago. With the advent of motion picture and sound tracks, it has become possible to document history as it is happening. Video has taken this capacity even further with its versatility and portability. In his book, Jolly answers such questions as to when is video an appropriate alternative to or addition to sound recording, photography, and film for documenting and exhibiting history; what place does video fill in the program of a historical society; at what point does video technology impinge on the historical society's main work; and how can video be integrated into an exhibit so that the tapes enrich rather than detract from the visitor's response? Jolly provides answers to these questions as well as providing information on the technology, the hardware, the use of the equipment, the uses of video for oral history, training and information and the use of video in archiving.

Kammen, Carol. *On Doing Local History.* 2nd ed. Walnut Creek, CA: AltaMira Press, 2003.

> Kammen defines local history as "the study of past events, or of people or groups in a given geographic area - a study based on a wide

variety of documentary evidence and placed in a comparative context that should be both regional and national." Generally a historian coordinates a local history project following general rules of historic inquiry - open-mindedness, honesty, accountability, and accuracy, providing an understanding of the past. In this revision of her first edition, Kammen intends to identify problems that are particular to the field of local history and discuss them for those working on local history projects. Some of the topics she discusses include revising what is held as true, censorship, journalists and historians, document exchanges, adult local history workshops, and more.

Key, Betty McKeever. *Exploring Oral History: a How, a Why, a Who Manual: Maryland Manual of Oral History*. Baltimore: Maryland Historical Society, 1979.

Especially good on how to organize a whole program, keep track of what you get and apply for funding.

Kyvig, David E. and Myron A. Marty. *Nearby History: Exploring the Past Around You*. 2nd ed. Walnut Creek, CA: AltaMira Press, 2000.

This is a general introduction to historical research which includes building an archives, oral history, building preservation, etc. It has practical suggestions about how to read historical documents, photographs, and other source material, as well as how to collect information from a variety of sources from traditional archives to the World Wide Web.

---. *Your Family History: A Handbook for Research and Writing*. Arlington Heights, IL: AHM, 1978, 1986.

Every family has a pattern of their own customs and traditions, Kyvig and Marty assist the writer in putting these family patterns down in print for their children and heirs. This guide aids the writer in defining how far back in the past to take the story, how to do the research, what kind of questions to ask and try to get answered, what kind of dangers they might encounter in the gathering process and how much information is enough. Forms for data collecting and organizing the family structure are given at the end.

Lance, David. *An Archive Approach to Oral History*. London: Imperial War Museum, 1978.

Practical details on how to select interviewees, keep records as the project progresses. Especially good on how to encourage the use of tapes rather than transcripts.

Lanman, Barry A. and George L. Mehaffey. *Oral History in the Secondary School Classroom*. Los Angeles: Oral History Association, no. 2, 1988.

> This pamphlet gives examples of oral history projects done by students and gives teachers some guidelines for organizing them.

— and Laura M. Wendling. *Preparing the Next Generation of Oral Historians: An Anthology of Oral History Education*. Lanham, MD: AltaMira Press, 2006.

> Aimed primarily at educators, *Preparing the Next Generation* seeks to bring the art of oral history alive for students of all levels. Step-by-step descriptions have been drawn from the personal experiences of oral historians and educators who have successfully integrated oral history into classroom assignments. An overview of oral history is combined with practical suggestions for creating curricula, engaging students, gathering community support and meeting educational standards. At the end of the text are resources for the educator, which include a collection of thought questions, a sample syllabus, a bibliography of research studies, books and articles, and the Principles and Standards of the Oral History Association.

Larmour, Judy. *How to Do Oral History*. Heritage Notes, Number 11. Alberta, Can: Government of Alberta, 1994.

> This is a short, easy-to-read guide on doing oral history and has examples of how to ask questions.

Lawrence, Kenneth R., comp. *Oral History, the Complete Guide to Interviewing and Transcription*. 2nd rev. ed. Shreveport, LA: Archival Services, 2002.

> This workbook provides a step-by-step procedure for constructing an oral history. It illustrates the interview techniques and suggests possible questions. The book is designed specifically for church oral historians. It also provides suggested legal forms.

Lichtman, Allan J. *Your Family History: How to Use Oral History, Personal Family Archives, and Public Documents to Discover Your Heritage*. New York: Vintage Books, 1978.

> Lichtman offers a research plan for those doing family histories. Chapters give an overview of oral history and provide basic information on techniques and how to conduct interviews, maintain

taped records and interpret transcripts. Genealogical resources such as family records, photos, tax and census records, and heirlooms are also included.

LoVerde, Mary. *Touching Tomorrow: How to Interview Your Loved Ones to Capture a Lifetime of Memories on Video or Audio.* New York: Fireside, 2000.

Growing older brings the realization that one is losing touch with the past and leaving behind stories that should have been preserved for future generations. LoVerde offers over 200 questions designed to gather information from parents, grandparents and other relatives to safeguard precious family memories. She also provides tips on preparing both yourself and the person to be interviewed on both the technical and emotional process of interviewing. Real life stories from people who have already preserved memories on tape are offered as examples. Suggestions for types of equipment to use in different situations are also discussed, as is the process for setting up a successful oral history project.

Lummis, Trevor. *Listening to History: the Authenticity of Oral Evidence.* London: Hutchinson Education, 1987, 1988.

This discusses the performance and appraisal of interviews and the proper use and purpose of oral histories in our culture.

Marcombe, David. *Sounding Boards: Oral Testimony and the Local Historian.* Nottingham: Dept. of Adult Education, University of Nottingham, 1995.

Beginning with a chapter on the origins of oral history, Marcombe follows up with a jargon free guideline on how to conduct an interview and the processes the oral historian, be they amateur or professional, needs to know. Simple guidance is offered on locating respondants, structuring the interview, the interview technique, and storage, analysis and transcription.

McCracken, Jane, ed. *Oral History: Basic Techniques.* Winnipeg: Manitoba Museum of Man and Nature, 1974.

Though dated, McCracken's outline of how to do an oral history is still relevant and is condensed to a quickly read, easily followed guide of the most important features of the interview and follow-up process. A sample release form and an example of tape indexing are also included, as well as an outline of sample question ideas.

McGoldrick, Monica. *You Can Go Home Again: Reconnecting With Your Family*. New York: W. W. Norton & Company, 1995, 1997.

Beyond simply genealogy, *You Can Go Home Again* is a book of family assessment. A psychological study in which the study of family and knowing family history can aid in the reconnection to home. Assisting in research of the family, this book also aids in reconciliation. It demonstrates how knowing the details of family history can be more important than simply tracing the family tree. In addition, each chapter has questions at the end which facilitate putting together the family history and in constructing a question base for use in oral histories.

McLaughlin, Paul. *A Family Remembers: How to Create a Family Memoir Using Video and Tape Recorders*. Bellingham, WA: Self-Counsel Press, 1993.

A Family Remembers is about creating a family heirloom. Utilizing the camcorder or tape recorder, McLaughlin provides easy to follow information on how to set your subject at ease, what type of questions to ask, interviewing and production tips from experts in the field, and what he calls 'survival techniques' for using the camcorder and tape recorder. McLaughlin provides and organized and readable outline of the oral history technique and how to use the equipment. He lists sample questions and examples of various stages of the interview process, as well as emphasizing the research and preparation stages of the process.

McMahan, Eva and Kim L. Rogers, eds. *Interactive Oral History Interviewing*. Hillsdale, NJ: Lawrence Erlbaum Associates, Publishers, 1994.

This book is designed not as a guide to doing oral histories, but more as a guide to illustrate how social and cultural influences affect the practice. Each chapter is written by experts in the field and they define oral history from a variety of vantage points. Grele discusses political ideology which may underlie and manipulate the process and Clark shows how events may be used to construct stories the interviewer wishes to achieve. Other chapters discuss the use of trauma in narrative construction, social psychological aspects, feminist social research, and racial and ethnic variables, as well as the use of photographs for generating personal and public memories.

Meckler, Alan M. and Ruth McCullin, eds. *Oral History Collections.* New York: R. R. Bowker Company, 1975.

This is a definitive guide to both oral history source materials and programs in the United States and abroad.

Mercier, Laurie and Madeline Buckendorf. *Using Oral History in Community History Projects.* Los Angeles: Oral History Association, Pamphlet No. 4, 1992, 2007.

This pamphlet offers suggestions for planning, organizing, and conducting oral history in community settings. It provides a guide to planning and establishing project objectives, identifying resources, and securing funding, and addresses common problems of oral history projects and presents case studies of successful projects.

Montell, W. Lynwood and Barbara Allen. *From Memory to History: Using Oral History Sources in Local Historical Research.* Nashville, TN: American Association for State and Local History, 1981.

The goal of this publication is to take the oral histories you have taped and guide you through the evaluation and writing process. It deals with using local history, to evaluate oral histories, testing for validity, recognizing folkloristic elements, personal and group bias, corroboration from written sources, physical artifacts, identifying attitudes about the past, community values and beliefs embodied in nonfactual accounts and suggestions for incorporating oral histories into written manuscripts.

Moss, William W. *Oral History Program Manual.* New York, Praeger, 1974.

This is an account of the concepts and practices of the oral history program at the John F. Kennedy Library, Waltham, Massachusetts. Though this is a specialized example of a specific library, it provides a guideline for setting up and planning an oral history program. Mr. Moss shares his experiences in organizing this program including a general discussion of an oral history program and methodology, a definition of who should be interviewed and who should conduct the interviews, interview techniques, the processing of interviews, the research potential for interviews, record processing, and the staffing and equipping of an oral history program. In the appendices of this book, Moss includes a basic transcription manual, a copy of the program statement of the John F. Kennedy Library Oral History Program, the Goals and Guidelines of the Oral History Association, an outline of processing steps, and a questionnaire to determine the terms of use of oral history tapes and transcripts.

Mundell, Kathleen and Steven Zeitlin. *Life Review Projects: A Guide for Seniors and Senior Citizen Groups.* Spring Valley, NY: Arts Council of Rockland, 1987.

> Mundell and Zeitlin have put together a brief, but effective guide to help seniors relive the important moments in their lives for their children, grandchildren and friends. Giving instructions on how to start a life review project, this resource also provides questions and ideas for anyone wishing to interview and preserve the memories of older adults. Basic oral history instructions are given, as well as instruction for working with photographs, and other activities to stimulate memories.

Mungo, Raymond. *Your Autobiography: More Than 300 Questions to Help You Write Your Personal Story.* New York: Macmillan, 1994.

> The 300 questions in Mungo's book can be adapted for use in conducting an oral history. These questions cover birth, childhood, school years, college, love, children, friends, work and retirement. Writing tips are also included to assist in looking back on life to create a lasting legacy.

Nathan, Harriet. *Critical Choices in Interviews: Conduct, Use and Research Role.* Berkeley: University of California, Institute of Governmental Studies, 1986.

> Harriet Nathan has developed a very in-depth description of the oral history process. She discusses participants, interests and process; control and flexibility - who is in charge and why; ethics - trust and responsibility; technique - skills and suitability; editor and publisher - authority, responsibility, scrutiny; and whether to interview - why and when, pro and con. Full of information and useful tips, her work is also very intense and is not for the person looking for quick information on doing oral history.

Nelson, Hasker Jr. *Listening for Our Past: A Lay Guide to African American Oral History Interviewing.* Cincinnati, OH: Heritage Research Creations, 2000.

> The logical beginning for most genealogical research is the oral history. Oral interviews uncover information that many of us have never heard before. Though a skilled interviewer, in his first interview with his mother, Nelson discovered that preparation is very necessary for beginning oral research of your family. In *Listening for Our Past*, Nelson writes of the questions he wishes he had asked in that first interview he did with his mother. He

discusses how to develop the questions, how to prepare for the interview, recording your own recollections, how to use family reunions for interview times, funerals and cemeteries, and photos and family documents. Nelson offers sample questions on such topics as ancestors, childhood memories, school days, courtship, marriage, descendants, work, looking back, life today, favorites, and generation spanning questions. He also, spends a few pages discussing how to put the oral history information together in a comprehensive form after it has been collected.

Neuenschwander, John A. *Oral History and the Law.* 4th ed. New York: Oxford University Press, 2009.

This small book in invaluable as a resource for guiding the oral historian through the ramifications of the legal aspects of utilizing oral history. The guide talks about invasion of privacy, defamation, how to avoid legal problems, sealed interviews, copyright, ownership and transfer, deeds of gift, drafting agreements, contractual agreements, and explaining legal issues to interviewees.

---. *Oral History as a Teaching Approach.* Washington, DC: National Education Association, 1976.

With interest in oral history increasing, it has become recognized as a teaching tool. First hand stories are considered primary sources and as such of importance to historians. As a teaching tool it stimulates interest in an area which may otherwise be viewed with less than vital interest. One word of caution, however, oral histories include each persons' perspective and as such may also include some exaggerations, therefore it is best to get several views of the same story if possible.

O'Hanlan, Elizabeth, O.P. *Oral History for the Religious Archives: The Sinsinawa Collection.* Sinsinawa, WI: Sinsinawa Dominican Archives, 1978.

Sister Elizabeth describes the concept of oral history and how it applies to the religious institution. She offers advice on prioritizing the interview process, and defining what should be collected. Though it is slanted to the Catholic viewpoint, it should be helpful for any religious institution. Samples of interviews are included, as well as a job description for an oral historian, sample questions, and release agreements.

Oral History Association. *Oral History Evaluation Guidelines.* Rev. ed. Carlisle, PA: Oral History Association, 2001.

> The Oral History Association has published guidelines for conducting oral history interviews, and in them includes a guide to social, legal, historical and ethical issues involved in the practice of oral history.

Pengra, Nancy. *Family Histories: An Easy, Step-by-Step Guide to Capturing Your Family's Precious Memories Now, Before They're Lost.* St. Paul, MN: Family Histories, 1995.

> Nancy Pengra developed this book after the death of her grandfather brought the realization that many of her family's stories had been lost with his death. Written with genealogists in mind, she presents an easy to follow guide for getting stories down on paper. She includes hundreds of ideas for jogging memories and triggering stories, ways to add variety to stories, tips for organizing the stories and memorabilia including techniques for writing and publishing, over forty pages of 'trigger' questions and samples of what others have done, a list of historical dates since 1900 on what has been done or invented, and creative ways of sharing the stories.

Perks, Robert and Alistair Thomson, eds. *The Oral History Reader.* 2nd ed. London: Routledge, 2006.

> Designed for the serious student of oral history, this reader is an anthology of key writings on the theory, method and use of oral history. Arranged by theme, the *Reader* discusses the issues in the theory and practice of oral history, from the creation of the history to the analysis of the information. Key debates in oral history are highlighted, such as the problems of interviewing, ethics, politics of empowerment, analytical strategies for interpreting memories, and the concerns of archiving and public history. Each section discusses the key issues of that section and relevant literature.

Reimer, Derek, ed. *Voices: A Guide to Oral History.* Victoria: Provincial Archives of British Columbia, 1984.

> This manual offers detailed information on doing an oral history, aimed at radio broadcast quality interviews, it provides information of equipment and recording methods.

Reminiscing: The Game for People Over Thirty and the Younger People They Let Play. The Millennium Edition. Itasca, IL: TDC Games, Inc., 1998.

> A game of memories, the time period is from the 1940s to 1990s. Made up of four player books and one Reminiscing book, fill-in-the blank flashback questions are asked along with a corresponding set of clues. When required, a person must tell a story from their own personal past related to one of the subjects. As the point of this game is to stimulate memories, the questions may be easily adapted to an oral interview format, particularly useful for generating memories of the social times of the interviewees' life.

Ritchie, Donald A. *Doing Oral History: A Practical Guide.* 2nd ed. Oxford: Oxford University Press, 2003.

> This book discusses both audio and video taping oral history. It describes the equipment, starting a project, doing interviews, processing interviews, using interviews as independent research, preserving them in libraries and archives, and teaching and presenting the interviews in various forms.

Rosenbluth, Vera. *Keeping Family Stories Alive: A Creative Guide to Taping Your Family Life & Lore.* 2nd ed. Point Roberts, WA: Hartley & Marks, 1997.

> This book by including materials on memory and advice for jogging memories for the interviewer and interviewee. Examples are given from real interviews. Practical advice is also given on handling the recording equipment as well as suggestions for interview techniques and questions.

Ross, Ronald D. *Your Family Heritage: A Guide to Preserving Family History.* Parker, CO: Ronald D. Ross, 1988.

> This book is designed to go beyond the simple family tree. Ross, a Presbyterian minister, presents an instructional manual for doing audio or video tape histories of your family, and in addition discusses photographic images to assist with this project. He also discusses the preservation of photos and family documents and how to record your own oral history. Included in his book are many pages of possible questions and topics, as well as information on transcribing and editing the history after it is recorded.

Schorzman, Terri A., ed. *A Practical Introduction to Videohistory: The Smithsonian Institution and Alfred P. Sloan Foundation Experiment.* Malabar, FL: Krieger Publishing Co., 1993.

> This book teaches video skills for recording video oral histories. It tends to be on the technical side. Probably the most valuable part of this book to the oral historian would be the appendices which discuss and outline steps for project planning and production. Set design is also discussed in one chapter.

Shedden, David B. *Preserving a Newspaper's Past: A Guide to Developing a Newspaper Oral History Program.* St. Petersburg, FL: Poynter Institute for Media Studies, 1992.

> Developed to preserve the story of newspapers, this guide also provides the basics for preparing for and conducting an oral history interview. Shedden explains how an oral history can be important for a newspaper, how it is used in journalism, and what is involved in developing a program for a newspaper. The same considerations that go into the newspaper program that Shedden describes can be easily adjusted to any interview situation. The advantage of his presentation is that it is short and in outline format that make it clear and easy to follow. He discusses the points - who is going to be interviewed, who is the audience, what kind of equipment is needed, when to interview, where to interview, legal releases (and includes a sample release form), guidelines for conducting a successful interview, post-interview guidelines, and suggests newspaper oriented topics.

Shumway, Gary L. *Oral History in the United States; a Directory.* New York: Oral History Association, 1971.

> A much dated resource, but it gives a list of several institutions, colleges, historical societies, etc., in each state which maintains oral history programs. This resource is in great need of updating.

--- and William G. Hartley. *An Oral History Primer.* Salt Lake City: Primer Publications, 1973, 1978.

> This booklet is a guide suggesting procedures for the various phases of the oral history process. Part one covers the preparation, conducting the interview, and making the taped information usable. Part two provides topic ideas to consider for the formulation of questions for biographical type interviews.

Sitton, Thad, George L. Mehaffy and O.L. Davis, Jr. *Oral History: A Guide for Teachers (and Others.)* Austin, TX: University of Texas Press, 1983.

> The authors examine techniques common to historiography that work in the classroom. Descriptions of the *Foxfire* project in Georgia are given. Chapters include project options for field work, including instruction on note taking, and obtaining legal releases. This guide also contains a thorough bibliography. This is a very thorough, "heavy" reading book, not recommended for a project needing a quick overview to start.

Sommer, Barbara W. and Mary Kay Quinlan. *The Oral History Manual.* 2nd ed. Lanham, MD: Altamira Press, 2009.

> Step-by-step directions, checklists, full-size reproducible forms, sample planning documents, project descriptions, and summary sheets assist anyone planning an oral history project to "think like an oral historian." Chapters in this manual include such topics as project overview and planning; legal and ethical considerations; recording technology; budgeting and financial support; interview preparation, setting and process; processing and care of the interview results; follow-up; and oral history resources. Appendices containing forms, suggestions for video and audio interviews, evaluation guidelines, a glossary of terms and a bibliography.

Stephenson, Shirley E. *Editing & Indexing: Guidelines for Oral History.* (2nd printing.) Fullerton, CA: Oral History Program, California State University, 1983.

> The objective of this short guide is to provide instruction in improving the appearance and editorial continuity of oral history transcripts. There are conflicting views of what to do with oral histories, leave them in their original "pure" form, or to edit them into a clean, concise, usable format. Though possibly a costly process, editing eliminates false starts and irrelevant asides which can detract from the intention and meaning of the history. This guide provides assistance in identifying what can be safely eliminated, and rules of editing, style and indexing the finished product.

Thompson, Paul R. *The Voice of the Past: Oral History.* 3rd ed. New York: Oxford University Press, 2000.

> This book combines the theory of oral history with the technical processes involved. Chapters one through four discuss the theory, and chapters five through eight serve as an oral history manual including examples. Included at the end are sample questions for interviewers.

Turner, Geneva. *How to Plan a Spectacular Family Reunion: Discovering Relationships: From Picnics and Talent Shows to Oral Histories and Family Themes, Genealogy and Family Inve$tment$.* Columbus, GA: Family Projects Publishers/TACF, 1993.

This manual provides a personal one-stop, resource for creative, fun, easy, and low cost activities that will encourage every family member to participate. Information is provided on obtaining oral and written histories; ideas for a family newsletter; and other ideas; along with easy to follow examples and explanations. Chapter 3 focuses on videotaping and photos, and chapters 8 to 10 and 13 discuss the processes for gathering information and conducting and writing up oral interviews. Included in the appendix are forms for family inventories, personal history, and ancestor charts.

Tyrrell, William G. *Tape-Recording Local History. Technical Leaflet No. 35.* Nashville, TN: American Association for State and Local History, 1978.

This short technical leaflet provides the general rational for developing an oral history project, as well as a brief, concise description of the interview process and preparing for the interview. The use of oral history in the classroom is briefly discussed as is the editing process.

United States Holocaust Memorial Museum. *Oral History Interview Guidelines, United States Holocaust Memorial Museum.* Washington, DC: U.S. Holocaust Memorial Museum, 1998.

Though directed specifically in the question structure section towards the questioning of Holocaust survivors, the instructional parts of this manual are an excellent guide in how to construct and do an oral history interview. The guidelines provide instruction in all aspects of conducting the interview, making the first contact with the interviewee, conducting background research, preparing questions, preparing the technical aspects of the interview for both audio and video taping, and interrelationships which develop between the interviewer and interviewee. Each chapter begins with a chapter overview, and the parts of the chapter are clearly outlined and easy to find if you are browsing for specific aspects of the process. Information forms have been created which could be adapted for other types of interview situations, transcription information and tips, references to other Holocaust and non-Holocaust resources, and samples of completed oral history transcripts. This is an excellent and clearly written resource which would be an asset to anyone who spends a lot of time doing oral histories.

Vansina, Jan. *Oral Tradition; a Study in Historical Methodology.* London: Routledge & Kegan Paul, 1965, 2006.

> This study is more in the line of how to record the oral testimonies of native peoples who have not previously had a written culture. While beneficial from the point of view of learning how oral history is transmitted within the cultural setting, it is not the "how-to" book that would be employed by someone learning how to do an interview in a modern setting. The focus in on African natives and the reading style is very scholarly and pedantic. What it does do well, is to point out how stories can change from generation to generation with differing cultural influences, and how hearsay can creep into a tradition over time.

Walker, Glen. *Create Your Own Life's Story: The Simple Way to Record Your Personal History.* San Leandro, CA: Bristol Publishing Enterprises, Inc., 1992.

> This workbook provides questions from life to guide you in writing your own story. A time line is also included at the end of the book to jog your memory of important events that happened during your lifetime. These questions could also be used as a guide for creating an oral history interview.

Whistler, Nancy. *Oral History Workshop Guide.* Denver, CO: Denver Public Library, 1979.

> Defining oral history and its uses and different types of oral history projects, Whistler takes the reader through the oral history process from beginning to end. Though equipment has progressed greatly since this was written, the process parts are excellent. She also includes a variety of forms for use by the historian, including letters, questionnaires, topic lists, and release forms.

Wind, James P. *Places of Worship: Exploring Their History.* Walnut Creek, CA: AltaMira Press, 1997.

> This volume focuses on congregational history, exploring in detail a number of different approaches to congregational history writing. These approaches are demonstrated by using congregations with a variety of traditions, i.e. Methodist, Jewish, Catholic, etc. as case studies. These studies can help distinctive Lutheran features of your own story become more visible. In addition to providing examples of how various parts of a historical project are done, the book has several pages of questions that can help shape your own projects.

Yow, Valerie R. *Recording Oral History: A Guide for the Humanities and Social Sciences*. Walnut Creek, CA: AltaMira Press, 2005.

> In her in-depth study of oral history, Yow shows the oral historian how to select interviewees, phrase questions, build rapport with the interviewee, use the equipment, deal with difficult situations, analyze the tapes and write up the project. Ethical and legal issues are covered in detail, and she elaborates on three different types of oral history projects, community studies, biographies, and family histories. Oral history guidelines for programs, interviewers, and finished products are included in the index, as well as sample release legal forms.

Zeitlin, Steven J., Amy J. Kotkin and Holly C. Baker. *A Celebration of American Family Folklore: Tales and Traditions from the Smithsonian Collection*. New York: Baker, Pantheon Books, 1982.

> Primarily a book highlighting the culmination of what can be done using the research from the collecting of a family's history, the last chapter focuses on the actual collecting, recording and techniques for putting together oral history and family memories. The remainder of the book is a wonderful example of the things you can do with the information you have collected from your trip through your family's memories, photos and memorabilia.

Zimmerman, William. *How to Tape Instant Oral Biographies*. New York: Bantam Books, 1999.

> Written for young, inexperienced practitioners, this book is simple to understand, suggests questions and techniques for conducting interviews, and discusses potential ideas and topics for inclusion in an oral history. A variety of family history sheets for use in conjunction with a family history are included.

---. *Instant Oral Biographies: How to Interview People & Tape the Stories of Their Lives*. New York: Guarionex Press, 1981, 1988.

> This book presents a method to help one become an instant biographer or reporter and to save the stories of your family or friends. The concept behind this work is that anyone, adult or child can easily prepare an oral biography by using the equipment that is traditionally used for home audio and video recording. The guides in this book were developed by the author out of his 20 years experience as a journalist. Suggestions are made on how to interview, what questions to ask, and family charts are given to help clarify what should be asked.

Heritage Photography

Photography as we know it has been around since the 1830s. There were of course camera like inventions prior to that, but what we think of as photography began in the late 1830s. The earliest style that we recognize is the daguerreotype which is a fixed image on a sheet of silver-plated copper. Some still have these in their family archives. If you haven't seen the earliest forms of photography, you will find them in many museums. The next most famous style (and there were of course, others created by a variety of photographers throughout history) is the tintype. The tintype used a thin sheet of iron as a base for light-sensitive material. Wet plate negatives followed and these, made of glass, were a more stable medium for photos. By 1879, dry plate negative and hand-held cameras were being invented, this allowed for more flexible settings for photographers. In 1889, George Eastman invented film which was unbreakable and could be rolled, and cameras could more easily be reproduced. By the 1940s, color films became commercially available, and cameras had greatly reduced in price, making them more readily available for hobby photographers.[2] There are many books available to help you learn how to preserve these older photographs if you own some of these.

This brings us to our current predicament! Most of us have boxes and albums full of either unlabeled or poorly labeled photographs. We may know the person or place in the photo, but not the date; we may know the date, but not the person. Fortunately, there are several books available which can help us date photos from the clothing worn, or maybe the development of an area. The family farm is now an apartment complex...you can check the county records and find out when the farm was sold and the apartments went up. Clothing changes over time, and there are always books being written on fashion and costumes. Photographs also tell stories of organizations, cultural events; they can be used for instruction, marketing, propaganda, advertising, study, research and any other use you can imagine. There are even books written to specifically help date photos for genealogical purposes.

Photographs can be an extremely important part of oral history and genealogy. For oral history, it can get a person talking and reminiscing. If you use a photo as a memory jogger, and you are taping the interview,

---

[2] http://inventors.about.com/od/pstartinventions/a/stilphotography.htm

please remember to describe the photo for the tape. If you are videotaping the interview, do a close-up shot of the photo so the viewers can see what you are discussing. In genealogy and family history writing, photographs can be used to supplement your research or to illustrate your text. Having photos of people on the family tree can make it infinitely more interesting for a stranger.

If you have boxes of unlabeled photographs, do not lose anytime in making contact with family members who might remember the content or people in the photos. It doesn't take many years before there isn't anyone around who can remember what a photo may be about. Don't let them lose their meaning.

There are several archival supply companies who will help you to preserve your photographs safely. If you already have them stored in those "magnetic" sticky albums, take them out as soon as possible. They will get discolored and sooner or later will become permanently attached to the pages. You will find books in this bibliography which will deal with most facets of preservation and identification in photography.

Author's collection: Graveyard at Kells, Ireland, 2010

Heritage Photography Books

Alesse, Craig. *Don't Take My Picture!: How to Take Fantastic Photos of Family and Friends (and Have Fun!)* 4th ed. Buffalo, NY: Amherst Media, 2005.

Generously illustrated with examples, Alesse's book features how to get great shots - catching the moment, getting great group shots, pointers on making anyone look good, photographing special times and celebrations, taking self portraits, jump shots, special portraits and more. He also includes chapters on choosing a camera, film, composition, lighting and other tricks for taking great pictures. Looking at the pictures in this book is half the fun!

Bannister, Shala M. *Family Treasures: Videotaping Your Family History. A Guide for Preserving Your Family's Living History as an Heirloom for Future Generations.* Hays, KS: Clearfield Co., 1994.

Bannister has put together a very basic book for the family wishing to video tape family memories and stories. She briefly discusses various settings and learning how to use the equipment, then makes suggestions for items that might be included on film such as memorabilia to make the filming more interesting and visually appealing. She suggests locations, props, the interview process, following a logical progression within the interview and wrapping up. The bulk of the book is made up of lists of questions covering almost every conceivable time period within a person's life. Finally at the end is a basic family tree chart and record sheet.

Davies, Thomas L. *Shoots: A Guide to Your Family's Photographic Heritage.* Danbury, NH: Addison House, 1977.

Photographs provide a portable and rich part of one's heritage. Memories may be triggered by seeing a shot long forgotten. Photos are a time machine, providing a window into the past. Photographs are delicate, but properly preserved and organized, they need not take up much room, and can last a hundred years. Photographs can tell genealogy sometimes more readily than a family member or about the people who have been close family friends, they also provide talking points for interviewing relatives for oral history or genealogical information. By organizing and detailing the information in photographs, a valuable legacy will be left for succeeding generations.

Frisch-Ripley, Karen. *Unlocking the Secrets in Old Photographs.* Salt Lake City, UT: Ancestry, 1990.

In her straight-forward, personable book, Karen Frisch-Ripley illustrates the methods of detection that go into finding names to go with the unidentified faces in your mother's photo album. She discusses the identification of photographs, the keeping of accurate records, utilizing public sources of information, recognizing the different types of photographs, the care and preservation of photographs, and how to locate family photos. Using her own family and photos as her subject, she sprinkles tips and 'how-tos' liberally throughout her text.

Frost, Lenore. *Dating Family Photos, 1850-1920.* Essendon, Victoria: L. Frost, 1991.

Photographs are an important part of identifying relatives and important events within a family's history. Frost's work illustrates the techniques needed to date and identify nineteenth and twentieth century photographs and put them in historical and social context. She also offers guidelines for preservation for these irreplaceable artifacts. Within part one she discusses photographers and studio backgrounds and then goes on to discuss the various types of photos such as daguerreotypes, ambrotypes, stereographs, and more. She also talks about photo albums, examining photos and copies. Part two discusses dating by men's and women's costumes, children, wedding shots, riding habits, work clothes, and mourning clothes. The last part discusses the issues of preservation.

Hazen, Ryne and Teresa. *Decorating with Family Photographs: Creative Ways to Display Your Treasured Memories.* New York: Sterling Publishing Co., Inc., 2001.

The Hazen's have created a book of suggestions on the alternative to putting your photos in a shoe box on the shelf or in the photo album only to be looked at every few years. Suggestions for interior decorating with photos include: painting a wall, stenciling it with "frames" and placing the pictures inside the "frames;" using photos instead of name cards for placing guests at dinner parties; choosing special matting and frames; and other ideas for displaying photos around the home. Advice on choosing the right pictures, picture treatments and picture enhancements are suggested. Numerous illustrations in the book serve as ideas and suggestions for making more extensive use of your pictures.

Heffler, Ira. *How to Create a Video Biography: A Legacy for Your Family*. Lake Arrowhead, CA: Arrowhead Publishing, 1999.

>   Most of us have seen photos of our grandparents, great-grandparents, and other relatives that we have never known personally, stories of them have been handed down from our parents, but many of us have never actually been able to talk to or hear their own stories. In his work *How to Create a Video Biography*, Heffler provides instructions and scripting for creating a video to pass down to our descendants. Videos are more personal and are able to convey more actual information than a scrapbook or photo album. A video reveals not only what the person looks like but what they sound like, it makes history truly alive. Heffler discusses the equipment, lighting, audio, how to create a good video, pre-tape hints, advice on what to wear, how to put the subject at ease, what to do in the pre-interview before taping, creating a profile sheet, how to direct the action, the actual taping process, the editing process, scripting for both adults and children, and the finished product. The scripts suggested by Heffler also provide numerous questions which would be useful for other oral history situations.

Hirsch, Julia. *Family Photographs: Content, Meaning, and Effect*. New York: Oxford University Press, 1981.

>   Family photographs can tell a great deal of information about the background of the family and the time period in which they lived. They are a rich source of the social aspect of past lives. Hirsch examines the conventions of the background, poses, and facial expressions to show how the reactions of the people photographed as well as the objects around them and the arrangement of the objects provide important clues to the photographer's message. Photos can reveal the internal politics of the families photographed, or illustrate conventions in group portraiture deemed suitable by each generation.

Hirsch, Marianne. *Family Frames: Photography, Narrative, and Postmemory*. Cambridge, MA: Harvard University Press, 1997.

>   Hirsch, in her work *Family Frames*, discusses photography in the context of what photographs tell about the family process. She attempts to answer the question of what photographs and albums do to mediate family relationships and family representations. She traces the intersections of private and public memories using photographs to study the cultural memory and stories they present. Her work is detailed and more for the person looking for meanings behind types of photographs, the serious student of sociology and

psychological reasoning behind photos. She discusses mourning and postmemory; the human family romance; unconscious optics; past lives and other images created by photography.

Housenbold, Jeffrey and Dave Johnson. *The Shutterfly Guide to Great Digital Photos.* New York: McGraw-Hill/Osborne, 2005.

This guide provides a step-by-step process for taking great digital pictures. They begin with the essentials of photography - composition and lighting, action shots, and close-ups. They then proceed to editing, enhancing and organizing the images, getting film quality prints and sharing your photos with others. Projects such as creating greeting cards, wrapping paper and other items are also included.

How to Produce Video Portraits. Videocassette. Colorado Springs, CO: Pikes Peak Library District, 1990.

Producing a video portrait, is much like doing an oral history, but it goes further. The actual interviewing parts are edited out so that only the subject of the interview remains. Where an oral history is simply memories of the interviewee, a portrait adds pictures of the times discussed, people, places, etc. so that the memories can be brought alive and visualized. This video tells the basics of what is involved in doing a video portrait, without going into the details.

Huberman, Rob and Laura Janis. *Video Family Portraits: The User Friendly Guide to Video Taping Your Family History and More.* Bowie, MD: Heritage Books, Inc., 1987.

Video Family Portraits provides interviewing and video tips, a family history question guide, a section on copying home movies onto video, and a guide to videotaping special occasions. Helpful hints and tips assist the amateur and professional video taper in the techniques best suited to dealing with family histories.

Jolly, Brad. *Videotaping Local History.* Nashville, TN: American Association for State and Local History, 1982.

Photographers and historians have been using film to capture historical events and stories since photography was invented. Matthew Brady chronicled the Civil War in still photos well over 100 years ago. With the advent of motion picture and sound tracks, it has become possible to document history as it is happening. Video has taken this capacity even further with its versatility and portability. In his book, Jolly answers such questions as to when is video an appropriate alternative to or addition to sound recording, photography, and film for documenting and exhibiting history; what place does video fill in the program of a historical society; at what point does video technology impinge on the historical society's main work; and how can video be integrated into an exhibit so that the tapes enrich rather than detract from the visitor's response? Jolly provides answers to these questions as well as providing information on the technology, the hardware, the use of the equipment, the uses of video for oral history, training and information and the use of video in archiving.

Langford, Martha. *Suspended Conversations: The Afterlife of Photographic Albums.* Montreal& Kingston, CAN: McGill-Queen's University Press, 2001, 2008.

This is not a "how-to" book, but a book describing the importance of photo albums and memories in our society. Langford discusses what makes photo albums important, and speaks of its importance as a collection of past history. She discusses it's function as a memoir, a travelogue, the idea of family, and the importance of including history with photography to bring life to the photographs themselves. This work may not belong in this collection, but it is an important historical study of the relevance of photo album collections to family and family histories.

LeDoux, Denis. *The Photo Scribe: A Writing Guide: How to Write the Stories Behind Your Photographs.* Lisbon Falls, ME: Soleil Press, 1999.

The Photo Scribe assists in helping to learn more about yourself, your family and your photos by acquiring the writing skills to photo scribe your albums, creating a legacy for your family and descendants. Not only does this book assist in showing how to "talk" the pictures, but it also enhances your photographing styles by suggesting how to "manage" the picture, getting into it what you want and leaving out what you don't want, in the words of a photographer - photo composition.

McClure, Rhonda. *Digitizing Your Family History: Easy Methods for Preserving Your Heirloom Documents, Photos, Home Movies, and More in a Digital Format.* Cincinnati, OH: Family Tree Books, 2004.

Even if you don't choose to put your family's history out on the Internet for everyone to visit, you still may want to digitize your research and photo history to share your relatives. In her book, McClure will share easy methods for choosing and using scanners, copiers, digital cameras, and the software to keep and share your research. Instructions will be given on using a scanner to create duplicates of old photos, tintypes, fragile papers, slides and negatives; choosing the right digital camera for yourself; mastering software fundamentals; and the use of PDAs as an easy way to take your materials with you. Illustrations and quick tips are a feature of Family Tree Books which help to make their series very workable.

Miller, Ilene C. *Preserving Family Keepsakes: Do's and Don'ts.* Yorba Linda, CA: Shumway Family History Services, 1995.

Family mementos and treasures are a big part of compiling a family history. If you intend to pass these on to future generations, however, they need to be taken care of properly. Miller provides a working guide to the preservation of all sorts of family keepsakes including photographs, documents, fabrics and other items of value. In individual chapters on the different types of keepsakes, she discusses what is important in the care of each type of medium. She talks of what to stay away from and what types of materials should be used to get the optimum life from your treasures. Her non-technical approach makes this a resource that can be used by anyone, and also includes information on how to correct mistakes that may have been made in the past storage of your treasured items.

Moorshead, Halvor, ed. *Family Chronicle's Dating Old Photographs, 1840-1929.* Toronto, CAN: Moorshead Magazines, Ltd., 2000.

Dating Old Photographs provides a short introductory section discussing the dating of old photographs and the types of old photographs from this time period. They give short descriptions of daguerreotypes, ambrotypes, tintypes, carte-de-visites and cabinet cards. Following the descriptive section, there is a section which talks about what to look for in old photographs. Following this section are samples of photographs from each decade so that you may compare the photo you have to the ones in the book, hopefully getting a rough estimate of when your photo was produced.

Nickell, Joe. *Camera Clues: An Handbook for Photographic Investigation.* Lexington, KY: The University Press of Kentucky, 1994.

The person behind the camera knows the reason the picture was taken and the subject of the picture, but what do you do when that person is no longer around or you don't even know who took the picture? Nickell, a former investigator for a detective agency, explains investigative methods for identifying and dating out photographs, enabling historians, genealogists, and amateur sleuths to trace a photo's past. He uses new and old techniques for identifying not only photo periods, but also the detection of fakes or copies, and also the restoration of deteriorating images. There are even a couple chapters on the world of UFO's, supernatural creatures and psychokinetic photography.

Noren, Catherine. *The Way We Looked: The Meaning and Magic of Family Photographs.* New York: Lodestar Books, 1983.

Noren discusses what to look for in photographs when compiling family albums. She shows how to evaluate the photos and determine valuable information from poses, backgrounds, clothing, and gestures. Suggestions include where to look for family photos, how to interview family members utilizing photos, and how to write interesting and revealing text about the photos. She also gives tips in documenting your family for posterity. This book is especially good for working with children and youth.

Rabiger, Michael. *Directing the Documentary.* 5th ed. Burlington, MA: Focal Press, 2009.

This book illustrates the methodology for planning documentary films. For those planning to video tape oral or family histories, this will help the amateur filmmaker in producing a more professional looking video. It is an introductory guide and gives instructions in crew and performer direction, editing, documentary aesthetics, and equipment. Rabiger offers step-by-step advice in addition to diagrams, sketches, and checklists to help make the experience a good one.

Reilly, James M. *Care and Identification of 19th-Century Photographic Prints.* Rochester, NY: Eastman Kodak, 1986

Reilly's work was the first and most comprehensive reference book on all aspects of care and identification of nineteenth century photographic prints. Intended for the serious collector, it will also be of interest to anyone with an interest in preserving old pictures, family historians, professional collectors, librarians, archivists and curators. Working with photos from the 1800s involves knowing the photographic history of the print process from 1840 to 1900, identification of different forms of deterioration, stability of specific print materials, collection management, proper handling, storage and display. An *Identification Guide* is included with the book to help the user identify the different types of photo processes during the nineteenth century. Various chapters discuss more specifically the evolution of the photographic process and different types of papers and printing styles used during the century. While technical, the book is at a readable level for the interested lay person.

Sartore, Joel and John Healey. *Photographing Your Family: And All the Kids and Friends and Animals Who Wander Through Too.* Washington, DC: National Geographic, 2008.

World class National Geographic photographer, Joel Sartore, illustrates how to take fantastic pictures of your family, pets and friends that enhance the family album. The instruction involves simple suggestions on composition and lighting using his own photographs as examples. Digital photographic tips on editing, album innovations, archiving methods and printing are part of this work.

Schorzman, Terri A., ed. *A Practical Introduction to Videohistory: The Smithsonian Institution and Alfred P. Sloan Foundation Experiment.* Malabar, FL: Krieger Publishing Co., 1993.

This book teaches video skills for recording video oral histories. It tends to be on the technical side. Probably the most valuable part of this book to the oral historian would be the appendices which discuss and outline steps for project planning and production. Set design is also discussed in one chapter.

Schultz, Arthur W. and Huntington T. Block. *Caring for Your Collections.* New York: Harry N. Abrams, Inc., 1992.

This work compiles advice by notable experts in the field of collecting to assist the private collector in correctly caring for and preserving their collections. It is divided into chapters according to the type of collectible - art, paper, photos, stamps, textiles, ceramics and glass, stone, musical instruments, etc. The authors concentrate on preventive maintenance, outlining the dos and don'ts of routine care such as cleaning, displaying, shipping and storage. They also cover what to do in the case damage does or has occurred. Additional chapters cover environmental guidelines, security, insurance, appraisal values, authentication, and tax coverage for owning and donating collections.

Shull, Wilma S. *Photographing Your Heritage.* Salt Lake City, UT: Ancestry Publishing, 1988.

Shull discusses heritage photography from a direction not usually taken. She offers instructions for current photographers on taking pictures to hand down to future generations. She discusses such topics as choosing a camera, getting to know it, film and photographs, filters and other photo apparatus, tripods and copy stands, copying photographs, photocopiers, taking the photograph, and taking meaningful people pictures. She also discusses photographing your heirlooms, lighting, and traveling with your camera.

Smith, Barbara. *The Art and Craft of Keepsake Photography: Engagements & Weddings*. New York: AmPhoto Books, 2007.

Smith, a wedding photographer, has put together this guide to wedding and engagement photography which goes from advising amateur and professional photographers on getting the most of their wedding and engagement party shots, to preserving those shots in attractive handmade albums. She suggests simple step-by-step projects to create treasured mementos, cards, invitations; discusses digital or alternative photo processes that can be used to turn photos into works of art; illustrates the techniques for professional looking layouts; demonstrates the creation of professional looking personalized stationery for the bride and groom; and other artistic ways of utilizing the photographs from that special day.

Smith, Roger L. *Heirloom Images: The Professional Guide to Copying and Restoring Old Photographs*. South Bend, IN: Heirloom Images, 1984.

This short book was written for those needing to produce quality copies of old photographs, primarily black and white. This book is really for those who want to do their own copying, not for those planning to have it professionally done. It discusses the equipment and skills needed to reproduce photos and negatives which will last through future generations.

Stanton, Katherine. *Make a Family Video Album From Old Photos, Slides, or Home Movies*. St. Paul, MN: Edgewater Productions, 1989.

Katherine Stanton discusses creative ideas and easy to follow instructions for producing a family video album from photos, slides, films, and ephemera such as postcards, maps, family heirlooms, or newspaper clippings. While she is discussing film technology which is for the most part, no longer used, the process is still relevant with more modern film technologies. Stanton also discusses how to decide on what pictures to include in a video, organization, adding music, deciding on the theme of the video, determining the storyline, narration techniques, film quality, creating a sound track, and many other suggestions for a successful family video.

Stephani, Julie. *More Than Memories: The Complete Guide for Preserving Your Family History.* Iola, WI: Krause Publications, 1998.

More Than Memories instructs on how to organize and protect photos and negatives, how to display photos and memorabilia in unique ways, and how to write captions to tell the story of the photo's history. Called scrapbooking, the process of putting photos in albums is enhanced by adding the stories that tell the history and background of the photo, thereby preserving the memory of the time and family history for future generations. Chapter one discusses the actual process of how to scrapbook correctly and how to find and use the correct supplies. The rest of the chapters discuss the various important events in a person's life that might be chronicled by scrapbooking.

---. *More Than Memories II: Beyond the Basics: Creative Techniques for Preserving Your Family History.* Iola, WI: Krause Publications, 1999.

Part two of the *More Than Memories* series continues the instruction on the proper way of preserving photographs. It discusses keeping photos in a safe environment, temperature control, humidity, dust, sunlight, "magnetic" albums, and contact with materials of high acidity. The ideas in scrapbooking and journaling in this text will stimulate creativity and help to maintain your favorite photos for your descendents.

---. *More Than Memories III: Mastering the Techniques.* Iola, WI: Krause Publications, 2000.

A continuation of the *More Than Memories* series, this volume continues with techniques for organizing, journaling, creative cutting and using texture, dimension, stickers and paper dolls.

Sturm, Duane and Pat Sturm. *Video Family History.* Salt Lake City, UT: Ancestry, Inc., 1989.

Written from their experience in putting together a video family history of their own, the Sturms explain the process of using home video equipment to produce a quality family video. They also offer many tips in making your video as interesting and creative as possible. The primary method they suggest is to use as many audio and visual sources as possible. Photographs, home movies, slides and live video can be mixed with a sound track consisting of narrations, music, and the recorded voices of family members. Each chapter offers a selection of options which can be used as best suits your family, and other chapters offer advice on equipment, the process of planning and getting ready for the shoot, editing techniques, packaging and much more.

Taylor, Maureen Alice. *Preserving Your Family Photographs: How to Organize, Present, and Restore Your Precious Family Images.* Cincinnati, OH: Betterway Books, 2001.

Whether or not you are a genealogist, or just want to safely store your family's photo history, this guide illustrates how to organize and store photos so that future generations can enjoy them. Discussion focuses on how to care for photographs, how to identify different types of damage, learning basic conservation techniques, buying the proper storage materials, and organization and the display of photos. Taylor also, discusses how and when to use a professional conservator and digital photography.

---. *Uncovering Your Ancestry Through Family Photographs.* 2nd ed. Cincinnati, OH: Betterway Books, 2005.

Taylor instructs the genealogist on how to determine clues to their heritage from old family photos. She offers instruction in identifying and verifying the people in the photos by using details such as poses, props, and print material to determine dates and places, she also shows how to track down the photography companies who shot the pictures. She offers advice on locating additional family photos, creating worksheets for every photo that confirms and validates your findings, and helps to expand your genealogical skills to include a working knowledge of the resources related to photo research.

---. *Your Family Story in Photographs: Capturing Memories.* Provo, UT: Ancestry Publishing, 2007.

All of us have used the camera to record the important parts of our past. Maureen Taylor as a photographic family historian discusses the photographic gear and gadgets available without getting too technical for the non-photographic professional and offers practical advice on composing and lighting your family photographs. She also discusses the photography of historic documents and using the current technology to restore the old family movies and videos to current formats. In addition to the technical photographic advice, Taylor assists with suggestions on using your photographs to tell a story using backgrounds, lighting, color, props and subject placement to highlight what your story is trying to portray.

Tuttle, Craig A. *An Ounce of Prevention: A Guide to the Care of Papers and Photographs.* Highland City, FL: Rainbow Books, Inc., 1995.

>Beginning each chapter with a historical overview of the medium he is discussing, Tuttle guide the reader in the preservation techniques to be used with such family treasures as letters, documents, works of art on paper, greeting cards, sports cards, scrapbooks, books, magazines, comic books, stamps, photographs and posters. Issues discussed in their preservation include temperature and humidity control; fungi, insects and rodents; light exposure; pollution and water; framing and lamination; mechanical disfigurement; and fire and theft. Tuttle who is a University Archivist and consultant/lecturer recommends preservation supplies and suppliers, and provides various sources of information with which to plan your preservation projects.

Weinstein, Robert and Larry Booth. *Collection, Use and Care of Historical Photographs.* Nashville, TN: American Association for State and Local History, 1981.

>Photographs are a very volatile medium, beginning to deteriorate almost as soon as they are processed. Weinstein and Booth discuss both the technical side of preserving photographic materials, as well as the philosophical side of why they should be preserved and the historical importance of preserving them. They give advice on cleaning daguerreotypes, distinguishing them from tintypes, the prevention of flaking of collodian plates, identifying the different types of photographic mediums, and identifying the time spans during which different photographs were made. They also discuss how to properly display photographs, their uses in historic research and illustrations, and how to make them available to the public, with information on procedures, usage fees, copyright and related topics.

Wilhelm, Henry G. and Carol Brower. *The Permanence and Care of Color Photographs: Traditional and Digital Color Prints, Color Negatives, Slides and Motion Pictures.* Grinnell, IA: Preservation Publishing Co., 1993.

>Twenty years of research have gone this work which evaluates the light fading and dark fading/yellowing characteristics of color transparency films, color negative films, and color papers. Wilhelm and Brower make recommendations as to longer lasting products and other imaging techniques to make photographs last longer. Storage techniques for preservation are discussed as well as conservation matting, mount boards, framing, slide pages, negative

and print enclosures, storage boxes, densitometric monitoring of black-and-white and color prints in museum and archive collections, and the discoloration and cracking of prints and other preservation techniques for the various forms of photographic media. This book is highly detailed and technical and would be of the most interest to the professional photographer.

Author's collection: Björbak family

Tracing Your Family Tree: Beginning Genealogy

Rapidly becoming America's past-time, the search for the family roots, or genealogy, is one of the fastest growing hobbies of this generation. In a time where many feel the study of history is no longer important, this provides another avenue of instruction in our historical roots.

Genealogy can be a daunting endeavor, it starts out easily, you begin with yourself and work out from there. List and chart those of your family you know as far back as you can. Then talk to your parents, aunts, uncles, cousins and garner the names of family members that they can remember. Once you have completed this level, you are ready to go on to the more difficult steps. While you are doing this step, pursue your family's history. Find out the contexts of their lives while you still have your living relatives to talk with. Finding out place names and the historical events going on during the lives that you have immediate access to assists in your search as you continue back from the living to the deceased. The Internet is now a great help in assisting research, but you must know the right questions to ask, and if you are planning to take this to the next logical step beyond the simple family tree, writing the family history, you need to know the context of the times in which your family lived.

The Internet has become a magnificent tool for researching the family and posting questions for finding lost family members. However, there are many things that you must retrieve in your research which are not actually "on" the Internet. Many primary source records, especially the older ones, such as birth, baptismal, marriage, and death certificates; divorce records; deeds and land records; census records; and others; are not on the Internet, though there are instructions there on how to obtain them and records of which records are housed in what locality. Many passenger lists are now on the Internet, though in many cases, it costs quite a bit to obtain them in this fashion. The Ellis Island site (www.ellisisland.org) charges $25 to $35 to copy and mail a page from a passenger list. However, balanced against what it would cost for someone from out of state to travel to Ellis Island to photocopy this page, that may not be a bad deal at all! There are a multitude of genealogy how-to books being published today which list mail addresses and websites from which vital records may be obtained. Many of these also, list sample letters to show how to frame your request and the type of information the records office needs to process your request.

There are also, many secondary source records which are helpful in doing genealogical research. These include published genealogies, county histories, obituaries, census records and death certificates. Death certificates were also, mentioned as a primary source. Their value, however, as a primary source diminishes if a distant relative or non-relative is the person filling out the death certificate. If someone has outlived their immediate family, the extended family or friends surviving might not have the correct, or enough information to fill out the complete form. In this case, the death certificate loses its value as a primary document. Published genealogies and county histories are only as good as the amount of research their authors put into them, and while a lot of valuable information can be found there, one should always check a second source for verification. Obituaries too, fall into the category of the death certificate. Inaccuracies may occur, or as is now the case in many newspapers across the country, if the family is not willing to list the cause of death, the newspaper will not list the next-of-kin. Thereby making the obituary of little value for the verification of relationships. In the case of census records, the earlier forms of these were hand copied, making them prone to human error, such as spelling errors, or the juxtaposition of numbers, and some are so poorly written that they are next to illegible. Microform copies of these are sometimes even more difficult to read.

Those said about the various types of records available, and despite the fact that some of these may be inaccurate, once you have obtained access to these records, make yourself a copy. If you are seriously pursuing your genealogy, you must accept that not only can this be a compulsive hobby, but it is not a cheap one! Copy any record you find, or pay to have it copied, if you have verified that it is your relative. If you do not finish this job, one of your children might and this will help them not have to revisit your work. Many of the records you find, you will want to refer to more than once, and so it is prudent to have them in your possession. A piece of information on a birth certificate that did not seem all that important a week ago might suddenly be crucial tomorrow. Also, if you make notations on copies of documentation, note that these are your comments, so that someone else looking at them later will not take them as part of the original documentation. On or with your copies, be sure to note where you got them from, the date on which they were obtained, and if from a particular book or microfilm - the title of that source, as well as the page. It is very time consuming to have to track a document back to its original source after the fact, and if you are writing your family history you may need this citation, or someone later may need to know where it was discovered. Put as much detail into the citation as possible, and make them clear enough that someone years from now will know what you meant. If it is an original document or copy which you do not want to write on, make a note on another piece of paper (preferably acid free) and attach it to the document with a plastic clip. Never use staples or metal paper clips, they tend to rust.

An important fact to remember when you have started the research past the remembered family members is that names have a tendency to evolve over the years, spellings change for various reasons, immigration officials have been known to spell something the way they thought it sounded; people have shortened lengthy names, or anglicized names to better fit into a community. If you reach a dead end, start looking at variant spellings.

Organization is important when you are researching your genealogy. If this becomes a serious endeavor for you, you will begin to have a lot of paperwork. Many of the how-to books have suggestions for organizational systems or you can create one which works for you. The main thing is to organize. Keep a log of your research, and there are suggested methods for doing this. The more involved you become, the easier it is to lose track of what you have done already. Make a list of what you are looking for and note when it is finished and where you have filed the information. This becomes time consuming and you do not want to go over the same ground twice.

There are many places which hold resources from which genealogical information may be obtained, libraries, archives, genealogical societies, historical societies and the Internet. Before approaching the Internet, collect everything you can from home and family members. The more information you have in hand, such as names, dates, and places, the easier it is when you go online. Also, the Internet is not the only place you need to search. In many cases, the Internet can tell you where you need to go to find the necessary sources, but not everything has been retrospectively converted to machine readable files yet, and ...may never be. Many archives, libraries, genealogical and historical societies, however, have what they call "finding aids" available online so that you can determine before leaving home, where you need to go. This allows you to make the best use of your physical travel time.

Before choosing your physical destination, search the Internet sites available. There are many different Internet sites that may be surfed for information. There are actually thousands of different, yet similar sites available now online. Five of the leading ones include CyndisList, Ancestry.com, Genealogy.org, Rootsweb.com, and Familysearch.org. These sites have a wide variety of information available and link to many other thousands of sites. Once involved in a search, be sure to keep a record of your search strategy. If you have to stop in the middle of a search, write down the exact keywords you were using as even altering a word by adding an "s" to the end, can skew your search the next time you go in looking. Also, record the URL of the website so that you can return to it again easily. The Web is still somewhat unstable and a website which was there yesterday may not be there tomorrow. Also, do not check just one site, browse around and check your information on other sites; they do not all have the same data. And ... be prepared to pay for some of the information you wish to receive, not everything on the Internet is free. Sometimes you are asked to pay for information; at that point, you will need to decide if you wish to put in your credit card number or if you wish to visit the physical site, such as a historical society, to obtain that particular piece of information.

Once you have determined that you need to visit a physical site, be sure you take with you the necessary information to get the job done. Bring a file with the questions you want answered, the dates you have found, and names you wish to research. You do not want to do the research twice! Do not bring a brief case or anything you are unwilling to be without while you are in the research room. Most facilities will ask you to put bags or cases into lockers. Bring sharpened pencils, ink pens are usually not allowed into archival research rooms. Also, bring paper on which to take notes, and take good notes, you may not get back to this facility, so be sure to cite titles, pages and publishing information from the sources you have accessed. This has been said before, but cannot be repeated too often!

When you have finished your research at the archives or library, be sure to thank any of the staff who has assisted you. Any added politeness to those assisting you makes them more willing to help both you and those who come after you, and a word of thanks always brightens a day!

From Author's collection: Boca Grand Lighthouse and Ghost

Genealogy Tips

1. Begin with yourself.
    - Create your family tree as far back as you can remember.
    - Solicit input from family members in the generation before yours, and any remaining aunts, uncles, cousins and grandparents.
    - Learn as much about the time periods in which your ancestors existed; if you are planning to write a family history, this will help greatly with the background material.

2. Examine existing primary source records for the people you have identified.
    Birth records
    Baptismal records
    Marriage certificates
    Divorce records
    Death certificates
    Deeds, land records
    Passenger lists
    Vital records

3. Search out secondary source records
    Published genealogies
    County histories
    Obituaries
    Census records

4. Try to get a copy of every piece of paper created by or about your ancestors.
    - Don't make editorial corrections to copies unless you note that they are *editorial comments!*

5. Always cite your sources, ***immediately!*** (It is very difficult to either remember or retrace your steps after the fact!) Detail as much information as you can, making citations clear enough that someone else could find the material.
    - If it is an original document which you do not want to write on, make a note on another piece of paper (acid free) and plastic clip it to the document.

6. Remember, names evolve over the years, and during immigration processes, so check variant spellings.

7. Keep your research organized. How-to books have suggestions for organizational systems, or create one which works for you.

8. Keep a log of your research, the more involved you become, the easier it is to lose track of whether you have answered a particular question or not!

9. Where to look for information: Go prepared; collect everything you can possibly obtain from your family sources before visiting a research center. Have names, dates, and places already in hand if possible.
    Libraries
    Archives
    Genealogical societies
    The Internet

10. Call ahead if possible. Not all libraries have genealogical collections, and some with genealogical collections have restricted hours of use.

11. Tools:
    How-to-books
    Forms
     Pedigree charts
      Family group sheets
      Research and correspondence logs
      Census forms
    The Internet
    Vital records
    Census records
    Genealogy source books

13. Joining a genealogical society provides other people with like interests who can be used as resources, offer membership privileges which will help with research such as workshops or on-site reference sources.

12. If you are interested, but do not want to do the work yourself, you can hire a professional genealogist. The Board of Certified Genealogists provides lists of genealogists across the country.

Genealogy Books

Allen, Desmond W. *First Steps in Genealogy: A Beginner's Guide to Researching Your Family History.* Cincinnati, OH: Betterway Books, 1998.

> Allen breaks the study of genealogy down into easy to follow, achievable steps. He explains how and where to collect information, and how to transform the names and dates you uncover into people you can relate to. Allen outlines how to locate the information you have at hand in your family scrapbook or attic, census information, courthouse and church records, how to organize the information, and how to study the events of history to help direct your research and expand your insights. She also includes sample forms, the resources needed to get started, a glossary of terms, and a directory of archives, libraries and organizations.

American Genealogical Research Institute Staff. *How to Trace Your Family Tree.* New York: Dolphin, 1975.

> A beginners guide to researching your family tree, *How to Trace...*, assists in formulating a search strategy. Family members can tell you a number of things about your history and the Institute staff has made suggestions of how and what type of questions one needs to ask. Local, state, and federal government sources are suggested, as well as print sources that can assist in a search. Other sections of this book include information on heraldry, genealogical societies, and how to organize your findings. While this book is older, it contains basic and valuable information to get started in organizing family tree research.

Arnold, Jackie S. *Kinship: It's All Relative.* 2nd ed. Baltimore, MD: Genealogical Publishing Co., Inc., 2000.

> Defining family and kinship, Arnold discusses many things and events through life that affect the search for genealogy. Chapters include topics such as marriage, divorce and live-ins; types of familys; family orientation and procreation; family law; adoption; grandparents; and vital statistics among others. These are areas all of which need to be considered when doing genealogical research. Tips on dealing with the multitude of relationships are given in this work.

Askin, Jayne and Molly Davis. *Search: A Handbook for Adoptees and Birthparents.* 3rd ed. Phoenix, AZ: Oryx Press, 1998.

> Finding that she needed to know information from her birth family, Jayne Askin instituted a search. Because the birth records were sealed by the court, she had to devise a plan to help her around the closed doors. In this greatly detailed book, she not only shares the methodology of her search, but shares details on costs, the rights of the adoptee, legal rights and laws, the need for moral support, reference resources, primary sources of data, alternate sources of data, search groups and consultants, and other groups helpful in a search. She provides checklists, state-by-state listing of agencies and groups, and reference sources.

Austin, Jeannette H. *Family History Center Research Handbook.* Fayetteville, GA: J. H. Austin, 1994.

> This book is an introduction to using the research materials available in the Family History Research Centers of the Church of Jesus Christ of the Latter Day Saints. Collecting information has been a passion with this organization and as such, they have one of the most comprehensive genealogical history collections in the world. Austin provides much bibliographical information on other genealogy materials as well as how to search and compile the information and chart it when finished. She also discusses all the various records that are useful to the genealogist and where to obtain them.

Bailey, Elaine B. *Genealogy Quest: Tracing Your Family Tree.* Carrollton, GA: J-LAINA Publishing, 1991.

> Bailey turns her own family quest into a guidebook for the beginning genealogist to follow. Tracing one clue and then another to the next branch of the tree provides a fascinating quest which for many almost becomes an obsession. Gathering names for charts is not the only part of the process, interviewing existing relatives is also important. Bailey takes the genealogist step-by-step through the research from how to begin, key questions to ask relatives, photographs, correspondence, charts, treasures and other family memories to court house records, cemetery records, vital statistics, and auxiliary needs such as interpreting old handwriting and seeing through nicknames. Numerous sources are defined and suggested in the later chapters, and sample forms and letters are provided.

Baxter, Angus. *Do's and Don'ts for Ancestor Hunters.* Baltimore, MD: Genealogical Publishing Co., Inc., 1988.

> A professional genealogist, Angus Baxter shares his tips on how to do genealogical research. Baxter aims his advice at those who have never even thought about tracing their ancestors, those who have just started the journey, and those who have reached a dead-end. Any questions you have, Baxter should be able to answer.

---. *In Search of Your British & Irish Roots: A Complete Guide to Tracing Your English, Welsh, Scottish, and Irish Ancestors.* Toronto, CAN: M & S, 2000.

> Baxter begins his work by detailing how to set up a family tree using resources close at hand. He also discusses continuing the search via correspondence with family history societies, record offices and other organizations which he lists, and concludes with the possibility of an actual trip to Britain or Ireland. He also discusses the transfers of important genealogical records to various records centers, the reorganization of counties in England, and Wales, the establishment of the Irish Genealogical Project and other important changes in records management throughout the British Isles.

---. *In Search of Your Canadian Roots: Tracing Your Family Tree in Canada.* 3rd ed. Baltimore, MD: Genealogical Publishing Co., Inc., 2000.

> As in his other books, Baxter describes how to get started searching for Canadian family histories. He instructs the user in researching historical records such as census returns, church registers, civil registration, land and homestead records, cemetery inscriptions, voters' lists, local newspaper indexes, and the files kept by the Church of the Latter-Day Saints. Baxter gives a province-by-province listing of where to find Canadian history records.

---. *In Search of Your European Roots: A Complete Guide to Tracing Your Ancestors in Every Country in Europe.* 3rd ed. Baltimore, MD: Genealogical Publishing Co., 2001.

> This is one of the most comprehensive guides for tracing genealogy in Europe, covering both personal visits and correspondence. Explanations are given of European politics and wars and their effects on genealogical records. Locations of archives from the national to municipal levels are given; the location of church records and census returns; the systems of civil registration of

births, marriages, and deaths; and how to find and use certificates of domicile, foundling books, orphan lists, guild records, internal passport lists, confirmation records and even vaccination lists. Thirty European countries are covered in this volume. The book begins with an introduction to Europe, and then includes chapters on Mormon records and Jewish records before going into a country by country breakdown of records centers. European genealogical organizations are listed at the end.

---. *In Search of Your German Roots: A Complete Guide to Tracing Your Ancestors in the Germanic Areas of Europe.* 4th ed. Baltimore, MD: Genealogical Publishing Co., Inc. 2008.

This guide by Angus Baxter is designed to teach the tracing of Germanic ancestry, not only in Germany, but in all the German speaking areas of Europe from the Baltic to the Crimea and from the Czech Republic to Belgium. It is designed so that you seldom have to leave home and shows how to conduct your research by correspondence. In addition to the basic how to search abroad information, it also lists resources for searching libraries, records of church and state, and archives in the Germanic countries.

Beard, Timothy F. and Denise Demong. *How to Find Your Family Roots.* New York: McGraw-Hill Book Company, 1977.

Beard and Demong's work is an extensive compilation of instructions on tracing your family's history. Now only do they guide you through the search process, but they list extensive resources for finding information in the United States and in foreign countries.

Beasley, Donna. *Family Pride: The Complete Guide to Tracing African-American Genealogy.* New York: Macmillan, 1997.

The legacy of slavery has made genealogy and the tracing of family more difficult for many African-Americans. *Family Pride* is designed to provide step-by-step directions on how to research African-American family history and genealogy. The basic techniques such as how to gather names, places, relationships, and family documents are highlighted, as well as the best places to find information, from interviews with relatives to census reports and church records, the National Archives and the Internet. Beasley details ways in which to overcome the barriers unique to African-American searches, tracing the impact of slavery and the Great Migration on family history. She also demonstrates how to write and publish the completed family history. Numerous sources for further information are given in the appendices.

Beller, Susan P. *Roots for Kids: A Genealogy Guide for Young People.* 2nd ed. White Hall, VA: Betterway Publications, 2007.

    Based on a twelve week course developed for a fourth grade class, *Roots for Kids* teaches children how to create a simple family tree and gives them the tools and tips to learn more about their roots and to uncover stories and events that define their families. Beller introduces them to genealogy, introduces them to the discussion of family histories, teaches them how to ask questions in an oral history format, and introduces them to searching local, state and national records using libraries and historical societies.

Blatt, Warren. *FAQ: Frequently Asked Questions About Jewish Genealogy.* Teaneck, NJ: Arotaynu Inc., 1997.

    In his book of *FAQ*'s, Blatt suggests starting with other more comprehensive works by Arthur Kurzweil - *From Generation to Generation* (listed elsewhere in this bibliography) and Dan Rottenberg's *Finding our Fathers.* He suggests these as the two pioneering works on Jewish genealogy. As with all genealogy, he advises starting with what you already know, working backwards from the present. He discusses Jewish publications, web sites, the JewishGen Family Finder, other useful books, vendors, Jewish genealogical societies, seminars, the National Archives, vital records, the social security death index, passenger lists, finding your ancestral town, naturalization records, the LDS Family History Centers, other archives, Holocaust research, the Jewish Genealogical People Finder, Jewish names, the JewishGen Discussion group, and computers and genealogy. Within each of these chapters other related books and web sites are listed.

Blockson Charles L. and Ron Fry. *Black Genealogy.* Englewood Cliffs, NJ: Prentice-Hall, 1977.

    African-Americans face unique hurdles when it comes to pursuing their genealogy. Countless records have been lost or destroyed, many slaves were only known by first names - which many changed upon gaining their freedom, and migration to the North frequently broke up family ties and scattered records throughout the continent. Some advantages do exist however, records of Black families have often been abstracted from census reports, many local histories and directories still exist, and records of churches and benevolent societies are often complete. Blockson describes how to interview relatives to find information that may be missing, how to organize and document your findings to make your search easier, and how to construct a family tree. He suggests specific types of documents to look for - birth and death certificates, wills, deeds, organizations such as the Freedman's Bureau, the National Archives, plantation records, and manumission papers. The appendix lists local and international sources which can be written to or visited, and provides a directory of African libraries and universities, Black research collections, historical and genealogical societies and other resources.

Burgeson, Nancy and Aija Janums. *My Family History.* Mahwah, NJ: Troll Associates, 1993.

Designed for a child, this short booklet defines how to start a family tree and poses easy to answer questions for engaging your children's interest in family history. Simple charts and exercises in addition to the questions assist a child in putting together a fairly comprehensive family history.

Burns, Robert A. *Out of Your Tree!: Crazy About Genealogy.* Videocassette. Austin, TX: Rondo Films, 1993.

Internationally known filmmaker, Robert Burns takes the viewer on a fun-filled, frequently irreverent tour of libraries, courthouses, and cemeteries. He also uses historic recreations to illustrate that genealogy can be a fun pursuit.

Burroughs, Tony. *Black Roots: A Beginners Guide to Tracing the African American Family Tree.* New York: Fireside Books, 2001.

Designed for those who have little or no previous experience in searching out family history, *Black Roots* highlights some of the special problems, solutions, and sources unique to African Americans. Burroughs explains everything needed to get started: where to search close to home, where to write for records, how to make the best use of libraries and the Internet, how to organize research, how to analyze historical documents, and how to write the family history. Included in the guide are real case histories, more than 100 illustrations and photographs of actual documents and records that will be encountered during a search, samples of worksheets and forms needed to keep research in order, and a list of traps that even experienced researchers fall into that hamper research.

Cache Genealogical Library. *Handbook for Genealogical Correspondence.* Logan, UT: Everton Publishers, Inc., 1974.

This second edition of the *Handbook* has been expanded and includes analyses of the problems and procedures encountered in genealogical correspondence. Poor letters are often the reason for closed doors in the genealogical search. This guide assists in setting up the proper formats and questions to be used in accessing genealogical information by mail. It also guides the user in locating and contacting the best sources for their search. While American and English genealogical research receives the heaviest concentration, tips are given for other countries as well.

Carlberg, Nancy Ellen. *Researching in Salt Lake City.* Anaheim, CA: Carlberg Press, 1987.

Carlberg discusses the research trip to Salt Lake City. The mecca of genealogists, the Library of the Church of the Latter-Day Saints (LDS) contains records in one place that one would have to search for in a variety of states and courthouses. Carlberg illustrates how to organize your research and tells what you need before going to Salt Lake City. She leads you through the library describing the site and the materials found there. Forms for doing research and organizing your family structure are also included.

Carmack, Sharon D. *A Genealogist's Guide to Discovering Your Female Ancestors: Special Strategies for Uncovering Hard-to-Find Information About Your Female Lineage.* Cincinnati, OH: Betterway Books, 1998.

Researching our foremothers can be infinitely more challenging than researching our forefathers. They shaped our family identities, were pioneers and political activists, yet throughout history, they have frequently gone unrecorded. This work provides strategies for overcoming the obstacles in researching the female side of your family, which includes a source checklist for researching female ancestors, a complete case study, and a detailed bibliography with more than 200 sources.

---. *A Genealogist's Guide to Discovering Your Immigrant & Ethnic Ancestors: How to Find and Record Your Unique Heritage.* Cincinnati, OH: Betterway Books, 2000.

Most Americans have a culturally mixed background. Uncovering where these ancestors came from can sometimes be a challenge. Part one of Carmack's book shows how to collect your family's oral history, and separate the fact from the fiction; understand the historical trends that might affect your research; develop strategies for tracing your ancestors back to their arrival in America; locate and interpret naturalization, immigration and emigration records;

and how to identify sources to help continue the research in the ancestor's homeland. Part two discusses major ethnic groups in America, discussing the forty-two distinct ethnic groups, including African Americans and Native Americans; helps to determine when your ancestors arrived and where and why they most likely settled, and provides resources to assist with further research. Part three discusses turning the results of this research into a written narrative for future generations.

---. *Organizing Your Family History Search: Efficient & Effective Ways to Gather and Protect Your Genealogical Research.* Cincinnati, OH: Betterway Books, 1999.

Carmack adds to her guides on how to do genealogical research with this sequel on how to organize the research and use it more logically once you have it. Reproducible charts and forms guide you through each step of your research. She assists in creating filing systems, organizing correspondence, planning research trips, defining goals and projects, developing storage systems, preparing essentials for trips, protecting documents, artifacts and photographs, and other organizational tricks to make research easier.

Carpenter, Cecelia S. *How to Research American Indian Blood Lines: A Manual on Indian Genealogical Research.* Bountiful, UT: Heritage Quest, 2000.

Through her research into her own American Indian blood lines, Carpenter has been able to assist others who must make this search. She lists three reasons for needing this information, basic genealogical searching, to enroll in an Indian tribe, and to establish and satisfy a personal satisfaction of identity. Organized in basic outline form, her book explains the reasons mentioned above for searching, creating an organizational system, how to begin the research, research problems encountered, using library materials, a listing of major libraries containing Indian materials, federal materials available, Indian materials available, and miscellaneous Indian materials to investigate. Carpenter lists the archival depositories across the United States, as well as Indian tribal listings and genealogical forms which might be used.

Carr, Peter E. *Guide to Cuban Genealogical Research: Records and Sources.* Chicago, IL: Adams Press, 1991.

For the past twenty-five years Carr has been accumulating records relating to Cuba. He has learned to get around the restrictions that the U.S./Cuban relations create. This guide will assist the person looking for their Cuban roots to do so as much as possible within the confines of international relations. He discusses the types of records available and how to go about accessing them.

Cerny, Johni and Arlene Eakle. *Ancestry's Guide to Research: Case Studies in American Genealogy.* Salt Lake City, UT: Ancestry Incorporated, 1985.

A companion to *The Source* also published by Ancestry, this *Guide to Research*, provides the basics for getting started. Using case studies, the text gives the researcher instructions and suggested methods for pursuing research in genealogy. Very detailed and amply supplied with example charts and illustrations, this volume even has a chapter on tracing the women in your family which is often one of the more difficult searches to pursue. The book is comprehensive in searching all sorts of areas, not only women, but military, occupations, colonial times, ethnicity, and immigrants.

Chamberlin, David C. *The Conceptual Approach to Genealogy: Organization, Processing, and Compilation of Genealogical Records.* Bountiful, UT: Heritage Quest, 1998.

Along with the concepts and techniques to do effective genealogical research, David Chamberlin concentrates on the organization, evaluation and the compilation of information that makes up a family genealogical project. Along with genealogical basics, he provides exercises to assist in learning the process and principles, and numerous supplemental materials which provide examples of how to do your genealogical research.

Charting Your Family History (Includes Software.) N.p.: Millennia Corporation, 1998.

Charting Your Family History which comes with a CD-Rom, provides a system which will gather into one place the significant events, images, and vital records comprising your family tree. The accompanying text provides step-by-step instructions for use of the software and creation of your online family tree. Beginning with installation instructions and a tutorial, the guide discusses using online searching and importing and merging files, doing family research and adding pictures and sound. It even includes instructions for submitting a template of your research to the Latter-Day Saints collection for assistance to others who may be looking for information on your branch of the family.

Chorzempa, Rosemary A. *My Family Tree Workbook: Genealogy for Beginners.* NY: Dover, 1982.

> Designed for beginning genealogists and young children interested in tracing their family history, Chorzempa has arranged this book as a workbook in which the user can participate in researching, recording and constructing their pedigree. Pages provide space for documenting information, including photos; instructions are provided for making a basic family tree chart; and important rules of research method and etiquette in genealogical techniques are given. Other sections include information on autographs, family tales, heraldry, geography, foreign languages, ethnic crafts, foods and customs, a sample filing system, correspondence record, glossary, bibliography, and ideas of further projects.

Clifford, Karen. *The Complete Beginner's Guide to Genealogy, the Internet, and Your Genealogy Computer Program.* Baltimore, MD: Genealogical Publishing Co., 2001.

> Clifford's book is a 'modern manual for genealogy.' It combines the fundamentals of genealogical research with the new technologies offered by computers and the Internet. Clifford shows how to combine the traditional research methods used in libraries and archives with today's technology. She shows how to conduct research in courthouse records, censuses, and vital records using the Internet and appropriate Web sites. She shows how to get started in family research, how to organize the family papers, how to enter information into a computer genealogy program, how to analyze data, and how to place the data in charts, forms and tables; and how to put together a family history notebook from computer sources, while still using those conventional sources which have not yet been digitalized.

Colwell, Stella. *Tracing Your Family History.* 3rd ed. London: Teach Yourself, 2007.

> Centering on the British Isles, *Tracing Your Family History* is a practical and comprehensive guide covering everything needed to trace a family history. It gives advice on planning the research and establishing the information needed, discusses interviewing the relatives, drawing up a family tree, and how to use the resources available for finding information. In addition to listing sources available for family research, Colwell also provides case studies of famous people in order to show how problems in research can be resolved.

Crandall, Ralph. *Shaking Your Family Tree: A Basic Guide to Tracing Your Family's Genealogy.* 2nd ed. Boston, MA: New England Historic Genealogical Society, 2001.

Each chapter of Dr. Crandall's book focuses on a single research area with tips on how to proceed. Chapters include such topics as interviewing family members; getting the most out of local and small-town library resources; locating and interpreting immigration records; interpreting the 'finds of the attic;' interpreting vital records, church records, cemetery records, wills and other court documents, land records, census records, and military records. He also includes a chapter on putting it all together in a finished form. Dr. Crandall's book is designed both for the amateur and professional genealogist.

Crawford-Oppenheimer, Christine. *Long-Distance Genealogy: Researching Your Family History From Home.* Cincinnati, OH: Betterway Books, 2000.

Many are unable to afford to travel to distant places to do the necessary research on their genealogy. Crawford-Oppenheimer has designed this genealogical search guide particularly for those researchers who cannot travel frequently to search for information. She shares techniques for locating and obtaining documents through correspondence, library research, inter-library loans, Family History Centers, archival repositories, microfilm and the Internet. Information in this work includes how to get birth, marriage, and death records; federal and state census records, estate files, land records, and military records; copies of original documents; locate others who are researching your family history; get maximum results from a research trip; locate where ancestors are buried; conduct interviews; and knowing when to consult a professional genealogist.

Croom, Emily A. *The Sleuth Book for Genealogists: Strategies for More Successful Family History Research.* Cincinnati, OH: Betterway Books, 2000, 2008.

Called the *Sleuth Book*, Croom suggests that the genealogist must be both a researcher and a detective in the hunting down of ancestors. She offers tips on pinpointing what you know in order to deduce your next step, identifying clues in the records searched, using "cluster genealogy," documenting evidence, considering the evidence and drawing valid conclusions, determining if your information proves your case, and other methods of detection. She provides case studies as research examples to take you step-by-step through the solving of frustrating research problems. Every chapter includes tips to help you avoid common mistakes and appendices include a guide to documentation and a listing of research basics.

---. *Unpuzzling Your Past: The Best-Selling Basic Guide to Genealogy.* 4th ed. Cincinnati, OH: Betterway Books, 2001.

Unpuzzling Your Past provides a basic handbook to begin your genealogy. It gives interview formats, sample letters, work sheets, multi-generation forms, census extraction forms, a comprehensive resource section, bibliographies and case studies. Croom also discusses the use of public sources such as censuses, courthouse records, federal government resources and computers in genealogy.

Crowe, Elizabeth P. *Genealogy Online: Researching Your Roots.* 2nd ed. New York: Windcrest/McGraw-Hill, 1996.

The Internet has rapidly become a fertile field for genealogy research. Many families are posting information on websites, and libraries around the world have their catalogs online so that one may do initial research and determine where to go without expending a lot of effort, thus saving years of expense and travel. Crowe's guide assists the researcher in gaining access to genealogical bulletin boards, newsgroups, genealogy forums, web pages, library catalogs and many other Internet resources. Crowe walks the user through computer systems and methodology for getting the most efficient uses out of a computerized genealogy search.

Curran, Joan Ferris. *Numbering Your Genealogy: Basic Systems, Complex Families, and International Kin.* Rev. ed. Arlington, VA: National Genealogical Society, 1999, 2008.

Many genealogists come up with their own numbering systems when creating their family histories. Curran discusses four of the common systems that people use which should fit the needs of most genealogists. Two are descending genealogies - those that trace the descendants of an early forebear, and two are ascending genealogies - those that present all the ancestors of a more-recent individual. People working with computer genealogical programs will usually find the programs use one of these four systems.

Currer-Briggs, Noel. *Worldwide Family History.* London, UK: Routledge & Kegan Paul, 1982.

Tracing ancestors is more difficult if you have to go overseas to do so; Currer-Briggs has compiled this book which discusses searching for ancestry in Europe. This book concentrates on the non-English world. The first part discusses the political and linguistic structure of Europe and includes chapters on genealogy in all European countries. The second part deals with colonial shipping in the seventeenth and eighteenth centuries and the settlement of the Americas. Chapters discuss peoples of Spanish, Italian, Polish, German, French and Slav backgrounds. It also, discusses the early settlement of Europeans in Australia, South Africa and New Zealand. There is also a chapter on heraldry.

David, Jo. *How to Trace Your Jewish Roots: Discovering Your Unique Heritage.* New York: Kensington Publishing Corp., 2000.

Speaking directly to Jewish genealogists, Rabbi Jo David has created a guide specific to the Jewish heritage which allows for the creation of a family tree to at least four to six generations. Enhanced with illustrations and document forms, she also, lists useful books, Internet and research sources for taking the research to the next level. Chapters provide information on family tree construction, using cyberspace, utilizing the living relatives, documenting your family, and the Holocaust. She also, provides ideas for including the entire family in the process, such as using children to interview older family members.

Doane, Gilbert H. and James B. Bell. *Searching for Your Ancestors: The How and Why of Genealogy.* 6th ed. Minneapolis, MN: The University of Minnesota, 1992.

This text was written for the beginning genealogist. It discusses family papers, searching professional organizations, cemeteries, libraries, overseas research and how to arrange your genealogy.

Dollarhide, William. *Genealogy Starter Kit.* 2nd ed. Baltimore, MD: Genealogical Publishing Co., 1998.

William Dollarhide reduces the process of genealogical research to its basic essentials in this starter kit. It allows the beginner to be brought up to speed without the necessity of spending days reading the longer reference works on the subject. Divided into three sections, it features a *how to start* section, a *where to find* section, and a set of *master forms* for keeping track of the genealogical information. The family group sheet, pedigree chart and family data sheet are designed to be photocopied. Dollarhide provides a seven step system for gathering the essential facts and doing beginning research, he also provides names and addresses of the places to find vital records and the more important genealogical resource centers in the country. He also provides a list of the top genealogical reference books.

———. *Getting Started in Genealogy Online.* Baltimore, MD: Genealogical Publishing Co., Inc., 2006.

This new work by Dollarhide is a very basic introduction to using the Internet for genealogical research. It is only 64 pages of basic computer instruction on finding your family history online. It also provides names and web addresses of the most important record repositories and sample forms for organizing your research.

———. *Grow a Family Tree: Seven Simple Steps.* North Salt Lake, UT: Heritage Quest, 2000.

Dollarhide has condensed his genealogical assistance to seven steps which include: organizing home and family sources; conducting family history interviews; writing for death records; following up on death record clues; searching federal censuses; searching state and county records; and using genealogical libraries and services. In this short and quickly read guide he emphasizes that before starting a search you must know the full name of your ancestor, the approximate dates of any vital events, and the places of the events.

———. *Managing a Genealogical Project: A Complete Manual for the Management and Organization of Genealogical Materials.* Rev. ed. Baltimore, MD: Genealogical Publishing Co., Inc., 1999.

Managing a Genealogical Project focuses on a particular method for organizing research materials. It offers a unique system for organization from the preliminary note-taking stage of research to the final presentation of your work as a report or book. Photocopy ready forms are included which Dollarhide suggests as valuable in helping to organize the research, they include relationship charts, reference family data sheets, compiled family data sheets, master data sheets, research log, ancestor table (to twelve generations), pedigree ancestor index (to 5 generations), reference journal and a correspondence log. This organizational method was designed for both the amateur and professional genealogist.

Douglas, Ann. *The Family Tree Detective: Cracking the Case of Your Family's Story.* Toronto, CAN: Owl Books, 1999.

Written for children or adults who want a quick, easy to read and colorful overview, this book gives tips and suggestions for discovering your family's history. Interview tips are given, places to search for information, suggestions for letters and e-mail questions, how to work with video and audio tapes, and numerous other suggestions and questions for developing the family history.

Drake, Paul E. *In Search of Family History - A Starting Place.* 2nd ed. Bowie, MD: Heritage Books, 1992.

Drake has written a basic workbook for finding ancestors and proceeding with genealogical research. He will guide the researcher from their first family interview through exploring cemeteries, churches, local libraries, courthouses and the National Archives. He gives advice for evaluating the information found, and warns of pitfalls that may be encountered. Thirty documents provide examples of what may be found during research and will help to familiarize the researcher with what they might be finding. There is also a special section on how to read early English with all its 'swirls and flourishes.' A pedigree chart, family unit chart, and census forms are given in the appendices, information on how to make a National Archives search easier, and names and addresses of the most popular and respected genealogical societies, periodicals and directories are included.

---. *You Ought to Write All That Down: A Guide to Organizing and Writing Genealogical Narrative.* Rev. ed. Bowie, MD: Heritage Books, 2004.

Drake provides instructions in writing one's genealogical history, the first chapter features organizing the information, defines each element in writing a book, and the correct way for using Roman and Arabic numerals. Further information is given on how to correctly use charts, forms and illustrations; how to test for the soundness of evidence; and how to get more information out of the sources. Sample forms and a list of addresses for state archives are included. There is also a section on wills and estates. This guide is also useful in showing how to search for genealogical materials.

— and Margaret G. Driskill. *Genealogy: How to Find Your Ancestors.* Rev. ed. Bowie, MD: Heritage Books, 2000.

This is a revision of Drake's 1992 edition of *In Search of Family History.* In this how-to book, he guides the researcher through interviews with relatives, the searching of cemeteries, church records, the library, courthouse, and National and State archives. A new chapter deals with how to use the Internet for genealogical hunting. Margaret Driskill instructs genealogists in the genealogical aspects of online searching. Appendices include common forms for families and censuses, forms for use in the National Archives, and the names and addresses of the best societies and associations to contact for assistance.

Draznin, Yaffa. *Family Historian's Handbook: A Complete How-to-Guide for Tracing Your Roots - Whatever Your Ethnic Background.* New York: Jove Publications, 1978.

Once the hobby of descendants of the Mayflower, genealogy has now become popular with people everywhere. Draznin, a veteran genealogist, shares her tips on how to interview, where to look for documents, how to get what you need from relatives, what to do if family records no longer exist, specialists in different ethnic sources, how to organize your research and queries, and how to publish what you find.

Durrant, George D. and Larene Gaunt. *Family History for the Clueless.* Salt Lake City, UT: Bookcraft, 2000.

Clueless: those who are beginners. Durrant and Gaunt have provided a basic how-to manual for those researchers just getting started in genealogy. Written with a down-to-earth style, the authors use anecdotes and cartoons to maintain an upbeat feeling. They discuss the basics and the "where-to-go-next" steps. Nine appendices are filled with information and resources, and blank forms which can be photocopied for use and to assist in organization of materials.

Eakle, Arlene. *Do Your Family Tree.* Videocassette. Provo, UT: Horizon Home Video, 1991.

Professional genealogist Arlene Eakle presents this video which illustrates the important steps in completing the family tree, how to fill out pedigree charts, what information to ask your family, how to verify family and public information, and which public records to search. The information is illustrated around an actual family tree and the video comes with a blank pedigree chart and graphics to help understand the family tree. Instructions on using the library for researching information is included, as well as the addresses of where to write for birth, marriage and death certificates for all fifty states.

—. *Do Your Family Tree: Advanced Research.* Provo, UT: Horizon Home Video, 1992.

Dr. Arlene Eakle, who recorded *Do Your Family Tree* part 1, will guide the researcher through this series of advanced steps in family tree research. In this video she demonstrates how to research the U.S. census records utilizing actual records from 1860 to 1900, discusses new information about the 1920 census released in 1992, and how to use family group sheets and county histories. She also discusses how researching the ancestor's occupations can extend the family pedigree. In the last part she discusses search dimensions such as locality, relationships, surname strategies, and what evidence can be substituted for documents which have been lost. The length of this video is 75 minutes.

---. *How to Trace Your Pedigree Ladies.* Salt Lake City, UT: Family History World, 1988.

Finding what used to be called the 'distaff' side of one's heritage is not always an easy task. In her work on searching for female genealogy, Eakle provides a guide to the principal indexes available, complete with addresses and how to follow-up information on women. Some sources which might be utilized to find women ancestry information include work identification permits, bastardy bonds, marriage certificates, census records, city court and police records, list of nurses, newspaper gossip columns and numerous other sources. She provides three separate checklists by time period and outlines of eight strategies for tracing women complete with examples. Also provided is an extensive annotated bibliography of sources for women, special research collections, and periodicals.

Eastman, Richard. *Your Roots: Total Genealogical Planning on Your Computer.* Emeryville, CA: Ziff-Davis Press, 1995.

Eastman's *Your Roots* with its accompanying CD assists the researcher in tracking, researching and organizing family history. *Your Roots* presents and explains the plethora of genealogical assistance and tools that can be found using a computer. It describes and presents some evaluation and provides sampling on the CD. He shows how to use a computer to plan major genealogical research; how to access the listing of over 5,000 genealogical societies, libraries and archives; organize genealogical research obtained from traditional book sources; look up census records; digitalize and restore family photos using photo CDs, and provides demonstrations of genealogy software.

Everton, Sr., George B., ed. *The Handy Book for Genealogists.* Tenth edition. Logan, UT: The Everton Publishers, 2002.

> First published in 1947, this tenth edition includes maps for every state, information on nineteen foreign countries, and websites for genealogical research. All the data has been updated from previous editions and much of it has been expanded. The volume is organized by state, with general information about the state - history, records, genealogical societies, libraries, periodicals, and publications on genealogy. After the state information, information will be given on counties, including counties which no longer exist. This section gives information on where to find records stored at the county level.

Fears, Mary L. Jackson. *Slave Ancestral Research: It's Something Else.* Bowie, MD: Heritage Books, Inc., 1995, 2007.

> Mary Fears chronicles her search for her slave ancestors. She found it to be a confusing, frustrating treasure hunt. African American research is often compounded by the fact that many ancestors were held as slaves and listed in the family accounts sometimes only by sex and age. Names were recorded casually, if at all and often changed. Last names were often not listed by owners, some took the last name of their owners when freed, and some simply made up a last name. Fears' search will help to assist others who are doing slave research while hunting for their ancestors. Copies of documents are included so people searching can see what some of the documents you may come across in your research look like.

Field, D. M. *Step-By-Step Guide to Tracing Your Ancestors.* London: British Tourist Authority, 1982.

> Field leads the researcher through birth, death and marriage records, census, the public records office, parish records, wills, printed sources, emigrants, trades and professions, property and taxes and other resources, in a brief step-by-step fashion, spending a few pages discussing each source of information and how to obtain it.

Finnegan, Ruth and Michael Drake, eds. *From Family Tree to Family History: Studying Family and Community History: 19th and 20th Centuries, Volume 1.* Cambridge: Cambridge University Press, 1994.

> This four volume series is aimed at stimulating the development of personal research in family and community history. Volume one moves from a focus on individual families to the broader patterns of population, household structures, domestic economies, family

relationships, and family myths. It has a brief section discussing oral history. Other volumes in the series include: *From Family History to Community, Communities and Families,* and *Sources and Methods for Family and Community Historians: A Handbook.*

Flinn, Cherri M. *Genealogy Basics Online: A Step-by-Step Introduction to Finding Your Ancestors Through the Internet.* Cincinnati, OH: Muska & Lipman Publishing, 2000.

Flinn demonstrates how to tap into the wealth of information available on the World Wide Web. She discusses birth, death and marriage certificates; census and population data; adoption information; military databases; immigration records and others. She also discusses organizing your data; learning Internet search techniques; meeting other researchers and exchanging information online; utilizing web directories and search engines; finding the best sites for further research, online genealogy lessons, and locating genealogy newsgroups and bulletin boards. The guide is amply illustrated with screen examples.

Galeener-Moore, Laverne. *Collecting Dead Relatives: An Irreverent Romp Through the Field of Genealogy.* Baltimore, MD: Genealogical Publishing Co., Inc., 1987.

Collecting Dead Relatives provides a bird's-eye view of the genealogical search from the experiences of one who has been there. Illustrating the steps to research, as well as the pitfalls along the way, Galeener-Moore tells entertaining stories of her research while telling of the techniques necessary to obtain genealogical information.

Galford, Ellen. *The Genealogy Handbook: The Complete Guide to Tracing Your Family Tree.* Pleasantville, NY: The Reader's Digest Association, Inc., 2001, 2005.

Ellen Galford and Reader's Digest have joined to create an easy to use guide to doing genealogy. Tips given in this work include straightforward instructions to guide you through the process of tracing ancestors, interpreting and recording discoveries, sharing what was learned, and preserving this knowledge for future generations. The book features real-life research notes from researchers to help guide you through the research experience, tips for searching the Internet, and includes a comprehensive international directory of public and private archives, genealogical associations, ethnic specialists, and Internet sites. Practical starting tips are given to research for amateurs, but the references will also, be of assistance to experienced genealogists. This is a very visually pleasing book, which discusses the essentials of genealogy in a simple, easy to understand format, with graphics and illustrations of the types of records for which a genealogist will be looking.

Genealogical Research at the Library of Congress. Washington, DC: Library of Congress, 1999, 2001.

This small booklet walks the reader through organizing the research trip to the Library of Congress. It offers in the introduction a step-by-step background research method you should employ before beginning at the Library. This allows you to identify the materials you will need when you get there. It discusses the Reader Registration Card you must apply for and then the resources available at the Library and how to use them.

Genealogy by Genetics, Ltd. *Family Tree DNA.* Houston, TX, 2001?

Family Tree DNA has come up with a 21 marker test to help people connect with relatives when conventional paper trails come to an end. For more information on this testing device, email: info@FamilyTree DNA.com.

Greene, Bob and D. G. Fulford. *To Our Children's Children: Preserving Family Histories for Generations to Come.* New York: Doubleday, 1993.

This is a guidebook of questions that makes recording a personal history as easy as writing a letter. After a brief introduction the rest of the book consists of chapters of engaging questions designed to open the doors of memory.

Greenwood, Val D. *The Researcher's Guide to American Genealogy.* 3rd ed. Baltimore, MD: Genealogical Publishing Co., Inc., 2000.

Frequently used as a genealogy text, this work teaches the principles of genealogical research. It identifies the various classes of records used, explains their uses, and evaluates them for use in the research process.

Grenham, John. *Tracing Your Irish Ancestors: The Complete Guide.* 23rd ed. Baltimore, MD: Genealogical Publishing Co., 2006.

Grenham provides a comprehensive guide for people tracing Irish ancestors. Common genealogical search instructions are compiled in part one, which discusses civil records, census records, church records, and land records. There is a comprehensive series of maps covering the Catholic parishes of Ireland. Part two examines sources with a narrower application such as wills, the genealogical office, emigration, the registry of deeds, newspapers, and directories; and part three is a reference guide which provides access to a range of reference materials including county by county source lists, printed family history, occupations and Church of Ireland records.

Hale, Duane K. *Researching and Writing Tribal Histories.* Grand Rapids, MI: Michigan Indian Press, Grand Rapids Inter-Tribal Council, 1991.

Encompassing tribes in both the United States and Canada, this guide illustrates the process necessary for doing genealogical research among the Native American tribes. Information covered includes: library resources for researching Native Americans, a list of Native American periodicals, a bibliography of related genealogical materials, methodology for recording oral histories, and an outline of writing techniques.

Harris, Maurine and Glen, comp. *Ancestry's Concise Genealogical Dictionary.* Salt Lake City, UT: Ancestry Publishing, 1989.

Don't know what the word grimgrabber is in the record you found on great-granddad? Check out the Harris's *Concise Genealogical Dictionary!* As much as language changes over the generations and is influenced by cultural differences across the continent, this dictionary is a valuable tool for finding unfamiliar words encountered in a genealogical search. It contains thousands of words and their meanings, some obsolete; some belonging to the jargon of the medical, legal or governmental arenas; as well as the Latin terminology found in probates, deeds and church records.

Harvey, R. *Genealogy for Librarians.* 2nd ed. London, UK: Library Association Publishing, Ltd., 1992.

Harvey, a librarian himself, has written a guide to assist genealogists in identifying sources for genealogical research. His overview contains chapters on preliminary and ancillary materials, published secondary sources, records of births, marriage records, death records, career records, and records on crime, poverty, litigation, and migration. This coverage is primarily of records in Great Britain.

Heiderer, Michele. *Before the Search: An Adoption Searcher's Primer.* Indianapolis, IN: Ye Olde Genealogie Shoppe, 1997.

For many, tracing their family histories and genealogies involves finding a family that has not been a part of their life from birth. For adoptees, there are many reasons for finding their family history, some simply to find the answers to unanswered questions, others for more drastic medical reasons. Whatever the reason for finding a birth family, Heiderer has put together a guide for doing family research for the adopted. Chapter one provides a glossary of words and phrases unique to adoption and the search process. Chapter two instructs on locating state laws that pertain to the release of information from the adoption file. In chapter three instructions are given on obtaining copies of the appropriate birth certificates and how to read the information found on them. Chapter four explains the information which may be found in an adoption file and how to use it. Chapter five explains how to use the International Soundex Reunion Registry. Chapter six discusses the different type of search assistance available and how to locate a professional adoption searcher for assistance. Sources of "how to search" books are included. And finally, chapter seven provides a detailed listing of the requirements to initiate a search in each state and the District of Columbia.

Heisey, John W. *Genealogy: Helps, Hints, & Hope.* Morgantown, PA: Masthof Press, 1995.

The articles in this book were originally written for *Antique Week/Tri-State Trader* of Knightstown, Indiana. In his articles, Heisey describes the methods and sources for research in what has become America's favorite pastime. He describes family records, genealogical correspondence, tombstone inscriptions, wills, and records (state, local and federal), census information, church records, military and pension records, and more. Heisey goes beyond the usual how-to books to go into greater detail on the resources of such institutions as the National Archives, Library of Congress, and the D.A.R. Library, the use of county histories, migration patterns, immigration and naturalization, suggestions for building up a personal genealogical library, and much, much more.

Helmbold, F. Wilbur. *Tracing Your Ancestry: A Step-By-Step Guide to Researching Your Family History.* Birmingham, AL: Oxmoor House, Inc., 1976. 1978.

Another step-by-step guide to the construction of a family history, Helmbold's book illustrates how to use records in libraries, archives, churches, genealogy and historical societies, and lineage societies. He also explores the problems that searchers run into during the search process. The various chapters explore the different types of records and searches that can be done while tracing a family history.

Herber, Mark D. *Ancestral Trails: The Complete Guide to British Genealogy and Family History.* Stroud, UK: Sutton, 2004.

Tracing the family in Britain is the subject of *Ancestral Trails*. The early chapters instruct the researcher in the basics of genealogical research, obtaining information from the living relatives, drawing family trees, and starting to research the records of birth, marriage and death. The later chapters guide the researchers in finding things like wills, parish registers, civil and ecclesiastical court records, pool books and property records. This book is recommended for both the beginning and advanced researcher.

Hilton, Suzanne. *Who Do You Think You Are? Digging For Your Family Roots.* Philadelphia: Westminster Press, 1976.

Designed for use with children and youth, Hilton's book begins with instructions on how to make a simple family tree and expand from there with family group records and research charts. She discusses the interview process with family members, where to write for information, and how to find one's way around a genealogical library. She also assists in tracing the 'hard to find' ancestors and illustrates how to document facts and statistics.

Hinckley, Kathleen W. *Locating Lost Family Members & Friends: Modern Genealogical Research Techniques for Locating the People of Your Past and Present.* Cincinnati, OH: Betterway Books, 1999.

Computers have made the location of the lost much more convenient for the average person. This has rapidly enhanced the process of genealogy and the popularity of doing genealogy as more people are able to accomplish more research in the privacy of their own homes. Hinckley, a professional private investigator and a Certified Genealogical Record Specialist, has combined her skills to produce this guide to assist in easing the genealogical searching. She demonstrates how to find such information as telephone and city directories; birth and death certificates; marriage and divorce records; social security documentation; licenses and registrations; military records; real estate transactions; high school and college transcripts; census records and more. Instruction is provided for conducting Internet research and she details how to overcome common twentieth-century problems such as privacy acts, record destruction, and more.

—. *Your Guide to the Federal Census for Genealogists, Researchers, and Family Historians.* Cincinnati, OH: Betterway Books, 2002.

>Census information is a primary source of genealogical information once you have tapped all your family's memories. Census provides such family history data as names, addresses, place of birth, race, land ownership, military service, and more. In this work, Hinckley shows how to use federal census to document families, communities and social histories. She provides step-by-step instructions for finding the census records and indexes you need; details about the information contained in the census records from 1790 to 1930; procedures for obtaining more recent census information; guidelines for working with non-population schedules, including agriculture, industry and manufacturing, mortality, social statistics, veteran, and dependent classes; tracing hard to find populations such as slaves, nuns, monks, military personnel, Native Americans, and more; and advice for coping with census irregularities. Also included are a glossary of census terms and extraction forms based on each census year to make the recording of information easier.

Hinshaw, William W. *Encyclopedia of American Quaker Genealogy.* Baltimore, MD: Genealogical Publishing Co., Inc., 1969. (CD version, 2003)

>Researching the Society of Friends, aka Quakers, is not an easy task. Records to this group are hidden in voluminous minutes and meeting records located in various places in assorted states. Though these records have been kept since the formal date of the organization of the Society, many of these records are held in private by the descendants of those who began keeping the records. The records when found contain birth, marriage and death information. This volume contains all the records that have been collected or ever belonged to the North Carolina Yearly Meeting of Friends which are known to be in existence.

Horowitz, Lois. *Dozens of Cousins: Blue Genes, Horse Thieves, and Other Relative Surprises in Your Family Tree.* Berkeley, CA: Ten Speed Press, 1999.

>Containing information on how to begin tracing your family tree, Horowitz's *Dozens of Cousins*, shows how family tree research can be fun, revealing how interrelationships within families work, and the complexities of many relationships. Interspersed with research tips and secrets for genealogical searching, Horowitz has put

genealogical facts about well known people and their families. She also shows how to make a family relationship chart, shares sample family trees, and suggests templates to get the research started.

Howell, Barbara T. *How to Trace Your African-American Roots: Discovering Your Unique History.* Secaucus, NJ: Carol Publishing Group, 1999.

Howell presents a practical guide showing how to use the basic resources of genealogy to trace African-American ancestors. Recognizing the deprivation of slavery on the African-American family, *How to Trace* emphasizes the importance of oral history in the rich African and African-American tradition and explains how to bridge the gap when written records are few or non-existent. Howell provides worksheets, genealogy charts and over 200 questions to ask relatives on everything from personal data and education to family life and military service. Sources for finding information are also listed and Howell guides the user in where to find and what to look for in birth records, marriage certificates, deeds, death records, wills, and even census. Word processing software and genealogical computer programs are also discussed.

Irvine, Sherry. *Your English Ancestry: A Guide for North Americans.* Rev. ed. Salt Lake City, UT: Ancestry, 1998.

Irvine wrote this book because she felt that other books on researching English ancestry did not always focus on a logical search routine for the most efficient way of finding the information. When looking for genealogical sources, the searcher needs to remember that every genealogical source has the following components: the time period it covers, the geographical period it covers, how it is organized, the information needed to access it, the new information it should provide and the availability. The researcher should provide room in each citation for this information so as to make the organization of information more efficient. Irvine provides a basic how to chapter and then goes on to explain the various resources available for searching out English ancestors.

Jacobus, Donald L. *Genealogy as Pastime and Profession.* 2nd ed. Baltimore, MD: Genealogical Publishing Co., 1986.

One of the classics in the genealogy field, *Genealogy as Pastime and Profession* was originally published in 1930. Jacobus considered genealogy in all its aspects - the use of source materials, the evaluation of evidence, the cultural and social aspects, the origin of the American colonies, the conditions of the genealogical profession, and the compilation of family history. Tight and intense in presentation - yes, tiny type too, the book covers such issues as early nomenclature, royal ancestry, genealogy as a profession, source materials - printed and original, how to compile a family history, the law, and how to trace your ancestry. This is probably a book for the deeply involved genealogist, not the hobbyist.

Jamison, Sandra L. *Finding Your People: An African-American Guide to Discovering Your Roots.* New York: Perigee Books, 1999.

African-Americans sometimes face unique challenges in searching for their ancestors, particularly those whose families came from a slave background. Jamison explains how to negotiate these obstacles and discusses finding lineage and pedigree documents; finding slave trade chronologies; alternate spellings of common surnames; interviewing methods; setting goals and keeping records; public versus "alternate" records; African-American research sources; local, national, and international resources; organizing family reunions; creating pedigree charts and family group sheets and using census information. The first five chapters discuss genealogy and the whys and hows of doing it, and the next seven chapters discuss resources and the location of information, as well as planning the family reunion. Numerous addresses and websites are given for finding statistical and genealogical information.

Johnson, Anne E. and Adam M. Cooper. *A Student's Guide to African American Genealogy.* Phoenix, AR: Oryx Press, 1996.

Johnson and Cooper's *Guide to African American Genealogy* begins with a basic history of African Americans, their language, their culture, and their arrival in America. Chapters four through eight discuss the basics of doing genealogy, discussing both how to do it and some of the common sources available and how to use them. Specifics are given on how to do research within slave and ownership records, use of oral history, military records and other sources affecting African Americans in the United States. The final chapter of this guide deals with the preservation of family history, both producing the family tree and compiling a written family narrative. Comprehensive bibliographies also give ideas for obtaining further information both about African American history in general and other genealogical sources.

Katers, Lynda F. *Family History Made Easy: A Complete Workbook and Directory: An Easy, Step-by-Step Workbook and Directory to Help Everyone Compile Their Family History: Includes Forms, Addresses, and Internet Sites.* St. Paul, MN: Family Histories, 2000.

Lynda Katers provides the beginning genealogist with an easy to follow guide which follows a logical sequence in developing the family history. Each chapter includes copies of the necessary charts and forms for whichever part of the search sequence is being conducted. Chapter topics include: beginning the search for your family history; pedigree and group charts; churches and cemeteries; vital records; names; censuses; immigration and naturalization records; national archives; ship passenger arrival records; military records; other countries; probate court records; genealogy libraries; national and international sources; the Internet; land records and the Social Security Death Index.

Kavasch, E. Barrie. *A Student's Guide to Native American Genealogy.* Phoenix, AR: Oryx Press, 1996.

Kavasch's *Guide to Native American Genealogy* begins with a basic history of Native Americans and their mythology. Chapters three through six discuss the basics of doing genealogy, discussing both how to do it and some of the common sources available and how to use them. Specifics are given on how to do research within tribal records and other Native American sources. Comprehensive bibliographies also give ideas for obtaining further information both about Native American history in general and other genealogical sources.

Kurzweil, Arthur. *From Generation to Generation: How to Trace Your Jewish Genealogy and Family History.* New York: HarperCollins, 1994, 2001.

From Generation to Generation provides a definitive guide to doing Jewish genealogical research. It provides a step-by-step guide to gathering family history from family members and family papers, doing Holocaust research, immigration and naturalization records, cemetery research and more. Originally published in 1980, this revised edition has new and updated information. Other information discussed includes how to find birth, marriage, and death records; passenger lists for steamships to the United States; how to do research in Eastern Europe, how to organize research findings; and how to obtain information on Jewish records from the Mormon Church. Lists of books and societies dealing with Jewish ancestry in particular are listed within this text.

Kyvig, David E. and Myron A. Marty. *Nearby History: Exploring the Past Around You.* 2nd ed. Walnut Creek, CA: AltaMira Press, 2000.

> This is a general introduction to historical research which includes building an archive, doing oral history, building preservation, etc. It has practical suggestions about how to read historical documents, photographs, and other source material.

Latham, William. *How to Find Your Family Roots: The Complete Guide to Searching for Your Ancestors.* Santa Monica, CA: Santa Monica Press, 1994.

> Beginning with a brief overview of American immigration, Latham provides a guide for tracing family history in a simple, easy and inexpensive manner. His book features how to organize research materials; how to interview family members; where to look for family treasures and relics; how to conduct library research; what to ask; where to obtain church records, vital records, and government resources; how to search in foreign countries; and how to write up your findings. He also provides a state-by-state list of sources and a country-by-country list of resources.

--- and Cindy Higgins. *How to Find Your Family Roots and Write Your Family History.* Rev. ed. Santa Monica, CA: Santa Monica Press, 2000.

> This revision of the 1994 edition of *How to Find Your Family Roots* has been updated to include the latest Internet resources and includes a section on writing up your research. Subjects covered in this edition include how to interview family members, where to look for family memorabilia, using the Internet, what questions to ask librarians, where to obtain church records, how to search for vital records, how to use government resources, looking for ancestors in foreign countries, a country-by-country list of sources, a state listing of resources, organizing your research, incorporating history and storytelling into writing your history, designing and printing your history and how to share this history with friends and relatives.

Lichtman, Allan J. *Your Family History: How to Use Oral History, Personal Family Archives, and Public Documents to Discover Your Heritage.* New York: Vintage Books, 1978.

> Lichtman offers a research plan for those doing family histories. Chapters give an overview of oral history and provide basic information on techniques and how to conduct interviews, maintain taped records and interpret transcripts. Genealogical resources such as family records, photos, tax and census records, and heirlooms are also included.

Linder, Bill R. *How to Trace Your Family History.* New York: Everest House, 1978.

> Linder's book provides an overview on the steps to take in constructing your family history. He discusses the interview process with family members, sources of information like vital statistics, genealogical libraries and records offices, and the preparation of the materials found and publishing the results.

Marelli, Diane. *The Beginners' Guide to Tracing Your Roots.* 2nd ed. Oxford, UK: How to Books, Ltd., 2007.

> Diane Marelli uses her own family research to walk the fledgling genealogist through the process of doing family research. Written in a diary format, it includes real life "adventures" and the joys of discovery as well as the pitfalls that the researcher can fall into along the way. Through her four year journey to find her ancestors, Marelli offers tips on using the internet, church records and private archives.

McClure, Rhonda. *The Complete Idiot's Guide to Online Genealogy.* Indianapolis, IN: Alpha, 2002.

> Without forgetting that not everything may be found online, McClure's introduction to working with genealogy online helps one get started with the fundamentals of using the Internet to work with genealogy. If you haven't used the Internet before, she provides an introductory chapter with an Internet overview. Also provided is instruction on how to communicate online with other genealogists. She gives the user a step-by-step guide to getting the most out of online research and how to use the Internet to find the things that will need to be visited in person.

—. *Genealogist's Computer Companion.* Cincinnati, OH: Betterway Books, 2002.

> The Internet has rapidly become the most popular spot for looking for any matter of information and in particular, genealogical searching and posting. McClure assists genealogists in mastering the basics of online research in an efficient, versatile manner. Most importantly, she provides guidelines for verifying existing research and finding new information. Areas of coverage in this work are the accession of library catalogs and databases; genealogical software; preservation of records, documents and photographs electronically; using online resources to prepare for site visits; verifying Internet findings; and accessing newsgroups, bulletin boards, mailing lists and commercial sites.

McClure, Tony M. *Cherokee Proud: A Guide for Tracing and Honoring Your Cherokee Ancestors.* Somerville, TN: Chunannee Books, 1999.

Tony McClure takes the Indian researcher through the steps necessary to trace records looking for Cherokee ancestry. The basic search strategies should be comparable for any Native American searches where similar record collections exist. He details how to start a search, searching the Cherokee census rolls, other records, provides addresses for selected archives, lists recommended texts, discusses pre-colonial/colonial era inter-marriages, gives a brief history of the Cherokee people and discusses the heritage.

McGlone, Mary T. *The Bare-Bones Guide to Genealogy: Researching and Recording Your Family History.* Greenport, NY: Pilot Books, 1998.

This book is designed to get you started on your genealogical research, illustrating how to do the basic starting steps and making sure you have the correct information when you start. She discusses basic records and shows information sheets for organizing your information as you find it. McGlone talks about using charts, getting organized, genealogy by computer, naming practices, family records, library research, public records, census records, immigrant ancestors, African American and Native American ancestors, preserving family treasures, and gathering family stories.

McGoldrick, Monica. *You Can Go Home Again: Reconnecting With Your Family.* New York: W. W. Norton & Company, 1995.

Beyond simply genealogy, *You Can Go Home Again* is a book of family assessment. A psychological study in which the study of family and knowing family history can aid in the reconnection to home. Assisting in research of the family, this book also aids in reconciliation. It demonstrates how knowing the details of family history can be more important than simply tracing the family tree. In addition, each chapter has questions at the end which facilitate putting together the family history.

Melnyk, Marcia D. Y. *Family History 101: A Beginner's Guide to Finding Your Ancestors.* Cincinnati, OH: Family Tree Books, 2005.

Marcia Melnyk is a professional genealogist and author of several books on genealogy. In this work, she provides beginning genealogists with a simple, step-by-step guide to doing family history. She discusses tips on tapping the information available on the Internet; checklists, forms, case studies, and illustrations to help get you started; assistance on maximizing the use of existing information, finding more and what it means; and tips and techniques for recording and sharing the information with your family.

———. *The Genealogist's Question & Answer Book.* Cincinnati, OH: Betterway Books, 2002.

Getting started in genealogy means asking lots of questions and knowing the questions to ask. Melnyk provides a starting point by listing 150 answers to the most commonly asked genealogical questions. The questions are grouped according to the type of resources used in genealogy, such as: census, church registers, immigration records, oral histories, web sites, electronic databases, and more. She illustrates what to look for in the different type of documents that assist in genealogical research, what kind of information can be found in the different documents and the next step in your search. In addition to discussing the various types of records and the information they contain, she tells how to conduct and oral history interview, and how to record and properly store documents.

———. *The Weekend Genealogist.* Cincinnati, OH: Betterway Books, 2000.

Most of us do not have time to do genealogy full-time. Melnyk here provides a guide which helps those of us who have to "pick it up, and put it down," piecing it together a little at a time. She shows how to get the most mileage out of short periods of time. Using case studies and timesaving tips for organizing time and research she provides sidebars, sample letters, and blank forms to assist in learning: how to implement organizational techniques for streamlining research and creating a timesaving filing system for notes, documents, and forms; how to get information by efficiently using mail, Fax and e-mail; how to utilize local historical and genealogical societies, relatives and microform rental programs; how to effectively search the Internet; how to use organizational forms such as pedigree charts and correspondence logs; how to effectively use the documents you find by learning the ten questions to 'ask' each document; how to find and access research facilities such as the National Archives and Records Administration, vital records offices, and libraries; how to plan research trips; and how to create a network among other genealogists.

Miller, Robert L. *Researching Life Stories and Family Histories.* Thousand Oaks, CA: Sage, 2000.

Robert Miller has designed his *Researching Life Stories and Family Histories* for those interested in doing biographical, life history or family historical research. The main section of Miller's book covers methods and instruction for collecting and analyzing family and life histories. Exercises are provided to illustrate this methodology. He uses three approaches to teach biographical methods. The first is the realist approach, this focused on techniques of interviewing; second is the neo-positivist, more structured interview techniques; and the third is narrative, emphasizing the active construction of life stories through the interplay between interviewer and interviewee.

Mills, Elizabeth S., ed. *Professional Genealogy: A Manual for Researchers, Writers, Editors, Lecturers, Librarians.* Baltimore, MD: Genealogical Publishing Co., 2001.

This manual was put together by professional genealogists for anyone interested in doing, or assisting someone in doing genealogy. It provides standards and instructions for those undertaking their own research and it gives guidelines for those considering hiring professionals to do the research. For librarians who are suddenly dealing with genealogy amateurs, this provides a bridge to methodology, sources and details of history often needed by researchers. For the professional genealogist, this book can provide assistance in enhancing their skills and assist them in their business of genealogy. Topic areas written by the twenty-nine professional genealogist who contributed to this manual include research skills, the analysis of evidence, writing and compiling genealogical research, the core genealogy collection, genealogical ethics and standards, editing and publishing, and other topics of interest in genealogy.

Milner, Paul and Linda Jonas. *A Genealogist's Guide to Discovering Your English Ancestors: How to Find and Record Your Unique Heritage.* Cincinnati, OH: Betterway Books, 2000.

Milner and Jonas have written a step-by-step guide for researching English ancestry. They not only show what records will be needed and how to find them, but also, why the records were created and how they can reveal more about an ancestor's life. Following their instructions, one should be able to focus and maximize research results by setting goals and keeping organized; find information without leaving home by utilizing the Internet, public libraries, and Family History Centers; search major indexes with speed and efficiency; locate crucial records such as civil registration, census returns, parish registers and probate materials by using the International Genealogical Index and the FHL catalog; analyze documents and records to determine their accuracy using their visual examples; and understand special challenges such as geographic and political terms, unstandardized records, and social and historical issues. Case studies are used to explain different features of genealogical searching and to illustrate the sources.

Mokotoff, Gary. *How to Document Victims and Locate Survivors of the Holocaust.* Teaneck, NJ; Avotaynu, 1995.

> Mokotoff wrote this book after having discovered how many of his relatives were actually lost during the Holocaust. Though it was widely believed that the Germans destroyed most of the records of Jewish existence, it was discovered that many of the records do in fact, still exist. Many of these have surfaced since the collapse of communism in Eastern Europe, the Soviets having seized great quantities of German records during the war. Mokotoff provides assistance in finding and accessing these records. He discusses the basics, provides a checklist for Holocaust research, discusses yizkor books, testimony, international tracing services, how to locate survivors, landsmanshaftn societies, oral testimonies and provides a case study of his own family. The second part of the book discusses facilities which have collections of Holocaust materials.

--- and Warren Blatt. *Getting Started in Jewish Genealogy.* Bergenfield, NJ: Avotaynu, Inc. 2000.

> Most people think Jewish genealogy is difficult as most Jews today do not live anywhere near where their ancestors did. The Holocaust and migration have conspired to make Jewish ancestry hard to trace. This however, has become a myth. There is a strong Jewish presence on the Internet, more than eighty Jewish societies throughout the world, approximately fifty books on tracing Jewish ancestry, a quarterly magazine called *Avotaynu*, and government census and vital records, many of which were not destroyed in the Holocaust simply because they were government records. This book has answers to the many questions about where to look for Jewish records and numerous listings of the appropriate source materials.

Moody, David. *Scottish Family History.* Baltimore, MD: Genealogical Publishing Co., Inc., 1988, 2002.

> Not only about researching the Scottish family, this book is also a guide to the family as it has developed in Scotland from the time of the clans to the present day. While it is not the step-by-step guide to genealogy provided by many other sources, this would be a good companion to one of those as one studies the structure of family in Scotland. As well as providing sources of information within Scotland, it delves into customs and traditions of the Scottish clans.

Morris, Christine M. *Tracing Your Ancestors: An Illustrated Guide to Compiling Your Family Tree.* New York: CLB, distributed by Quadrillon Publishing, Inc., 1999.

Christine Morris has created an interactive guide for searching out and constructing your family tree. Accompanied by a CD which contains forms and reports, genealogical data, templates in a variety of languages, and instructions on importing files from local archives and Internet sites around the world; this book is geared to both the amateur and experienced genealogist. Morris's guide is fully illustrated with pictures and examples of what is discussed, and not so long that the beginning researcher needs to feel bogged down at the beginning of their search. Each section is designed to work progressively through each step in the genealogical research method. Morris explains in text and illustration how to draw up a family tree, organize research, the use of documented records - including civil registers, censuses, parish records, indexes and many other unusual materials. Along with the enclosed CD, she provides advice on using computers in genealogy, selecting the appropriate software, and surfing the Internet. Addresses of useful organizations are listed at the end of the book, as well as a bibliography of further readings and a comprehensive index.

Nelson, Lynn. *A Genealogist's Guide to Discovering Your Italian Ancestors.* Cincinnati, OH: Betterway Books, 1997.

Discovering Your Italian Ancestors is a step-by-step guide suitable for beginning genealogists as well as experienced genealogists for locating Italian ancestors as far back as the 1700s. As well as general genealogical guidelines, it includes how to use the major American records such as census, naturalization, ship passenger lists and passport applications; minor American records such as family letters, church and cemetery records, and newspapers; Italian vital records - civil documents recording birth, marriages and deaths; interpreting margin notations in Italian records; and how to interview relatives.
Information is also given on Italian naming traditions, how to interpret foreign handwriting, tips on using English/Italian dictionaries, and a letter writing guide to use for requesting data from Italian officials.

Parker, J. Carlyle. *Going to Salt Lake City to do Family History Research.* 3rd ed. Turlock, CA: Marietta Publishing Co., 1996.

Salt Lake City has long been the mecca for genealogical research, the Church of Jesus Christ of Latter-Day Saints (LDS) maintaining and constantly updating the premier genealogical collection in the world.

Parker teaches his readers how to prepare for a trip to the Family History Library maintained by the LDS and how to use the library once they arrive. There are now numerous branches of the Family History Library in major cities around the country. The scope of the Family History Library is worldwide with its greatest strengths being the United States, Canada and Western Europe. In many cases, family research may be done cheaper and more efficiently by simply going to Salt Lake City than by traveling to various cities and courthouses around the country. Most of your routine organization should be done before going to Salt Lake City, and Parker explains what is to be done in the organizational portion of your search.

Pengra, Nancy. *Family Histories: An Easy, Step-by-Step Guide to Capturing Your Family's Precious Memories Now, Before They're Lost.* St. Paul, MN: Family Histories, 1995.

Nancy Pengra developed this book after the death of her grandfather brought the realization that many of her family's stories had been lost with his death. Written with genealogists in mind, she presents an easy to follow guide for getting stories down on paper. She includes hundreds of ideas for jogging memories and triggering stories, ways to add variety to stories, tips for organizing the stories and memorabilia including techniques for writing and publishing, over forty pages of 'trigger' questions and samples of what others have done, a list of historical dates since 1900 on what has been done or invented, and creative ways of sharing the stories.

Perl, Lila. *The Great Ancestor Hunt: The Fun of Finding Out Who You Are.* Boston: Houghton Mifflin, 1989.

While aimed at children with the intent of stimulating their interest in genealogy, this book provides a lot of interesting information in a very accessible format. For the beginning genealogist of any age, it is an easy to follow first step and much less intimidating than many books that claim to be for beginners. Perl suggests numerous sources of information that may be garnered within the family circle as well as suggesting sources that take a little more effort, as in writing away for more difficult to obtain information and governmental records.

Pomery, Chris. *Family History in the Genes: Trace Your DNA and Grow Your Family Tree.* Surrey, UK: The National Archives, 2007.

DNA testing is not something only associated with solving crimes or determining paternity suits. It can also be used in a family history search. There are now more than a dozen companies which will do tests targeted at family historians. This test can be used to determine if families who share names are actually related to each other. This book offers practical advice on when to pursue this avenue of family searching and is filled with tips, techniques and case studies.

Powell, Kimberly and William G. Hartley. *The Everything Family Tree Book: Research and Preserve Your Family History.* 2nd ed. Avon, MA: Adams Media Corporation, 2006.

Power and Hartley's *Everything Family Tree Book*, covers almost every aspect of creating a family tree and history. Complete with sample charts and instructions, this easy to read and understand guide also provides information on tracking down outside sources, researching religious and ethnic organizations, soliciting remembrances from family members, collecting and preserving family records, and writing your family history. He also lists organizations and sources of genealogical information, as well as preservation and archival supplies. One chapter is on end products that can be created from the information that has been collected besides writing your history.

Recording Historic Cemeteries: A Guide for Historical Societies and Genealogists. Columbia, SC: Chicora Foundation, Inc., 1998.

The Chicora Foundation has developed a small publication detailing identification, and mapping of historic cemeteries, preservation planning, and conservation treatment of stones and ironwork. Many cemeteries are no longer in use and are in great need of care. This booklet discusses getting permission to work in cemeteries, the necessary supplies, what should be recorded, and information which may be obtained from the inscriptions.

Richley, Pat. *The Everything Online Genealogy Book: Use the Web to Discover Long-lost Relations, Trace Your Family Tree Back to Royalty, and Share Your History with Far-flung Cousins.* Holbrook, MA: Adams Media Corporation, 2000.

One of the more inexpensive genealogical guides available, this book should appeal to the beginning genealogist. It provides basic genealogical guidelines for surfing the Internet for genealogical resources.

Roberts, Ralph. *Genealogy Via the Internet: Tracing Your Family Roots Quickly and Easily.* 2nd ed. Alexander, NC: Alexander Books, 2003.

Genealogy is one of the most rapidly growing hobbies worldwide. The Internet has been instrumental in opening up this fascination with family history providing a library in your own home. This book contains tips on which genealogical programs are the easiest and best to use; how to hook your computer up to the world via your telephone; resources available through the Internet and other online services; places to find reference materials and guides of all kinds; and online databases you can search for your own family information. Numerous websites are given for searching various ancestry listings.

Robl, Gregory. *A Student's Guide to German American Genealogy.* Phoenix, AZ: Oryx Press, 1996.

Robl begins his *Guide to German American Genealogy* with a basic history of Germany and German emigration. Chapters three through six discuss the basics of doing genealogy, discussing both how to do it and some of the common sources available and how to use them, chapter three delving into the specific German sources for searching. There is also a glossary of German-English genealogical terms. Comprehensive bibliographies also give ideas for obtaining further information both about German history in general and other genealogical sources.

Rogers, Colin D. *Tracing Your English Ancestors: A Manual for Analyzing and Solving Genealogical Problems, 1538 to the Present.* 2nd ed. Manchester, UK: Manchester University Press, 1989.

Rogers has structured his book more around the need for solving problems than in instructing on the ways to use genealogical records themselves. He approaches the three basic problems of genealogy in his work, the need to find parents, marriage information and death information. For example, the section on marriage discusses why you may be failing to find a marriage record and what can be done about it. This book was written both for the amateur and the professional genealogist. Rogers addresses the reasoning for beginning genealogical research, asking questions and getting organized in his preamble. Parts two through four concentrate on looking for parents, marriage and death information. Within the second part he deals with birth certificates from 1837 to the present, problems that might occur, finding more than one possible birth, alternative sources, and other records which might relate to birth records. He also deals with the census from 1801 to the present and what to do if you cannot find the information you are looking for in the census records; and church records from 1538 to the present which deal with baptisms and other church related information. Part three introduces looking for marriage information, marriage certificates from 1837 to the present and failure to find a certificate; marriage in the church from 1538 to the present and unrecorded marriages; and finding alternative sources when parish registers are not available. Part four deals with looking for deaths. Death certificates from 1837 to the present and what to do if the death is not registered; other death related records which may be searched; church burial from 1538 to the present and finding more than one possible burial site; and probate records which discuss wills proved both before 1858 and from 1858 to the present including lost wills and other probate information. Appendices list such topics as family history societies, registration districts in England and Wales, principle records offices, and how to employ professional help.

Rose, Christine and Kay G. Ingalls. *The Complete Idiot's Guide to Genealogy.* Indianapolis, IN: Alpha Books, 2005.

Beginning a genealogical search can be a daunting process. *The Complete Idiot's Guide*'s are designed to make tasks easier, and the genealogist's version illustrates quick and easy ways to unlock the secrets of public records, choosing a research strategy that works for you, avoiding common mistakes, keeping accurate records with complete citations, writing effective query letters, and getting past dead-ends. It also provides clues for finding family documents, money saving ideas for planning investigative trips, hints on using electronic records, and lists of genealogical repositories and archives.

Ryskamp, George R. *Finding Your Hispanic Roots.* Rev. ed. Baltimore, MD: Genealogical Publishing Co., 1997.

The first four chapters in this work are the basics on how to do genealogy from the Hispanic viewpoint, how to begin, how to set up a filing system and how to understand the Sosa numbering system, (Sosa was a Spanish genealogist who set up a genealogical numbering system in 1676 which has been adopted worldwide,) selecting a computer program, and using the Church of Jesus Christ of Latter-Day Saints family history centers. The remainder of the book explains specific aspects of using Hispanic materials, including languages, handwriting, naming systems, and civil, church, military, and notary records in Hispanic countries. A listing of Hispanic genealogical societies in the United States is also included. The 1984 edition also includes a listing of sample letters and forms.

--- and Peggy Ryskamp. *A Student's Guide to Mexican-American Genealogy.* Phoenix, AZ: Oryx Press, 1996.

> Part of Oryx Press's American Family Tree series, the Ryskamps' book follows the pattern of those dealing with other nationalities. It begins with a section on Mexican-Americans exploring family history, understanding their heritage, ancestors, identity, surnames, and resources for Mexican-Americans; the second section discusses the actual Mestizo society and the history of Mexicans in the United States and Mexico; chapter three discusses how to do genealogical research for this ethnic group, both general research and specific research to the heritage; chapter four includes chars and computer information, discussing the organization of the research and findings; chapter five discusses working with Mexican documentation; chapter six discusses other documents such as census records, notarial records and other resources; chapter seven discusses Mexican Archives, research groups, genealogical societies and other resources for research; and chapter eight discussed writing the family history. Within each chapter other books and resources are listed for further research on the chapter's subject matter.

Smith, Jessie C., ed. *Ethnic Genealogy: A Researcher's Guide.* Westport, CT: Greenwood Press, 1983.

> *Ethnic Genealogy* provides an introduction to those problems confronting persons searching for ancestors who are American Indian, Asian-American, black-American, or Hispanic. The first half of the book provides information on general genealogical research and the second half contains extended information on each of the groups mentioned above. The locations of sources for the different groups are listed; lists of periodicals, directories or societies and repositories, and a bibliography is provided for each chapter.

Smith, Lorna D. *Genealogy is More Than Charts.* Ellicott City, MD: Lifetimes, 1991.

> Smith has designed this book as what she calls a compilation of fifteen books, rather than fifteen chapters. Each can stand alone as a subject, or be combined with any of the others as a genealogy project or search. The books provide ideas and activities for genealogists with all levels of experience from beginners to pros and suggest ways to communicate, record and turn memories into family histories. The chapters include such topics as the rewards of genealogy; celebrating life; the display of heirlooms; creating memories; preserving community; writing; and many other family oriented topics.

Smolenyak, Megan and Ann Turner. *Trace Your Roots With DNA: Using Genetic Tests to Explore Your Family Tree.* Emmaus, PA: Holtzbrinck Publishers, 2004.

There are so many people in the world with the same last names, and they can't all be related! It is now possible to use DNA technology to find out if that person you met with your last name is related to you. With this new technology it is possible to find out if you are related to a person who's name you share, find out what region your ancestors came from, if the family rumors of adoption are true, if you have an American Indian ancestor and much more. Tests are private, easy and this book tells how to use them, where to get them and how to read the results.

Stern, Malcolm H. *First American Jewish Families: 600 Genealogies, 1654-1988.* Rev. ed. Baltimore, MD: Ottenheimer Publishers, 1991.

Stern's goal has been to compile the genealogies of Jewish families established in the United States and Canada prior to 1840, tracing the descendants wherever possible to the present. The year 1840 was chosen because by that time there were an estimated 10,000 Jews settled in America. Within twenty years, an additional 200,000 Jews had immigrated to America. This work provides a basic stepping stone for those of Jewish heritage to make a beginning to the exploration of their family histories.

Stevenson, Noel C. *Genealogical Evidence: A Guide to the Standard of Proof Relating to Pedigrees, Ancestry, Heirship, and Family History.* Rev. ed. Laguna Hills, CA: Aegean Park Press, 1989.

Drawing on legal citations and case histories, Stevenson gives practical advice on verifying genealogical evidence. His work provides information concerning such things as legitimacy, illegitimacy, marriage, death, birth, age and identity. He gives suggestions for locating critical facts and examples of the type of evidence necessary to prove or disprove facts which may concern pedigree, heirship, inheritance, and will contests.

Stone, Elizabeth. *Black Sheep and Kissing Cousins: How Our Family Stories Shape Us.* New York: Times Books, 1988.

Family stories are instrumental in shaping our identities. They provide a sense of place in the world, give us values, inspirations, warnings, and incentives. Weaving her own family stories among stories of over a hundred other people, Stone clarifies predictable types of family legends, provides ways for interpreting our own stories, and the stories role in our lives. She examines stories of birth, death, work, money, romantic adventure in the context of the family storytelling ritual. She shows how the stories of ancient ancestors may provide answers in our current lives, as well as how new events in our lives create new stories to be passed down to future generations. While this book doesn't really qualify as a "how-to" book, it illustrates what can be done in writing down and preserving the stories that have been told throughout the generations.

Streets, David H. *Slave Genealogy: A Research Guide with Case Studies.* Bowie, MD: Heritage Books, Inc., 1986, 2004.

Emphasizing non-plantation slave genealogy, Streets provides a clear discussion and case studies drawn from Wayne County, Kentucky records. He illustrates the search methods and types of analysis that are needed, as well as the importance of researching both owners and slaves. The case studies are supported by charts and diagrams, and extracts from original sources to show the methodology and type of records used. Chapter one discusses research methodology and the difficulty of tracking down slave genealogy and tells how to use a variety of the record sources in the search. Chapter two lists the various types of records and how to use them effectively, and chapter three highlights three case studies.

Stryker-Rodda, Harriet. *How to Climb Your Family Tree: Genealogy for Beginners.* Rev. ed. New York: J. B. Lippincott, 1995.

This introduction to the methods and principles of genealogical research is written for the beginning researcher. It illustrates how to get started and how to find clues in family treasurers and memorabilia. It also describes the important sources of information such as census records, church records, vital records of birth, marriage, death, probate, and land records, and the infinite array of public records.

Sturdevant, Katherine S. *Bringing Your Family History to Life Through Social History.* Cincinnati, OH: Betterway Books, 2000.

Social history is a facet of everyday life and as such, an important part of getting a feel for your family's history. Sturdevant illustrates how this can be used to fill out your family history and also to assist in the searching for family history. In this work she shows how to fill out the background of daily lives; how to find, acquire, care for analyze, copy and display family photographs; how to record your family's oral traditions and folklore, as well as formulating the questions; how to collect artifacts and materials from within the family such as heirlooms, memorabilia and photographs; and how to do research, such as writing letters for historical information, using libraries, and creating the cultural context to learn how your ancestors lived. Each chapter has tips, charts, examples, and checklists to guide you through the research process.

Swan, James. *The Librarian's Guide to Genealogical Services and Research.* New York: Neal-Schuman Publishers, 2004.

The *Librarian's Guide* offers both a how to section and a resource section for genealogists getting started in developing their family histories. Beginning with a concise introduction to basic procedures with anecdotes, practical advice, checklists, and examples; it continues through resources lists and lists of the latest methods and tools. Also included are: reproducible forms for genealogy, contact and collections information for major genealogical institutions, descriptions and evaluations of major genealogical software, Websites and listservs, hints on hiring a professional researcher and how to evaluate his performance, and more.

Szucs, Loretta D. *Family History Made Easy: A Step-by-Step Guide to Discovering Your Heritage.* Salt Lake City, UT: Ancestry, Inc., 1998.

Suggesting the obvious, that is, working backwards from the present generation to the past, Szucs clearly lays out the strategy for the family historian. Chapters include information on researching at home; published sources and libraries; local, state and federal records; genealogical societies; foreign, ethnic, and religious research; computers and the Internet; and how to organize and preserve what you have found. The text is clear and well written and sources for further information and addresses are given when appropriate and are abundant.

--- and Sandra H. Luebking, eds. *The Source: A Guidebook of American Genealogy.* 3rd ed. Salt Lake City, UT: Ancestry, 2006.

Designed for genealogists of various skill levels, *The Source* is a complete reference of the vast collection of significant record sources from Colonial times to the present. It details search techniques and provides creative ideas for continuing research. By using *the Source*, the genealogist can determine which records exist for a particular time period, what information can logically be obtained, where the records may be located, and how they might best be put to use.

Taylor, Maureen. *Through the Eyes of Your Ancestors: A Step-by-Step Guide to Uncovering Your Family's History.* Boston: Houghton Mifflin, 1999.

> Taylor instructs genealogists on how to utilize a variety of resources including vital records, cemetery records, land records, citizenship papers, passenger lists, church records, newspapers, city directories, military records, web sites, and genealogical libraries. This book is directed to children and youth who are interested in looking into their family's background. Each chapter begins with an anecdote to entice young researchers with what might be hidden in their family's pasts. The initial chapters include information on interviewing and record keeping, and offer sample questions and organizational charts.

Vandagriff, G. G. *Voices in Your Blood: Discovering Identity Through Family History.* Kansas City, MO: Andrews and McMeel, 1993.

> A practical guide to genealogy, Vandagriff outlines all the steps to creating a family history, from interviewing the relatives to using computer software without getting lost. Though now several years old by computer standards, she introduces the reader to the computer research tool *Family Search*, this introduction can be transferred in general to the multitude of other family search software which has sprung up since. Chapters deal with asking questions (and sample questions are listed); evaluating information received; obtaining records through correspondence; using census records; using new technologies; using the Family History Library; and surname research among other tips.

Walker, James D. *Black Genealogy: How to Begin.* Athens: University of Georgia Center for Continuing Education, 1977.

> Compiling Black genealogy is in the main, no different that compiling genealogy of any other nationality. However, since many African-Americans were brought to America as slaves, and names were frequently changed to reflect those of their owners or location, complications can arise in research. Searching for slave ancestors takes a different set of records than is typically used in most searches. As slaves were considered property, references are frequently found in property records of the owners or in plantation records. The varying status of Blacks in the early history of the country complicates the search for ancestry. Names cannot be assumed to have remained consistent from generation to generation, slaves often took the names of their owners, last owner, the owner

who gave them manumission, were assigned names by the Freedman's Bureau or even on occasion chose their own names. Walker's book covers the process of searching within these complications.

Wallace, Arthur and Shirley Bousfield. *Successful Family Organizations, Record-Keeping, and Genealogy in Family Activities.* 3rd ed. Los Angeles, CA: LL Company, 1978.

Published by the Church of the Latter-Day Saints (LDS), this book while heavily into LDS theology, celebrates the family unit and provides not only information on organizing the family reunions and gatherings, but on collecting and maintaining the family genealogical heritage. Each section is very detailed in organizing the family structured genealogy project and includes putting together and publishing your materials when you have them collected.

Walton-Raji, Angela Y. *Black Indian Genealogy Research: African American Ancestors Among the Five Civilized Tribes.* Bowie, MD: Heritage Books, Inc., 1993, 2007.

Throughout early history, it was not uncommon for African Americans to wind up living with Indian tribes. It came about in a variety of ways. In some cases, escaped slaves were taken in and became a part of the tribe and some Indian tribes kept slaves, both black and white. In 1907, when the Indian Territory became the state of Oklahoma, qualification for payments and land allotments set aside for the Five Civilized Tribes caused the former slaves of these nations to apply for official enrollment. This produced testimonies of value for today's genealogists. Walton-Raji shows where to find and how to use the Indian Freedman Records, discusses Black Indians, and Tri-Racial groups from the Upper South. She has also, added two lists of family names: Freedman Surnames from the Final Rolls of the Five Civilized Tribes, and Surnames of Tri-Racial families of the Upper South.

Warren, James W. and Paula S. Warren. *Getting the Most Mileage from Genealogical Research Trips.* 3rd ed. St. Paul, MN: Warren Research & Marketing, 1998.

This short guide assists in planning research trips for genealogists. The Warrens provide step-by-step suggestions and checklists for preparing genealogical travels. Practical on-the-road tips are offered, as well as creative ideas for beginning to advanced genealogists for tracking down the hard to locate ancestor. Bibliographic information and Internet sites are included.

Weitzman, David. *My Backyard History Book.* Boston: Little, Brown & Co., 1975.

> Also known by the title, *Brown Paper School Presents My Backyard History Book*, Weitzman had created a book for children and young people who are interested in exploring their family histories. In it he presents activities and projects such as making time capsules, rubbings of cemetery markers, tracing genealogy and illustrating how finding the past begins at home. He shows how to use photographs, objects and places from daily life that are commonly ignored by children in teaching the young how to do genealogy and family history.

Westin, Jeane E. *Finding Your Roots: How to Trace Your Ancestors at Home and Abroad.* Los Angeles, CA: J. P. Tarcher, Inc., 1998.

> Westin has published a comprehensive work on how to utilize almost every form of genealogical search tool, from your attic to the Internet. Finding your family begins with your family and she discusses how to research and gather your basic family records, the information to gather from them for searching public records, and how to search out your roots abroad in your ancestral homeland. From home, records offices and cyberspace, she takes you to family reunions and uniting your family and to the final step of writing and publishing your family history. Several appendices are attached with an extensive list of sources for enhancing a search.

Whitaker, Beverly D. *Beyond Pedigrees: Organizing and Enhancing Your Work.* Salt Lake City, UT: Ancestry, 1993.

> Genealogists rapidly uncover great quantities of information. Whitaker has compiled ideas on organizing these reams of information into manageable forms. She discusses how to manage research on different family lines at once, even when traveling; how to better manage all aspects of your research, expenses, correspondence and workspace; how to enlist the help of family members and others; how to thoroughly research the historical setting and geography associated with the family line; how to collect and study family photographs and memorabilia; sharing your work with others; and how to compile a genealogy to pass down to future generations. She includes reproducible charts, a search checklist, a research bibliography, a correspondence calendar, a census checklist and more.

Willard, Jim and Terry Willard. *Ancestors: A Beginner's Guide to Family History & Genealogy.* Boston: Houghton Mifflin, 1997. (Also on video.)

> A companion to the PBS ten part television show on researching your family tree, this book offers an easy-to-follow instruction on the basics of family research. It discusses resources and techniques, tools, charts and everything needed to do effective research. Included in the appendix are archives, libraries, historical societies, church record sources and genealogical societies in each state.

Wolfman, Ira. *Do People Grow on Family Trees? Genealogy for Kids & Other Beginners: The Official Ellis Island Handbook.* New York: Workman Publishers, 1991, 2002.

> Designed for children, this is also a good book for the beginning genealogist. Wolfman's book explains genealogy in an easy to read format, discussing the various concepts of genealogy and provides a step-by-step guide on utilizing your family treasures and memories in constructing your past. It also discusses finding and using the sources that are not immediately at your fingertips, how to organize a search for when you go to visit resource centers and records offices, where to write for information, and how to chart and organize what you have found.

Woodtor, Dee P. *Finding a Place Called Home: A Guide to African-American Genealogy and Historical Identity.* New York: Random House, 1999.

> Written in a conversational style, Woodtor provides an accessible, step-by-step guide to finding out who your family was and where the family came from. Showing the research process beginning with your immediate family, she guides one through the steps necessary to digging up the past. Interviewing family members, using census records, slave schedules, property deeds and courthouse records are some of the tools Dr. Woodtor discusses. Using the Internet is also discussed. She helps put together the family tree while learning the history of African-Americans, not only in the Americas, but also the Caribbean. Using the research gained on the family history she also discusses the growing trend towards family reunions and other methods for celebrating newly discovered family history.

Wright, Norman E. *Preserving Your American Heritage: A Guide to Family and Local History.* Provo, UT: Brigham Young University Press, 1981.

> Putting genealogy and family history in the proper perspective is Wright's first instruction in conducting genealogical research. Good for beginning and advanced genealogists alike, his guide provides practical and workable methods of research. He illustrates the various documents needed in a search and explains them in chapters on the fundamental concepts of searching vital, church, cemetery, census, court, land and military records. His information is very in-depth and he concludes with a bibliography of resources for investigating genealogy.

Wright, Raymond S. *The Genealogist's Handbook: Modern Methods for Researching Family History.* Chicago, IL: American Library Association, 1995.

> After spending years as a librarian helping genealogists, Wright realized there was so much more to genealogy than simply finding one's ancestors. He realized that this was the entrance to discovering the family history. In this resource he assists the researcher in discovering not only who the ancestors were, but how they lived. The goal of this book is to discover the lives of the ancestors in original and other records and to put them into the context of their times. He also discusses the role of computer searching in genealogy. Chapters include Genealogy and Family History; Getting Started; Computers and Genealogy; Family and Neighborhood Records; Town, County and State Records; National Sources; Learning about Your Ethnic Origins; Writing Family History and an appendix which lists genealogical research centers and ethnic and immigration research centers. This could be a somewhat imposing book for someone looking for a quick start method, though his detail is in-depth, it does not go to extremes, making this a good book for someone who wants to get a little more involved in the historical part of a family search.

Genealogical Resouce Books

Allen, Desmond W. and Carolyn E. Billingsley. *Social Security Applications: A Genealogical Resource.* Conway, AR: Research Associates, 1995.

Allen and Billingsley have written a guideline on how to search the Social Security Administration (SSA) files for your ancestors. They remind the researcher that even though the SSA is a recent program, many persons born earlier registered late for Social Security benefits or just a Social Security number. On this application alone, there are many facts of interest to the genealogist, father's full name, mother's full name including the maiden name, date of birth, place of birth and present mailing address. If you do not already have a Social Security number, they also give tips for locating the number. They tell what the numeric portions of the number mean and tell about new trends in Social Security numbers.

American Association for State and Local History. *Directory of Historical Organizations in the United States and Canada.* 15th ed. Walnut Creek, CA: AltaMira Press, 2002.

This *Directory of Historical Organizations* lists approximately 13,000 organizations. Listing such agencies as state offices, university and college history departments, genealogical resources, libraries, museums, archives and others, the listings incorporate location, type of agency, information as to whether it is a historic site in and of itself, collections, programs, and personnel. The organizations are listed alphabetically by state, city name and organization name. Part 2 lists state offices, Part 3 lists historical organizations of Canada, Part 4 lists product and service vendors, and Part 5 is a quick reference index to major program areas.

American Indians: A Select Catalog of National Archives Microfilm Publications. Washington, DC: National Archives Trust Fund Board, 1998.

This listing indexes all the microform collections within the National Archives which pertain to American Indians. Records microfilmed include Civilian Agency records and Military Establishment records. These are each broken down into more specific details.

Arends, Marthe. *Genealogy on CD-ROM*. Baltimore, MD Genealogical Publishing Co., 1999.

> A growing amount of genealogical sources are being stored on CD-ROM. This book shows what is available on CD-ROM in all major categories. In particular, biographies, genealogical references, historical references, and dictionaries; journals, newspapers, and dictionaries; geographical finding aids; immigration and naturalization records; military records; African American and Native American records; U.S. resources; international resources; compiled family histories and genealogies; indexes; and bible records may all be found on CD. The guide is organized by subject, each CD listing, except for the census records, includes the title, publisher, prices, system requirements, and a description of the contents.

—. *Genealogy Software Guide*. Baltimore, MD: Genealogical Publishing Co., 1998.

> Arends reviews all the popular genealogical software programs published prior to 1998. Before reviewing each program, she answers questions regarding why one should use genealogical software, what kind of equipment is needed, how to choose and evaluate a program, what are the different types of software available and where can one purchase the software. Following the discussions on these questions, she lists genealogy database programs, genealogy utilities and research tools, Macintosh and other genealogy software, database comparison charts, software vendors, locating old files, Internet software resources, a list of programs not reviewed, GEDCOM, and computer genealogy publications. The database reviews include basic information about the program and running requirements, program information, reports which may be generated, sources, and comments. Illustrations are also provided introducing the ways in which some of the program screens look and the report formats.

Askin, Jayne and Molly Davis. *Search: A Handbook for Adoptees and Birthparents*. 3rd ed. Phoenix, Oryx Press, 1998.

> Finding that she needed to know information from her birth family, Jayne Askin instituted a search. Because the birth records were sealed by the court, she had to devise a plan to help her around the closed doors. In this greatly detailed book, she not only shares the methodology of her search, but shares details on costs, the rights of the adoptee, legal rights and laws, the need for moral support, reference resources, primary sources of data, alternate sources of

data, search groups and consultants, and other groups helpful in a search. She provides checklists, state-by-state listing of agencies and groups, and reference sources.

Balhuizen, Ann R. *Searching on Location: Planning a Research Trip.* Salt Lake City, UT: Ancestry, Inc., 1992.

Searching on Location is a step-by-step guide to planning your genealogical research trip. Beginning with a discussion of what your should do at home to prepare for the trip, which is everything possible!, to what you need for approaching libraries, archives and record centers, Balhuizen covers the round trip from the front door to back again. Three things she says are of critical importance are your files and equipment which provide a foundation for your work; your knowledge of basic techniques and skills in dealing with people and institutions; and an attitude of openness and friendliness to new experiences combined with a professional and systematic approach to your research.

Basch, Reva. *Researching Online for Dummies.* Foster City, CA: IDG Books Worldwide, 2000.

Strategy is very important when researching online. Basch, in her book, *Researching Online for Dummies*, discusses specialty search engines, subject-based catalogs, reference sites, online libraries, and for-pay information services. She teaches search strategies, instructing in the construction of an effective search. To do this, you need to develop goals, determine your strategy, know what you are searching for and sometimes even discover new strategies along the way. She explains the difference between surfing the net and doing online searching. She also discusses the importance of evaluating the information retrieved, and how to determine if it is not only relevant, but accurate.

Baxter, Angus. *In Search of Your Canadian Roots: Tracing Your Family Tree in Canada.* 3rd ed. Baltimore, MD: Genealogical Publishing Co., Inc., 2000.

As in his other books, Baxter describes how to get started searching for Canadian family histories. He instructs the user in researching historical records such as census returns, church registers, civil registration, land and homestead records, cemetery inscriptions, voters' lists, local newspaper indexes, and the files kept by the Church of the Latter-Day Saints. Baxter gives a province-by-province listing of where to find Canadian history records.

---. *In Search of Your European Roots: A Complete Guide to Tracing Your Ancestors in Every Country in Europe.* 3rd ed. Baltimore, MD: Genealogical Publishing Co., Inc., 2001.

> This is one of the most comprehensive guides for tracing genealogy in Europe, covering both personal visits and correspondence. Explanations are given of European politics and wars and their effects on genealogical records. Locations of archives from the national to municipal levels are given; the location of church records and census returns; the systems of civil registration of births, marriages, and deaths; and how to find and use certificates of domicile, foundling books, orphan lists, guild records, internal passport lists, confirmation records and even vaccination lists. Thirty European countries are covered in this volume. The book begins with an introduction to Europe, and then includes chapters on Mormon records and Jewish records before going into a country by country breakdown of records centers. European genealogical organizations are listed at the end.

---. *In Search of Your German Roots: A Complete Guide to Tracing Your Ancestors in the Germanic Areas of Europe.* 4th ed. Baltimore, MD: Genealogical Publishing Co., Inc. 2008.

> This guide by Angus Baxter is designed to teach the tracing of Germanic ancestry, not only in Germany, but in all the German speaking areas of Europe from the Baltic to the Crimea and from the Czech Republic to Belgium. It is designed so that you seldom have to leave home and shows how to conduct your research by correspondence. In addition to the basic how to search abroad information, it also lists resources for searching libraries, records of church and state, and archives in the Germanic countries.

Beard, Timothy F. and Denise Demong. *How to Find Your Family Roots.* New York: McGraw-Hill, 1977.

> Beard and Demong's work is an extensive compilation of instructions on tracing your family's history. Now only do they guide you through the search process, but they list extensive resources for finding information in the United States and in foreign countries. It is also especially good for resources on Native American research.

Bentley, Elizabeth P. *County Courthouse Book.* 2nd ed. Baltimore, MD: Genealogical Publishing Company, 1995.

Having surveyed county courthouses and other jurisdictions, Bentley provides a list of all names, addresses, phone numbers and dates of organization of all county courthouses and for the sixty-five percent that responded to the survey, she provides a concise summary of record holdings, personnel, and services. Besides genealogical use, this book can be used for land title searches, legal investigations, and questions of property rights and inheritance.

---. *Directory of Family Associations.* 4th ed. Baltimore, MD: Genealogical Publishing Co., 2001.

The *Directory of Family Associations* compiles information solicited from family associations, reunion committees, and one-name societies, providing access to approximately 6,500 family associations across the United States. Since some of these groups only exist for a short period of time or are not fully staffed, Bentley has supplemented the available information with details obtainable in standard family journals and newsletters. This alphabetical listing of associations gives addresses, phone numbers, contact persons, and publications (if any) for the family associations listed. Cross referencing of similar surnames is also provided.

---. *Genealogist's Address Book.* 5th ed. Baltimore, MD: Genealogical Publishing Company, 2005.

This essentially national yellow pages is classified by subject, cross-referenced, and alphabetized. It included all the key sources of genealogical research, providing names, addresses, phone numbers, FAX numbers, e-mail addresses, web sites, contact persons and business hours of more than 25,000 libraries, archives, genealogical societies, historical societies, government agencies, vital records offices, professional bodies, religious organizations, surname registries, research centers, special interest groups, periodicals, newspaper columns, publishers, booksellers, services, databases, and more.

Berry, Ellen T. and David A. Berry. *Our Quaker Ancestors: Finding Them in Quaker Records.* Reprint. Baltimore: Genealogical Publishing, 1996.

George Fox developed a system of record keeping for the Quakers in 1675, little dreaming that it would become a wealth of information for

Quakers searching for their ancestors years later. The Berrys begin with a short history of the Quaker movement and a discussion of the organization and structure. Later chapters discuss the migrations to and within America, the special types of records available for research, specifically Quaker repositories, non-Quaker repositories, and sources outside of the United States for Quaker research.

Billingsley, Carolyn E. and Desmond W. Allen. *How to Get the Most Out of Death Certificates.* Conway, AR: Research Associates, 1991.

Death certificates are very important to genealogists as they provide much valuable information. This small volume shows where to write for death certificates, and how to order one, how much they cost. It also tells, why a death certificate might not be found, what you can do if you can't find one, and how a funeral home can help. Billingsley and Allen tell what types of information might be found on death certificates, and where to go if you cannot always read the handwriting or understand the jargon. They also discuss, delayed death certificates, alternate sources of proof of death and provide a checklist of information to look for on the death certificate.

Black Studies: A Select Catalog of National Archives Microfilm Publications. Rev. ed. Washington, DC: National Archives Trust Fund Board, 2007.

Black Studies provides a listing and explanation of the microform resources available at the National Archives. The different types of records held are described in detail as well as summaries of what is contained on the various pieces of microfilm and in each record grouping.

Bonner, Laurie and Steve Bonner. *Searching for Cyber-Roots.* Salt Lake City, UT: Ancestry, 1997.

Cyber-Roots begins with an introduction to the Internet for novice users. If you aren't a novice Internet user, you can skip this section on go on to the more advanced chapters on how to get the most out of online searching. It will also, suggest software that allows you to put the results of your search online when you are ready so that other researchers can find you and gain from your results. The appendix has a particularly useful list of websites to assist in searching.

Bremer, Ronald A. *Compendium of Historical Sources: The How and Where of American Genealogy.* 8th ed. Bountiful, UT: 1996.

Bremer has criss-crossed the United States 37 times and inventoried hundreds of records offices to provide the materials for this compendium. He claims to have visited almost every 'town and hamlet!' This book answers almost any question a genealogist might have, as well as contains approximately ninety percent of all resources needed to locate American ancestors. Some of the questions answered include what is the best way of keeping records, what sources are the most valuable, where can I find church records, which are the most important reference works for genealogists, and many others. Section one deals with the how-to and research structure. Section two discusses the repositories of genealogical information. Section three discusses the various types of records. Section four lists special information, museums, sources and place names; and section five lists maps, forms and a glossary.

Burek, Deborah M., ed. *Cemeteries of the U.S.: A Guide to Contact Information for U.S. Cemeteries and Their Records.* Detroit, MI: Gale Research, 1994.

One of Gale Research's many comprehensive reference tools; *Cemeteries of the U.S.* lists and describes more than 22,600 cemeteries covering all 50 states, U.S. territories and foreign countries containing major military cemeteries that have interred U.S. citizens. Contact information is provided for about 2,000 state and county genealogical and historical organizations and libraries, and citations are listed for publications which provide detailed information on individual cemeteries in particular geographical areas. Cemeteries may be located within the book by state, county, cemetery name, former or alternate names, city, and affiliations (i.e. National military or religion.)

Byers, Paula K., ed. *African American Genealogical Sourcebook.* Detroit, MI: Gale Research, Inc., 1995.

Divided into two parts, this resource offers explanations and tips on accessing records of such institutions as the Freedman's Bureau, records of religious orders, archives, and other genealogical repositories. Part one gives an overview of immigration and migration, basic genealogical methodology, and problems endemic to African-American researches. Part two lists the resources for finding the information, libraries, archives, public and private organizations, print resources, and other media that hold relevant materials for genealogists.

---, ed. *Asian American Genealogical Sourcebook.* Detroit, MI: Gale Research, Inc., 1995.

> The *Asian American Genealogical Sourcebook* provides the first step in researching the Asian American heritage and provides the guidance for setting up a genealogical research project. Part one combines the historical data and practical genealogical advice, as well as basic immigration and migration patterns, traditions and customs, and basic genealogical records and examples. Part two lists the resources and places specific to where Asian American research information may be found, and part three provides author, title and organization indexes to part two and a subject index to part one.

---, ed. *Hispanic American Genealogical Sourcebook.* Detroit, MI: Gale Research, Inc., 1995.

> This resource is divided into two parts, part one contains essays on immigration and migration, basic genealogical methods and resources, and problems specific to ethnic genealogy. Part two consists of a 'directory of genealogical information' listing libraries, archives, public and private organizations, print resources, and other media relevant to genealogical research. The libraries and archives are listed geographically. Explanations and tips for accessing the various records are given, especially in relation to the Inquisition, records of religious orders, and an overview of newspaper ads and Hispanic heraldry. Tables, examples and an extensive bibliography are included.

---, ed. *Native American Genealogical Sourcebook.* New York: Gale Research, 1995.

> This book is designed to be a first step in researching a person of Native American background. Part one contains essays combining historical data and practical genealogical advice and suggest the steps for a logical search of information. Part one also includes information on migration patterns, traditions and customs, basic genealogical records, and concrete examples of what might be found. Part two lists information resources which can provide help specific to Native American research, and part three consists of author, title and organization indexes, and a subject index to part one.

Carangelo, Lori. *The Ultimate Search Book: Worldwide Adoption, Genealogy and Other Search Secrets.* Rev. ed. Bountiful, UT: Heritage Quest, 2002.

> Adoption makes finding genealogical information about biological parents near impossible. This resource enables the adoptee to

conduct a search. Chapter one discusses the basics of searching and legal ramifications, chapter two discusses missing and runaway children, chapter three talks about family trees and traditional research sources for genealogy, chapter four talks about divorce and separation and questions to be asked among the known family, chapter five discusses computerized searching. Following these chapters are keys to searching within each state with adoption and support groups, searching within U.S. possessions and territories, and international searching. Addresses and letter writing suggestions are included to help get the best possible responses and information.

Carmack, Sharon DeBartolo and Erin Nevius, eds. *The Family Tree Resource Book for Genealogists: The Essential Guide to American County and Town Sources.* Cincinnati, OH: Family Tree Books, 2004.

Even an expert genealogist needs guidance occasionally. Carmack and Nevius have provided a resource book with research summaries, tips and techniques for searching for family tree information across the United States. The book includes maps for every state; detailed county-level data; web sites and contact information for libraries, archives, genealogical societies, and historical societies; bibliographies for each state; and contributions from top genealogists Emily Anne Croom, David A. Fryxell, Rhonda R. McClure, Maureen Taylor and James W. Warren. The format of the text is divided by state, with an introduction by a renowned genealogist, state map; a listing of resources, and a break-out section of towns with basic information such as courthouse or town hall address, web site, county, comments, and types of records with their jurisdictions.

—. *The Genealogy Sourcebook.* Los Angeles: Lowell House, 1998.

The sources of genealogical information consist of letters, books, periodicals, personal interviews, and other records. Carmack's work guides the researcher from the beginning of research - starting with the known, to the search for the unknown. *The Genealogy Sourcebook* provides information on genealogical associations which give information on lineage, family associations, and ethnic societies that can help in the search for ancestors.

—. *Your Guide to Cemetery Research.* Cincinnati, OH: Betterway Books, 2002.

Cemeteries have always provided clues in not only history, but in family research, providing birth and death dates and sometimes even a peek into the person's personality via tombstone inscriptions. Carmack illustrates how to do cemetery research from determining an ancestor's final resting place to decoding headstone symbols. She tells how to use a cemetery to determine when and where a family member died, how to locate the exact cemetery in which a family member is interred, how to analyze headstones and markers, how to conduct cemetery surveys, and how to use cemeteries to locate living relatives. She also provides information on the interpretation of funerary art and tombstone iconography, including symbols, epitaphs, and inscriptions, as well as illustrating how to do a rubbing or a cast of the tombstone or marker without damaging it. Information is also provided on, American burial customs, attitudes towards death, and funeral rites for a variety of ethnic and religious denominations. Sidebars are included in the text which give helpful hints on gravestone art, symbols, and emblems; and appendices, a glossary and a time line provide information on medical facts, and the episodes of deadly diseases and epidemics throughout history.

Carter, Fran. *Searching American Military Records.* 2nd ed. Bountiful, UT: American Genealogical Lending Library, 1993.

Listing all America's conflicts since Colonial times, Carter's book shows where to find military records, and other sources including the records of veteran's homes, national cemeteries and burial grounds, and where to get pension and bounty land warrants. Also included, are the types of records created as a result of these conflicts, where to find them and how to use them.

---. *Searching American Probate Records.* Rev. Bountiful, UT: American Genealogical Lending Library, 1993.

In her work, *Searching American Probate Records*, Carter describes the types of genealogical information that can be accessed. Probate records can answer many genealogical questions, proving relationships as bequests are often detailed as to which family member is receiving something under the will. She shows where to find the records, explains the probate process, and how to use the records once they are found. Nearly every courthouse in the U.S. has a master index to estates or to probate cases which provides help if the surname and approximate date of death are known. What is of greatest concern to the family historian is the location and analysis of the final settlement of the estate. The steps leading to this process may leave different records involved in the process stored in different locations within the courthouse. Carter shows in her book how to bring these together with the greatest benefit to the researcher.

Cerny, Johni and Wendy Elliott. *The Library: A Guide to the LDS Family History Library.* Salt Lake City, UT: Ancestry Publishing, 1988.

> This comprehensive description of the Mormon Library system details not only the main research library of the Church of Jesus Christ of Latter Day Saints, but also their hundreds of branch Family History Libraries spread across the world. By consulting *The Library*, the researcher can determine what records have been collected, what times they span and how to access them. The all-inclusive charts provide information on the library's holdings for nearly every country in the world. Everyone is welcomed at the Family History Libraries, but assistance is limited, making this book a critical first step in using the facilities. *The Library* provides information on chronological histories of states and foreign countries, including genealogically important facts and dates; explanations of settlement and migration patterns; concise descriptions of record groups and what they contain; tips for accessing the collection and saving time; extensive bibliographies; what can and cannot be accessed at the branches; information available by correspondence, facilities and services offered by the libraries and much more.

Chorzempa, Rosemary A. *Polish Roots/Korzenie Polskie.* Baltimore, MD: Genealogical Publishing Co., Inc., 1993.

> Poland is a country that has been made and unmade many times throughout history. The Polish people include many nationalities such as Austrians, Germans, Lithuanians, Russians and Ukrainians who represent countries who at one time or another had dominion over the Polish nation. People of other nationalities have also called it home, making it a genealogical mosaic. Chorzempa's work on Polish family history has been designed to aid the American researcher with the information needed to make a search for Polish roots successful. Chapters within this work discuss where to find the more common records such as church records; cemetery and gravestone records; church anniversary books; naturalization records; and many more; libraries and resouce centers that can assist with Polish research; Polish Genealogical Societies; life in Poland; ethnic groups in Poland; geographic and ethnic areas of Poland; maps and gazetteers; Polish records; records of Polish churches; Polish civil records; surnames; Christian or first names; working with other languages; writing to Poland; and visiting Poland.

Clemens, William M., ed. *American Marriage Records Before 1699.* Baltimore, MD: Genealogical Publishing Co., Inc., 1979, 1998.

>The marriage records in this compilation go back to the early days of American settlement with the arrival of the first emigrants in James Town, New Netherlands, and Plymouth through the year 1700. Family names are spelled as accurately as records allowed. Names are listed in alphabetical order, with either married name or maiden name first and then the spouse's name. For example, the first entry reads: Abbott, Benjamin and Sarah Farnum, 22 April 1685, Andover, Mass. Under the F's you will find Farnum, Sarah and Benjamin Abbott, 22 April 1685, Andover, Mass. So, whether you are looking up the wife or the husband, you should find the couple either way.

Cole, Trafford R. *Italian Genealogical Records: How to Use Italian Civil, Ecclesiastical and Other Records in Family History.* Salt Lake City, UT: Ancestry, Inc., 1995.

>Discussing the history and development of Italian record keeping, he describes the various sorts of records found in Italian repositories. These include civil vital records; ecclesiastical records; and notary and military records. He tells of the unique aspects of using Italian sources and how to approach the task of obtaining these source wherever they might be found. Sample letters for corresponding with Italian repositories are shared, as well as information on the significance of Italian surnames and relevance of Italian noble families to your search of Italian roots.

Colletta, John P. *Finding Italian Roots: the Complete Guide for Americans.* 2nd ed. Baltimore, MD: Genealogical Publishing Co., Inc., 2003.

>This guide focuses on using the resources available in the United States for identifying the places of origin of Italian ancestors, and identifying repositories in Italy, including archives, religious records and libraries. Colleta gives practical tips for research and travel. An expert in Italian ancestry, Colleta provides easy to follow information both for the beginner and the expert genealogist. He provides a great deal of detail when discussing sources and also includes a glossary of Italian terms that researchers are likely to encounter. Examples of birth, baptismal and marriage registers are given, along with two line maps of modern and pre-unification Italy.

---. *They Came in Ships: A Guide to Finding Your Immigrant Ancestor's Arrival Records.* 3rd ed. Orem, UT: Ancestry Incorporated, 2002.

For four hundred years our ancestors came to America by the millions and are still coming. Ships of all sorts arrived along the coastlines of the Atlantic, Pacific, Gulf of Mexico and the Great Lakes. Many of the passenger lists of these ships still exist. *They Came in Ships* is designed to make the access to these lists easier. Colletta provides step-by-step instructions to determining what ships to look for, to researching passenger manifests and how to use the available indexing and alternative resources for finding an ancestor's name. One chapter in this work focuses on finding a ship if it is not listed in the National Archives index. More than sixty lists relating to ship lists and listed and described in the bibliography.

Cosgriff, John and Carolyn Cosgriff. *Turbo Genealogy: An Introduction to Family History Research in the Information Age.* Salt Lake City, UT: Ancestry, Inc., 1997.

The Cosgriffs have written a primer for beginning genealogists to unlock the secrets of finding sources on the computer. Showing how to make computer technology yield valuable information faster and easier, they provide investigative techniques and sources for finding up-to-date information on genealogy. They also offer pointers on software, hardware and networking. They also discuss all of the typical genealogical record sources and tell where to look for those that cannot be obtained via the computer.

Croom, Emily Anne. *The Genealogist's Companion and Sourcebook: A Beyond-the-Basics, Hands-on Guide to Unpuzzling Your Past.* 2nd ed. Cincinnati, OH: Betterway Books, 2003.

A companion work to her *Unpuzzling Your Past*, this volume highlights the different types of primary and secondary source materials. It shows how to get past obstacles such as public records lost to fire or flood, and explores sources that are not always the first thought of such as church and funeral home records. She also explains how to use government records, court records, newspapers and maps. Included are bibliographies of materials and sources, case studies, census forms, and information on major archival and library sources.

---. *The Unpuzzling Your Past Workbook: Essential Forms and Letters for All Genealogists.* Cincinnati, OH: Betterway Books, 1996.

> Forty tear-out forms are provided in this workbook for the genealogist who isn't sure what type of form they need send for uncovering information. In addition to the tear-out forms, there are numerous other forms and examples of how to fill them out. There are also, explanations of what the forms are for and how to use them. Some of these forms are for abstracting and indexing records, interviewing relatives, family group sheets, and others. She also offers, ideas of sources to search, tips to help write effective genealogical letters, and references to other information.

Crowe, Elizabeth P. *Genealogy Online: Researching Your Roots.* 8th ed. New York: Windcrest/McGraw-Hill, 2008.

> The Internet has rapidly become a fertile field for genealogy research. Many families are posting information on websites, and libraries around the world have their catalogs online so that one may do intitial research and determine where to go without expending a lot of effort, thus saving years of expense and travel. Crowe's guide assists the researcher in gaining access to genealogical bulletin boards, newsgroups, genealogy forums, webpages, library catalogs and many other Internet resources. Crowe walks the user through computer systems and methodology for getting the most efficient uses out of a computerized genealogy search. The 2000 Millennium edition is available online through NetLibrary.

Crume, Rick. *Plugging Into Your Past: How to Find Real Family History Records Online.* Cincinnati, OH: Betterway Books, 2004.

> Crume unlocks the Internet for enterprising genealogists by providing step-by-step instructions to help make the most of electronic databases and digital records. Many things may now be found online and they include marriage and census records, tombstone transcriptions, and military and immigration records among others. Search strategies for finding these records are explained; assistance with difficult databases is provided; local, county, state and federal sources on databases are identified; a directory of real records, books and abstracts in electronic form is provided; and help with interpreting and applying the records you find is provided.

Culligan, Joseph J. *You, Too, Can Find Anybody: A Reference Manual.* Miami, FL: Hallmark Press, Inc., 1998.

    Private Investigator, Joseph Culligan, has put together a book of resources to help track down all manner of information. Sources listed in his book include - drivers license departments in all fifty states; registration and title departments in all the states; state police agencies; hunting and fishing license departments; birth, death, marriage, and divorce records ordering information; Armed Forces records departments; information on Death Master File searches; Nationwide Telephone listings; Social Security Number updates; and how to use the Postal Service's policy to find adddresses for Post Office boxes and more. Each chapter starts with a brief introduction on the type of record discussed and how to access the record, and then lists the addresses or access points for accessing the records.

Davenport, Robert Ralsey. *Hereditary Society Blue Book.* 7th ed. Beverly Hills, CA: Eastwood Publishing Co., 1999.

    The *Heritage Society Blue Book* contains information on Hereditary, Lineage, and Patriotic Societies; and lists a *Who's Who* or *Social Register* of the society's leading members. It should be available at every major genealogical library. It includes information on each society, the insignia, membership requirements, and the national address of each organization.

DesJardins, Dawn Conzet., ed. *Gale's Guide to Genealogical & Historical Research: A Gale Ready Reference Handbook.* Detroit. MI: Gale Group, 2000.

    Gale has provided a reference work which gives access to associations, libraries, publishers, research centers, databases, online services, periodicals, directories, and newsletters that provide information about genealogical and historical family research. Over 4,200 genealogical and family related sources are listed in this volume. Each of the citations contains, where possible, names, addresses, phone/Fax numbers, and e-mail addresses/URLs for the organization listed, as well as descriptions and other pertinent details. The volume is divided into three sections: organizations, publications, and databases. There is also, a geographic index and master index with an alphabetic listing of all entries and important keywords from within the listings.

Dollarhide, William and Ronald A. Bremer. *America's Best Genealogy Resource Centers*. Bountiful, UT: Heritage Quest, 1999.

> There are numerous resource centers around the country ranging from local public libraries to genealogical association collections to the Family History Library of the Church of Jesus Christ of the Latter Day Saints. Dollarhide and Bremer identify the major resource facilities with genealogical collections by local, state, regional and national levels. The top ten genealogical sites are listed first, followed by the best genealogy resource centers for each state. Following the state listings chapters identify the regional branches of the National Archives and the vital statistics offices for each state. A summary of holdings is given for each repository. Comparisons of over three thousand sites visited have resulted in this select group of about 600 facilities considered the best in America.

---. *The Census Book: A Genealogist's Guide to Federal Census Facts, Schedules and Indexes*. Bountiful, UT: Heritage Quest, 2000.

> A comprehensive guide to the census, this work provides a review of census schedules and identifies every known index of censuses ever published. *The Census Book* gives a complete tabulation of all the US Federal Censuses including non-population census schedules and tells where census records are located. Twenty-nine census extraction forms are included for 1790 to 1930, enabling one to copy and track ancestors information as one views original source documents. This publicaton also includes a CD-Rom to assist in printing forms, searching the publication, and quickly retrieving items of interest. Many unknown facts and pecularities of census records are also given.

Eichholz, Alice, ed. *Red Book: American State, County and Town Sources*. 3rd ed. Provo, UT: Ancestry, 2004.

> The *Red Book* is designed to assist in doing research in each of the fifty states and Washington, DC Though nothing replaces an on-site visit, this provides information on what is available in the various locations, including the microform collections. Each state is listed alphabetically and topics are arranged methodologically within each state. A map accompanies each state entry detailing the political divisions and geographic features. Vital records are listed first in each chapter. Also listed are census records, local history, maps, land records, probate records court records, tax records, cemetery records, church records, military records, and periodical, newspaper, and manuscript collections. Each states archival societies and libraries are listed; special focus catagories list information on immigration,

naturalization, Black Americans, and Native Americans; and county resources are listed. There is also a short bibliographical section under the regional sections listing other sources for that area.

Elliott, Wendy L. *Using Land Records to Solve Research Problems.* Bountiful UT: American Genealogical Lending Library, 1987.

Land records may often be helpful in genealogical research. Knowledge of areas where the family owned land can help one trace the history of the family movements and ownership details. Elliot's work explains the various terms and information needed to research land records during various time periods and parts of the country. Some of the areas covered include public domain survey layouts, deed showing relationships, deed listing heirs, land entry showing wife's given name, deed listing grantee physical description and several other types of land records.

Everton, George B. and Louise M. Everton. *The Handy Book for Genealogists: United States of America.* 10th ed. Logan, UT: Everton Publishers, 2002.

First published in 1947, this nineth edition includes maps for every state, information on nineteen foreign countries, and websites for genealogical research. All the data has been updated from previous editions and much of it has been expanded. The volume is organized by state, with general information about the state - history, records, genealogical societies, libraries, periodicals, and publications on genealogy. After the state information, information will be given on counties, including counties which no longer exist. This section gives information on where to find records stored at the county level.

Family History Library [Microform]. Salt Lake City, UT: Corporation of the President of the Church of Jesus Christ of Latter-Day Saints, 1989.

These microforms issued by the Family History Department of the Church of Jesus Christ of Latter-Day Saints (LDS), encompass catalogs of genealogical sources. These may be found in the Family History Center in Salt Lake City or in the various Family History Centers the LDS maintains around the country. The microform collection is made up of an author/title catalog of 865 microfiche, a surname catalog of 278 microfiche, a locality catalog of 936 microfiche, and a subject catalog of 52 microfiche.

Ferraro, Eugene. *How to Obtain Birth, Death, Marriage, Divorce & Adoption Records.* Santa Ana, CA: Marathon Press International, 1989.

> Birth, death, marriage, divorce, and adoption records are all what are referred to as vital records. At least one of these records exist for every person. To obtain these records, one must write to the appropriate state or local office in the area in which the pertinent event occurred, for instance to obtain a birth record, one must write to the county or city where the birth occurred. To ensure the fastest and most accurate answer the following steps should be followed. 1.) Write to the appropriate office; 2.) determine if a fee is required, and include it; 3.) type or print any names for which information is required; and 4.) give as much information in the request as you have access to, this will make it easier for the office to determine the person for whom you are looking. Ferraro's book lists the type of information required for each type of record needed as well as which offices within a state to write for the particular type of record requested. He includes the offices and fees up to the date of 1989. While many phone numbers and fees have changed over the years, most of the addresses should have remained the same. He also provides information on sending for foreign records, valid social security numbers, and agencies and offices which deal with adoptions.

Filby, P. William. *Passenger and Immigration Lists Index: A Guide to Published Arrival Records of About 500,000 Passengers Who Came to the United States and Canada in the Seventeenth, Eighteenth, and Nineteenth Centuries.* Detroit, MI: Gale Research Company, 1993.

> This set contains the early passenger and arrival records of immigrants who came to America prior to 1820.

Fleming, Ann Carter. *The Organized Family Historian: How to File, Manage, and Protect Your Genealogical Research and Heirlooms.* Nashville, TN: Rutledge Hill Press, 2004.

> Every genealogist needs to be well organized, or one soon has a state of chaos! Fleming discusses how to organize your "stuff." She talks about family history files, photographs, heirlooms, family interviews, assembling to-do lists, sharing your research with others, expanding your research, analyzing data using forms and charts, planning research trips, and other preservation tips. There are also forms provided that assist with genealogical organization.

Frywell, David A., Brad Crawford, and Erin Nevius, eds. *The Family Tree Guide Book: Everything You Need to Know to Trace Your Genealogy Across North America.* Cincinnati, OH: Betterway Books, 2002.

A genealogical travelogue, *the Family Tree Guide Book* provides essential genealogy guidelines, online directories, and regional travel information to help make the search for family history more efficient, fun and more importantly, successful. Instructions assist with using the Internet to access distant resources and to decide where to go for physical searching. Major genealogical search experts have lent their expertise to the book's content. In the text, the book is divided into seven sections on the U.S. and Canada. Each section is introduced with a brief history and resource guide and basic methods of finding and using regional records. The state-by-state listing includes thousands of web sites, family history centers, archives and libraries, in-depth city guides, and maps of every state and province. Sections on African American and Native American ancestry are also included.

Gibson, Jeremy S. W. *General Register Office and International Genealogical Indexes: Where to Find Them.* Birmingham, Eng: Federation of Family History Societies, 1987.

Gibson's small guide discusses various genealogical indexes and resources available in the British Isles and how to use them. Many of the genealogical resources have been microfilmed and made available at various locations around Britain so that going to London to obtain these materials is no longer necessary. His main discussion centers around the General Register Office indexes, the International Genealogical Index, who holds what (the counties of the United Kingdom), and Scotland's Old Parochial Register Index.

Glazier, Ira A. and William P. Filby, eds. *Italians to America: Lists of Passengers Arriving at U.S. Ports, 1880-1899.* Wilmington, DE: Scholarly Resources, 2000.

Italians to America is a compilation of ship's lists presented in chronological order by each ship's date of arrival. They provide the name of the ships, ports of departure and arrival, and debarkation dates. When available, the passenger's age, sex, occupation, village or origin, and destination may be given. An index of Italian surnames for the ships' passengers is included in each volume, these indexes include approximately 750,000 names nof the 1880-1899 period and will facilitate finding an ancestor's family name when the exact date of entry or port is unknown. There is also an introduction to the history of Italian migration to the United States given, with statistical data showing the total Italian migration to other selected countries such as to Europe, Brazil, and Canada.

Grannum, Karen and Nigel Taylor. *Wills and Other Probate Records: A Practical Guide to Researching Your Ancestors' Last Documents.* Surrey, UK: The National Archives, 2004.

Most families have wills and almost all estates must go through some form of probate, thus creating documentation which can be valuable in adding to the story of your ancestors. Wills and probate records help us to find out more about an ancestor's life, family, livelihood, and sometimes their personality. Written in England, but applicable to any country that records wills and final documents, this book helps in illustrating how to research the location and meaning of wills. It tells where they might be found from county records to church records, and how to read them and explains much of the legal terminology involved in a will. In direct relation to English wills, the text discusses wills as sources, ecclesiastical courts, the different county courts in England, wills before 1858, inventories, death duties, litigation, other probate records, and other United Kingdom countries.

Greenwood, Val. *The Researcher's Guide to American Genealogy.* 3rd ed. Baltimore, MD: Genealogical Publishing Company, 2000.

Divided into two parts, part one of Greenwood's book deals with the basic principles of genealogical research in American ancestry. Part two deals with the records in which the genealogist will do most of their research. The records are examined in detail as to their use and value to a genealogist. Greenwood has put an extensive amount of detail into explaining the research and how to do it, as well as in her discussion of each type of record and how it may be used and located.

Groene, Bertram H. *Tracing Your Civil War Ancestor.* 4th ed. Winston-Salem, NC: John F. Blair, Publisher, 1995.

Designed particularly for those who are descended from Civil War veterans, this book may also be useful to collectors of Civil War memorabilia. Groene discusses how to take relics handed down from a Civil War ancestor and use them to trace the owner's history and activities. Primarily, he provides names and addresses for all the state archives, names and addresses of institutions which hold microform service records from the national archives, names and publishers of useful Civil War reference books, names and publishers of sourcebooks for identifying Civil War weapons and accoutrements, and much more.

Guide to the Records of the United States House of Representatives at the National Archives, 1789-1989. Washington, DC: National Archives and Records Administration, 1989.

In 1880, the Rules of the House directed all committees to turn over their records to the Clerk within three days of the final adjournment of Congress. These records were in turn transferred to the Library of Congress. In 1934, the National Archives was formed to be a depository for the records of all three branches of the Federal Government. Since 1959, the National Archives has published an inventory of its record holdings. The purpose of this guide is to analyze and describe the records of the House of Representatives in a manner that makes them accessible to Congressional staff, Government officials, historians, and non-academic researchers. Each chapter is a survey of the records from each agency/committee under the House's jurisdiction.

Guide to the Records of the United States Senate at the National Archives, 1789-1989. Washington, D. C.: National Archives and Records Administration, 1989.

Beginning in March 1937, the U.S. Senate began to send records of its committees and agencies to the National Archives. Prior to that, storage and retention had been relatively haphazard. This guide to the Senate records at the National Archives is divided into six sections. Section 1 guides the researcher through effective research procedures. Section 2 describes the records of each of the Senate's standing committees. Section 3 describes the records of the Senate select and special committees and joint committees of Congress. Section 4 concerns non-committee records and executive proceedings of the Senate. Section 5 discusses the committee records since 1969 which are still closed to public use, and section 6 includes the appendices and indexes.

Gunderson, Ted and Roger McGovern. *How to Locate Anyone, Anywhere Without Leaving Home.* Rev. ed. New York: Penguin Books, 1996.

Missing or hard-to-locate relatives can be found without leaving the comfort of your own home by following Gunderson's techniques for finding anyone. He offers proven techniques which show you how to map out a search plan and follow the paper trail most people leave, how to use the computer and Internet in your search, the proper way to contact organizations that may hold valuable information and many more information finding techniques. This reference features comprehensive listings of federal, state, and local agencies, as well as listings of the index of valid Social Security numbers, runaway hotlines, and genealogical libraries. He also provides up-to-date information on how to conduct adoptee/birth parent searches.

Haines, Gerald K. and David A. Langbart. *Unlocking the Files of the FBI: A Guide to Its Records and Classification System.* Wilmington, DE: Scholarly Resources, Inc., 1993.

This is a guide to the content, organization, location, and access to the records of the Federal Bureau of Investigation, providing a history of the Bureau's recordkeeping from 1909 to the present. By court order, the National Archives and Records Administration (NARA) was instructed to analyze the FBI's files and make recommendations for retention and destruction. These reviews are to be conducted at five year intervals and those records which may be declassified are transferred to NARA's care and are available for use. These records are classified by the same system derived from law, such as Kidnapping, Ethics in Government, etc. The book is organized by these classifications and provides background information on the classification number, title, background on when it was established, changes over time, and description of typical files.

Hanks, Patrick and Flavia Hodges. *A Dictionary of Surnames.* New York: Oxford University Press, 1988.

Intended as a reference work for surname researchers, genealogists, family historians and others interested in name searching, this dictionary contains entries for most major surnames of European origin, as well as many rarer ones. A surname is defined as a hereditary name borne by members of a single family and handed down from father to son. The names in this dictionary are 'nested' in groups under a main entry. The simple form of the names are usually preferred as the main entry. The entry explains the linguistic origins and the peculiarities of its history, current distribution, and other relevant facts. There is an extensive introduction which discusses names and how names in many of the European countries were formulated. A list of the abbreviations used in the dictionary precedes the alphabetical listing of names, and finally an index which alphabetically lists all of the names in the dictionary and the main references under which they appear.

Hatcher, Patricia Law. *Locating Your Roots: Discover Your Ancestors Using Land Records.* Cincinnati, OH: Betterway Books, 2003.

Land was a major motivation for most of the immigrants who came to America from abroad, especially in the early days prior to the 20th century. Records that are frequently overlooked during genealogical research, yet are frequently a goldmine of information are land records, including deeds, grants, mortgages, wills and more, as they are some of the most common and most reliable documents existing. Hatcher shows where to find land records and how to use them to prove ancestry and family relationships. They also provide new avenues of research and will illustrate how your ancestors lived. This book shows how to locate records in a courthouse and online; how to maximize your search results with microforms and published abstracts; how to interpret and record what you find; how to figure out land transfers from one owner to another; the use of maps, atlases, and gazetteers to find the correct areas; and how to work from home with online land records and the Family History Library Catalog. Also provided, is a glossary of related terms and guidelines for utilizing state references and other general resources.

Helm, Matthew L. and April L. Helm. *Genealogy On-line for Dummies.* 5th ed. Hoboken, NJ: Wiley Pub., 2008.

This is an excellent introductory guide to doing genealogical research online. Helm explains how to lay the groundwork for doing efficient online genealogy, locating the best Internet sources, how to swap data with other online researchers, how to tap into public records and how to use *Family Tree Maker* software. He also, discusses how to involve your children in your genealogical project and make it a family hobby. It includes a useful directory to great sites for collecting genealogy information from the WWW, mailing lists, newsgroups, and sever of the on-line service providers. It explains how to use a home computer to maintain and publish your genealogy information.

___ and ___. *Your Official America Online Guide to Genealogy.* 3rd ed. New York: Wiley, 2002.

The Helms have produced several guides to doing online genealogy. This guide to utilizing America Online illustrates how to find the best family history resources on AOL, as well as how to map a strategy for searching these resources, and evaluating genealogical software. This book provides assistance in building a multi-media family tree, building a family history website, and even assists in organizing family reunions. Online resources beyond genealogical websites which are discussed include message boards, chat rooms and newsgroups. The Helms guide shows how to do almost any family construct you can image online and a CD installation package is included.

Hendrickson, Nancy. *Finding Your Roots Online.* Cincinnati, OH: Betterway Books, 2003.

> Everything is on the Internet now...well, not quite, but it has become a valuable search resource for many things, not the least of them being genealogy. Nancy Hendrickson has put together a valuable resource which not only gives basic tips for all facets of genealogy, but also list most of the major online resources for a genealogical researcher. She discusses the sites and search engines which assist in reading pedigree charts and conducting family interviews; gathering reliable evidence; getting the most out of the Internet resources; evaluating when researching online is not the best option; accessing military, marriage and land records; and finding useful maps, historical data, migration patterns and more.

Herber, Mark D. *Ancestral Trails: The Complete Guide to British and Family History.* 2nd ed. Baltimore, MD: Genealogical Publishing Co., 2005.

> Tracing the family in Britain is the subject of *Ancestral Trails*. The early chapters instruct the researcher in the basics of genealogical research, obtaining information from the living relatives, drawing family trees, and starting to research the records of birth, marriage and death. The later chapters guide the researchers in finding things like wills, parish registers, civil and ecclesiastical court records, pool books and property records. This book is recommended for both the beginning and advanced researcher.

Hoffman, Marian. *Genealogical and Local History Books in Print.* 5th ed. Baltimore, MD: Genealogical Publishing Co., 1997.

> This is a four volume set which lists most genealogical reference works in print. The set is broken into two volumes of US Resources, a General Reference and World Resources volume, and a Family History volume. The listings of books and resources are selectively annotated, and the price of the book is given when available. Vendor numbers for each are listed at the ends of the citation and there is a list of the vendors at the beginning of the volume.

Holt, Dean W. *American Military Cemeteries: A Comprehensive Illustrated Guide to the Hallowed Grounds of the United States, Including Cemeteries Overseas.* Jefferson, NC: McFarland and Co., 1992.

Holt has published a survey of American military cemeteries which should be of immense value to local military historians and genealogists. He has served as director of the National Cemetery System and in his book identifies and describes each of the sites administered by the Veterans Administration. Medal of Honor recipients, lists of cemetery directors and the circumstances of each cemeteries founding are also included. Brief stories on notable individuals interred in the National Cemetery System are also included.

Hone, E. Wade. *Land and Property Research in the United States.* Salt Lake City, UT: Ancestry Publishing, 1997.

A frequently overlooked source for genealogical material, land records may provide clues back further in time than many of the records genealogists usually use. These records generally apply to more people than any other type of written record and seem to be not as frequently "lost" than many other types of records. Insights into family relationships may be gained by tracing the ownership of land from family member to family member, and is often a place for finding women's maiden names. The coverage for this work goes back to pre-U.S. possession days. It also covers state lands, federal lands, and individual lands, and has a section on Native American land records.

Horowitz, Lois. *A Bibliography of Military Name Lists From Pre-1675 to 1900: A Guide to Genealogical Sources.* Metuchen, NJ: The Scarecrow Press, Inc., 1990.

This bibliography is designed to assist the researcher in identifying a person through their military service in American wars from the seventeenth century to the late nineteenth century. This bibliography has compiled the sources which contain lists of payrolls, musters, and honor rolls; as well as account books, obituaries, pension and bounty land records and other military related records in various archives, libraries and historical and genealogical societies. The order of the book is chronological, with the names of various conflicts within each time period listed at the beginning of that period, and then broken out by state and county. As many counties no longer exist or have changed names, it is up to the researcher to have obtained that information prior to using this source. Under each state or county breakdown is a bibliographic entry giving the pertinent information for the publication in which that particular piece of information may be found.

Howells, Cyndi. *Cyndi's List: A Comprehensive List of 70,000 Genealogy Sites on the Internet.* 2nd ed. Baltimore, MD: Genealogical Publishing Co., 2001.

Cyndi's List is a hardcopy compilation of the sources she has on her Internet site. For a more expanded and up-to-date listing of these sources, go online to www.CyndisList.com. This hardcopy list gives the genealogist who is not totally comfortable online a chance to scan through what type of sources are available before going online to search. URLs are provided for each type of genealogical online search area. However, do not forget that website addresses change frequently, so for the most current information, see Cyndi's online webpage.

---. *Netting Your Ancestors: Genealogical Research on the Internet.* Baltimore, MD: Genealogical Publishing Co., Inc., 1997.

Cyndi's List is by far, the most complete starting point on the Internet for doing family research. Her site address is http://www.CyndisList.com. Howells shows the Internet researcher how to effectively use the Internet for genealogical research. She discusses each facet of utilizing the computer for research: e-mail, mailing lists, newsgroups and the worldwide web with strategies to use each most effectively.

Humling, Virginia. *U.S. Catholic Sources: A Diocesan Research Guide.* Salt Lake City, UT: Ancestry, 1995.

Humling's list provides a state-by-state listing of all the archdiocese and diocese in the United States and the archdiocese for the military. Within each diocese listing is given the address, phone number, archivist (at the time of publication), area included in the diocese, a brief history of the diocese, fees, and in some diocese a fairly detailed collection description. When a publication is attached to the diocese, it is listed. At the end of the book is a list of the diocese whose collections have been microfilmed by the Genealogical Society of Utah. The records contained in most diocesan archives include records of religious sacraments - baptism, marriage, etc.; and other ecclesiastical records which provide information for family research.

Humphrey, John T. *Understanding and Using Baptismal Records.* Washington, DC: Humphrey Publications, 1996.

Different denominations and religions produce different types of baptismal records. These records have different meanings and carry different implications. Humphrey explores the baptismal beliefs of different religious denominations which established churches in Colonial America and illustrates how to interpret their particular records.

Jacobus, Donald L. *Index to Genealogical Periodicals: Together with "My Own" Index.* 1973. Baltimore, MD: Genealogical Publishing Co., 1981, 1997.

This is a three volume collection in one, indexing genealogical periodicals and periodicals with significant historical interest to genealogists. To use it, look in part one for the surname you want. If this does not work check part two for the place name where your ancestor lived, trying town, county and state. There are also, listings in part two for *Passenger Lists, Revolutionary War and Soldiers, French and Indian Wars, Loyalists, England, Germany,* etc. There is a key which gives full names of the periodicals indexed, with references to volume and page. There is also, a list of general reference sources included.

Jarboe, Betty. *Obituaries: A Guide to Sources.* 2nd ed. Boston: G. K. Hall, 1989.

Obituaries are a valuable source of biographical material, particularly for the ordinary person. For many, they are the only printed source for obtaining information about a person. This guide indexes books and articles which either index or abstract obituaries and death notices from newspapers and periodicals. It also includes references to annuals and yearbooks which contain necrology sections. For the most part, this reference does *not* index civil records, church or parish registers, cemetery records, mortuary records or Bible records which may be found easily in county offices or parish offices. There are however, some ecclesiastical necrologies for foreign countries indexed here. The arrangement of the book is geographical, but in addition to scanning the books from a given state, also, search the general index as a back-up. There are 3,547 entries in this reference, and a new section has been added to this edition featuring tombstone inscriptions.

Johnson, Keith A. and Malcolm R. Sainty. *Genealogical Research Directory: National & International.* Melbourne, AU: Genealogical Research Directory, 2005-.

In its twenty-fifth year of publication, the *Genealogical Research Directory* has become the largest worldwide surname index. The 1990-1999 edition is also available on CD-ROM. There are maps at the beginning for the countries of France, Germany, Spain, England

and Wales, and Scotland. Following the maps is a feature article discussing British pedigrees, a calendar of genealogical events, abbreviations which may be found in the lists, and an explanation of how to use the listing. The sections of the book contain a listing of surnames, which is the largest component. The surnames are followed by the time period in which they were found, where they were at that time, and a reference number which indexes who contributed the name. The second section is a list of subject entries submitted by the contributors which include such subjects as general, individuals, migration, military, occupations, places, religion, and shipping and ships. Items within these categories are not linked to anything but the person contributing them. The third section contains the addresses of the contributors. This is to enable contact for those doing family research. One is asked not to phone these people unless they have listed their phone numbers. Section four is called 'One Name Studies.' These are persons or organizations interested in all references to a surname or particular area. The listings here include the name being researched, the name and address of a contact person, plus information such as whether a reunion is being planned, new information is welcomed, etc. Section five is a listing of Genealogical Societies, and section six lists archives, major libraries and research organizations.

Johnson, Richard S. and Debra Johnson Knox. *How to Locate Anyone Who Is or Has Been in the Military: Armed Forces Locator Directory.* 8th ed. Burlington, NC: Spartenburg, SC: MIE Publishing, Inc., 1999.

Members of the military may be located by a great variety of methods, and Johnson has tried to bring together in his work all of those methods. They include: locating by social security number and service number; locating active duty military; locating members of the Reserve and National Guard; locating retired members; locating veterans of the Armed Forces and former members of the Reserve and National Guard; locating and obtaining military records, unit and ships' rosters and organizational records; locating people for a military reunion; locating persons through state governmental records; locating a deceased person; and locating anyone - civilian or military. Also included are directories of Armed Forces World-Wide Locators, Base and Post Locators, Fleet Post Offices, APO's of all overseas bases, Military, Patriotic and Veterans Organizations, Military Unit Reunion Associations, Driver's License, MVR and Vital Statistics Offices.

Kemp, Thomas J. *The American Census Handbook.* Wilmington, DE: Scholarly Resources, 2001.

> Kemp, who has put together several other guides to using vital records and government resources, now offers this guide to utilizing the federal, state, and county census indexes for genealogical research. Arranged by geographically, by year, and by topic this manual will assist users in the detail found in census information.

—. *The Genealogist's Virtual Library: Full-Text Books on the World Wide Web.* Wilmington, DE: Scholarly Resources, 2000.

> This bibliography lists all the full-text genealogical books available on the web as of the publication date. Included is a CD-ROM with hot links to the sites listed in the book. This resource shows what is available for specific areas of interest and identifies thousands of genealogies, biographies and local histories.

---. *International Vital Records Handbook.* 4th ed. Baltimore, MD: Genealogical Publishing Company, 2004.

> *International Vital Records* provides a complete, up-to-date collection of vital records applications forms from nations throughout the world, simplifying and speeding up the process by which vital records may be obtained. The book is divided into three parts covering sixty-seven countries and territories. The application forms cover a variety of civil registration offices and current procedures for obtaining a birth, marriage or death certificates which may be photocopied. Data pages give the addresses and fees for the appropriate records offices.

---. *Virtual Roots 2.0: A Guide to Genealogy and Local History on the World Wide Web.* Rev. and updated. Wilmington, DE: Scholarly Resources, 2002.

> *Virtual Roots* is a roadmap to genealogy and historical sites on the Internet. There are over 30 million sites on the Web that can assist with genealogical research and this guide focuses on the most valuable of those. This first edition lists the sites of the best libraries, archives, institutions, genealogical, and historical societies, and family associations around the world as well as e-mail addresses, complete mailing addresses, and Fax and phone number. It's only drawback, is that in the world of the web, site addresses change frequently, so this source will need to be updated frequently.

Kirkham, E. Kay. *Our Native Americans and Their Records of Genealogical Value.* 2 volumes. Logan, UT: Everton Publishers, 1980.

The purpose of the two volumes in this set is to provide information to the beginner and expert in Indian research. Kirkham recommends beginning the research by reading and studying the glossary of Indian records in the second chapter of this book. It defines the type of information contained and different periods of time covered. As with other genealogical research, Indian research starts with the records of your immediate family and builds from there. Be sure to record all the information you have immediate access to fully as this will help in further searches of published records. Indian names do not always indicated whether they refer to male or female. Indians also usually have more than one name throughout their lives - be sure to make a record of these as they are found. In some records, numbers follow the names, these will be used as reference numbers to further record groups, so be sure to record them when found. Other instructions of this nature are given in Kirkham's set, as well as the sources for locating records of Indian relatives and how to use them.

---. *Some of the Military Records of America, before 1900: Their Use and Value in Genealogical and Historical Research.* Washington, DC: Kirkham, 1963.

The compilation by Kirkham lists the better known military records for the time period before 1900. Treated on a limited scale are records that were compiled as a result of military service, pensions, and bounty land warrants. Examples and definitions of these records are included.

---. *A Survey of American Church Records.* 4th ed. Logan, UT: Everton Publishers, 1978.

While not a comprehensive source for the entire United States, and not even cumulative from one edition to the next (it is recommended that earlier additions also be checked for information,) this source lists church records if they may be found in archival collections. For those records not found in archival sources, one must search out the individual churches and request the assistance of the pastor, church secretary, or parish clerk. The first part of the book gives a brief summary and chronology of the major denominations in the U.S. The second part gives a brief summary of the states, a bibliography of religious record statistical books, and a list of churches and contact points which maintain archival collections. Some states include timelines where the information was available on the progress of different denominations within the state.

Klunder, Virgil L. *Lifeline: The Action Guide to Adoption Search.* Cape Coral, FL: Caradium Publishing, 1991.

According to studies of adoption, one in every ten persons is in some way affected by adoption. Approximately 80% of these people have tried to do research into their biological family history, whether for a sense of curiosity and connection or for the need to obtain medical records and information. An adoptee with a need to find the medical information of his birth parents, Klunder offers tips in this step-by-step guide for adoptees. Over 100 tested techniques which have successfully obtained results are listed; sample letters, documents and checklists are included; and a detailed twenty-one point directory of search tips for all fifty states is provided which includes current laws, personal guidance, and instruction from local search experts and contacts to over 1,000 organizations set up exclusively to assist adoptees. Tips on searching internationally are also included.

Knox, Debra Johnson. *WWII Military Records: A Family Historian's Guide.* Spartanburg, SC: MIE Publishing, 2003.

Designed for the genealogist doing military research, Knox's book on military records is a comprehensive guide for both novice and professional researcher. She shows how to access information on personnel records, casualty reports, WWII draft registrations, burial sites, awards and medals, and unit and ship histories.

Kurzweil, Arthur and Miriam Weiner, eds. *The Encyclopedia of Jewish Genealogy.* Northvale, NJ: J. Aronson, 1991, 1996.

Volume one of this encyclopedia provides a listing of sources on Jewish genealogy available in Canada and the United States. Information covered includes immigrations and naturalization records, passenger and steamship research, and a guide to institutional resources. State by state and province by province listings include addresses and telephone numbers for libraries, funeral homes, cemeteries, synagogues, and local, state and federal government record centers. A synopsis of the types of records held in each repository is included. Volume two covers resources in Europe, South America, Australia, Israel, and South Africa. The third volume is to be arranged by topic.

Lackey, Richard S. *Cite Your Sources: A Manual for Documenting Family Histories and Genealogical Records.* Jackson: University of Mississippi Press, 1980, 1985.

> Like Turabian, or the MLA Handbook, this is a citation guide. Lackey seeks to provide genealogists with an uncomplicated, academically acceptable guide to basic citations. Though there are many other acceptable citation formats available, this one was constructed with genealogists in mind. Part one discusses standard formats, using reference notes, citing the source being used, making cross references, how to add information to explain why a source was used, and making acknowledgements. Part two illustrates the actual citation forms and goes into detail on punctuation, capitalization, abbreviation, commonly used abbreviations, and other miscellaneous information. Citation details are given on each of the various types of genealogical sources which might be used in the research. Part three discusses the use of short notes and other reference forms.

Lainhart, Ann S. *State Census Records.* Baltimore, MD: Genealogical Publishing Company, Inc., 1992.

> State censuses frequently ask different questions than federal censuses do, so this is further census source to pursue. In her book, Lainhart has inventoried state census records state by state, year by year, county by county, and district by district to assist the researcher in identifying available information. It also helps the researcher to find out what types of information is available.

Lancour, Harold. *A Bibliography of Ship Passenger Lists, 1538-1825; Being a Guide to Published Lists of Early Immigrants to North America.* New York: New York Public Library, 1963.

> This is a bibliography which lists the works which exist listing ships lists for the American ports between the arrival years of 1538 and 1825. Beginning with the 'generic' works covering multiple ports, the book is then subdivided into states, beginning with Maine in the Northeast and following down the coastline to Louisiana. Within each category, the listings are chronological. Annotations are given when possible. There is an index of ship names at the end of the book leading back to the pages which include bibliographies pertaining to that ship.

Lawson, Sandra. *Generations Past: A Select List of Sources for Afro-American Genealogical Research.* Washington, DC: Library of Congress, 1988.

The purpose of *Generations Past* is to make available the names of published sources available for researching Afro-American genealogy. This is a selected list of books in collections of the Library of Congress for researchers of Afro-American lineage. Included are guidebooks, bibliographies, genealogies, collective biographies, United States local histories, directories, and other works relating specifically to Afro-Americans Emphasis is on books that contain information about lesser-known individuals of the nineteenth-century and earlier. The selected books are usually ones which contain genealogical information: names, dates, places and relationships. Other books provide historical background or information where other information may be found. The book is broken into sections, first with a listing of books on genealogical research, then family histories, and finally, listings by state. Following the state listings are sections dealing with genealogical periodicals, biographies and directories, bibliographies, catalogs to collections, newspaper sources, genealogical organizations and an author/title index.

McClure, Rhonda R. *Finding Your Famous {& Infamous} Ancestors: Uncover the Celebrities, Rogues, and Royals in Your Family Tree.* Cincinnati, OH: Betterway Books, 2003.

Did you ever wish you were descended from someone famous? Related to a famous movie star? Worried about that outlaw in the family tree? Well, actually, if the outlaw was far enough back . . . he sort of becomes romantic! McClure shares techniques for proving or disproving your family's rumored relationships; unearthing the family black sheep; finding famous figures from your past; tracing connections to real royalty; creating a family tree for your favorite celebrity; and working with the Titanic passenger log. Looking to find your lost inheritance or castle? Maybe this source will help you find it!

Meyerink, Kory M., ed. *Printed Sources: A Guide to Published Genealogical Records.* Salt Lake City, UT: Ancestry, 1998.

A major new guidebook for genealogists, *Printed Sources* discusses all aspects of genealogical sources including recent publications on compact disc. A comprehensive introduction is followed by detailed chapters discussing every possible published genealogical source. Explanations include the how and why each record was created, how to use it, and where to find it, while cautioning the researcher on the limitations of the records. Each chapter also includes bibliographies listing further sources for each topic. *Printed Sources* is a sequel to the book *The Source: A Guidebook of American Genealogy*. Chapter topics include: general reference; instructional materials; geographic tools - maps, atlases, and gazetteers; ethnic sources; bibliographies and catalogs; published indexes; vital and cemetery records; church sources; censuses and tax records; published probate records; printed land records; court and legal records; military sources; immigration sources; documentary records; family histories and genealogies; county and local histories; biographies; genealogical periodicals; medieval genealogy; and appendices which list CD-ROMS, major genealogical libraries and genealogical publishers and booksellers.

Milner, Anita C. *Newspaper Indexes: A Location and Subject Guide for Researchers*. Metuchen, NJ: The Scarecrow Press, Inc., 1977-.

This index provides location information to libraries around the country for finding which library has which newspaper index. Questionnaires were sent to over 800 libraries with the questions: what newspaper indexes do you have and for what years, what subjects are covered in the indexes, what is the charge for having a staff member check the index for a requested reference, what is the cost of photocopying an article, are newspapers available on interlibrary loan, is there a catalog or other publication available and what is its price? From these questions, information on 300 repositories was compiled. Though this information is somewhat out of date, it gives the researcher a rough idea of what to find in the way of newspaper indexes for these 300 libraries.

Mokotoff, Gary. *How to Document Victims and Locate Survivors of the Holocaust*. Teaneck, NJ: Avotaynu, 1995.

In documenting his own family, Mokotoff learned that contrary to his past belief, his entire family had not been safe from the Holocaust. In researching his family, he found that over 250 members of the family were murdered in the Holocaust. This discovery led him to find what information sources are available on the fate of those victims. In this work, he publishes the sources he has found that assist in finding family histories for people who have perished in the Holocaust of World War II. He begins the book with how to do Holocaust research and where to find the records, providing a checklist on what to use and look for in the research process. The rest of the work describes the sources and places available which provide the materials needed to do the family research from this time period.

Moore, Dahrl E. *The Librarian's Genealogy Notebook: A Guide to Resources.* Chicago, IL: American Library Association, 1998.

This book discusses the growth of one of America's fastest growing hobbies, genealogy. Moore has compiled a guide to a range of resources, including a basic genealogy bibliography; state, county, city, town and area sources; large genealogical societies; genealogical records such as vital records, passenger lists, land records, wills and probate; and computer databases, Internet sites, and the World Wide Web. These sources provide the librarian and researcher with information on location and access. Checklists give the researcher a guide to looking for the right kind of information.

Morgan, George G. *The Genealogy Forum on America Online: The Official User's Guide.* Salt Lake City, UT: Ancestry, 1998.

George Morgan, who has been working on his family's genealogy since the age of ten, has become one of the leading experts in the field of genealogy. Here he puts his expertise and his association with America Online's (AOL) Genealogy Forum to use by illustrating this preeminent research site. The AOL Genealogy Forum has over 150 people who contribute time and expertise to helping other AOL members in their research. The Genealogy Forum (GF) has an immensely diverse collection of research tools for doing genealogical research. Coverage includes: how-to articles and instructions for beginners; message boards for exchanging information with other genealogists; file libraries of lineage files (GEDCOM), historical files, maps, software programs, tools, forms, and many other types of information; articles for intermediate and advanced genealogists; information about doing research in many areas of the world; resources for African-American, Native-American, Hispanic, Jewish, and Huguenot researchers; regularly scheduled genealogical chats; an in-depth Internet area with easy-to-understand explanations and links to other Web sites, mailing lists and user groups; and online columns that share information and tips on a regular basis.

Morton Allan Directory of European Passenger Steamship Arrivals for the Years 1890 to 1930 at the Port of New York and for the Years 1904 to 1926 at the Ports of New York, Philadelphia, Boston, and Baltimore. Baltimore, MD: Genealogical Publishing Co., Inc., 1987.

This directory simply gives the year of arrivals, broken down by steamship companies and dates and ports of arrival. Behind each individual day is the name of the ship which arrived in port on that day.

Morton-Young, Tommie M. *Afro-American Genealogy Sourcebook.* New York: Garland, 1987.

> This sourcebook lists the types of materials used in Afro-American genealogy research, gives examples of these materials, and lists the locations of the research materials. Primary and secondary sources are included in the list. This work was compiled from a survey of over 200 libraries and genealogical collections. Part one includes background readings and basic sources, part two lists private resources, part three lists public resources, and part four is a directory of resources.

The MVR Book: Motor Services Guide. Tempe, AZ: BRB Publications, Inc., 1998-.

> Motor vehicle records may be used to search for genealogical information. The annual *MVR Book* shows how to access these records. The record information is listed by state. An introduction provides information on privacy laws and tells what types of information may be disclosed and to whom. While each state is different, it does help to read the basic regulations in the introduction first. Within the state listings one can find general help numbers, driver licensing facts, information on financial responsibility, suspensions and revocations, driver-related records, vehicle and plate information, and where to write for information on the previous issues. The appendices list various drivers programs and networks, professional agencies and institutions, the Driver's Privacy Protection Act, state reciprocity of records, state driver license format and records access, sate membership and compliance, and a glossary of common abbreviations.

National Archives and Records Administration. *Guide to Genealogical Research in the National Archives.* 3rd ed. Washington, DC: National Archives Trust Fund Board, 2000.

> The National Archives of the United States documents American history from the time of the first Continental Congress to the present and holds the records of all three of the branches of the federal government. One million cubic feet of records are located not only in Washington, DC, but also, in eleven regional archival branches located around the country. The guide lists the collections contained in the National repositories and records of genealogical value in the branches. It also contains photos and illustrations, citations to microform publications, and expanded and clarified descriptions of the records.

National Genealogical Society. *Special Aids to Genealogical Research in Northeastern and Central States.* Washington, DC: National Genealogical Society, 1962.

This is a collection of reprints from the National Genealogical Society's *Quarterly* prepared by experts familiar with the records of the Northeastern and Central States. These articles were intended to be helpful to those just beginning genealogical research in these regions. Written as magazine articles, they are considerably in-depth and not as easy to peruse as most of the more recent books for genealogical instruction. They do however; provide some tips from those who have done research in these areas.

National Genealogical Society. *Special Aids to Genealogical Research on Southern Families.* Washington, DC: National Genealogical Society, 1965.

This is a collection of reprints from the National Genealogical Society's *Quarterly* prepared by experts familiar with the records of the Southern States. These articles were intended to be helpful to those just beginning genealogical research in this region. Written as magazine articles, they are considerably in-depth and not as easy to peruse as most of the more recent books for genealogical instruction. They do, however, provide some tips from those who have done research in this area.

Neagles, James C. *Confederate Research Sources: A Guide to Archival Collections.* 2nd ed. Salt Lake City, UT: Ancestry Pub., 1997.

Written for the descendents of persons serving in the Confederate forces during the Civil War, this work may also be helpful to those whose ancestor may have been a civilian associated with some aspect of the Confederacy. Neagles identifies Confederate records available in the National Archives or other state archives and genealogical libraries, as well as provides a separate section for each of the eleven Confederate states, territories and Border States that contributed men to the armies and navies of the Confederacy. A historical background is given discussing the role each state played in the conflict, as well as the descriptions of the records and their locations. Chapter one discusses the Confederacy as a whole, chapter two discusses searching within the Confederate states, chapter three contains the border states, chapter four the National Archives, chapter five discusses searching in other publications, and the appendix discusses the Daughters of the Confederacy.

---. *The Library of Congress: A Guide to Genealogical and Historical Research.* Salt Lake City, UT: Ancestry Publishing, 1990.

> Neagles' guide is the definitive manual on what is available to the genealogist and historical researcher at the Library of Congress. Many genealogists' never venture beyond the Genealogical reading room. There is a lot more information available, however, in the other divisions of the library and Neagles delineates these in this work. Part one defines the Library of Congress and its research rooms and resources. Part two discusses the categories of research such as genealogies, biographies, local histories, and other records available at the Library. Part three details the key source materials by region and state which are available at the Library. Within each of these parts there is detailed information either discussing the type of material highlighted or telling how to use it in the most effective manner. This is a must read for the dedicated genealogist.

---. *U. S. Military Records: A Guide to Federal and State Sources from Colonial Times to the Present.* Salt Lake City, UT: Ancestry, Inc., 1994.

> Enlistment forms, muster rolls, pension applications are all records created as a result of spending time in the military service. These records contain detailed personal information including dates of birth, place of birth, places of residence, addresses of loved ones and more. In *U.S. Military Records*, Neagles describes the records that are available and where to find them.

--- And Lila Lee Neagles. *Locating Your Immigrant Ancestor: A Guide to Naturalization Records.* Rev. ed. Logan, UT: Everton Publishers, 1986.

> Finding that naturalization records of aliens prior to 1906 were almost impossible to locate lead the authors to undertake this work. The national government is not the only repository of naturalization records. Many of these are located in county court houses, especially those from the years prior to 1907. Chapters one through five discuss information dealing with the immigrants of numerous countries, the types of records that exist and how to use them. Chapter six is the listing by state of the locales of various immigration records and the years which may be found at each location.

--- and ---. *Locating Your Revolutionary War Ancestor: A Guide to the Military Records.* Rev. ed. Logan, UT: Everton Publishers, Inc., 1983.

Many persons researching their genealogy will eventually need to find and verify an ancestor who fought in the American Revolution. The Neagles' work attempts to compile resources which will assist in finding the military records from the Revolutionary period. The first chapters describe the military organization which was created during the Revolutionary War period and the events of the war itself. Other chapters discuss the section of the National Archives which holds the microfilm of the Revolutionary participants and the categories one needs to utilize them. There is also a checklist of publications for use at other libraries around the country to identify various sources for Revolutionary War information. This work compiles a listing of approximately 483 titles of publications which contain military lists of the Revolutionary War.

Nelson, Lynn. *A Genealogist's Guide to Discovering Your Italian Ancestors: How to Find and Record Your Unique Heritage.* Cincinnati, OH: Betterway Books, 1997.

Discovering Your Italian Ancestors is a step-by-step guide suitable for beginning genealogists as well as experienced genealogists for locating Italian ancestors as far back as the 1700s. As well as general genealogical guidelines, it includes how to use the major American records such as census, naturalization, ship passenger lists and passport applications; minor American records such as family letters, church and cemetery records, and newspapers; Italian vital records - civil documents recording birth, marriages and deaths; interpreting margin notations in Italian records; and how to interview relatives. Information is also given on Italian naming traditions, how to interpret foreign handwriting, tips on using English/Italian dictionaries, and a letter writing guide to use for requesting data from Italian officials.

Nevius, Erin, et. al. *The Family Tree Guide Book to Europe: Your Passport to Tracing Your Genealogy Across Europe.* Cincinnati, OH: Betterway Books, 2003.

The United States is very much a "migrant" nation. With the exception of the very earliest arrivals and Native Americans, many of us are only a generation or two removed from kinship ties to Europe, Asia and other parts of the world. Each of these world parts have different methods of registering descendants, some are matrilineal, some patrilineal. Some utilize first names of one or the other of the parents to create a surname. To do genealogy overseas, you must discover how each country utilizes the naming process and charts its genealogy. *The Family Tree Guide Book to Europe* will assist in this exploration. Each of the fourteen chapters is devoted to a specific region or country in Europe. In addition to a discussion of the traditions and histories of each area, the authors provide a listing of where to find essential records and resources for each country or area; provide a listing of online sites and print resources for Europe; and where to go in person if it becomes necessary.

Newman, John J. *American Naturalization Records, 1790-1990: What They Are and How to Use Them.* Bountiful, UT: Heritage Quest, 1998.

As with the use of any other genealogical search tool, it is important to know as much about the person you are searching for as possible. This information can help with the search for naturalization and immigration records. Understanding the process which an immigrant goes through to become a citizen is important in determining where to look for records. Knowledge of the naturalization process assists in determining if an ancestor was naturalized, where they were naturalized and what kind of documentation exists. This work gives a synopsis of the naturalization laws and processes in a few pages to assist in learning how to use these records. Other information which might contribute to finding naturalization records are such issues as placing them in a time, locality and neighborhood; the motivation for citizenship; a need to own land, vote, peer pressure; local traditions and conditions; and other issues all contribute to reasons why and when a person applied for naturalization. Understanding your ancestor's life helps in finding their history.

Nichols, Elizabeth L. *Genealogy in the Computer Age. Understanding Family Search (Ancestral File, International Genealogical Index, and Social Security Death Index.)* Salt Lake City, UT: Family History Educators, 1994.

Family Search is a set of genealogical programs and data files on computer disc. It was published by the Church of Jesus Christ of Latter-Day Saints (LDS, Mormons) and is available at the Family History Library in Salt Lake City, Utah and most of its over 2000 Family History Centers worldwide. *Ancestral File* is a pedigree-linked file which shares genealogies, focusing on people now deceased. Names are linked to family members and other ancestors and descendants. Anyone can contribute information to it. The *International Genealogical Index* is a file of over 200 million names from over 90 countries extracted from vital records. Links do not attach records. The *U.S. Social Security Death Index* is a brief index of those whose death was reported to the Social Security Administration. The file is made available through the Freedom of Information Act. This book gives details and illustrations that assist in finding and retrieving the information from these files.

Parco, Vincent. *Researching Public Records: How to Get Anything on Anybody.* New York: Citadel Press Book, 1994.

Public records are a main source of information to the genealogist. However, they show more than most of us imagine. They can tell information about credit ratings, unpaid tickets, criminal, corporate, and real estate records among much other information. Parco's book also illustrates ways of finding information not documented by public records by using the various "detection" techniques of surveillance, interviews and interrogation. This book will be especially useful to adoptees, birthparents, researchers and of course, genealogists.

Periodical Source Index. Fort Wayne, IN: The Allen County Public Library Foundation, 1987-.

This is a comprehensive place, subject, and surname index to current genealogical and local history periodicals. Originally compiled by the Allen County Public Library in Fort Wayne, Indiana to go with their genealogy collection, it has become a standard index useful in any library containing a significant collection of genealogical periodicals. It is also, now available on CD-ROM. A retrospective compilation has also been done, indexing the years from 1847 to 1985. PERSI as it is known is divided into five parts, a places section, a family section, a Canadian places section, a section for other foreign places, and a section on research methodology citations to articles for assistance in improving research skills. Listed record types include: biography, cemetery, census, church, court, deeds, directories, history, institutions, land, maps, military, naturalization, obituaries, passenger lists, probate, school, tax, vital records, voter, wills, and a section for records which do not fall under the above categories.

Pfeiffer, Laura Szucs. *Hidden Sources: Family History In Unlikely Places.* Provo, UT: Ancestry, 2000.

Pfeiffer has provided a listing of over 100 sources with overviews which help amateur to professional genealogists to determine whether or not a particular source will be useful for them to pursue when tracing their family history. Some of these sources include adoption records, coroner's inquests, orphan asylum records, court records, diaries and journals, holocaust records, licenses, slavery records, patent records and many more. She also indicates where these records might be found in libraries and other record centers and provides a short bibliography at the end of each type of resource. Websites and URLs are also included which provide further areas of research and some "hidden" areas to research.

Porter, Pamela Boyer and Amy Johnson Crow. *Online Roots: How to Discover Your Family's History and Heritage with the Power of the Internet.* Nashville, TN: Rutledge Hill Press, 2003.

There are many ways to do genealogy, but the Internet has revolutionized how we do almost any searching for information in the twenty-first century. Porter and Crow have compiled a practical guide to make Internet genealogy more effective for the family researcher. They will also help the researcher to evaluate the accuracy of what may be found via the Internet. This guide offers advice in searching historic and current records around the United States and the world; locating photographs online; finding clues to sources which are not on the web; contacting distant relatives who may have needed information; learning about different types of records and searching methods; and how to share your research with others.

Reid, Judith Prowse and Simon Fowler. *Genealogical Research in England's Public Record Office: A Guide for North Americans.* 2nd ed. Baltimore, MD: Genealogical Publishing Co., Inc., 2000.

One of the richest genealogical repositories in the world, the Public Record Office (PRO) in London contains records all the way back to the *Doomsday Book* of 1086. From 1086 to the present, records include census records, probate documents, and emigration records. The purpose of this book is to make it easier for North Americans to access these records. This book provides an introduction to the major PRO record classes of special interest to a North American researcher and helps them to make the most efficient use of their time if they go to London. However, it also, identifies the important PRO records available in large North American institutions such as the Family History Library in Salt Lake City, Utah, the Library of Congress in Washington, DC, and the National Archives of Canada in Ottawa. Topics covered in this book are emigration and immigration records, censuses, nonconformist church records, birth, death, and marriage records, and military, taxation, court and Parliamentary records. A list of the principle

PRO offices is given, as well as a list of the addresses for genealogical research in North American and the British Isles, and a checklist of information you will need before going to the PRO.

Renick, Barbara and Richard S. Wilson. *The Internet for Genealogists: A Beginner's Guide.* 4th ed. La Habra: CA: Compuology, 1998.

The Internet has become a vast resource for the genealogist. Second only to a library, and often referred to as a virtual library, the Internet provides the genealogist with access to finding people (dead or alive), research, software, education and training, travel help, language aids, finding calendars for genealogy events, locating societies (historical and genealogical), and purchasing products and services. Throughout the book are tips and explanations of how to effectively search the Internet for genealogy, as well as popular site addresses and descriptions of these sites.

Rising, Marsha Hoffman. *The Family Tree Problem Solver: Proven Methods for Scaling the Inevitable Brick Wall.* Cincinnati, OH: Family Tree Books, 2005.

Designed for an intermediate or experienced genealogist, Rising has put together a guide to help genealogists delve into areas that commonly cause problems when searching for that elusive family link. She guides the researcher in locating missing documents, overcoming census omissions, discovering, recognizing and using "collateral kin" and neighbors, interpreting court and probate records, interpreting property records, distinguishing between individuals with the same name and finding ancestors who lived prior to 1850.

Roberts, Ralph. *Genealogy Via the Internet: Tracing Your Family Roots Quickly and Easily: Computerized Genealogy in Plain English.* 2nd ed. Alexander, NC: Alexander Books, 2002.

Roberts explains how to use your personal computer to trace your family roots, he goes into genealogical programs - which are best, which are easiest to use; how to hook your computer up to the world via the telephone; resources available through the Internet and other online services; places to find reference materials and guides of all sorts; and online databases you can search for your own family history.

Robl, Gregory. *A Student's Guide to German American Genealogy.* Phoenix, AZ: Oryx Press, 1996.

Robl begins his *Guide to German American Genealogy* with a basic history of Germany and German emigration. Chapters three through six discuss the basics of doing genealogy, discussing both how to do it and some of the common sources available and how to use them, chapter three delving into the specific German sources for searching. There is also a glossary of German-English genealogical terms. Comprehensive bibliographies also give ideas for obtaining further information both about German history in general and other genealogical sources.

Ryan, James G. *Irish Records: Sources for Family and Local History.* Rev. ed. Salt Lake City, UT: Ancestry, Inc., 1997.

Records for the late eighteenth to mid nineteenth centuries are very sparse. Few written records were kept among the small tenant farmers and laborers of this period. Births, marriages and deaths were not consistently recorded until after 1864. *Irish Records* provides a resource which facilitates Irish family history research with a comprehensive listing of the record sources available for each county in Ireland. Records include such sources as civil registers, censuses, land records, and church records. Heritage centers providing search services are listed and indicate which parish registers, gravestone inscriptions and other sources have been indexed by each. The introduction discusses the various types of records and what they can be used for and then the rest of the work is divided by counties.

Sankey, Michael L. and Carl R. Ernst. *The Librarian's Guide to Public Records: The Complete State, County, and Courthouse Locator.* Tempe, AZ: BRB Publications, Inc., 1998, 2000.

Over 11,500 major federal, state, and county record locations are listed in this reference book. Section one lists the county records, section two - state, and section three - federal. Each section is alphabetical by state and then broken down by county for the county portion, state agency in the sate section and the federal is listed by US Court of Appeals, Federal Records Centers, and District and Bankruptcy courts. Each individual entry has the name of the office or agency, address, and phone number as well as a list of the types of records held by that office. This is an excellent source for tracking down the offices pertinent to your records search.

— and —. *The Sourcebook of County Court Records.* 4th ed. Tempe, AZ: BRB Publications, Inc., 1998.

> Within this resource is a listing of over 5,340 primary and secondary county courts throughout the United States. Listed alphabetically by state, each state chapter begins with a summary of the state court system, state vital records, and the state criminal record repository. A list of county seats is also included, and each chapter ends with an extensive city to county cross reference index. Tips are listed on how to obtain information from the county courts whether it is done by letter or by phone. The over 11,500 addresses and phone numbers provide access to county recorders, county assessors, and probate courts.

— and —. *The Sourcebook of State Public Records: The Definitive Guide to Searching for Public Record Information at the State Level.* 3rd ed. Tempe, AZ: BRB Publications, 1997.

> Listing more than 5,000 locations in a state by state file, *The Sourcebook* provides details where nineteen different types of information may be found. Most of this information can be found elsewhere, but not in the comprehensive manner provided by this collection. The information locations listed here include offices, agencies, and bureaus which maintain public records; these records include criminal, corporation, trademark, Uniform Commercial Code, workers' compensation, driver and accident, birth, death, marriage and divorce, licenses, registrations and permits, and state legislation. Addresses, phone numbers, Fax numbers, department names, hours, and description of the records held are also given; as is the procedure for obtaining records, the costs and the turn-around time.

Saul, Pauline A. and F. C. Markwell. *The A-Z Guide to Tracing Ancestors in Britain.* 4th ed. Baltimore, MD: Genealogical Publishing Co., 1992.

> This resource is arranged alphabetically and contains definitions, explanations, bibliographies, sources, addresses, and guides to almost every conceivable topic of interest to the historian looking for family information in Britain. A breakdown as to where records are located is given in the appendix as well as record listings for Wales, Scotland and Northern Ireland.

Schaefer, Christina K. *The Center: A Guide to Genealogical Research in the National Capital Area*. Baltimore, MD: Genealogical Publishing Co., 1996.

>Washington, DC is the home to the largest body of accessible research materials in the world. It is the central repository of primary source records making it the premier location for genealogical research. It lists the various records available in the Capitol, the building in which they may be found and how best to access them. In Washington, one can find not only the resources of the federal government, but those of societies and associations; ethnic, cultural, and religious groups; military records; university archives and special collections; and specialized genealogical research libraries. Locations are also listed for the Maryland and Virginia areas around Washington. Citations for the resources contain information on addresses, telephone and Fax numbers; public transportation and parking; rules of access, copy facilities, hours and online addresses; and general information on the collections.

---. *Genealogical Encyclopedia of the Colonial Americas: A Complete Digest of the Records of All the Countries of the Western Hemisphere*. Baltimore, MD: Genealogical Publishing Co., 1998.

>Schaefer's work *Genealogical Encyclopedia of the Colonial Americas* is the most complete listing of records of all the countries in the western world covering the time period from 1492 to 1775. Part one is a chronological timeline of historical events in the Western Hemisphere, part two lists the countries of Latin American, part three indexes the Caribbean, part four the thirteen colonies of the United States plus Maine and Vermont, part six, the other states with settlements prior to the American Revolution, and part six indexes Canada. Part seven provides resources for further research. There are many maps included for the colonial time period as well. Each country or state has a brief introduction with a list of resources, and suggested further readings about its history. For the Latin American countries and the Caribbean the dates of independence in the 1800s are also included.

---. *The Great War: A Guide to the Service Records of all the World's Fighting Men and Volunteers*. Baltimore, MD: Genealogical Publishing Co., 1998.

>The Great War, World War I, has passed from living history, so now provides a genealogical challenge. The records of the millions of men who participated in various aspects of this war are difficult to find, in

this work, Schaefer has compiled a guide to WWI service records. She covers soldiers from Britain, Germany, France, Russia, Canada, the United States, Brazil, India, Australia, Japan, South Africa and more. She begins with the history of the war and research tips. Then she lists the countries and sources within each alphabetically. The next chapter discusses casualties and prisoners of war and new countries. She also discusses Internet research on military records in the appendix.

---. *Guide to Naturalization Records of the United States.* Baltimore, MD: Genealogical Publishing Co., 1997.

Naturalization records are similar to census records and include such information as place and date of birth, foreign and current places of residence, marital status, names, ages, and places of birth of other family members, occupation, port and date of entry into the United States, and more. Naturalization records can be processed by any court of record, thereby making them difficult to track down. Schaefer has provided a practical guide for locating these widely scattered records. She has identified all the major repositories of these records, indicating the types of records held by each, their dates of coverage, and the location of the original and microfilm records. The Guide also pinpoints the location of federal court records in all National Archives facilities. The book is organized by state, with a brief description of the state's history, a list of statewide records available, and then a list of records by county. At the end of the county listing is a list of important addresses and phone numbers as well as a list of suggested readings for that state.

---. *The Hidden Half of the Family: A Sourcebook for Women's Genealogy.* Baltimore, MD: Genealogical Publishing Co., 1999.

In most societies, by law or by custom, women's individual identities have been subsumed by those of their husbands. In these societies, for centuries, women were not allowed to own real estate in their own names, sign a deed, devise a will, or enter into contracts, and in some places even their citizenship and their position as heads of households have been in doubt. This makes finding a women's ancestry very difficult sometimes as many of the conventional sources do not fully report on women. Schaefer recommends looking at parts of the law which mandate female interaction in the legal process for finding information on female ancestors. She says the legal status of women at any given time is the key to finding information. Therefore, this work highlights those laws, both federal and state which indicate that a woman could do any of the above activities in their own names. The first part of the book, deals with the way in which women are dealt with in federal records such as immigration records, passports, naturalization records, census enumerations, land records, military records, and records dealing with minorities. Also discussed are nongovernmental records such as newspapers, cemetery records, city directories, church records, and state laws covering such issues as common law marriages, and marriage and divorce registrations. The bulk of this work, however, deals with individual states, showing laws, records, and resources which may be used in determining female identity. Each state section begins with a time line of events important in that state's history, followed by a detailed listing of these eight key categories of information: Marriage and Divorce - marriage and divorce laws and where to find marriage and divorce records; Property and Inheritance - women's legal status as reflected in statute law, code and legislative acts; Suffrage - information as to when voting rights were granted prior to the ratification of the 19th Amendment in 1920; Citizenship - dates when residents of an area became U.S. citizens; Census Information - special notes on searching federal, state, and territorial enumerations; Other - information on welfare, pensions, and other laws affecting women; Bibliography - books and articles relating to women in state, historical and biographical resources and publications regarding legal history and jurisprudence; and Selected Resources for Women's History - addresses of state archives, historical societies, and libraries, women's studies programs, history programs and more.

---. *Instant Information on the Internet! A Genealogist's No-Frills Guide to the British Isles.* Baltimore, MD: Genealogical Publishing Co., 1999.

Designed to make the Internet more accessible, this guide identifies the top Internet resources on Great Britain, Wales, Scotland and Ireland. The guide is organized by country and following that by county. As applicable, each county listing includes the record office of facility that holds official records such as local authority archives, larger public library archives, and parish and Non-conformist archives; libraries, museums, societies, and other resources (in alphabetical order); a section of information sites listing how-to information, local history sources, and other materials; a selection of indexes, documents, maps and publications in digitalized form; and sites containing links to other sites. A reminder in the Internet age is also important, when researching the Internet, be sure to keep a paper trail as sites and addresses change frequently.

---. *Instant Information on the Internet! A Genealogist's No-Frills Guide to the 50 States and the District of Columbia.* Baltimore, MD: Genealogical Publishing Co., 1999.

The Internet has rapidly become one of the most valuable sources of information to genealogists as more and more research materials and library holdings become accessible on the web, as well as numerous postings and web pages being constructed by private individuals listing their personal family information. Schaefer's guide lists the URLs (addresses) for what she considers the best websites for genealogical research in each of the fifty states and the District of Columbia. It tells how and where to locate records, contact information for other researchers, how to exchange information, and how to locate indexes which may be searched free of charge from a home computer. Arranged by state, the guide provides Internet listings for the state departments of vital records; the state archives, historical society, and library; any National Records Center branch within the state; other state or regional libraries, archives, and societies and additional resources; sites listing how-to or instructional information; a selection of indexes, documents, and publications in digitalized form; and sites which link to other sites.

Schafer, Louis S. *Tombstones of Your Ancestors.* Bowie, MD: Heritage Books, 1991.

Tombstones frequently hold a fascination for people whether or not they are doing genealogy research or just browsing a cemetery looking at artistic creations of past ages. In the first part of her text, Schafer examines the historical development of tombstones, their materials, styles, artwork and epitaphs, as well as devoting one chapter to interesting epitaphs she has found. Genealogists can find much interesting information on a tombstone and methods for searching this out are detailed. She provides lists of abbreviations used, definitions of Latin phrases, and an explanation of the different dating systems that have been used. Symbolic images of artwork are also discussed. The second part of the text defines the process for creating a clear reproduction of a grave markers message, from the proper techniques for cleaning a marker, to what materials to use and how to preserve the final product. Shafer discusses the techniques for tombstone photography, highlighting, chalking, tracing, rubbing, dabbing, foiling, and transferring.

Smith, Juliana Szucs. *The Ancestry Family Historian's Address Book.* 2nd ed. Salt Lake City, UT: Ancestry, Inc., 2003.

> The *Address Book* provides a comprehensive list of local, state and federal agencies, institutions and ethnic and genealogical organizations. Beginning with a listing of national societies; archives, libraries and museums; ethnic and ecclesiastical resources and websites; military and federal government agencies; National Archives and Records Administration; and other helpful websites; the bulk of the book provides listings alphabetically by state. The state listings give a breakdown of all the state offices and addresses of the previous list, also including LDS Family History Centers, newspaper repositories, and specific state websites.

The Sourcebook of Federal Courts, U.S. District and Bankruptcy: The Definitive Guide to Searching for Case Information at the Local Level Within the Federal Court System. 2nd ed. Tempe, AZ: BRB Publications, Inc., 1996.

> This reference points the researcher to the courts where public records may be found. In this volume there are 300 U.S. District Courts, 192 U.S. Bankruptcy Courts, and 14 Federal Records Centers listed. It provides information detailing the federal court structure, standard record keeping practices, searching tips, and full explanation of electronic access and worksheets. There is also an alphabetical county list for every state, cross referencing the applicable courts. Court-by-court descriptions of each court are given including how each court indexes case records, specific search information, and how to use the electronic access programs. County maps for every multiple judicial district state showing the court locations. Section one tells how to use the court system, section two lists the courts and their descriptions by state, and section three lists and describes the Federal Records Centers.

Sperry, Kip. *Abbreviations & Acronyms: A Guide for Family Historians.* Rev. 2nd ed. Orem, UT: Myfamily.com, Inc., 2003.

> Acronyms and abbreviations are encountered constantly in everyday life, and genealogical research is no exception to this rule! No one can possibly know all of them, so Sperry has provided a comprehensive listing of those abbreviations and acronyms found most commonly in genealogy and family history searching. He provides the meanings for not only abbreviations and acronyms, but also alphabetic symbols, initials, contractions and shortenings of words. They are listed alphabetically and appear just as they would in an original document.

Stein, Lou. *Clues to Our Family Names.* Bowie, MD: Heritage Books, Inc., 1988.

> Hundreds of names are listed in Stein's book of *Clues to Our Family Names.* Many have descriptions of their use-origins and the root from which they came. In addition, the text has anecdotes about the origins of phrases and words commonly used today. Chapters also cover, why surnames came into existence, types of surnames, names developed from nicknames, names from occupations, names evolved from parent's first names, and names which came from addresses. There is also a chapter on what to do if your name is not included in this book.

Streets, David H. *Slave Genealogy: A Research Guide with Case Studies.* Bowie, MD: Heritage Books, 1986.

> Emphasizing non-plantation slave genealogy, Streets provides a clear discussion and case studies drawn from Wayne County, Kentucky records. He illustrates the search methods and types of analysis that are needed, as well as the importance of researching both owners and slaves. The case studies are supported by charts and diagrams, and extracts from original sources to show the methodology and type of records used. Chapter one discusses research methodology and the difficulty of tracking down slave genealogy and tells how to use a variety of the record sources in the search. Chapter two lists the various types of records and how to use them effectively, and chapter three highlights three case studies.

Szucs, Loretto Dennis. *They Became Americans: Finding Naturalization Records and Ethnic Origins.* Salt Lake City, UT: Ancestry Inc., 1998.

> The naturalization process creates significant historical records about the individuals who immigrate to America. Immigrants have to record their biographical data as they enter the country. Over the years this data has gone from no more than writing their name on a piece of paper to filling out detailed forms. Szucs addresses the complexity of naturalization records and uses illustrations and examples to explain them. She provides the historical background to the naturalization process, shows how to find the records, discusses naturalization courts and the processes, discusses published naturalization records and indexes, talks about the Immigration and Naturalization Service, discusses naturalization records in the National Archives, shows how to find naturalization information on the Internet and provides other forms, addresses and a chronology of immigration.

--- and Sandra Hargreaves Luebking. *The Archives: A Guide to the National Archives Field Branches.* Salt Lake City, UT: Ancestry Publishing, 1988.

>Over 1,000,000 cubic feet of records are housed and maintained by the National Archives in Washington and its many field branches. Visiting the various field branches of the National Archives, Szucs and Luebking did a detailed study and inventory of the holdings of each. This inventory will guide the user through the holdings found at each site describing the various individual field branches, listings of the microfilm copies held by each branch, printed descriptions and inventories, histories of the agencies and their records, cross-references to microfilm holdings, suggestions for research topics and much more.

---, eds. *The Source: A Guidebook of American Genealogy.* Rev. ed. Salt Lake City, UT: Ancestry, 1997.

>Designed for genealogists of varying skill levels, *The Source* is a complete reference of the vast collection of significant record sources from Colonial times to the present. It details search techniques and provides creative ideas for the next step of research. By using *the Source*, the genealogist can determine which records exist for a particular time period, what information can logically be obtained, where the records may be located, and how they might best be put to use.

Tepper, Michael. *American Passenger Arrival Records: A Guide to the Records of Immigrants Arriving at American Ports by Sail and Steam.* Baltimore, MD: Genealogical Publishing Co., 1993.

>Tepper's *Passenger Arrival Records* contain listings of passengers arriving on various ships in the American Ports. Prior to the 1820s many of these lists were compiled from baggage lists which were kept for some unknown reason. After 1819, legislation was passed regulating passengers in the various ports which provided for more accurate arrival lists. The lists provide the names of the passengers, ships and arrival dates. Tepper has published several port specific passenger arrival lists also, such as *Passenger Arrivals at the Port of Philadelphia, 1800-1819 (1986).*

Thode, Ernest. *Address Book for Germanic Genealogy.* 6th ed. Baltimore, MD: Genealogical Publishing Co., Inc., 1997.

>This address book for doing German genealogical research contains a listing of genealogical, historical and German-related societies outside of Europe in a state-by-state listing, by locality or area, by

other related country or ethnic group, and by whether they are European or American. It also, lists archives in the United States; German-American religious organizations; German-American and/or American genealogical booksellers and importers; foreign offices in North America; German-language newspapers in North America; map sources; ship and riverboat records; German national archives and organizations; European national and state archives; European stat or provincial archives; European religious archives; European national and regional genealogical and historical societies; European genealogical publishers and booksellers; national and regional libraries and museums; genealogists, sample form letters; and German genealogy on the Internet.

Thorndale, William and William Dollarhide. *Map Guide to the U.S. Federal Censuses 1790-1920.* Rev. ed. Baltimore: Genealogical Publishing Company, Inc., 2000.

Though federal censuses have always been taken by county, county lines have not always stayed the same. This work shows all the U.S. county boundaries from 1790 to 1920. Each of the 400 maps has the old county lines superimposed over the modern ones to highlight the boundary changes at ten-year intervals. Also included are: a history of census growth; the technical facts about each census; a discussion of census accuracy; an essay on the available sources for each state's old county lines; and a statement accompanying each map stating which county lines still exist and which have been lost. There is also a list of all present day counties as well as a list of defunct and renamed counties.

Tillman, Norma M. *How to Find Almost Anyone, Anywhere.* Rev. ed. Nashville, TN: Rutledge Hill Press, 1998.

Norma Tillman, a private investigator, discusses the techniques she uses that may be used by the average searcher to find persons and information. Among other types of searching, she has a specific chapter on doing genealogical searching which includes a basic how-to explanation of getting started on family tree research, using birth certificates and death records, census records, immigration and naturalization records, libraries, and Native American ancestry information. She also provides details and website addresses for doing searches on the Internet.

Walch, Timothy. *Our Family, Our Town: Essays on Family and Local History Sources in the National Archives.* Washington, DC: National Archives and Records Administration, 1987.

>Practical advice is offered on how to use federal records in family and local history research. Military pension records, census schedules, ship passenger lists, and court documents are among the materials discussed.

Warren, Paula Stuart and James W. Warren. *Your Guide to the Family History Library: How to Access the World's Largest Genealogy Resource.* Cincinnati, OH: Betterway Books, 2001.

>The Family History Center in Salt Lake City, Utah, is the largest and probably best known collection of genealogy and family history in the world. The Warrens have put together a guide to help the beginning genealogist make the best use of this resource both on-site and from a distance or online. Included in their guide are tips for making the most of limited research time; guidelines for accessing the collection of the Utah site or the more than 3,400 Family History Centers worldwide; overviews of their records; a traveler's guide to Salt Lake City; and advice on using what you the materials you find.

Wehmann, Howard H., comp. *A Guide to Pre-Federal Records in the National Archives.* Washington, DC: National Archives and Records Administration, 1989.

>Though the Constitution went into effect in 1789, there were a hundred plus years preceding that time for which records were generated in what became the United States. This guide will assist in tracking down the records from pre-constitutional America. While not a complete listing, this guide identifies and describes bodies of records in the Archives holdings which contain documents from prior to 1789. These include records of the Continental and Confederation Congresses, the Constitutional Convention, and records from the predecessors to the Departments of State, Treasury, Office of the Chief of Engineers, Quartermaster General, Bureau of Land Management, Adjutant General, Veterans Administration and other agencies.

Where to Write for Vital Records: Births, Deaths, Marriages, and Divorces. Washington, DC: U.S. Department of Health and Human Services, 2005.

>This publication provides information about individual vital records maintained only on file in State or local vital statistics offices. These offices should have certificates recording every birth, death,

marriage and divorce which occurs in the U.S. This guide also provides instructions for obtaining access to these records. Each state is listed in alphabetical order with the price charged for the copying of each record. There are also instructions at the end for obtaining records from overseas offices.

Witcher, Curt B. *African American Genealogy: A Bibliography and Guide to Sources.* Fort Wayne, IN: Round Tower Books, 2000.

The introduction in this bibliography is designed to provide the basic how-to information for the beginning researcher in African American genealogy. Research strategies and methodologies are outlined, significant record groups are highlighted and reproductions of documents typically encountered are illustrated. The bibliography which comprises the bulk of this book is arranged in standard format beginning with the author. As this was built around the collection of the Allen County Public Library in Fort Wayne, the citations also contain a call number or location identifier for that library. The first section is General Sources, and cites works which do not have a specific geographic focus. The general section is followed by lists of sources for each state, and by citations pertaining to Canada, several Caribbean countries, and Liberia. There are also, numerous plantation record collections listed.

Zubatsky, David S. and Irwin M. Berent. *Sourcebook for Jewish Genealogies and Family Histories.* Rev. ed. Teaneck, NJ: Avotaynu, 1996.

First published in 1984, Zubatsky's resource provides information on approximately 12,000 family names gathered from over 22,000 sources. Primary source material includes materials from national archive records from American and foreign archives and libraries; collections of family papers; catalogs; and published and unpublished genealogies. Qualification for inclusion was that information had to span at least three generations. The entries are organized alphabetically mainly by family names with locations of related resources.

Localized Genealogical Resources

This section includes a limited number of general genealogical guides and journals which have been written about specific states. There are numerous works done for each state and listed in the National Library catalog, but it is impossible to list them all here. These are sources that encompass whole state or regional interest, they have not been evaluated for quality, they were simply inclusive for the state rather than limited to selected topics or city/county area within a state. Much of the additional material to be found are on individual counties or cities, census, probate records, birth, death and marriage records, or books about individual families. There are also many single page bibliographies available to local census materials for different states. Following the state listings are journal selections for Canada and Mexico, our nearest North American neighbors and then journal listings for various countries around the world.

United States & Canada:

Andriot, John L. *Township Atlas of the United States.* McLean, VA: Androit Associates, 1991.

Barsi, James C. *The Basic Researcher's Guide to Homesteads and Other Federal Land Records.* Colorado Springs, CO: Nuthatch Grove Press, 1994.

Bockstruck, Lloyd DeWitt. *Revolutionary War Bounty Land Grants Awarded by State Governments.* Baltimore, MD: Genealogical Publishing Co., 1996.

Carlson, Jone. *The USA Search Resources Directory: State by State Listings Including Puerto Rico & the Virgin Islands; for Adoptees and Birth Families Separated by Adoption.* Fort Lauderdale, FL: J. E. Carlson and Associates, 1992.

Church of Jesus Christ of Latter-Day Saints. Family History Library. *Family History Library Catalog.* Salt Lake City, UT: The Genealogical Society of Utah, 1990-.

Directory of United States Cemeteries. San Jose, CA: Cemetery Research, 1974-.

Dollarhide, William. *Map Guide to American Migration Routes, 1735-1815.* Bountiful, UT: Heritage Quest, 1997.

Filby, P. William. *American and British Genealogy and Heraldry: A Selected List of Books*. 3rd. ed. Boston: New England Historical and Genealogical Society, 1983.

---. *A Bibliography of American County Histories*. Baltimore, MD: Genealogical Publishing Co., 1987, 2005.

---. *Directory of American Libraries with Genealogy or Local History Collections*. Wilmington, DE: Scholarly Resources, Inc., 1988.

Grundset, Eric G. and Steven B. Rhodes. *American Genealogical Research at the DAR*. 2nd ed. Washington, DC: Daughters of the American Revolution, 2004.

Hatcher, Patricia L. *Abstract of Graves of Revolutionary Patriots*. 4 volumes. Dallas, TX: Pioneer Heritage, 1987-1988.

Hewett, Janet. *The Roster of Confederate Soldiers, 1861-1865*. 16 volumes. Wilmington, NC: Broadfoot, 1995-1996.

---. *The Roster of Union Soldiers, 1861-1865*. Wilmington, NC: Broadfoot, 1997-2000.

Kot, Elizabeth G. and James D. Kot. *United States Cemetery Address Book, 1994-1995*. Vallejo, CA: Indices Publishing, 1994.

List of Pensioners on the Roll, January 1, 1883... 5 volumes. 1883. Baltimore, MD: Genealogical Publishing Co., 1970.

Meyer, Mary K. *Meyer's Directory of Genealogical Societies in the U.S.A. and Canada*. 11th ed. Mt. Airy, MD: Mary K. Meyer, 1996.

National Archives and Records Administration. *1900 Federal Population Census*. 1978. Washington, DC: National Archives Trust Fund Board, 2000.

---. *The 1910 Federal Population Census*. 1982. Washington, DC: National Archives Trust Fund Board, 1996.

---. *The 1920 Federal Population Census*. Washington, DC: National Archives Trust Fund Board, 1998.

---. *Federal Population Censuses, 1790-1890*. Washington, DC: National Archives Trust Fund Board, 2001.

National Archives and Records Service. *Guide to Genealogical Research in the National Archives.* 3rd ed. Washington, DC: National Archives and Records Administration, 2000.

New York Public Library. *United States Local History Catalog: A Modified Shelf List Arranged Alphabetically by State, and Alphabetically by Locality Within Each State.* Boston: G. K. Hall, 1974.

Roll of Honor: Names of Soldiers Who Died in Defense of the American Union Interred in the National Cemeteries, 1865-1871. 11 volumes. Baltimore, MD: Genealogical Publishing Co., 1994.

White, Virgil D. *Genealogical Abstracts of Revolutionary War Pension Files.* 4 volumes. Waynesboro, TN: National Historical Publishing, 1990-1992.

---. *Index to Indian Wars Pension Files, 1892-1926.* 2 volumes. Waynesboro, TN: National Historical Publishing, 1987.

---. *Index to Mexican War Pension Files.* Waynesboro, TN: National Historical Publishing, 1989.

---. *Index to Old War Pension Files, 1815-1926.* 2 volumes. Waynesboro, TN: National Historical Publishing, 1959.

---. *Index to Pension Applications for Indian Wars Service between 1817 and 1898.* Waynesboro, TN: National Historical Publishing, 1997.

---. *Index to Revolutionary War Service Records.* 4 volumes. Waynesboro, TN: National Historical Publishing, 1995.

---. *Index to U.S. Military Pension Applications of Remarried Widows for Service Between 1812 and 1911.* Waynesboro, TN: National Historical Publishing, 1999.

---. *Index to War of 1812 Pension Files.* 3 volumes. Waynesboro, TN: National Historical Publishing, 1989.

Journals:

Genealogical and Historical Magazine of the South
National Genealogical Society Quarterly
New England Historical and Genealogical Register
NGS Newsletter
Southern States Armchair Researcher
Surname Research Directory

Alabama:

Alabama Marriages, Early to 1825: A Research Tool. Bountiful, UT: Precision Indexing, 1991.

Armstrong, Zella. *Notable Southern Families.* 6 volumes. 1918-1933. Baltimore, MD: Genealogical Publishing Company, 1993-2000.

Barefield, Marilyn D. and Yvonne Shelton Crumpler, eds. *Researching in Alabama: A Genealogical Guide.* Rev. ed. Birmingham, AL: Birmingham Public Library Press, 1998.

Boddie, John B. and Mrs. John B. Boddie. *Historical Southern Families.* 23 volumes. 1957-1980. Baltimore, MD: Genealogical Publishing Company, 1967-.

Brewer, Willis. *Alabama, Her History, Resources, War Record, and Public Men, From 1540 to 1872.* Baltimore, MD: Clearfield Co., 1995.

Cemetery Records of Alabama. 6 volumes. LDS Church in Alabama, 1946-64.

Clark, Murtie June. *Colonial Soldiers of the South, 1732-1774.* 1983. Baltimore, MD: Genealogical Publishing Company, 1999.

Connick, Lucille M. *Lists of Ships' Passengers, Mobile, Alabama.* Mobile, AL: L. M. Connick, 1988-.

Davis, Robert Scott. *Tracing Your Alabama Past.* Jackson, MS: University Press of Mississippi, 2003.

Elliott, Wendy L. *Research in Alabama.* Rev. ed. Bountiful, UT: W. L. Elliott, 1987.

Foley, Helen S. *Marriage and Death Notices from Alabama Newspapers and Family Records, 1819-1890.* 1981. Greenville, SC: SHP, 2005.

Foscue, Virginia O. *Place Names in Alabama.* Tuscaloosa, AL: University of Alabama, 1989.

Hageness, MariLee B. *Alabama Church & Family Cemeteries.* Anniston, AL: MLH Research, 1995-.

Long, John Hamilton and Peggy T. Sinko. *Alabama Atlas of Historical County Boundaries.* New York: Charles Scribner's Sons, 1996.

Read, William A. *Indian Place Names in Alabama.* Rev. ed. University, AL: University of Alabama Press, 1984, 1994.

Remington, W. Craig, and Thomas J. Kallsen. *The Historical Atlas of Alabama.* 2nd ed. Tuscaloosa, AL: University of Alabama, 1999-.

Journals:

Alabama Family History and Genealogy News
AGE: Alabama Genealogical Exchange
Alabama Genealogical Quarterly
Alabama Genealogical Society Magazine
Central Alabama Genealogical Society Quarterly
Deep South Genealogical Quarterly
Natchez Trace Traveler
Newsletter, Alabama Genealogical Society, Inc.
Pioneer Trails
Randolph County Alabama Roots
Southeast Alabama Genealogical Society
The Southern Genealogists Exchange Quarterly
Southern Roots and Shoots
Tap Roots
Valley Leaves

Alaska:

Alaska-Yukon Gold Book: A Roster of the Progressive Men and Women Who Were Argonauts of the Klondike Stampede... Seattle, WA: Sourdough Stampede Association, 1930.

Bradbury, Connie Malcolm. *Alaska People Index.* 2 volumes. Anchorage: Alaska Historical Commission, 1986.

— and David Albert Hales. *Alaska Sources: A Guide to Historical Records and Information Sources.* North Salt Lake, UT: Heritage Quest, 2001.

Ferrell, Ed, ed. *Biographies of Alaska-Yukon Pioneers, 1850-1950.* Bowie, MD: Heritage Books, 1994-2004.

Index of Alaska Obituaries from Various Sources with a Supplement of Obituaries from Sources in the Ketchikan Area Collected by Patricia Roppel. Ketchikan, AK: P. Roppel, 1996.

Merrell, Bruce. *Alaska Territorial Telephone Books, 1906-1958: A Collection on Microfiche.* Anchorage, AK: Anchorage Municipal Libraries, 1989.

Parnham, R. Bruce. *How to Find Your Gold Rush Relative: Sources on the Klondike and Alaska Gold Rushes, (1896-1914.)* Juneau, AK: Alaska Gold Rush Centennial Task Force, 1997.

Schorr, Alan Edward, ed. *Alaska Place Names.* 2nd ed. Juneau, AK: University of Alaska, 1980.

Ulibarri, George S. *Documenting Alaskan History: Guide to Federal Archives Relating to Alaska.* Fairbanks, AK: University of Alaska Press, 1982.

Journals:
Anchorage Genealogical Society Quarterly
North Star Nuggets: Fairbanks Genealogical Society Quarterly
The Taproot

Arizona:

Arizona Death Records: An Index Compiled from Mortuary, Cemetery, and Church Records. 3 volumes. Tucson, AZ: Arizona State Genealogical Society, 1976-1982.

Barnes, Will C. *Arizona Place Names.* Tucson, AR: University of Arizona Press, 1988.

Beers, Henry P. *Spanish and Mexican Records of the American Southwest: A Bibliographical Guide to Archives and Manuscript Sources.* Tucson, AZ: University of Arizona Press, 1979.

Bibby, Carolyn M. *Surname and Locality Index.* Glendale, AZ: Family History Society of Arizona, 1984.

Gabbert, Howard M. *The "Rough Riders": A Brief Study and Indexed Roster of the 1st Regiment, U.S. Volunteer Cavalry, 1898.* Tucson, AZ: Arizona State Genealogical Society, 1992.

Mexican Census - Pre-Territorial (Arizona.) Tucson, AZ: Arizona State Genealogical Society, 1986-.

Spiros, Joyce V. Hawley. *Genealogical Guide to Arizona and Nevada.* Gallup, NM: Verlene Pub., 1983.

Walker, Henry P. and Don Bufkin. *Historical Atlas of Arizona.* 2nd ed. Norman, OK: University of Oklahoma Press, 1986.

Fulcher, Richard Carlton and Linda Carolyn Allen Suber. *Arkansas Records*. Brentwood, TN: Fulcher Pub. Co., 1993.

Hallum, John. *Biographical and Pictorial History of Arkansas*. 1887. Easley, SC: Southern Historical Press, 1980.

Index to the Wills and Administrations of Arkansas from the Earliest to 1900. Jonesboro, AR: National Society, Daughters of the American Revolution, 1986.

Norris, Rhonda S. *Arkansas Links: A Comprehensive Guide to Genealogical Research in the Natural State*. Russellville, AR: Arkansas Genealogical Research, 1999.

Shinn, Josiah Hazen. *Pioneers and Makers of Arkansas*. 1908. Baltimore, MD: Genealogical Publishing Co., 1999.

> *Journals*:
>
> AGS Newsletter
> Arkansas Family Historian
> Arkansas Genealogical Register
> Arkansas Historical Quarterly
> Arkansas Pioneers
> Family Pedigrees
> Frontier Research
> The Genie
> Melting Pot Genealogical Society Quarterly
> The Southern Genealogists Exchange Quarterly

California:

Bancroft, Hubert Howe. *California Pioneer Register and Index, 1542-1848, Including Inhabitants of California, 1769-1800 and List of Pioneers, Extracted from Hubert Howe Bancroft's History of California*. 1884-90. Baltimore, MD: Genealogical Publishing Co., 1990.

Gudde, Erwin G. *California Place Names*. 4th ed. Berkeley, CA: University of California Press, 2004.

Kot, Elizabeth Gorrell and Shirley Pugh Thomson. *California Cemetery Inscription Sources: Print & Microform*. Vallejo, CA: Indices Pub., 1994.

Parker, J. Carlyle. *Index to Biographies in the 19th Century California County Histories*. Detroit, MI: Gale Research, 1979.

Journals:

Arizona State Genealogical Society News: Copper Filings
Copper State Bulletin
Copper State Journal
Family Connections
Journal of Arizona History
Sands of Time
Sun Cities Genealogist
Yesteryears News Today

Arkansas:

Allen, Desmond W. *Arkansas' Damned Yankees: An Index to Union Soldiers in Arkansas Regiments.* 2nd ed. Conroy, AR: Arkansas Research, 2000.

---. *Arkansas Death Record Index: 1914-1948.* 4 volumes. Conway, AR: Arkansas Research, 1996-1999.

---. *Arkansas Union Soldiers Pension Application Index.* Conroy, AR: Arkansas Research, 1987.

---. *Index to Arkansas Confederate Soldiers.* 3 volumes. Conroy, AR: Arkansas Research, 1990.

Armstrong, Zella and Janie Preston Collup French. *Notable Southern Families.* 6 volumes. 1918-1933. Baltimore, MD: Genealogical Publishing Company, 1993-2000.

Arnold, Morris. *Colonial Arkansas, 1686-1804.* Fayetteville, AR: University of Arkansas Press, 1991.

Baker, Jack D., transc. *Cherokee Emigration Rolls, 1817-1835.* Oklahoma City, OK: Baker Pub. Co., 1977.

Boddie, John B. and Mrs. John B. Boddie. *Historical Southern Families.* 23 volumes. 1957-1980. Baltimore, MD: Genealogical Publishing Company, 1994-1998.

Clark, Murtie June. *Colonial Soldiers of the South, 1732-1774.* 1983. Baltimore, MD: Genealogical Publishing Company, 1999.

Elliott, Wendy L. *Arkansas Research Guide.* Rev. ed. Bountiful, UT: American Genealogical Lending Library, 1987.

Quebedeaux, Richard. *Prime Sources of California and Nevada Local History: 151 Rare and Important City, County and State Directories, 1850-1906.* Spokane, WA: Arthur H. Clark Co., 1992.

Rasmussen, Louis J. *San Francisco Ship Passenger Lists. Volume 1, 1850-1864.* 1965. Baltimore, MD: Genealogical Publishing Co., 1978-.

Strong, Gary E., ed. *Local History and Genealogy Resources of the California State Library.* Sacramento, CA: California State Library Foundation, 1991.

> *Journals:*
>
> Ancestors West
> Ash Tree Echo
> California History
> Orange County Genealogical Society Journal
> San Diego Leaves and Saplings
> Santa Clara Connections
> The Searcher: Official Monthly Periodical of the Southern California Genealogical Society
> Valley Quarterly

Colorado:

Bright, William and George R. Eichler. *Colorado Place Names: Communities, Counties, Parks, Passes with Historical Lore and Fact Plus a Pronunciation Guide.* Boulder, CO: Johnson Pub., 1980.

Colorado Families: A Territorial Heritage. Denver, CO: Colorado Genealogical Society, 1981.

Colorado Resource Handbook. Rev. ed. Denver, CO: Colorado Council of Genealogical Societies, 1999.

Elliott, Donald R., comp. and Doris L. Salmen Elliott, ed. Place *Names of Colorado.* Denver, CO: Colorado Council of Genealogical Societies, Inc., 1999.

Hinckley, Kathleen W. *Genealogical Research in Colorado.* Arlington, VA: National Genealogical Society, 1989.

Joy, Carol M. and Terry Ann Mood, comps. *Colorado Local History: A Directory.* Denver, CO: Colorado Historical Society, 1986.

Peters, Bette D., Mary Crackel, and Jane Johnson. *Genealogical Index to the Records of the Society of Colorado Pioneers.* Denver, CO: Colorado Genealogical Society, 1990.

Wynar, Bohdan and Roberta J. Depp, eds. *Colorado Bibliography.* Littleton, CO: Libraries Unlimited for the National Society of Colonial Dames of America in the State of Colorado, 1980.

Journals:

Boulder Genealogical Society Quarterly
Colorado Genealogist
Colorado Heritage
Inquirer
Pinon Whispers

Connecticut:

Anderson, Robert C., et. al. *The Great Migration Begins: Immigrants to New England, 1620-1633.* 3 volumes. Boston: New England Historic Genealogical Society, 1995-.

—, George F. Sanborn, Jr. and Melinde L. Sanborn. *The Great Migration, 1634-1635, Volume 1: A-B.* Boston: New England Historic Genealogical Society, 1999-.

Hughes, Arthur H. and Morse S. Allen. *Connecticut Place Names.* Hartford, CT: Connecticut Historical Society, 1976.

Jacobus, Donald L. *Families of Ancient New Haven: 1922-32.* Reprint. Baltimore, MD: Genealogical Publishing Co., 1974, 1994.

Johnston, Henry P. *Record of Service of Connecticut Men in the I. War of Revolution, II. War of 1812, III. Mexican War.* Boston: New England Historic Genealogical Society, 1998.

Kemp, Thomas J. *Connecticut Researcher's Handbook.* Detroit, MI: Gale Research Co., 1981.

Lainhart, Ann S. *Digging for Genealogical Treasure in New England Town Records.* Boston: New England Historic Genealogical Society, 1996.

Long, John Hamilton and Gordon DenBoer, eds. *Atlas of Historical Boundaries: Connecticut, Maine, Massachusetts, Rhode Island.* New York: Simon and Schuster, 1994.

Manwaring, Charles. *A Digest of Early Connecticut Probate Records.* 3 volumes. 1904. Baltimore, MD: Genealogical Publishing Co., 1995.

Melnyk, Marcia. *Genealogist's Handbook for New England Research.* 4th ed. Boston: New England Historic Genealogical Society, 1999.

Roberts, Gary B., ed. *English Origins of New England Families, From the New England Historical and Genealogical Register, First Series.* 3 volumes. Baltimore, MD: Genealogical Publishing Company, 1984. Second Series. 3 volumes, 1985, 2004.

— and Judith McGhan. *Genealogies of Connecticut Families from the New England Historical and Genealogical Register.* 3 volumes. Baltimore, MD: Genealogical Publishing Co., 1983,1998.

Sperry, Kip. *Connecticut Sources for Family Historians and Genealogists.* Logan, UT: Everton Publishers, 1980.

White, Lorraine C., ed. *The Barbour Collection of Connecticut Vital Records.* Baltimore, MD: Genealogical Publishing Co., 1994-2002.

Journals:

Connecticut Ancestry
Connecticut History
Connecticut Maple Leaf
Connecticut Nutmegger
The Great Migration Newsletter
New England Ancestors
New England Historical and Genealogical Register

Delaware:

Bendler, Bruce A. *Colonial Delaware Assemblymen 1682-1776.* Westminster, MD: Family Line Publications, 1989.

Biographical and Genealogical History of the State of Delaware. 2 volumes. Chambersburg, PA: J. M. Runk and Co., 1899.

Burr, Horace. *The Records of Holy Trinity (Old Swedes) Church, Wilmington, Del., From 1697 to 1773.* 2 volumes. 1890, 1919. Baltimore, MD: Genealogical Publishing Co., 1983.

Clark, Raymond B. *Delaware Church Records: A Collection of Baptisms, Marriages, Deaths, and Other Records and Tombstone Inscriptions, From 1686-1880, Five Important Religious Groups: Baptist, Episcopal, Methodist, Presbyterian, and Quaker, with Historical Sketches of the Churches or Groups, and With Illustrations of the Churches.* St. Michaels, MD: R. B. Clark, 1986.

Doherty, Thomas P. *Delaware Genealogical Research Guide.* 3rd ed. Wilmington: Delaware Genealogical Society, 2002.

Ferris, Benjamin. *A History of the Original Settlements on the Delaware.* 1846. Wilmington, DE: Delaware Genealogical Society, 1987.

Heck, L. W. *Delaware Place Names.* Washington, DC: U.S. Government Printing Office, 1966.

Long, John Hamilton, ed. *Atlas of Historical County Boundaries: Delaware, Maryland, and District of Columbia.* New York: Charles Scribners Sons, 1996.

Society of Colonial Wars in the State of Delaware, Register of Members, Nos. 1 thru 338. Baltimore, MD: Genealogical Publishing Co., 1998.

    Journals:

    Delaware Genealogical Society Journal
    Delaware History
    Maryland and Delaware Genealogist

District of Columbia:

Angevine, Erma. *Research in the District of Columbia.* Arlington, VA: National Genealogical Society, 1992.

Bagley, Charlotte, H. Byron Hall, et. al. *Lest We Forget: A Guide to Genealogical Research in the Nation's Capitol.* 8th ed. Annandale, VA: Annandale Stake, Church of Jesus Christ of Latter-day Saints, 1992.

Cook, Eleanor M. V. *Guide to the Records of Your District of Columbia Ancestors.* 4th ed. Silver Spring, MD: Family Line Publications, 1990.

Long, John Hamilton, ed. *Atlas of Historical County Boundaries: Delaware, Maryland and District of Columbia.* New York: Charles Scribners Sons, 1996.

Pippenger, Wesley E. *District of Columbia Ancestors: A Guide to Records of the District of Columbia.* Rev. Westminster, MD: Family Line Publications, 2000.

---. *District of Columbia Marriage Licenses, Register 1: 1811-1858.* 1994. Westminster, MD: Family Line Publications, 2000.

---. *District of Columbia Marriage Licenses, Register 2: 1858-1870.* Lovettsville, VA: Willow Bend Books, 1996.

---. *District of Columbia Marriage Records Index: June 28, 1877 to October 19, 1885.* Arlington, VA: W. E. Pippenger, 1997.

—. *District of Columbia Marriage Records Index: October 20, 1885 to January 20, 1892.* Arlington, VA: W. E. Pippenger, 2003.

Provine, Dorothy S. *Index to District of Columbia Wills, 1801-1920.* Baltimore, MD: Genealogical Publishing Co., 1992.

Florida:

Armstrong, Zella. *Notable Southern Families.* 6 volumes. 1918-1933. Baltimore, MD: Genealogical Publishing Company, 1993-2000.

Bertalan, John J. *A Survey of Major Genealogical Holdings in Florida, 1988-89.* Tallahassee, FL: Florida Department of State, 1990.

Clark, Murtie June. *Colonial Soldiers of the South, 1732-1774.* 1983. Baltimore, MD: Genealogical Publishing Company, 1999.

Davidson, Alvie L. *Florida Land: Records of the Tallahassee and Newnansville General Land Office, 1825-1892.* Bowie, MD: Heritage Books, 1989.

Feldman, Lawrence H. *The Last Days of British Saint Augustine, 1784-1785: A Spanish Census of the English Colony of East Florida.* Baltimore, MD: Genealogical Publishing Co., 1998.

Florida Department of State, Division of Library and Information Services. *The Black Experience: A Guide to Afro-American Resources in the Florida State Archives.* Rev. Tallahassee, FL: Florida Department of State, 2002.

Hartman, David W. and David Coles. *Biographical Rosters of Florida's Confederate and Union Soldiers, 1861-1865.* 6 volumes. Wilmington, NC: Broadfoot Publishing Co., 1995.

Historical and Genealogical Holdings in the State of Florida. Boca Raton, FL: The Florida Library Association, 1992.

Knetsch, Joe. *Land Grants in Florida and Their Uses in Genealogy.* N.p., 1999.

Long, John Hamilton, Peggy Tuck Sinko, and Kathryn Ford Thorn, eds. *Atlas of Historical County Boundaries: Florida.* New York: Simon and Schuster, 1997.

Michaels, Brian E. *Florida Voters in Their First Statewide Election: May 26, 1845.* Tallahassee, FL: Florida State Genealogical Society, 1987.

Mills, Donna R. *Florida's First Families: Translated Abstracts of pre-1821 Spanish Censuses.* Tuscaloosa, AL: Mills Historical Press, 1992-.

—. *Florida Unfortunates. The 1880 Federal Census: Defective, Dependent, and Delinquent Classes.* Tuscaloosa, AL: Mills Historical Press, 1993.

Morris, Allen Covington. *Florida Place Names.* Coral Gables, FL: University of Miami Press, 1995.

Robie, Diane C. *Searching in Florida.* Costa Mesa, CA: ISC Publications, 1982.

Soldiers of Florida in the Seminole Indian, Civil, and Spanish-American Wars. 1903. Macclenny, FL: R. J. Ferry, 1983.

Taylor, Anne W. and Mary Barnes Harrell. *Florida Connections Through Bible Records.* Tallahassee, FL: Florida State Genealogical Society, 1993.

Journals:

Ancient City Genealogist
East-Florida Gazette
Florida Armchair Researcher
Florida Genealogical Society Journal
Florida Genealogist
Florida Historical Quarterly
Jacksonville Genealogical Society Magazine
South Florida Pioneers
The Southern Genealogists Exchange Quarterly

Georgia:

Adams, Marilyn. *Georgia Local and Family History Sources in Print.* Clarkston, GA: Heritage Research, 1982.

Armstrong, Zella and Janie Preston Collup French. *Notable Southern Families.* 6 volumes. 1918-1933. Baltimore, MD: Genealogical Publishing Company, 1993-2000.

Austin, Jeanette Holland. *Georgia Bible Records.* Baltimore, MD: Genealogical Publishing Co., 1985-.

---. *Georgia Intestate Records.* Baltimore, MD: Genealogical Publishing Co., 1986, 2005.

Brooke, Ted O. *In the Name of God, Amen: Georgia Wills, 1733-1860, an Index.* Atlanta, GA: Pilgrim Press, 1976.

---. and Robert Scott Davis, Jr. *Georgia Genealogical Workbook.* Atlanta, GA: Georgia Genealogical Society, 1987.

Clark, Murtie June. *Colonial Soldiers of the South, 1732-1774.* 1983. Baltimore, MD: Genealogical Publishing Company, 1999.

Cornell, Nancy Jones. *1864 Census for Re-organizing the Georgia Militia.* Baltimore, MD: Genealogical Publishing Co., 2000.

Davis, Robert S. Jr. *Georgia Research: A Handbook for Genealogists, Historians, Archivists, Lawyers, Librarians and other Researchers.* Atlanta, GA: Georgia Genealogical Society, 2001.

---. *A Researcher's Library of Georgia History, Genealogy, and Records Sources.* 2 volumes. Easley and Greenville, SC: Southern Historical Press, 1987-.

Dorsey, James E. *Georgia Genealogy and Local History: A Bibliography.* Spartanburg, SC: Reprint Co., 1983.

Hehir, Donald M. *Georgia Families: A Bibliographic Listing.* Bowie, MD: Heritage Books, 1993.

Henderson, Lillian. *Roster of the Confederate Soldiers of Georgia, 1861-1865.* 7 volumes. 1959-1964. N.p..: Georgia Division of UDC, 1994.

Krakow, Kenneth K. *Georgia Place-Names.* 1st ed. Macon, GA: Winship Press, 1975.

Overby, Mary McKeown. *Obituaries Published by the Christian Index.* 2 volumes. Macon, GA: Georgia Baptist Historical Society, 1975-.

Southern States Genealogical Resources: Alabama, Georgia, Kentucky, North Carolina, South Carolina, Tennessee, Virginia, West Virginia Research Sources and Bibliographies. Seattle, WA: Fiske Genealogical Foundation, 1991.

Warnock, Robert Holcomb. *Georgia Sources for Family History.* Atlanta, GA: Georgia Genealogical Society, 1995.

Journals:

Georgia Genealogical Magazine
Georgia Genealogical Society Newsletter
Georgia Genealogical Society Quarterly
Georgia Genealogical Survey
Northwest Georgia Historical and Genealogical Society Quarterly
The Southern Genealogists Exchange Quarterly
Southern Roots and Shoots

Hawaii:

Char, Wai J. And Tin-Yuke Char. *Chinese Historic Sites and Pioneer Families...* Honolulu: University of Hawaii Press, 1979-1988.

Conrad, Agnes C. *Genealogical Sources in Hawaii.* Honolulu, HI: Hawaii Library Association, 1974.

Duey, John V. and Rose Marie H. Lindsey Duey. *A Beginner's Guide for Genealogical Research in Hawaii.* Honolulu, HI: Alu Like, Inc., 1989.

Handy, E. S. Craighill and Mary Kawena Pukui. *The Polynesian Family System in Ka-'U, Hawaii.* Rutland, VT: Charles E. Tuttle, Co., 1972.

Lind, Andrew W. *Hawaii's People.* 4th ed. Honolulu: University of Hawaii Press, 1980.

Mardfin, Jean Kadooka. *Hawaiian Genealogy Project: Directory of Secondary Sources.* Honolulu: Office of Hawaiian Affairs, 1996.

Mckinzie, Edith K. and Ishmael W. Stagner. *Hawaiian Genealogies: Extracted from Hawaiian Language Newspapers.* 2 volumes. Laie and Honolulu, HI: Institute for Polynesian Studies, 1983-1999.

Pukui, Mary Kawena, Samuel H. Elbert and Esther T. Mookini. *Place Names of Hawaii.* Rev. and Enlarged ed. Honolulu, HI: University Press of Hawaii, 1974.

Searching Genealogical Records in Hawaii. Honolulu: Hawaii State Archives, 1982.

Journals:

Hawaiian Journal of History

Idaho:

Boone, Lalia Phipps. *Idaho Place Names: A Geographical Dictionary.* Moscow, ID: University of Idaho Press, 1988.

Lawless, Elaine J. *Guide to the Idaho Folklore Archives.* Boise, ID: Idaho Folklore Center, Idaho State Historical Society, 1983.

Schmick, Judy. *Idaho Surname Index.* Boise, ID: Idaho Genealogical Society, 1989.

Journals:

Heritage Chronicle
Idaho Genealogical Society Quarterly
Idaho Yesterday's: The Quarterly Journal of the Idaho State Historical Society
Lost and Found
Newsletter: Idaho Genealogical Society
Snake River Echoes

Illinois:

Adams, James N., comp. and William E. Keller, ed. *Illinois Place Names.* Springfield, IL: Illinois State Historical Society, 1989.

Cox, E. Evelyn. *Ancestree Climbing in the Midwest: Illinois, Indiana, Iowa, Kansas, Missouri, and Nebraska.* Rev. ed. Owensboro, KY: Cook & McDowell Publications, 1980.

Gooldy, Pat and Ray Gooldy. *Manual for Illinois Genealogical Research*. Indianapolis, IN: Ye Olde Genealogie Shoppe, 1994.

Guide to Public Vital Statistics Records in Illinois. 1941. Indianapolis, IN: Heritage House, 1976.

Long, John Hamilton. *Atlas of Historical County Boundaries: Illinois*. New York: Charles Scribners Sons, 1997.

Pence, Cheryl, ed. *Newspapers in the Illinois State Historical Library*. Springfield: Illinois State Library, 1998.

Reener, Lynn Boyd. *Illinois State Genealogical Society Family Bible Records*. Volumes 1 and 2. Springfield, IL: The Society, 1991, 1994.

Rochefort, Beth. *Prairie Pioneers of Illinois*. 2 volumes. Lincoln and Springfield: Illinois State Genealogical Society, 1986-1988.

Roll of Honor. Record of Burial Places of Soldiers, Sailors, Marines and Army Nurses of all Wars of the United States Buried in the State of Illinois... 2 volumes. Springfield: Illinois Military and Naval Departments, 1929.

Schweitzer, George Keene. *Illinois Genealogical Research*. Knoxville, TN: G. K. Schweitzer, 1997.

Sinko, Peggy Tuck. *Guide to Local and Family History at the Newberry Library*. Salt Lake City, UT: Ancestry, 1987.

Soldiers' Burial Places in State of Illinois (for Wars 1774-1898.) Microfiche. 1933. Springfield, IL: Secretary of State, Micrographics Division, 1975.

Szucs, Loretto D. *Chicago and Cook County: A Guide to Research*. Salt Lake City, UT: Ancestry, 1996.

Thackery, David. *Afro-American Family History at the Newberry Library: A Research Guide and Bibliography*. 1988. Chicago, IL: The Newberry Library, 1993.

Thompson, Joseph J. *The First Chicago Church Records, 1833-44*. 1920. Baltimore, MD: Gateway Press, 1988.

Walker, Harriet J. Revolutionary Soldiers Buried in Illinois. 1917. Baltimore, MD: Clearfield Co., 1999.

Volkel, Lowell M. and Marjorie Corrine Smith. *How to Research a Family With Illinois Roots.* Thomson, IL: Heritage House, 1977.

Journals:

Central Illinois Genealogical Quarterly
Discovering Family and Local History
Illiana Genealogist
Illinois Mennonite Heritage
Illinois State Genealogical Society Quarterly
Illinois State Genealogical Society Newsletter
Journal of Illinois History
Journal of the Illinois Historical Society
Koreny=Roots: Journal of the Czech & Slovak American
    Genealogical Society of Illinois
Newsletter: Afro-American Genealogical & Historical Society
    of Chicago
The Springhouse

Indiana:

Baer, M. Teresa, Geneil Breeze, Judith Q. McMullen, and Kathleen M. Breen. *Finding Indiana Ancestors: A Guide to Historical Research.* Indianapolis, IN: Indiana Historical Society Press, 2007.

Baker, Ronald L. *Indiana Place Names.* Bloomington, IN: Indiana University Press, 1975.

Beatty, John D. *Research in Indiana.* Arlington, VA: National Genealogical Society, 1992.

Carty, Mickey Dimon. *Searching in Indiana: A Reference Guide to Public and Private Records.* Costa Mesa, CA: ISC Publications, 1985.

Darlington, Jane Eaglesfield. *Indiana Tax Lists.* 2 volumes. N.p.: Jane E. Darlington, 1990.

Dorrel, Ruth. *Pioneer Ancestors of Members of the Society of Indiana Pioneers.* Indianapolis: Indiana Historical Society, Family History Section, 1983-.

Gooldy, Pat and Ray Gooldy. *Manual for Indiana Genealogical Research.* 2nd ed. Indianapolis, IN: P. Gooldy, 1993.

Heiss, Willard C. *Abstracts of the Society of Friends in Indiana.* 32 microfiches. Indianapolis: Indiana Historical Society, 1990.

An Index to Indiana Naturalization Records Found in Various Order Books of the Ninety-Two Local Courts Prior to 1907. Indianapolis: Indiana Historical Society, Family History Section, 1981.

Long, John Hamilton and Peggy Tuck Sinko, eds. *Indiana Atlas of Historical County Boundaries.* New York: Simon and Schuster, 1996.

Maps of Indiana Counties in 1876. Reprinted from Illustrated Historical Atlas of the State of Indiana. 1876. Indianapolis, IN.: Indiana Historical Society, 1968.

Miller, Carolynne L. Wendel. *Indiana Sources for Genealogical Research in the Indiana State Library.* Indianapolis, IN: Indiana Historical Society, Family History Section, 1984.

Miller, John W., Paul Brockman, and Patricia Lucken. *Indiana Newspaper Bibliography.* Indianapolis: Indiana Historical Society, 1982.

Newman, John J. *Research in Indiana Courthouses: Judicial and Other Records.* 1981. Indianapolis: Indiana Historical Society, 1990.

Riker, Dorothy Lois. *Genealogical Sources: Reprinted from the Genealogy Section, Indiana Magazine of History.* Indianapolis: Indiana Historical Society, Family History and Genealogy Section, 1979.

Schweitzer, George Keene. *Indiana Genealogical Research.* Knoxville, TN: G. K. Schweitzer, 1996.

Slater-Putt, Dawn. *Pre-1882 Indiana Births From Secondary Sources.* Fort Wayne, IN: Heritage Pathways, 1999-.

Taylor, Robert M., Jr. and Connie A. McBirney. *Peopling Indiana: The Ethnic Experience.* Indianapolis: Indiana Historical Society, 1996.

Waters, Margaret R. *Revolutionary Soldiers Buried in Indiana.* 2 volumes in 1. 1949, 1954. Baltimore, Genealogical Publishing Co., 1995.

Witcher, Curt Bryan. *A Bibliography of Sources for Black Family History in the Allen County Public Library, Genealogy Department.* Fort Wayne, IN: Allen County Public Library, 1989.

Journals:

Hoosier Genealogist
Hoosier Journal of Ancestry
Indiana Magazine of History

Iowa:

Church of Jesus Christ of Latter-Day Saints. Family History Library. *Research Outline: Iowa.* Salt Lake City, UT: Family History Library, 1988.

Cox, E. Evelyn. *Ancestree Climbing in the Midwest: Illinois, Indiana, Iowa, Kansas, Missouri, and Nebraska.* Rev. ed. Owensboro, KY: Cook & McDowell Publications, 1980.

Dilts, Harold E. *From Ackley to Zwingle: The Origins of Iowa Place Names.* 2nd ed. Ames, IA: Iowa State University Press, 1993.

Foresman, Sherry. *This is an Index to County Histories, Biographical Records, ...Covering All 99 Counties in the State of Iowa.* Menlo, IA: S. Foresman, 1980-1989.

Iowa Genealogical Society. *Iowa Genealogical Society Surname Index.* 5 volumes. Des Moines, IA: The Society, 1972-1990.

Long, John Hamilton and Gordon DenBoer, eds. *Atlas of Historical County Boundaries: Iowa.* New York: Charles Scribners Sons, 1998.

Meyer, Steve. *Discovering Your Iowa Civil War Ancestry.* Garrison, IA: Meyer Publishing, 1993.

Morford, Charles. *Biographical Index to the County Histories of Iowa, Vol. 1.* Baltimore, MD: Gateway Press, 1979.

Sopp, Elsie L. *Personal Name Index to the 1856 City Directories of Iowa.* Detroit, MI: Gale Research Co., 1980.

Journals:

Annals of Iowa
Hawkeye Heritage

Kansas:

Church of Jesus Christ of Latter-Day Saints. Family History Library. *Research Outline: Kansas.* Salt Lake City, UT: Family History Library, 1988.

Cox, E. Evelyn. *Ancestree Climbing in the Midwest: Illinois, Indiana, Iowa, Kansas, Missouri, and Nebraska.* Rev. ed. Owensboro, KY: Cook & McDowell Publications, 1980.

Long, John Hamilton. *Kansas Atlas of Historical County Boundaries.* New York: Charles Scribners Sons, 2000.

McCoy, Sondra Van Meter. *1001 Kansas Place Names.* Lawrence, KS: University Press of Kansas, 1989.

Official State Atlas of Kansas. 1887. N.p.: Kansas Council of Genealogical Societies, 1982.

Owen Jennie, Kirche Mechem, and Louise Barry, eds. *The Annals of Kansas, 1886-1925.* 2 volumes. Topeka: Kansas State Historical Society, 1954-1956.

Robertson, Clara Hamlett. *Kansas Territorial Settlers of 1860 Who Were Born in Tennessee, Virginia, North Carolina and South Carolina.* 1976. Baltimore, MD: Genealogical Publishing Co., 1999.

Smith, Patricia Douglass. *Kansas Biographical Index: State-Wide and Regional Histories: Citing More Than 35,500 Biographies from Sixty-eight Volumes of Kansas Biographical Sources.* Garden City, KS: P. D. Smith, 1994.

Socolofsky, Homer Edward and Huber Self. *Historical Atlas of Kansas.* Norman, OK: University of Oklahoma Press, 1988.

Journals:

Kansas History
Kansas Kin

Kentucky:

Armstrong, Zella. *Notable Southern Families.* 6 volumes. 1918-1933. Baltimore, MD: Genealogical Publishing Company, 1993-2000.

Chinn, George M. *Kentucky, Settlement and Statehood, 1750-1800.* Frankfort: Kentucky Historical Society, 1975.

Clark, Murtie June. *Colonial Soldiers of the South, 1732-1774.* 1983. Baltimore, MD: Genealogical Publishing Company, 1999.

Cook, Michael L. *Kentucky Index of Biographical Sketches in State, Regional and County Histories.* Evansville, IN: Cook Publications, 1986.

Filson, John. *The Discovery, Settlement, and Present State of Kentucky.* 1784. Whitefish, MT: Kessinger Pub., 2006.

Hehir, Donald M. *Kentucky Families: A Bibliographic Listing.* Bowie, MD: Heritage Books, 1993.

Hogan, Roseann Reinemuth. *Kentucky Ancestry: A Guide to Genealogical and Historical Research.* Salt Lake City, UT: Ancestry, 1992.

Jillson, Willard Rouse. *The Kentucky Land Grants: A Systematic Index to All of the Land Grants Recorded in the State Land Office at Frankfort, Kentucky, 1782-1924.* 1925. Baltimore, MD: Genealogical Publishing Co., 1994.

---. *Old Kentucky Entries and Deeds: A Complete Index to All of the Earliest Land Entries, Military Warrants, Deeds, and Wills of the Commonwealth of Kentucky.* 1926. Baltimore, MD: Genealogical Publishing Co., 1999.

King, J. Estelle Stewart. *Abstract of Early Kentucky Wills and Inventories: Copied From Original and Recorded Wills and Inventories.* 1933 Baltimore, MD: Clearfield Co., 2008.

Klotter, James C. *Genealogies of Kentucky Families From the Register of the Kentucky Historical Society.* 2 volumes. Baltimore, MD: Genealogical Publishing Co., 1981, 2000.

Long, John Hamilton and Gordon DenBoer, eds. *Atlas of Historical County Boundaries: Kentucky.* New York: Simon and Schuster, 1995.

Rennick, Robert M. *Kentucky Place Names.* Lexington, KY: University Press of Kentucky, 1984.

Schweitzer, George Keene. *Kentucky Genealogical Research.* Knoxville, TN: George K. Schweitzer, 1995.

Southern States Genealogical Resources: Alabama, Georgia, Kentucky, North Carolina, South Carolina, Tennessee, Virginia, West Virginia Research Sources and Bibliographies. Seattle, WA: Fiske Genealogical Foundation, 1991.

Sutherland, James F. *Early Kentucky Landholders, 1787-1811.* 1986. Baltimore, MD: Clearfield Co., 1997.

Teague, Barbara and Jane A. Minder. *Guide to Kentucky Archival and Manuscript Collections*. Frankfort, KY: Kentucky Department for Libraries and Archives, Public Records Div., 1988-.

Trapp, Glenda K. and Michael L. Cook. *Kentucky Genealogical Index: An Every Name Index to Kentucky Ancestors, Kentucky Genealogist, ...* Evanston, IL: Cook Publications, 1985.

Walker, Emma Jane and Virginia Wilson, eds. *Kentucky Bible Records*. 6 volumes. Lexington, KY: National Society Daughters of the American Revolution - Kentucky, 1962-1981.

> *Journals:*
>
> Bluegrass Roots
> The Bulletin
> Filson Club History Quarterly
> Kentucky Ancestors
> Kentucky Pioneer Genealogy and Records
> Register of the Kentucky Historical Society
> The Southern Genealogists Exchange Quarterly

Louisiana:

Armstrong, Zella. *Notable Southern Families*. 6 volumes. 1918-1933. Baltimore, MD: Genealogical Publishing Company, 1993-2000.

Arrigo, Jan and Laura A. McElroy. *Cemeteries of New Orleans: A Journey Through the Cities of the Dead*. Stillwater, MN: Voyager Press, Inc., 2005.

Boling, Yvette G. *A Guide to Printed Sources for Genealogical and Historical Research in the Louisiana Parishes*. Jefferson, LA: Y.G. Boling, 1985.

—. *A Guide to Printed Sources for Genealogical and Historical Research in the Louisiana Parishes: 1991 Supplement*. Jefferson, LA: Y. G. Boling, 1992.

Catholic Church. *Diocese of Baton Rouge, Catholic Church Records*. Baton Rouge, LA: Department of Archives, the Diocese, 1978-1994.

Clark, Murtie June. *Colonial Soldiers of the South, 1732-1774*. 1983. Baltimore, MD: Genealogical Publishing Company, 1999.

Deiler, J. Hanno and Jack Belsom. *The Settlement of the German Coast of Louisiana and Creoles of German Descent.* 1909, 1969. Baltimore, MD: Genealogical Publishing Co., 1998.

DeVille, Winston. *Gulf Coast Colonials: A Compendium of French Families in Early Eighteenth Century Louisiana.* 1968. Baltimore, MD: Genealogical Publishing Co., 1999.

---. *The New Orleans French, 1720-1733: A Collection of Marriage Records Relating to the First Colonists of the Louisiana Province.* 1973. Baltimore, MD: Genealogical Publishing Co., 1994.

Hebert, Donald J. *A Guide to Church Records in Louisiana, 1720-1975.* Eunice, LA: Donald J. Hebert, 1975.

Korn, Bertram Wallace. *The Early Jews of New Orleans.* Waltham, MA: American Jewish Historical Society, 1969.

Notre Dame University. *Guide to the Microfilm Edition of the Records of the Diocese of Louisiana and the Floridas, 1576-1803.* Notre Dame, IN: the Compilers, 1967.

Pierson, Marion J. B. *Louisiana Soldiers in the War of 1812.* 1963. Baltimore, MD: Genealogical Publishing Co., 1999.

Poret, Ory G. *History of Land Titles in the State of Louisiana.* 1973. Baton Rouge: Louisiana Department of Natural Resources, 1978.

Ryan, Clifton Earl. *Louisiana Plus Genealogy Resources.* Metairie, LA: C. E. Ryan, 1987.

Smith, Virginia Rogers. *Searching for Your Louisiana Ancestors...and All That Jazz!* Baton Rouge, LA: Virginia Rogers Smith, 1995.

West, Robert C. *An Atlas of Louisiana Surnames of French and Spanish Origin.* Baton Rouge, LA: Geoscience Publications, Louisiana State University, 1986.

Woods, Earl C., Charles C. Nolan and Dorenda Dupont. *Sacramental Records of the Roman Catholic Church of the Archdiocese of New Orleans.* New Orleans, LA: The Archdiocese, 1987-.

Journals:

The Genie
L'Heritage
Les Voyagers
Louisiana Armchair Researcher
Louisiana Genealogical Register
Louisiana History
Natchitoches Genealogist
New Orleans Genesis
The Southern Genealogists Exchange Quarterly
Terrebonne Life Lines

Maine:

Anderson, Robert C., et. al. *The Great Migration Begins: Immigrants to New England, 1620-1633.* 3 volumes. Boston: New England Historic Genealogical Society, 1995.

—, George F. Sanborn, Jr. and Melinde L. Sanborn. *The Great Migration, 1634-1635, Volume 1: A-B.* Boston: New England Historic Genealogical Society, 1999.

Banks, Charles Edward and Elijah Ellsworth Brownell. *Topographical Dictionary of 2,885 English Emigrants to New England, 1620-1650.* 1937. Baltimore, MD: Genealogical Publishing Company, 1981.

Crandall, Ralph J., ed. *Genealogical Research in New England.* Baltimore, MD: Genealogical Publishing Company, 1984.

Denis, Michael J. *Genealogical Researching in New England: An Address Guide to Connecticut, Maine, Massachusetts, New Hampshire, Rhode Island, and Vermont.* Oakland, ME: Michael Dennis, 1982.

---. *Maine Towns and Counties: What Was What, Where and When.* 3rd ed. Oakland, ME: Danbury House Books, 1988.

Fisher, Carleton Edward and Sue G. Fisher. *Soldiers, Sailors and Patriots of the Revolutionary War, Maine.* Louisville, KY: National Society of the Sons of the American Revolution, 1982.

Frost, John E. *Maine Genealogy: A Bibliographical Guide.* 2nd ed. rev. Portland: Maine Historical Society, 1985.

---. *Maine Probate Abstracts: Volume 1, 1687-1775; Volume 2, 1775-1800.* Camden, ME: Picton Press, 1991.

Gray, Ruth, Alice MacDonald Long, Joseph C. Anderson, II, and Lois Ware Thurston. *Maine Families in 1790.* 6 volumes. Camden, ME: Picton Press, 1988-.

Lainhart, Ann S. *Digging for Genealogical Treasure in New England Town Records.* Boston: New England Historic Genealogical Society, 1996.

Long, John Hamilton and Gordon DenBoer, eds. *Atlas of Historical County Boundaries: Connecticut, Maine, Massachusetts, Rhode Island.* New York: Simon and Schuster, 1994.

Melnyk, Marcia. *Genealogist's Handbook for New England Research.* 4th ed. Boston: New England Historic Genealogical Society, 1999.

Morris, Gerald E., ed. *The Maine Bicentennial Atlas.* Portland, ME: Historical Society, 1976.

Pope, Charles Henry. *The Pioneers of Maine and New Hampshire, 1623-1660, a Descriptive List.* 1908. Bowie, MD: Heritage Books, 2002.

Rutherford, Phillip R. *The Dictionary of Maine Place-Names.* Freeport, ME: Bond Wheelwright Company, 1970.

Savage, James, O. P. Dexter and John Farmer. *A Genealogical Dictionary of the First Settlers of New England, Showing Three Generations of Those Who Came Before May 1692...* 4 volumes. 1860-62. Baltimore, MD: Genealogical Publishing Company, 1994.

United States Office of Geographic Research. *Maine Geographic Names: Alphabetical Finding List.* Reston, VA: U.S. Geographical Survey, 1985.

Journals:

Downeast Ancestry
The Great Migration Newsletter
New England Ancestors
New England Historical and Genealogical Register

Maryland:

Heisey, John W. *Maryland Genealogical Library Guide.* Morgantown, PA: Masthof Press, 1998.

Jacobsen, Phoebe R. *Researching Black Families at the Maryland Hall of Records.* Annapolis: Maryland Hall of Records, Department of General Services, 1984.

Long, John Hamilton, ed. *Delaware, Maryland, District of Columbia Atlas of Historical County Boundaries.* New York: Charles Scribner's Sons, 1996.

Maryland, Delaware Atlas & Gazetteer. Freeport, MA: DeLorme Mapping, 1993.

Meyer, Mary Keysor. *Genealogical Research in Maryland: A Guide.* 4th ed. Baltimore, MD: Museum & Library of Maryland, Maryland Historical Society, 1992.

Schweitzer, George Keene. *Maryland Genealogical Research.* Knoxville, TN: G. K. Schweitzer, 1998.

Virdin, Donald Odell. *Maryland and Delaware Genealogies and Family Histories: A Bibliography of Books about Maryland and Delaware Families.* Bowie, MD: Heritage Books, 1993.

Journals:

Maryland and Delaware Genealogist
Maryland Genealogical Society Bulletin

Massachusetts:

Anderson, Robert C., et. al. *The Great Migration Begins: Immigrants to New England, 1620-1633.* 3 volumes. Boston: New England Historic Genealogical Society, 1995.

—, George F. Sanborn, Jr. and Melinde L. Sanborn. *The Great Migration, 1634-1635, Volume 1: A-B.* Boston: New England Historic Genealogical Society, 1999.

Banks, Charles E. *Topographical Dictionary of 2,885 English Emigrants to New England, 1620-1650.* 1937. Baltimore, MD: Genealogical Publishing Company, 1981.

Church of Jesus Christ of Latter-Day Saints. Family History Library. *Research Outline: Massachusetts*. Salt Lake City, UT: Family History Library, 1988.

Crandall, Ralph J., ed. *Genealogical Research in New England*. Baltimore, MD: Genealogical Publishing Company, 1984.

Davis, Charlotte Pease. *Directory of Massachusetts Place Names*. Lexington, MA: Bay State News, 1987.

Denis, Michael J. *Genealogical Researching in New England: An Address Guide to Connecticut, Maine, Massachusetts, New Hampshire, Rhode Island, and Vermont*. Oakland, ME: Michael Dennis, 1982.

—. *Massachusetts Towns and Counties*. Oakland, ME: Danbury House Books, 1984.

Galvin, William Francis. *Historical Data Relating to Counties, Cities, and Towns in Massachusetts*. 5th ed. Boston: New England Historic Genealogical Society, 1997.

Gardner-Westcott, Katherine A. *Massachusetts Sources*. Ashland, MA: Massachusetts Society of Genealogists, 1988.

Lainhart, Ann S. *Digging for Genealogical Treasure in New England Town Records*. Boston: New England Historic Genealogical Society, 1996.

Lindberg, Marcia Wiswall. *Genealogist's Handbook for New England Research*. 3rd ed. Boston, MA: New England Historic Genealogical Society, 1993.

Long, John Hamilton and Gordon DenBoer, eds. *Atlas of Historical County Boundaries: Connecticut, Maine, Massachusetts, Rhode Island*. New York: Simon and Schuster, 1994.

Melnyk, Marcia. *Genealogist's Handbook for New England Research*. 4th ed. Boston: New England Historic Genealogical Society, 1999.

Roberts, Gary B., ed. *English Origins of New England Families, From the New England Historical and Genealogical Register, First Series*. 3 volumes. Baltimore, MD: Genealogical Publishing Company, 1984. Second Series. 3 volumes, 1985.

Savage, James. *A Genealogical Dictionary of the First Settlers of New England, Showing Three Generations of Those Who Came Before May 1692.* 4 volumes. 1860-62. Baltimore, MD: Genealogical Publishing Company, 1986.

Schweitzer, George Keene. *Massachusetts Genealogical Research.* Knoxville, TN: G. K. Schweitzer, 1999.

Journals:

The Great Migration Newsletter
New England Ancestors
New England Historical and Genealogical Register

Michigan:

Church of Jesus Christ of Latter-Day Saints. Family History Library. *Research Outline: Michigan.* Salt Lake City, UT: Family History Library, 1988.

Detroit Public Library. *Sources for Black Genealogy in the Burton Historical Collection.* Detroit, MI: The Bruton Historical Collection, 1989.

Long, John Hamilton And Peggy Tuck Sinko, eds. *Atlas of Historical County Boundaries: Michigan.* New York: Charles Scribner's Sons, 1997.

McGinnis, Carol. *Michigan Genealogy: Sources & Resources.* 2nd ed. Baltimore, MD: Genealogical Publishing Co., 2005.

Romig, Walter. *Michigan Place Names: The History of the Founding and the Naming of More than Five Thousand Past and Present Michigan Communities.* 1973. Detroit, MI: Wayne State University Press, 1986.

Russell, Donna Valley. *Michigan Censuses 1710-1830 Under the French, British, and Americans.* Detroit, MI: Detroit Society for Genealogical Research, 1982.

Journals:

Michigan Genealogical Council Newsletter
MMGS Newsletter
The Pastfinder
WMGS Newsletter

Minnesota:

Bakeman, Mary Hawker. *A Guide to the Minnesota State Census Microfilm.* Roseville, MN: Park Genealogical Book Co., 1992.

— and Mai Treude. *Minnesota Land Owner Maps and Directories.* Brooklyn Park, MN: Park Genealogical Books, 1994.

Lind, Marilyn. *Continuing Your Genealogical Research in Minnesota.* Cloquet, MN: Linden Tree, 1988.

Long, John Hamilton and Gordon DenBoer, eds. *Atlas of Historical County Boundaries: Minnesota.* New York: Charles Scribner's Sons, 2000.

Minnesota Historical Society. *Genealogical Resources of the Minnesota Historical Society: A Guide.* 2nd ed. St. Paul, MN: Minnesota Historical Society Press, 1993.

Peterson, Ann H. *An Introduction to Minnesota Research Sources.* St. Paul, MN: Minnesota Genealogical Society, 1988.

Pope, Wiley R., Sara Fee, and Juanita J. Pope. *Minnesota Cemetery Locations.* 2nd ed. Saint Paul, MN: Minnesota Family Trees, 1998.

Warren, James W. *Minnesota 1900 Census Mortality Schedule.* St. Paul, MN: Warren Research & Marketing Publication, 1992.

Warren, Paula S. *Minnesota Genealogical Reference Guide.* 6th ed. rev. St. Paul, MN: Warren Research and Publishing, 2003.

Journals:

MGS Newsletter
Minnesota Genealogist
Newsletter - Minnesota Genealogical Society
The Scandinavian Saga

Mississippi:

Armstrong, Zella. *Notable Southern Families.* 6 volumes. 1918-1933. Baltimore, MD: Genealogical Publishing Company, 1993-2000.

Brieger, James. *Hometown Mississippi.* 3rd ed. Jackson, MS: Town Square Books, 2000.

Church of Jesus Christ of Latter-Day Saints. Family History Library. *Research Outline: Mississippi.* Salt Lake City, UT: Family History Library, 1988.

Clark, Murtie June. *Colonial Soldiers of the South, 1732-1774.* 1983. Baltimore, MD: Genealogical Publishing Company, 1999.

Long, John Hamilton and Peggy Tuck Sinko, eds. *Atlas of Historical County Boundaries: Mississippi.* New York: Charles, Scribner's Sons, 1993.

Northeast Mississippi Historical & Genealogical Society. *Mississippi Lineage Charts.* Columbia, MS: Northeast Mississippi Historical & Genealogical Society, 1984.

Webster, Anne L. and Kathleen S. Hutchinson. *Tracing Your Mississippi Ancestors.* Jackson: University Press of Mississippi, 1994.

Journals:

Family Trails
Mississippi Coast Historical & Genealogical Society (Magazine)
Mississippi Genealogical Exchange
The Northeast Mississippi Historical & Genealogical Society Quarterly
The Southern Genealogists Exchange Quarterly

Missouri:

Eddlemon, Sherida K. *The "Show Me" Guide to Missouri: Sources for Genealogical and Historical Research.* Bowie, MD: Heritage Books, Inc., 1999.

Cox, E. Evelyn. *Ancestree Climbing in the Midwest: Illinois, Indiana, Iowa, Kansas, Missouri, and Nebraska.* Rev. ed. Owensboro, KY: Cook & McDowell Publications, 1980.

Hehir, Donald M. *Missouri Family Histories and Genealogies: A Bibliography.* Bowie, MD: Heritage Books, 1996.

Kot, Elizabeth Gorrell and Shirley Pugh Thomson. *Missouri Cemetery Inscription Sources: Print & Microform.* Vallejo, CA: Indices Pub., 1995.

Schweitzer, George Keene. *Missouri Genealogical Research.* Knoxville, TN: G. Schweitzer, 1997.

Steele, Edward E. *Guide to Genealogical Research in St. Louis.* 4th ed. St. Louis, MO: St. Louis Genealogical Society, 1999.

> *Journals:*
>
> Genealogia
> Missouri State Genealogical Association Journal
> Northwest Missouri Genealogy Society Journal
> The Ozark Quarterly: Missouri Genealogy
> Pioneer Times
> Show Me State Genealogical News

Montana:

Church of Jesus Christ of Latter-Day Saints. Family History Library. *Research Outline: Montana.* Salt Lake City, UT: Family History Library, 1988.

Parpart, Paulette K. and Donald E. Spritzer, comps. *Montana Data Index: A Reference Guide to Historical and Genealogical Resources.* 2nd ed. Missoula, MT: Montana Library Association, 1992.

Richards, Dennis L. *Montana's Genealogical and Local History Records: A Selected List of Books, Manuscripts, and Periodicals.* Detroit, MI: Gale Research Co., 1981.

Stoner, Al. *First Families of Montana and Early Settlers.* Lewistown, MT: Montana State Genealogical Society, 2000.

> *Journals:*
>
> Big Sky Roundup
> Central Mountains Wagon Trails
> Smoke Signals from the Assiniboine Genealogical Society
> WMGS Newsletter

Nebraska:

Buller, Galen, et. al., eds. *Broken Hoops and Plains People: A Catalogue of Ethnic Resources in the Humanities: Nebraska and Surrounding Areas.* Lincoln, NE: Nebraska Curriculum Development Center, 1976.

Church of Jesus Christ of Latter-Day Saints. Family History Library. *Research Outline: Nebraska.* Salt Lake City, UT: Family History Library, 1988.

Cox, E. Evelyn. *Ancestree Climbing in the Midwest: Illinois, Indiana, Iowa, Kansas, Missouri, and Nebraska.* Rev. ed. Owensboro, KY: Cook & McDowell Publications, 1980.

Daniels, Sherrill F. *An Index to and Bibliography of Reminiscences in the Nebraska State Historical Society Library.* Lincoln, NE: University of Nebraska Dissertation, 1986.

Illustrated Biographical Album of Northeastern Nebraska. Philadelphia, PA: National Publishing Co., 1893.

Morris Sones, Georgene. *Nebraska: A Guide to Genealogical Research.* Lincoln, NE: Nebraska State Genealogical Society, 1984.

Nebraska State Historical Society. *Historical Resources for Genealogists in the Nebraska State Historical Society.* Lincoln, NE: Nebraska State Historical Society, 1986.

Nimmo, Sylvia and Mary Cutler. *Nebraska Local History and Genealogy Reference Guide: A Bibliography of County Research Materials in Selected Repositories, Library of Congress...* Papillion, NE: S. Nimmo, 1987.

Perkey, Elton. *Perkey's Nebraska Place Names.* Rev. ed. Lincoln, NE: Nebraska State Historical Society, 1995.

Sittler, Melvin. *Sittler Index of Surnames for Which Information has Been Abstracted from the (Lincoln) Nebraska State Journal, May 1873-December 1900.* 5 volumes. Lincoln, NE: Lincoln-Lancaster County Genealogical Society, 1983-1993.

Journals:

Ancestors Unlimited
Bridging the Years: Quarterly Newsletter
Homesteader
Leaves from Our Family Tree
Nebraska Ancestree
The Nebraska and Midwest Genealogical Record
Nebraska History
Roots and Leaves
The Wagoner Newsletter

Nevada:

Carlson, Helen S. *Nevada Place Names: A Geographical Dictionary.* Reno, NV: University of Nevada Press, 1974, 1985.

Ferrel, Jean and Roger Ferrel. *Nevada State Cemeteries.* Nevada: J. & R. Ferrel, 1997.

Greene, Diane E. *Nevada Guide to Genealogical Records.* Baltimore, MD: Clearfield, 1998.

Leigh, Rufus W. *Nevada Place Names: Their Origin and Significance.* Salt Lake City, UT: Desert News Press, 1964.

Parker, J. Carlyle and Janet G. Parker. *Nevada Biographical and Genealogical Sketch Index.* Turlock, CA: Marietta Publishing Co., 1986.

Quebedeaux, Richard. *Prime Sources of California and Nevada Local History: 151 Rare and Important City, County and State Directories, 1850-1906.* Spokane, WA: Arthur H. Clark Co., 1992.

Spiros, Joyce V. Hawley. *Genealogical Guide to Arizona and Nevada.* Gallup, NM: Verlene Pub., 1983.

Taylor, Richard B. *The Nevada Tombstone Record Book.* Las Vegas, NV: Nevada Families Project, 1986.

Journals:

Chart and Quill
Nevada Desert
Nevada Historical Society Quarterly
Nevada State Genealogical Society Newsletter
The Prospector

New Hampshire:

Anderson, Robert C., et. al. *The Great Migration Begins: Immigrants to New England, 1620-1633.* 3 volumes. Boston: New England Historic Genealogical Society, 1995-.

—, George F. Sanborn, Jr. and Melinde L. Sanborn. *The Great Migration, 1634-1635, Volume 1: A-B.* Boston: New England Historic Genealogical Society, 1999.

Banks, Charles E. *Topographical Dictionary of 2,885 English Emigrants to New England, 1620-1650.* 1937. Baltimore, MD: Genealogical Publishing Company, 1981.

Copeley, William. *Index to Genealogies in New Hampshire Town Histories.* Concord, NH: New Hampshire Historical Society, 1989.

Crandall, Ralph J., ed. *Genealogical Research in New England.* Baltimore, MD: Genealogical Publishing Company, 1984.

Denis, Michael J. *Genealogical Researching in New England: An Address Guide to Connecticut, Maine, Massachusetts, New Hampshire, Rhode Island, and Vermont.* Oakland, ME: Michael Dennis, 1982.

Farmer, John and Jacob Bailey Moore. *A Gazetteer of the State of New Hampshire.* Bowie, MD: Heritage Books, 1997.

Green, Scott E. *Directory of Repositories of Family History in New Hampshire.* Baltimore, MD: Clearfield Company, 1993.

Lainhart, Ann S. *Digging for Genealogical Treasure in New England Town Records.* Boston: New England Historic Genealogical Society, 1996.

Long, John Hamilton and Gordon DenBoer, eds. *Atlas of Historical County Boundaries: New Hampshire, Vermont.* New York, NY: Simon and Schuster, 1993.

Melnyk, Marcia Yannizze. *Genealogist's Handbook for New England Research.* 4th ed. Boston: New England Historic Genealogical Society, 1999.

Merrill, Eliphalet and Phinehas Merrill. *Gazetteer of the State of New Hampshire.* 1817. Bowie, MD: Heritage Books, 1987.

Noyes, Sybil, Charles T. Libby and Walter G. Davis. *The Genealogical Dictionary of Maine and New Hampshire.* 1928-29. Baltimore, MD: Genealogical Publishing Company, 1996.

Pope, Charles H. *The Pioneers of Maine and New Hampshire, 1623-1660, a Descriptive List.* 1908. Bowie, MD: Heritage Books, 1994.

Rollock, Rich. *New Hampshire Family Histories.* 4th ed. Meredith, NH: Past Tense Pub., 1996.

Savage, James, O. P. Dexter, and John Farmer. *A Genealogical Dictionary of the First Settlers of New England, Showing Three Generations of Those Who Came Before May 1692.* 4 volumes. 1860-62. Baltimore, MD: Genealogical Publishing Company, 1986.

Towle, Laird C. and Ann N. Brown. *New Hampshire Genealogical Research Guide.* Rev. ed. Bowie, MD: Heritage Books, 1983.

Wilson, Emily S. *Inhabitants of New Hampshire, 1776.* 1983. Baltimore, MD: Genealogical Publishing Company, 1993.

> *Journals:*
>
> Genealogical Sources in New Hampshire
> The Genealogist: Official Journal of the American-Canadian Genealogical Society of New Hampshire
> The Great Migration Newsletter
> Historical New Hampshire.
> New England Ancestors
> New England Historical and Genealogical Register
> The New Hampshire Genealogical Record
> New Hampshire Yesterday
> Newsletter (New Hampshire Society of Genealogists)

New Jersey:

Chambers, Theodore F. *The Early Germans of New Jersey: Their History, Churches, and Genealogies.* 1895. Baltimore, MD: Genealogical Publishing Company, 1982.

Epstein, Bette Marie, Daniel P. Jones and Karl J. Niederer, comps. *Guide to Family History Sources in the New Jersey State Archives.* 2nd ed. Trenton, NJ: Division of Archives and Records Management, 1990.

Gannett, Henry. *A Geographic Dictionary of New Jersey.* Baltimore, MD: Genealogical Pub. Co., 1978.

Guide to Family History in the New Jersey State Archives. 3rd ed. Trenton, NJ: Division of Archives and Records Management, New Jersey Department of State, 1994.

Jackson, Ronald Vern. *New Jersey Tax Lists, 1772-1822.* 6 volumes. Salt Lake City, UT: Accelerated Indexing Systems, 1981.

Klett, Joseph R., ed. *Genealogies of New Jersey Families: from the Genealogical Magazine of New Jersey.* 2 volumes. Baltimore, MD: Genealogical Publishing Company, 1996.

Lee, Francis Bazley, ed. *Genealogical and Memorial History of the State of New Jersey: A Record of the Achievements of Her People in the Making of a Commonwealth and the Founding of a Nation.* 4 volumes. 1910. Baltimore, MD; Genealogical Publishing Company, 2000.

Murrin, Mary R., comp. *New Jersey Historical Manuscripts: A Guide to Collections in the State.* Trenton, NJ: New Jersey Historical Commission, 1987.

Nelson, William. *New Jersey Marriage Records, 1665-1800.* 1900. Baltimore, MD: Genealogical Publishing Company, 1997.

New Jersey. Department of State. *Index of Wills, Inventories, Etc. in the Office of the Secretary of State Prior to 1901.* 3 volumes. 1912-1913. Englewood, NJ: Bergen Historic Books, 1996.

Ricord, Frederick W. *General Index to the Documents Relating to the Colonial History of the State of New Jersey.* 10 Vol. Baltimore, MD: Genealogical Research Society of New Orleans, 1994.

Rudner, Anna L. *A Guide to Genealogical Resources in New Jersey.* Rev. ed. Lincroft, NJ: A. L. Rudner, 1985.

Shourds, Thomas. *History and Genealogy of Fenwick's Colony (NJ).* 1876. Baltimore, MD: Clearfield Publishing Company, 1991.

Sinclair, Donald A. and Helen Maher. *New Jersey Biographical Index, Covering Some 100,000 Biographies...Published to About 1980.* Baltimore, MD: Genealogical Publishing Company, 1993.

Smeal, Lee and Ronald Vern Jackson. *Index to New Jersey Wills, 1689-1890: The Testators.* Salt Lake City, UT: Accelerated Indexing Systems, 1979.

Stillwell, John E. *Historical and Genealogical Miscellany: Data Relating to the Settlement and Settlers of New York and New Jersey.* 5 volumes. 1903-32. Baltimore, MD: Genealogical Publishing Company, 1998.

Stryker, William S. *Index, Record of Officers and Men of New Jersey in the Civil War, 1861-1865.* 2 volumes. 1876. Englewood, NJ: Bergen Historic Books, 1996.

— and James Wall Shureman Campbell. *Official Register of the Officers and Men of New Jersey in the Revolutionary War.* 1872, 1911. Baltimore, MD: Genealogical Publishing Company, 1997.

Stryker-Rodda, Kenn. *Revolutionary Census of New Jersey.* 1972. Lambertville, NJ: Hunterdon House, 1986.

Journals:

Genealogical Magazine of New Jersey
The Jersey Heritage: A Celebration of African American History & Genealogy
New Jersey Genesis
New Jersey History
Newsletter - Genealogical Society of New Jersey
Proceedings of the New Jersey Historical Society
The South Jersey Genealogist
South Jersey Magazine

New Mexico:

Beck, Warren A. and Ynez D. Haase. *Historical Atlas of New Mexico.* Norman, OK: University of Oklahoma Press, 1969.

Chavez, Angelico. *Origins of New Mexico Families: A Genealogy of the Spanish Colonial Period.* Rev. ed. Santa Fe, NM: Museum of New Mexico Press, 1992.

—. *Archives of the Archdiocese of Santa Fe, 1678-1900.* 6 microfiches. 1957. Socorro, NM: New Mexico Tech. Library, 1970.

Church of Jesus Christ of Latter-Day Saints. Family History Library. *Research Outline: New Mexico.* Salt Lake City, UT: Family History Library, 1988.

Esterly, Robert E. *Genealogical Resources in New Mexico.* 2nd ed. Albuquerque: New Mexico Genealogical Society, 2002.

Julyan, Robert Hixon. *The Place Names of New Mexico.* 2nd ed. Albuquerque, NM: University of New Mexico Press, 1998.

Myers, Christine. *New Mexico Local and County Histories: A Bibliography.* University Park, NM: New Mexico Library Association, 1983.

Olmsted, Virginia L. *Spanish and Mexican Colonial Censuses of New Mexico, 1790, 1823, 1845.* Albuquerque, NM: New Mexico Genealogical Society, 1975.

—. *Spanish and Mexican Censuses of New Mexico, 1750-1830.* Albuquerque, NM: New Mexico Genealogical Society, 1981.

Pearce, T. M. *New Mexico Place Names.* Albuquerque, NM: University of New Mexico Press, 1965.

Spiros, Joyce V. Hawley. *Handy Genealogical Guide to New Mexico.* Gallup, NM: Verlene, 1981.

> *Journals:*
>
> Herencua: The Quarterly Journal of the Hispanic Genealogical Research Center of New Mexico
> New Mexico Genealogist
> New Mexico Historical Review

New York:

Anderson, Robert C., et. al. *The Great Migration Begins: Immigrants to New England, 1620-1633.* 3 volumes. Boston: New England Historic Genealogical Society, 1995.

—, George F. Sanborn, Jr. and Melinde L. Sanborn. *The Great Migration, 1634-1635, Volume 1: A-B.* Boston: New England Historic Genealogical Society, 1999.

Banks, Charles E. *Topographical Dictionary of 2,885 English Emigrants to New England, 1620-1650.* 1937. Baltimore, MD: Genealogical Publishing Company, 1981, 2002.

Bowman, Fred Q. *8,000 More Vital Records of Eastern New York State, 1804-1850.* Rhinebeck, NY: Kinship, 1991.

—. *10,000 Vital Records of Central New York, 1813-1850.* Baltimore, MD: Genealogical Publishing Company, 1986.

—. *10,000 Vital Records of Eastern New York, 1777-1834.* Baltimore, MD: Genealogical Publishing Company, 1987.

—. *10,000 Vital Records of Western New York, 1809-1850.* Baltimore, MD: 1985.

— and Thomas J. Lynch. *7,000 Hudson-Mohawk Valley (NY) Vital Records, 1808-1850.* Baltimore, MD: Genealogical Publishing Company, 1997.

— and —. *Directory of Collections of New York Vital Records, 1726-1989.* Bowie, MD: Heritage Books, 1995.

Burke, Kate. *Searching in New York: A Reference Guide to Public and Private Records.* Costa Mesa, CA: ISC Publications, 1987.

Clint, Florence. *New York Area Key: A Guide to the Genealogical Records of the State of New York.* Elizabeth, CO: Keyline, 1979.

Crandall, Ralph J., ed. *Genealogical Research in New England.* Baltimore, MD: Genealogical Publishing Company, 1984.

Epperson, Gwenn F. *New Netherland Roots.* Baltimore, MD: Genealogical Publishing Company, 1994, 2008.

Foley, Janet Wethy, ed. *Early Settlers of New York State: Their Ancestors and Descendants.* 1934-1942. Baltimore, MD: Genealogical Publishing Company, 1993.

French, J. H. and Frank Place. *Gazetteer of the State of New York.* 1860. Baltimore, MD: Genealogical Publishing Co., 1995.

General Peter Gansevoort Chapter. Daughters of the American Revolution. *Revised Master Index to the New York State Daughters of the American Revolution Genealogical Records Volumes.* 2 volumes. Zephyrhills, FL: Jean D. Worden, 1998.

Guzik, Estelle M. *Genealogical Resources in the New York Metropolitan Area.* New York: Jewish Genealogical Society, 1989.

Hoff, Henry B. *Genealogies of Long Island Families from the New York Genealogical and Biographical Record.* 2 volumes. Baltimore, MD: Genealogical Publishing Company, 1987.

Inskeep, Carolee. *The Graveyard Shift: A Family Historian's Guide to New York City Cemeteries.* Orem, UT: Ancestry, 1999.

Lainhart, Ann S. *Digging for Genealogical Treasure in New England Town Records.* Boston: New England Historic Genealogical Society, 1996.

Long, John Hamilton and Kathryn F. Thorne, eds. *Atlas of Historical County Boundaries: New York.* New York: Simon and Schuster, 1993.

Melnyk, Marcia Yannizze. *Genealogist's Handbook for New England Research.* 4th ed. Boston: New England Historic Genealogical Society, 1999.

Reynolds, Cuyler. *Genealogical and Family History of Southern New York and the Hudson River Valley.* 3 volumes. 1914. Baltimore, MD: Clearfield Co., 1997.

Roberts, Gary B., ed. *English Origins of New England Families, From the New England Historical and Genealogical Register, First Series.* 3 volumes. Baltimore, MD: Genealogical Publishing Company, 1984. Second Series. 3 volumes, 1985.

Savage, James, O. P. Dexter and John Farmer. *A Genealogical Dictionary of the First Settlers of New England, Showing Three Generations of Those Who Came Before May 1692.* 4 volumes. 1860-62. Baltimore, MD: Genealogical Publishing Company, 1994.

Schweitzer, George Keene. *New York Genealogical Research.* Knoxville, TN: G. K. Schweitzer, 1995.

Spafford, Horatio Gates. *Gazetteer of the State of New York.* 1824. Interlaken, NY: Heart of the Lakes Publishing, 1981.

Stillwell, John. *Historical and Genealogical Miscellany: Data Relating to the Settlement and Settlers of New York and New Jersey.* 5 volumes. 1903-32. Baltimore, MD: Genealogical Publishing Company, 1998.

Yates, Melinde. *Gateway to America: Genealogical Research in the New York State Library.* 2nd rev. ed. Albany, NY: New York State Library, 1982.

Journals:

The Capital
De Halve Maen
The Great Migration Newsletter
The Mohawk
New England Ancestors
New England Historical and Genealogical Register
New York Genealogical and Biographical Record

New York History
Tree Talks
Western New York Genealogical Society Journal
Yesteryears

North Carolina:

Armstrong, Zella and Janie Preston Collup French. *Notable Southern Families.* 6 volumes. 1918-1933. Baltimore, MD: Genealogical Publishing Company, 1993-2000.

Bennett, William D. *North Carolina State Archives: State Agency Finding Aids of Interest to Genealogists.* Raleigh, NC: W. D. Bennett, 1997-.

Clark, David Sanders. *Index to Maps of North Carolina in Books and Periodicals.* Fayetteville, NC: The Author, 1976.

Clark, Murtie June. *Colonial Soldiers of the South, 1732-1774.* 1983. Baltimore, MD: Genealogical Publishing Company, 1999.

Hay, Gertrude M. S. *Roster of Soldiers from North Carolina in the American Revolution: With an Appendix Containing a Collection of Miscellaneous Records.* Baltimore, MD: Genealogical Publishing Company, 1988.

Hehir, Donald M. *Carolina Families: A Bibliography of Books About North and South Carolina Families.* Bowie, MD: Heritage Books, 1994.

Hofmann, Margaret M. *An Intermediate Short, Short Course in the Use of Some North Carolina Records in Genealogical Research.* Roanoke Rapids, NC: Margaret M. Hofmann, 1990.

—. *The Short, Short Course in the Use of North Carolina's Early County-Level Records in Genealogical Research.* Roanoke, NC: Margaret M. Hofmann, 1988.

Leary, Helen F. M., ed. *North Carolina Research: Genealogy and Local History.* 2nd ed. Raleigh, NC: North Carolina Genealogical Society, 1996.

Long, John Hamilton and Gordon DenBoer, eds. *Atlas of Historical County Boundaries: North Carolina.* New York: Simon and Schuster, 1998.

Mitchell, Thornton W. *North Carolina Wills: A Testator's Index, 1665-1900.* Rev. ed. Baltimore, MD: Genealogical Publishing Company, 1996.

North Carolina Atlas and Gazetteer: Topo Maps of the Entire State. 4th ed. Yarmouth, ME: DeLorme Mapping Company, 2000.

North Carolina Division of Archives and History. Archives and Records Division. *Guide to Research Materials in the North Carolina State Archives: County Records.* 11th ed. Raleigh, NC: Department of Cultural Resources, Division of Archives and History, Archives and Records Section, 1997.

Schweitzer, George Keene *North Carolina Genealogical Research.* Knoxville, TN: G. K. Schweitzer, 1996.

Southern States Genealogical Resources: Alabama, Georgia, Kentucky, North Carolina, South Carolina, Tennessee, Virginia, West Virginia Research Sources and Bibliographies. Seattle, WA: Fiske Genealogical Foundation, 1991.

> *Journals:*
>
> Journal of North Carolina Genealogy
> North Carolina Genealogical Society Journal
> North Carolina Historical Review
> The Southern Genealogists Exchange Quarterly

North Dakota:

Berg, Francie M. *Ethnic Heritage in North Dakota.* Washington, DC: Attiyeh Foundation, 1983.

Bye, John E. *Guide to Manuscripts and Archives.* Fargo, ND: North Dakota Institute for Regional Studies, 1985.

Register of North Dakota Veterans: World War II, 1941-1945, and Korean Conflict, 1950-1953. Bismarck, ND: Adjutant General's Office, 1968.

Register of North Dakota Veterans: Vietnam Conflict, 1964-1973. Bismarck, ND: Adjutant General's Office, 1981.

Sherman, William C. and Playford V. Thorson, eds. *Plains Folk: North Dakota's Ethnic History.* Fargo, ND: Institute for Regional Studies, 1988.

Slater, Sandra J. *Guide to Genealogical/Family History Sources.* Grand Forks, ND: Elwyn B. Robinson, Department of Special Collections, Chester Fritz Library, University of North Dakota, 1999.

State Historical Society of North Dakota. *Historical Data Project; Pioneer Biography Files.* Bismarck, ND: State Historical Society of North Dakota, 1936-1940.

Wick, Douglas A. *North Dakota Place Names.* Bismarck, ND: Hedemarken Collectibles, 1988.

Winistorfer, Jo Ann. *Tracing Your Dakota Roots: A Guide to Genealogical Research in the Dakotas.* 2nd ed. Bismarck, ND: Dakota Roots, 2006.

Journal:

The Dakota Homestead Historical Newsletter
Der Stammbaum=Genealogical Research
North Central North Dakota Genealogical Record
North Dakota History

Ohio:

Bell, Carol Willsey. *Master Index, Ohio Society Daughters of the American Revolution Genealogical and Historical Records.* Westlake, OH: Ohio Society DAR, 1985.

—. *Ohio Genealogical Guide.* 6th ed. Youngstown, OH: Bell Books, 1995.

—. *Ohio Guide to Genealogical Sources.* Baltimore, MD: Genealogical Publishing Company, 1988.

—. *Ohio Wills and Estates to 1850: An Index.* Columbus, OH: Carol Willsey Bell, 1981.

Green, Karen M. *Pioneer Ohio Newspapers, 1802-1818.* Galveston, TX: The Frontier Press, 1988.

Harter, Stuart. *Ohio Genealogy and Local History Sources Index.* Fort Wayne, IN: Stuart Harter, 1986.

Hehir, Donald M. *Ohio Families: A Bibliography of Books About Ohio Families.* Bowie, MD: Heritage Books, 1993.

Klaiber, Teresa Lynn Martin. *Ohio Cemeteries Addendum.* Mansfield, OH: Ohio Genealogical Society, 1990.

Long, John Hamilton and Peggy Tuck Sinko. *Atlas of Historical County Boundaries: Ohio.* New York: Charles Scribners Sons, 1998.

Miller, Larry L. *Ohio Place Names.* Bloomington, IN: Indiana University Press, 1996.

Nathan, Jean. *Ohio Marriages Recorded in County Courts, 1 Jan 1821 - 31 Dec 1830: an Index.* Mansfield, OH: Ohio Genealogical Society, 1997.

Schweitzer, George Keene *Ohio Genealogical Research.* Knoxville, TN: G. K. Schweitzer, 1999.

Smith, Maxine H. *Ohio Cemeteries.* 1978. Mansfield, OH: Ohio Genealogical Society, 1998.

Sperry, Kip. *Genealogical Research in Ohio.* 2nd ed. Baltimore, MD: Genealogical Publishing Co., 2003.

Thomson, Peter Gibson. *Bibliography of the State of Ohio, Being a Catalog of the Books and Pamphlets Relating to the History of the State, the West and Northwest.* Salem, MA: Higginson Book Co., 1993.

> *Journals:*
>
> Ohio Civil War Genealogy Journal
> Ohio DAR News
> Ohio Genealogical Society Newsletter
> Ohio History
> Ohio Records and Pioneer Families
> Ohio: the Crossroad of Our Nation
> The Report

Oklahoma:

Ashton, Sharron Standifer. *Guide to Cherokee Indian Records Microfilm Collection: Archives and Manuscript Division, Oklahoma Historical Society.* Norman, OK: S.S. Ashton, 1996.

Bell, George Morrison. *Genealogy of "Old and New Cherokee Indian Families."* Bartlesville, OK: George Bell, 1972.

Blessing, Patrick J. *Oklahoma: Records and Archives.* Tulsa, OK: University of Tulsa, 1978.

A Compilation of Records of the Choctaw Nation, Indian Territory. Microfilm. Oklahoma City, OK: Oklahoma Genealogical Society, 1976.

Dewitt, Donald L. *Guide to Manuscript Collections Western History Collections University of Oklahoma.* Bowie, MD: Heritage Books, 1994.

Elliott, Wendy L. *Oklahoma Research.* Rev. ed. Bountiful, UT: American Genealogical Lending Library, 1987.

First Families of the Twin Territories: Our Ancestors in Oklahoma Before Statehood. Oklahoma City, OK: Oklahoma Genealogical Society, 1997.

Goins, Charles Robert, Danny Goble and John W. Morris. *Historical Atlas of Oklahoma.* 6th ed. Norman, OK: University of Oklahoma Press, 2006.

Gray, Robert N. *The Cherokee Strip of Oklahoma: A Hundred Yesteryears.* Enid, OK: Sons and Daughters of the Cherokee Strip Pioneers Museum, 1992.

Huffman, Mary and Nancy Laub. *Family Histories: A Bibliography of the Collections in the Oklahoma Historical Society.* Oklahoma City, OK: Library Resources Division, Oklahoma Genealogical Society, 1991.

Koplowitz, Bradford S. *Guide to the Historical Records of Oklahoma.* Rev. ed. Bowie, MD: Heritage Books, 1997.

Mooney, Thomas G. *Exploring Your Cherokee Ancestry: A Basic Genealogical Research Guide.* 1990. Tahlequah, OK: Cherokee National Historical Society, 1996.

O'Brien, Mary Metzger. *Oklahoma Genealogical Research.* Sand Springs, OK: M. O'Brien Bookshop, 1987.

Pearcy, Deone K. and N. Dale Talkington. *Oklahoma Death Notice and Obituary Index to the Daily Oklahoman.* 2 volumes. Tehapi, CA: T. P. Productions, 1992.

Pierce, Barbara and Brian Basore. *Oklahoma Cemeteries: A Bibliography of the Collections in the Oklahoma Historical Society.* Oklahoma City, OK: Library Resources Division, Oklahoma Historical Society, 1993.

Shirk, George H. *Oklahoma Place Names.* 2nd ed. Norman, OK: University of Oklahoma Press, 1987.

Starr, Emmet and James Julian Hill. *Old Cherokee Families: Old Families and Their Genealogy.* Norman, OK: University of Oklahoma Press, 1968.

Wright, Muriel H. *A Guide to the Indian Tribes of Oklahoma.* 1951. Norman, OK: University of Oklahoma Press, 1986.

> *Journals:*
>
> Chronicles of Oklahoma
> Oklahoma Genealogical Society Quarterly
> Tree Tracers

Oregon:

Brandt, Patricia A. and Nancy Guilford. *Oregon Biography Index.* Corvallis, OR: Oregon State University, 1976.

Cemetery Survey for the State of Oregon. Salem, OR: Oregon Department of Transportation, 1978.

Lenzen, Connie. *A Guide to Oregon Church Records.* Portland, OR: Connie Lenzen, 1991.

—. *How to Find Oregon Naturalization Records.* Rev. ed. Portland, OR: Connie Lenzen, 1990.

—. *Oregon Guide to Genealogical Sources.* 3rd ed. Portland, OR: Genealogical Forum of Oregon, 1996.

—. *Research in Oregon.* Arlington, VA: National Genealogical Society, 1992.

McArthur, Lewis A. *Oregon Geographic Names.* 7th ed. Portland, OR: Historical Society, 2003.

Myers, Jane. *Honor Roll of Oregon Grand Army of the Republic, 1881-1935.* Cottage Grove, OR: Cottage Grove Genealogical Society, 1980.

Oregon Pioneers. 4 volumes. Eugene, OR: Oregon Genealogical Society, 1982-.

Robinson, Jeanne G. *Visitors Guide to Oregon Historic Cemeteries.*
S.l.: Oregon Historic Cemeteries Association, 1999.

Journals:

Beaver Briefs
Bulletin (Genealogical Forum of Oregon)
Oregon Genealogical Society Quarterly
Oregon Historical Quarterly
Rogue Digger

Pennsylvania:

Bell, Raymond M. *Searching in Western Pennsylvania.* 1968. Detroit, MI: Detroit Society for Genealogical Research, 1983.

Church of Jesus Christ of Latter-Day Saints. Family History Library. *Research Outline: Pennsylvania.* Salt Lake City, UT: Family History Library, 1988.

Dructor, Robert M. *Guide to Genealogical Sources at the Pennsylvania State Archives.* 2nd ed. Harrisburg, PA: Pennsylvania Historical and Museum Commission, 1998.

Elliott, Wendy L. *Pennsylvania Genealogical Research Guide.* Rev. ed. Salt Lake City, UT: W. L. Elliott, 1987.

Espenshade, Abraham Howry. *Pennsylvania Place Names.* Reprint. Baltimore, MD: Genealogical Publishing Co., 1970.

Genealogies of Pennsylvania Families: from the Pennsylvania Magazine of History and Biography. Baltimore, MD: Genealogical Publishing Company, 1983.

Gordon, Thomas Francis. *A Gazetteer of the State of Pennsylvania.* 1832. New Orleans, LA: Polyanthos, 1975.

Hazard, Samuel. *General Index to the Colonial Records, in 16 Volumes, and to the Pennsylvania Archives, in 12 Volumes.* 16 volumes. 1838-1853. New York: A.M.S. Press, 1976.

Hodge, Ruth E., ed. *Guide to African American Resources at the Pennsylvania State Archives.* Harrisburg: Pennsylvania Historical and Museum Commission, 2000.

Humphrey, John T. *Pennsylvania Births*. Washington, DC: Humphrey Publications, 1991-.

Iscrupe, William L. and Shirley G. M. Iscrupe, eds. *Pennsylvania Line: A Research Guide to Pennsylvania Genealogy and Local History*. 4th ed. Laughlintown, PA: Southwest Pennsylvania Genealogical Services, 1990.

Long, John Hamilton and Gordon DenBoer, eds. *Atlas of Historical County Boundaries: Pennsylvania*. New York: Simon and Schuster, 1996.

Munger, Donna B. *Pennsylvania Land Records: A History and Guide for Research*. Wilmington, DE: Scholarly Resources Inc., 1991.

Schweitzer, George Keene *Pennsylvania Genealogical Research*. Knoxville, TN: George K. Schweitzer, 1986.

Strassburger, Ralph Beaver and William John Hinke. *Pennsylvania German Pioneers: A Publication of the Original Lists of Arrivals in the Port of Philadelphia From 1727-1808*. 3 volumes. 1934. Camden, ME: Picton, 1992.

Virdin, Donald Odell. *Pennsylvania Family Histories and Genealogies*. Bowie, MD: Heritage Books, 1992.

Woodroofe, Helen Hutchison and Marion F. Egge. *A Genealogist's Guide to Pennsylvania Records*. Philadelphia, PA: Genealogical Society of Pennsylvania, 1994.

Yoder, Don. *Pennsylvania German Church Records of Births, Baptisms, Marriages, Burials, etc. from the Pennsylvania German Society Proceedings and Addresses*. 3 volumes. Baltimore: MD: Genealogical Publishing Company, 1983.

Journals:

Pennsylvania Genealogy Magazine
Pennsylvania Magazine of History and Biography
Pennsylvania Mennonite Heritage
Western Pennsylvania Genealogical Society Quarterly

Rhode Island:

Anderson, Robert C., et. al. *The Great Migration Begins: Immigrants to New England, 1620-1633.* 3 volumes. Boston: New England Historic Genealogical Society, 1995.

—, George F. Sanborn, Jr. and Melinde L. Sanborn. *The Great Migration, 1634-1635, Volume 1: A-B.* Boston: New England Historic Genealogical Society, 1999.

Austin, John Osborne and George A. Moriarity. *The Genealogical Dictionary of Rhode Island: Comprising Three Generations of Settlers Who Came Before 1690, with Many Families Carried to the Fourth Generation.* 1887. Baltimore, MD: Genealogical Publishing Company, 1995.

Banks, Charles Edward and Elijah Ellsworth Brownell. *Topographical Dictionary of 2,885 English Emigrants to New England, 1620-1650.* 1937. Baltimore, MD: Genealogical Publishing Company, 1981.

Bartlett, John Russell and Elijah Ellsworth Brownell. *Census of the Inhabitants of the Colony of Rhode Island and Providence Plantations, 1774.* 1858. Baltimore, MD: Clearfield Company, 1999.

Crandall, Ralph J., ed. *Genealogical Research in New England.* Baltimore, MD: Genealogical Publishing Company, 1984.

Denis, Michael J. *Genealogical Researching in New England: An Address Guide to Connecticut, Maine, Massachusetts, New Hampshire, Rhode Island, and Vermont.* Oakland, ME: Michael Dennis, 1982.

Lainhart, Ann S. *Digging for Genealogical Treasure in New England Town Records.* Boston: New England Historic Genealogical Society, 1996.

Lamar, Christine. *Genealogical Sources in the Rhode Island State Archives.* Providence, RI: Rhode Island State Archives, 1991.

Long, John Hamilton and Gordon DenBoer, eds. *Atlas of Historical County Boundaries: Connecticut, Maine, Massachusetts, Rhode Island.* New York: Simon and Schuster, 1994.

Melnyk, Marcia Yannizze. *Genealogist's Handbook for New England Research.* 4th ed. Boston: New England Historic Genealogical Society, 1999.

Pease, John Chauncey and John M. Niles. *A Gazetteer of the States of Connecticut and Rhode Island.* Hartford, CT: Heritage Books, 1991.

Parker, J. Carlyle. *Rhode Island Biographical and Genealogical Sketch Index.* Turlock, CA: Marietta Pub. Co., 1991.

Roberts, Gary Boyd, ed. *English Origins of New England Families, From the New England Historical and Genealogical Register, First Series.* 3 volumes. Baltimore, MD: Genealogical Publishing Company, 1984. Second Series. 3 volumes, 1985.

—. *Genealogies of Rhode Island Families: from the New England Historical and Genealogical Register.* 2 volumes. Baltimore, MD: Genealogical Publishing Company, 1989.

Savage, James and O. P. Dexter. *A Genealogical Dictionary of the First Settlers of New England, Showing Three Generations of Those Who Came Before May 1692.* 4 volumes. 1860-62. Baltimore, MD: Genealogical Publishing Company, 1986.

Sperry, Kip. *Rhode Island Sources for Family Historians and Genealogists.* Logan, UT: Everton Publishers, 1986.

Taylor, Maureen Alice. *Runaways, Deserters, and Notorious Villains From Rhode Island Newspapers, Volume I: The Providence Gazette, 1762-1800.* Camden, ME: Picton Press, 1995.

—. *Rhode Island Passenger Lists: Port of Providence, 1798-1808, 1820-1871; Port of Bristol and Warren, 1820-1871.* Baltimore, MD: Genealogical Publishing Company, 1995.

Journals:

The Great Migration Newsletter
New England Ancestors
New England Historical and Genealogical Register
Rhode Island History
Rhode Island Roots

South Carolina:

Armstrong, Zella and Janie Preston Collup French. *Notable Southern Families.* 6 volumes. 1918-1933. Baltimore, MD: Genealogical Publishing Company, 1993-2000.

Begley, Paul R., Steven D. Tuttle and Alexia J. Helsley. *African American Genealogical Research.* Columbia, SC: South Carolina Department of Archives and History, 1997.

Clark, Murtie June. *Colonial Soldiers of the South, 1732-1774.* 1983. Baltimore, MD: Genealogical Publishing Company, 1999.

Côté, Richard N. *Local Family History in South Carolina: A Bibliography.* 1981. Greenville, SC: Southern Historical Press, 1991.

Hehir, Donald M. *Carolina Families: A Bibliography of Books About North and South Carolina Families.* Bowie, MD: Heritage Books, 1994.

Hendrix, Ge Lee Corley. *Research in South Carolina.* Arlington, VA: National Genealogical Society, 1992.

Hicks, Theresa M. *South Carolina: A Guide for Genealogists.* Columbia, SC: Columbia Chapter, South Carolina Genealogical Society, 1995.

--- and Frances S. Osburn. *South Carolina, A Guide to County Records.* Columbia, SC: Peppercorn Publications, 1998.

Holcomb, Brent. *A Guide to South Carolina Genealogical Research and Records.* Rev. Columbia, SC: B. H. Holcomb, 2001.

Langdon, Barbara R. *South Carolina Marriages.* 7 volumes. Barnwell, SC: Langdon and Langdon, 1991-1999.

Long, John Hamilton, Gordon Den Boer, and Kathryn Ford Thorne, eds. *Atlas of Historical County Boundaries: South Carolina.* New York: Simon and Schuster, 1997.

Mills, Robert. *Mills' Atlas: Atlas of the State of South Carolina.* 1825. Easley, SC: Southern Historical Press, 1980.

Moss, Bobby G. *Roster of South Carolina Patriots in the American Revolution.* Baltimore, MD: 1983.

Schweitzer, George Keene. *South Carolina Genealogical Research.* Knoxville, TN: G. K. Schweitzer, 1993.

Southern States Genealogical Resources: Alabama, Georgia, Kentucky, North Carolina, South Carolina, Tennessee, Virginia, West Virginia Research Sources and Bibliographies. Seattle, WA: Fiske Genealogical Foundation, 1991.

Journals:

>Carolina Herald
>South Carolina Genealogical Register
>South Carolina Genealogical Society Newsletter
>South Carolina Historical Magazine
>South Carolina Magazine of Ancestral Research
>The Southern Genealogists Exchange Quarterly
>Upper South Carolina Genealogy and History

South Dakota:

Church of Jesus Christ of Latter-Day Saints. Family History Library. *Research Outline: South Dakota.* Salt Lake City, UT: Family History Library, 1988.

Winistorfer, Jo Ann B. and Cathy A. Langemo. *Tracing Your Dakota Roots: A Guide to Genealogical Research in the Dakotas.* Bismarck, ND: Dakota Roots, 1999.

>*Journals:*
>
>Black Hills Nuggets
>Pioneer Pathfinder
>South Dakota Genealogical Society Quarterly
>South Dakota History
>Tree Climber

Tennessee:

Armstrong, Zella and Janie Preston Collup French. *Notable Southern Families.* 6 volumes. 1918-1933. Baltimore, MD: Genealogical Publishing Company, 1993-2000.

Bamman, Gale Williams. *Research in Tennessee.* Arlington, VA: National Genealogical Society, 1993.

Bates, Lucy W. *Roster of Soldiers and Patriots of the American Revolution Buried in Tennessee.* Rev. Johnson City, TN: Tennessee Society, National Society, Daughters of the American Revolution, 1979.

Clark, Murtie June. *Colonial Soldiers of the South, 1732-1774.* 1983. Baltimore, MD: Genealogical Publishing Company, 1999.

Creekmore, Pollyanna. *Tennessee Newspaper Extracts and Abstracts: Marriage, Death and Other Items of Genealogical/Historical Interest, The Knoxville Press, Vol. 1 (1816-1830), Vol. 2 (1830-1839.)* Knoxville, TN: Clinchdale Press, 1995-.

Eddlemon, Sherida K. *Genealogical Abstracts From Tennessee Newspapers.* 3 volumes. Bowie, MD: Heritage Books, 1988-1991.

Fulcher, Richard Carlton. *Guide to County Records and Genealogical Resources in Tennessee.* Baltimore, MD: Genealogical Publishing Company, 1987.

Fullerton, Ralph O. *Place Names of Tennessee.* Nashville, TN: State of Tennessee, 1974.

Long, John Hamilton and Peggy Tuck Sinko, eds. *Atlas of Historical County Boundaries: Tennessee.* New York: Simon and Schuster, 2000.

Lucas, Silas E. and Ella L. Sheffield. *35,000 Tennessee Marriage Records and Bonds, 1783-1870.* 3 volumes. Easley, SC: Southern Historical Press, 1981.

Schweitzer, George Keene. *Tennessee Genealogical Research.* Knoxville, TN: G. K. Schweitzer, 1993.

Southern States Genealogical Resources: Alabama, Georgia, Kentucky, North Carolina, South Carolina, Tennessee, Virginia, West Virginia Research Sources and Bibliographies. Seattle, WA: Fiske Genealogical Foundation, 1991.

Tennesseans in the Civil War. 2 volumes. 1964. Knoxville, TN: University of Tennessee Press, 1996.

Tennessee Settlers and Their Descendants, Genealogical Data About Some of the Men and Women Who Helped Shape the Volunteer State. Memphis, TN: Tennessee Genealogical Society, 1994-2002.

Journals:

Ansearchin' News: The Tennessee Genealogical Magazine
Middle Tennessee Journal of Genealogy and History
Southern Roots and Shoots
Tennessee Ancestors

Texas:

Bockstruck, Lloyd DeWitt. *Research in Texas.* Arlington, VA: National Genealogical Society, 1992.

Brown, John Henry. *Indian Wars and Pioneers of Texas.* 1880. Greenville, SC: Southern Historical Press, 1994.

Carefoot, Jean. *A Guide to Genealogical Resources in the Texas State Archives.* Austin, TX: Texas State Library, Archive Division, 1984.

Day, James M. and Ann B. Dunlap, comps. *Maps of Texas, 1527-1900: Map Collection of the Texas State Archives.* Austin, TX: Texas State Library, 1962.

Dodd, Jordan R. *Texas Marriages, Early to 1850, a Research Tool.* Bountiful, UT: Precision Indexing Publishers, 1990.

Ericson, Carolyn R. *A Guide to Texas Research.* Nacogdoches, TX: Ericson Books, 1994.

Geue, Ethel Hander. *New Homes in a New Land: German Immigration to Texas, 1847-1861.* 1970. Baltimore, MD: Genealogical Publishing Company, 1982.

— and Chester William Geue. *A New Land Beckoned: German Immigration to Texas, 1844-1847.* Baltimore, MD: Genealogical Publishing Company, 2002.

Gracy, Alice Duggan, Jane Sumner, and Emma Gene Seale Gentry. *Early Texas Birth Records, 1838-1878.* Greenville, SC: Southern Historical Press, 1991.

Kennedy, Imogene Kinard and J. Leon Kennedy. *Genealogical Records in Texas.* 1987. Baltimore, MD: Genealogical Publishing Co., 2005.

Stephens, A. Ray, William M. Holmes and Phyllis M. McCaffree. *Historical Atlas of Texas.* Norman, OK: University of Oklahoma Press, 1989.

Tarpley, Fred. *1001 Texas Place Names.* Austin, TX: University of Texas Press, 1980.

Texas State Library and Archives Commission. Archives and Information Services Division. *Genealogical Resources at the Texas State Library.* Austin, TX: Texas State Library and Archives Commission, Archives and Information Services Division, 1996.

Williams, Villamae. *Stephen F. Austin's Register of Families.* 1984. Baltimore, MD: Genealogical Publishing Company, 1996.

   Journals:

   East Texas Family Records
   Footprints
   Genealogical Record
   The Genie
   Heart of Texas Records
   Northeast Texas Genealogy and History
   Our Heritage
   Stirpes, Texas State Genealogical Society Quarterly
   Yellowed Pages

Utah:

Church of Jesus Christ of Latter-Day Saints. Family History Library. *Research Outline: Utah.* Salt Lake City, UT: Family History Library, 1988.

Jaussi, Laureen Richardson and Gloria Duncan Chaston. *Genealogical Records of Utah.* Salt Lake City, UT: Deseret Book, 1974.

Hansen, Judith W. and Norma Lundberg. *Marriages in Utah Territory, 1850-1884.* Salt Lake City, UT: Utah Genealogical Association, 1998.

Van Cott, John W., comp. *Utah Place Names: A Comprehensive Guide to the Origins of Geographic Names.* Salt Lake City, UT: University of Utah Press, 1990.

   Journals:

   Utah Genealogical and Historical Magazine
   Utah Historical Quarterly

Vermont:

Anderson, Robert Charles., et. al. *The Great Migration Begins: Immigrants to New England, 1620-1633.* 3 volumes. Boston: New England Historic Genealogical Society, 1995.

—, George Freeman Sanborn, Jr. and Melinde Lutz Sanborn. *The Great Migration, 1634-1635, Volume 1: A-B.* Boston: New England Historic Genealogical Society, 1999.

Banks, Charles Edward and Elijah Ellsworth Brownell. *Topographical Dictionary of 2,885 English Emigrants to New England, 1620-1650.* 1937. Baltimore, MD: Genealogical Publishing Company, 1981.

Bartley, Scott A. *Vermont Families in 1791.* Volume 1. Camden, ME: Picton Press, 1992.

—. *Vermont Families in 1791.* Volume 2. St. Albans, VT: Genealogical Society of Vermont, 1997.

Crandall, Ralph J., ed. *Genealogical Research in New England.* Baltimore, MD: Genealogical Publishing Company, 1984.

Denis, Michael J. *Genealogical Researching in New England: An Address Guide to Connecticut, Maine, Massachusetts, New Hampshire, Rhode Island, and Vermont.* Oakland, ME: Michael Dennis, 1982.

Eichholz, Alice. *Collecting Vermont Ancestors.* Rev. ed. Montpelier, VT: New Trails, 1993.

Fisher, Carleton Edward and Sue G. Fisher. *Soldiers, Sailors, and Patriots of the Revolutionary War, Vermont.* Camden, ME: Picton Press, 1992.

Hyde, Arthur L. and Frances P. Hyde. *Burial Grounds of Vermont.* 3rd ed. Bradford, VT: Vermont Old Cemetery Association, 1998.

Lainhart, Ann S. *Digging for Genealogical Treasure in New England Town Records.* Boston: New England Historic Genealogical Society, 1996.

Leppman, John A. *A Bibliography for Vermont Genealogy.* 2nd ed. St. Albans, VT: Genealogical Society of Vermont, 2005.

Long, John Hamilton and Gordon DenBoer, eds. *Atlas of Historical County Boundaries: New Hampshire, Vermont.* New York, NY: Simon and Schuster, 1993.

Melnyk, Marcia Yannizze. *Genealogist's Handbook for New England Research.* 4th ed. Boston: New England Historic Genealogical Society, 1999.

Nichols, Joann H., Patricia Liddle Haslam and Robert M. Murphy. *Index to Known Cemetery Listings in Vermont.* 4th ed. Montpelier, VT: Vermont Historical Society, 1999.

Roberts, Gary Boyd, ed. *English Origins of New England Families, From the New England Historical and Genealogical Register, First Series.* 3 volumes. Baltimore, MD: Genealogical Publishing Company, 1984. Second Series. 3 volumes, 1985.

Savage, James and O. P. Dexter. *A Genealogical Dictionary of the First Settlers of New England, Showing Three Generations of Those Who Came Before May 1692.* 4 volumes. 1860-62. Baltimore, MD: Genealogical Publishing Company, 1986.

Swift, Ester Munroe. *Vermont Place-Names: Footprints of History.* Brattleboro, VT: Stephen Green Press, 1977.

Torrey, Clarence Almon and Elizabeth Petty Bentley. *New England Marriages to 1700.* Baltimore, MD: Genealogical Publishing Company, 1992.

Journals:

The Great Migration Newsletter
New England Ancestors
New England Historical and Genealogical Register
Vermont Genealogy
Vermont History

Virginia:

Armstrong, Zella and Janie Preston Collup French. *Notable Southern Families.* 6 volumes. 1918-1933. Baltimore, MD: Genealogical Publishing Company, 1993-2000.

Bockstruck, Lloyd DeWitt. *Virginia Colonial Soldiers.* Baltimore, MD: Genealogical Publishing Company, 1988.

Clark, Jewell T. and Elizabeth Terry Long. *A Guide to Church Records in the Archives Branch, Virginia State Library.* Richmond, VA: Archives Branch, Archives and Records Division, Virginia State Library, 1981, 1988.

Clark, Murtie June. *Colonial Soldiers of the South, 1732-1774.* 1983. Baltimore, MD: Genealogical Publishing Company, 1999.

Doran, Michael F. *Atlas of County Boundary Changes in Virginia, 1634-1895.* Athens, GA: Iberian Publishing, 1987.

Eckenrode, Hamilton James. *Virginia Soldiers of the American Revolution.* Richmond, VA: Virginia State Library and Archives, 1989.

Grundset, Eric. *Research in Virginia.* Arlington, VA: National Genealogical Society, 1998.

Hogg, Anne M. and Dennis A. Tosh, ed. *Virginia Cemeteries: A Guide to Resources.* Charlottesville, VA: University Press of Virginia, 1986.

McGinnis, Carol. *Virginia Genealogy: Sources & Resources.* Baltimore, MD: Genealogical Pub. Co.,1993.

Salmon, Emily J. and Edward D. C. Campbell, eds. *The Hornbook of Virginia History: A Ready-Reference Guide to the Old Dominion's People, Places, and Past.* 4th ed. Richmond, VA: The Library of Virginia, 1994.

Schweitzer, George Keene *Virginia Genealogical Research.* Knoxville, TN: G. K. Schweitzer, 1995.

Southern States Genealogical Resources: Alabama, Georgia, Kentucky, North Carolina, South Carolina, Tennessee, Virginia, West Virginia Research Sources and Bibliographies. Seattle, WA: Fiske Genealogical Foundation, 1991.

Virginia Atlas and Gazetteer. 6th ed. Freeport, ME: Delorme Mapping Co., 2005.

Virginia Genealogy: A Guide to Resources in the University of Virginia Library. Rev. ed. Charlottesville, VA: University of Virginia Press, 1983.

Vogt, John and T. William Kethley, Jr. 2nd ed. *Marriage Records in the Virginia State Library: A Researcher's Guide.* Athens, GA: Iberian Publishing Co., 1988.

Wardell, Patrick G. *Timesaving Aid to Virginia-West Virginia Ancestors: A Genealogical Index of Surnames from Published Sources.* 3 volumes. Athens, GA: Iberian Publishing Co., 1987.

Journals:

Central Virginia Heritage
Magazine of Virginia Genealogy
The Southern Genealogists Exchange Quarterly

Tidewater Virginia Families
Tyler's Quarterly Historical and Genealogical Magazine
Virginia Genealogical Society Newsletter
Virginia Genealogist
Virginia Magazine of History and Biography
William and Mary Quarterly

Washington:

Barnes, Judy and Chris Barnes. *Directory of Cemeteries and Funeral Homes in Washington State.* Orting, WA: Heritage Quest, 1989.

Genealogical Resources in Washington State: A Guide to Genealogical Records Held at Repositories, Government Agencies, and Archives. Olympia, WA: Secretary of State for Washington, Division of Archives, 1983.

McLean, Frank. *Washington State Cemeteries and Burial Plots.* Olympia, WA: Washington State Genealogy Society, 1997.

Phillips, James Wendell. *Washington State Place Names.* Seattle, WA: University of Washington Press, 1971.

Ruby, Robert H. and John Arthur Brown. Rev. ed. *A Guide to the Indian Tribes of the Pacific Northwest.* Norman, OK: University of Oklahoma Press, 1992.

Washington Pioneers. Olympia, WA: Washington State Genealogical Society, 1991.

Journals:

Appleland Bulletin
Bulletin of the Whatcom Genealogical Society
Eastern Washington Genealogical Society Bulletin
Family Backtracking
Pacific Northwest Quarterly
Pioneer Branches
The Researcher
Seattle Genealogical Society Bulletin

West Virginia:

Elliott, Wendy L. *Guide to Genealogical Research in West Virginia Records.* Rev. ed. Salt Lake City, UT: American Genealogical Lending Library, 1987.

Good, Rebecca H. and Rebecca A. Ebert. 4th ed. *Finding Your People in the Shenandoah Valley of Virginia.* Alexandria, VA: Hearthside Press, 1998.

Johnston, Ross B., ed. *West Virginians in the American Revolution.* 1939-1947. Baltimore, MD: Genealogical Publishing Company, 1990.

Lewis, Virgil. *The Soldiery of West Virginia.* 1911. Baltimore, MD: Genealogical Publishing Company, 1998.

McGinnis, Carol. *West Virginia Genealogy: Sources and Resources.* Baltimore, MD: Genealogical Publishing Company, 1988.

Southern States Genealogical Resources: Alabama, Georgia, Kentucky, North Carolina, South Carolina, Tennessee, Virginia, West Virginia Research Sources and Bibliographies. Seattle, WA: Fiske Genealogical Foundation, 1991.

Stinson, Helen S. *A Handbook for Genealogical Research in West Virginia: County Kanawha.* Rev. ed. South Charleston, WV: Kanawha Valley Genealogical Society, 1992.

Virginia and West Virginia: Atlas of Historical County Boundaries. New York: Simon and Schuster, 1998.

Wardell, Patrick G. *Timesaving Aid to Virginia-West Virginia Ancestors: A Genealogical Index of Surnames from Published Sources.* 3 volumes. Athens, GA: Iberian Publishing Co., 1985-.

Wisconsin:

Danky, James Philip. *Genealogical Research: An Introduction to the Resources of the State Historical Society of Wisconsin.* 5th print, rev. Madison: State Historical Society of Wisconsin, 1986.

Gard, Robert Edward and L. G. Sorden. *Romance of Wisconsin Place Names.* New York: Wisconsin House, 1968.

Herrick, Linda M. *Wisconsin Genealogical Research.* 3rd ed. Janesville, WI: Origins, 2002.

— and Wendy K. Unacapher. *Cemetery Locations in Wisconsin.* 2nd ed. Janesville, WI: Origins, 1999.

Long, John Hamilton and Gordon DenBoer, eds. *Atlas of Historical County Boundaries: Wisconsin.* New York: Charles Scribners Sons, 1997.

Moore, Dennis R. *Researching Your Civil War Ancestors in Wisconsin.* Manitowoc, WI: Bivouac Publications, 1994.

Russell, Donna Valley. *Michigan Censuses 1710-1830, Under the French, British, and Americans.* Detroit, MI: Detroit Society for Genealogical Research, 1982.

Ryan, Carol Ward. *Searching for Your Wisconsin Ancestors in the Wisconsin Libraries.* 3rd ed. Green Bay, WI: Carol W. Ryan, 2001.

> *Journals:*
>
> Wisconsin Magazine of History
> Wisconsin State Genealogical Society Newsletter

Wyoming:

Fremont County Genealogical Society. *Wyoming Genealogical Society Survey.* Riverton, WY: Fremont County Genealogical Society, 1986.

Spiros, Joyce V. Hawley. *Genealogical Guide to Wyoming.* Gallup, NM: Verlene Publications, 1982.

Urbanek, Mae Bobb. *Wyoming Place Names.* Missoula, MT: Mountain Press Publishing Co., 1988.

> *Journals:*
>
> Bits and Pieces
> Fremont County Nostalgia News

Canada:

Boudreau, Dennis M. *Beginning Franco-American Genealogy.* Pawtucket, RI: American French Genealogical Society, 1986, 1993.

Douglas, Althea. *Here Be Dragons! Navigating the Hazards Found in Canadian Family Research: A Guide for Genealogists: With Some Uncommon Useful Knowledge.* Toronto, CAN: Ontario Genealogical Society, 1996.

Elliot, Noel Montgomery. *The Atlantic Canadians, 1600-1900: An Alphabetized Directory of the People, Places, and Vital Dates.* 3 volumes. Toronto: Genealogical Research Library, 1994.

—. *The Central Canadians, 1600-1900: An Alphabetized Directory of the People, Places, and Vital Dates.* 3 volumes. Toronto: Genealogical Research Library, 1994.

—. *The French Canadians, 1600-1900: An Alphabetized Directory of the People, Places, and Vital Dates.* 3 volumes. Toronto: Genealogical Research Library, 1992.

—. *The Western Canadians, 1600-1900: An Alphabetized Directory of the People, Places, and Vital Dates.* 3 volumes. Toronto: Genealogical Research Library, 1994.

Gagné, Peter. *Links to Your Canadian Past, Volume 1: Acadia and the Maritime Provinces.* Pawtucket, RI: Quintin Publications, 1999.

—. *Links to Your Canadian Past, Volume 2: Quebec.* Pawtucket, RI: Quintin Publications, 1999.

—. *Links to Your Canadian Past, Volume 3: Ontario and the Canadian West.* Pawtucket, RI: Quintin Publications, 1999.

Merriman, Brenda Dougall. *Genealogy in Ontario: Searching the Records.* 4th ed. Toronto, CAN: Ontario Genealogical Society, 2008.

Punch, Terrence M. and George F. Sanborn, Jr. *Genealogist's Handbook for Atlantic Canada Research.* 2nd ed. Boston: New England Historic Genealogical Society, 1997.

Rayburn, Alan. *Dictionary of Canadian Place Names.* Oxford University Press, 1997.

Roy, Janine. *Tracing Your Ancestors in Canada.* 11th ed. Ottawa: Public Archives of Canada, 1992.

Tapper, Lawrence F. *A Biographical Dictionary of Canadian Jewry: 1909-1914: From the Canadian Jewish Times.* Teaneck, NJ: Avotaynu, Inc., 1992.

Taylor, Ryan. *Books You Need to Do Genealogy in Ontario: An Annotated Bibliography.* 2nd ed. Fort Wayne, IN: Round Tower Books, 2000.

Journals:

Acadian Genealogy Exchange
American-Canadian Genealogist
British-Columbia Genealogist
The Canadian-American Genealogical Digest
Canadian Federation of Genealogical & Family History
    Societies (Newsletter)
Families
Family History News: The Newsletter for Genealogical and
    Historical Researchers
The Genealogist: Official Journal of the American-Canadian
    Genealogical Society of New Hampshire
Generations: The Journal of the Manitoba Genealogical Society
Generations: Journal of the New Brunswick Genealogical Society
Journal of Canadian Queries
Mémoires de la Société Généalogique Canadienne-Française
Newfoundland Ancestor
Nova Scotia Genealogist
The Ontario Register
P.E.I. Genealogical Society Newsletter
Relatively Speaking
Saskatchewan Genealogical Society Bulletin

International:

Australia:

Burkhardt, G. A. *Researching Australian School Records: A Guide for Family Historians and Local History Enthusiasts.* Canberra, G. A. & J. A.: Burkhardt Old and Fine Books, 2004.

Guide to New South Wales State Archives Relating to Convicts and Convict Administration. Kingswood, N. S. W.: State Records Authority of New South Wales, 2006.

Kopittke, Rosemary and Deanna Robertson. *Guide to the Microform Collection in the Queensland Family History Society Library and Resource Center (includes all computer based records.)* Indooroopilly, Qld.: Queensland Family History Society, 2005.

Looking West: A Guide to Aboriginal Records in Western Australia. Perth, W. A.: Records Taskforce of Western Australia, 2004.

Loukakis, Angelo. *Who Do You Think You Are?: The Essential Guide to Tracing Your Family History.* Sydney, N.S.W.: Pan McMillan, 2008.

Reid, Ralph S. *Australian Family Histories: A Bibliography and Index.* Klama, N. S. W.: Ralph Reid in association with Gould Genealogy, 2007.

Sharp, Moya. *Family History & Local History on the Eastern Goldfields of Western Australia: Source Guide.* Kalgoorlie, W.A.: Goldfields Family History Society, 2006.

Tracking Family: A Guide to Aboriginal Records Relating to the Northern Territory. Canberra, A. C. T.: National Archives of Australia, 2006.

Vine Hall, Nick J. *Tracing Your Family History in New South Wales.* South Australia: Gould Genealogy in association with Nick Vine Hall, 2006.

Webster, Judy, ed. *Specialist Indexes in Australia: A Genealogist's Guide: 2006 Supplement to the 1998 Edition.* Brisbane, Qld: J. Webster, 2006.

 Journals:

 The Ancestral Searcher
 Australian Family Tree Connections
 Compiling Your Family History
 Descent
 Family History for Beginners
 The Genealogical Contact Reference
 The Genealogist
 The Kosher Koala: Newsletter of the Australian Jewish Genealogical Society
 Lost Links
 Pathfinder: Sources of Information in the State Library of NSW...
 South Australian Genealogist
 Western Ancestor: Journal of Western Australian Genealogical Society
 Your Family Tree

Austria:

Senekovic, Dagmar. *Handy Guide to Austrian Genealogical Records.* Logan, UT: Everton Publishers, 1979.

Skyte, Thea and Randol Schoenberg. *A Guide to Jewish Genealogy in Germany & Austria*. London, UK: Jewish Genealogical Society of Great Britain, 2001.

Journals:

Hof- und Besitzergeschichte zu den...Verliehenen Erhöfen Monatsblatt des Heraldisch-GenealogischenVereines "Adler"

Belgium:

DeBrabandere, Dr. Frans. *Etymological Dictionary of the Surnames in Belgium and North France*. 2 vols. Brussels: Uitgegeven door het Gemeentekrediet, 1993.

Drugy, Christophe and Guy Magdonelle. *Guide du Généalogiste en Belgigue et Dans Les Anciens Pays-Bas; Flandre, Artois, Hainaut, Luxembourg*. Paris, FR: Editions Christian, 2000.

Journals:

Belgium Laces
L'Intermediaire des Généalogistes De Middelaar Tussen de Genealogische Navorsers
Le Parchemin
Vlaamse Stam: Maandblad van de Vlaamse Vereniging Voor Familiekunde

Brazil:

Journals:

Origens: Boletim Informativo do Instituto Genealógico do Rio Grande do Sul
Revista do Instituto Genealógico Brasileiro

Chad:

Collelo, Thomas and Harold D. Nelson. *Chad: A Country Study*. 2nd ed. Washington, DC: Library of Congress, Federal Research Division, 1990.

Chile:

Church of Jesus Christ of the Latter Day Saints. *Genealogical Word List: Spanish*. 2nd ed. Salt Lake City, UT: Family History Library, 1997.

Church of Jesus Christ of the Latter Day Saints. *Research Outline. Latin America.* Salt Lake City, UT: Family History Library, 1992.

HLAS Online: Handbook of Latin American Studies. 49 volumes. Washington, DC: Library of Congress, 1995.
lcweb2.loc.gov/hlas/mdbquery.html

Hudson, Rex A. *Chile: A Country Study.* Washington, DC: Library of Congress, Federal Research Division, 1994.

Journals:

Origen
Revista de Estudios Históricos

China:

Chao, Sheau-yueh J. *In Search of Your Asian Roots: Genealogical Resources on Chinese Surnames.* Baltimore: Clearfield Company, 2000.

Worden, Robert L. and Andrea M. Savada. *China: A Country Study.* Washington, DC: Library of Congress, Federal Research Division, 1988.

Journals:

Pu Tieh Hsüeh Yen Chiu
Pu Tieh Lun Tsung
Pu Die Lun Cong
Pu Die Xue Yan Jiu
Yazhou Zu Pu Xue Shu Yan Tao Hui Hui Yi Ji Lu
Zhonghua Minguo Zong Quin Pu Xi Xue Hui Nian Kan

Columbia:

Church of Jesus Christ of the Latter Day Saints. *Genealogical Word List: Spanish.* 2nd ed. Salt Lake City, UT: Family History Library, 1997.

Church of Jesus Christ of the Latter Day Saints. *Research Outline. Latin America.* Salt Lake City, UT: Family History Library, 1992.

HLAS Online: Handbook of Latin American Studies. 49 volumes. Washington, DC: Library of Congress, 1995.
lcweb2.loc.gov/hlas/mdbquery.html

Costa Rica:

Garcia, Eduardo Fournier. *Orígenes de las Ramonenses: Familias Fundadores de San Ramón, 1843-1900.* Alajuela, CR: Museo Histórico Cultural Juan Santamaría, 1994.

Lobo, Tatiana and Mauricio Meléndez Obando. *Negros y Blancos: Todo Mezclado.* San José, CR: Editorial de la Universidad de Costa Rica, 1997.

Murchie, Anita Gregorio. *Imported Spices: A Study of Anglo-American Settlers in Costa Rica, 1821-1900.* San Jose, CR: Ministry of Culture, Youth and Sports, Dept. of Publications, 1981.

Obregón Loria, Rafael. *Familias Alajuelenses en los Libros Parroguiales: Parroguia de Alajuela 1790-1900.* Alajuela, CR: Museo Histórico Cultural Juan Santamaría, 1993-1999.

Stone, Samuel Z. *The Heritage of the Conquistadors: Ruling Classes in Central America from the Conquest to the Sandinistas.* Lincoln, NE: University of Nebraska Press, 1990.

Journals:

Colección Norberto de Castro
Revista de la Academia Costarricense de Ciencias Genealógicas

Croatia:

Eterovich, Adam S. *A Guide to Croatian Genealogy.* Palo Alto, CA: Ragusan Press, 1995.

Jerin, Robert. *Searching for Your Croatian Roots: A Handbook.* N.p.: R. Jerin, 2002.

Ljubovic, Enver. *Grbovik Gracke, Krbave, Like, Senja i Vinodola.* Senj: Senjsko, 2007.

Journals:

Vitezovic

Cuba:

Carr, Peter E. *Cuban Census Records of the 16th, 17th, and 18th Centuries.* Baltimore, MD: Clearfield, 2004.

Perera Diaz, Aisnara and María de los Ángeles Meriño Fuentes. *Nombrar las Cosas: Aproximación a la Onomástica de la Familia Negra en Cuba.* Guantánamo, Cuba: El Mar y la Montaña, 2006.

Piñón Cervera, Jorge. *Research Guide to Cuban Family History and Genealogy.* Coral Gables, FL: University of Miami, 2005.

Journals:

Correo
Raíces de la Perla: C. G. C. Journal
Revista

Czech Republic:

Milberger, Olivia Cleveland and Doris Fischer Obsta. *Checking Your Czech Ancestors: Seventy-five (and Maybe More) Resources for Tracing Your Czech Ancestors: A Guide for Beginning Czech Research.* Texas: N.p., 1990.

Miller, Olga K. *Genealogical Research for Czech and Slovak Americans.* Detroit: Gale Research Co., 1978.

Schlyter, Daniel M. *A Handbook of Czechoslovak Genealogical Research.* 2nd ed. Orem, UT: Genun Publishers, 1990.

Journals:

Heraldika a Genealogie: HG
Nase Dejiny
Nase Rodina=Our Families: Newsletter of the Czechoslovak Genealogical Society
Phoenix: Journal of Czech and Slovak Jewish Family and Community History
Rocenka= Yearbook of the Czechoslovak Genealogical Society
Sborník

Denmark:

Carlberg, Nancy Ellen and Norma S. Keating. *Beginning Danish Research.* Anaheim, CA: Carlberg Press, 1992.

Church of Jesus Christ of the Latter Day Saints. *Genealogical Word List: Danish.* Salt Lake City, UT: Family History Library, 1990.

---. *Major Genealogical Record Sources in Denmark.* Salt Lake City, UT: Church of Jesus Christ of the Latter Day Saints, 1968.

---. *Research Outline: Denmark.* Salt Lake City, UT: Family History Library, 1993.

---. *Scandinavian Vital Records Index: Denmark, Finland, Norway, Sweden.* Salt Lake City, UT: Church of Jesus Christ of the Latter Day Saints, 2001.

Douglas, Lee V. *Danish Immigration to America, an Annotated Bibliography of Resources at the Library of Congress.* Research Guide No. 28. Washington, DC: Library of Congress, Local History and Genealogy Reading Room, 1996.

Hart, Anne. *Tracing Your Baltic, Scandinavian, Eastern European, & Middle Eastern Ancestry Online: Finnish, Swedish, Norwegian, Danish, Icelandic, Estonian, Latvian, Polish, Lithuanian, Greek, Macedonian, Bulgarian, Armenian, Hungarian, Eastern European & Middle Eastern Genealogy (all Faiths.)* New York: ASJA Press, 2005.

Reed, Robert D. and Danek S. Kraus. *How & Where to Research Your Ethnic-American Cultural Heritage: Scandinavian Americans.* San Jose, CA: R & E Publishers, 1994.

Searching for Your Danish Ancestors: A Guide to Danish Genealogical Research in the United States and Denmark. Rev. St. Paul, MN: Danish Genealogy Group, 1994.

Smith, Frank and Finn A. Thomsen. *Genealogical Guidebook & Atlas of Denmark.* 4th ed. Provo, UT: Stevenson's Genealogical Center, 1998.

Thomsen, Finn A. *The Beginner's Guide to Danish Genealogical Research.* Bountiful, UT: Thomsen's Genealogical Center, 1984.

---. *Scandinavian Genealogical Research Manual.* Bountiful, UT: Thomsen's Genealogical Center, 1980.

Wellauer, Maralyn A. *Scandinavian Locational Guide: (Including Postal Numbers of Denmark, Norway and Sweden.)* Milwaukee, WI: M. Wellauer, 1980-81.

Journals:

Danish Genealogical Helper
Danmarks Adels Aarbog
Dansk Adel og Borgerstand
Dødsfald i Dankark i Aaret...
Fortid og Nutid (The Past and the Present)
Heraldiske Studier
Hvem Forsker Hvad (Who's Researching What)
Lekiskon Over Danske Familier
Personalhistorisk Tidskrift (Periodical and Serial of Personal History)
The Scandinavian Genealogical Helper

Dominican Republic:

Benzo de Ferrer, Vilma. *Pasajeros a La Española, 1492-1530.* Santo Domingo, República Dominicana: N.p., 2000.

Church of Jesus Christ of the Latter Day Saints. *Genealogical Word List: Spanish.* 2nd ed. Salt Lake City, UT: Family History Library, 1997.

Church of Jesus Christ of the Latter Day Saints. *Research Outline. Latin America.* Salt Lake City, UT: Family History Library, 1992.

HLAS Online: Handbook of Latin American Studies. 49 volumes. Washington, DC: Library of Congress, 1995.
lcweb2.loc.gov/hlas/mdbquery.html

Haggerty, Richard A. *Dominican Republic, A Country Study.* Washington, DC: Library of Congress, Federal Research Division, 1989.

Larrazábal Blanco, Carlos. *Familias Dominicanas.* Santo Domingo, Academia Dominicana de la Historia, 1967-.

Rodríguez Demorizi, Emilio. *Familias Hispanoamericanas.* Ciudad Trujillo, Editora Montalvo, 1959-.

Journals:

Raíces: Boletín Informativo del Instituto Dominicano de Genealogia, Inc.

Ecuador:

Church of Jesus Christ of the Latter Day Saints. *Genealogical Word List: Spanish.* 2nd ed. Salt Lake City, UT: Family History Library, 1997.

---. *Research Outline. Latin America.* Salt Lake City, UT: Family History Library, 1992.

Gomezjuarado Zevallos, Javier. *Genealogías Mestizas.* Quito, EC: Casa de la Cultura Ecuatoriana "Benjamín Carrión," 2008-.

HLAS Online: Handbook of Latin American Studies. 49 volumes. Washington, DC: Library of Congress, 1995.
lcweb2.loc.gov/hlas/mdbquery.html

Hanratty, Dennis Michael. *Ecuador, A Country Study.* Washington, DC: Library of Congress, Federal Research Division, 1991.

Larrea, Gregorio César de. *De Historia y Genealogía.* Quito, EC: Abya-Yala, 2003.

Journals:

Colección "Amigos de la Genealogía"
Estudios Historico Genealógicos
Publicación
S. A. G.

Egypt:

Legrain, Georges Albert. *Répertoire Généalogique et Onomastique du Musée du Caire.* Genève, SW: Société Anonyme des Arts Graphiques, 1908.

Metz, Helen Chapin. *Egypt, A Country Study.* Washington, DC: Library of Congress, Federal Research Division, 1991.

Journals:

Journal of Ancient Egyptian Studies

England:

Church of Jesus Christ of Latter-Day Saints. *Research Outline: England.* Salt Lake City, UT: Family History Library, 1999.

Colwell, Stella and Jane Cox. *The Family Records Centre: A User's Guide.* Kew, Surry, UK: Public Record Office, 2002.

Collins, Audrey. *Basic Facts About Using the Family Records Centre.* Bury, ENG: Federation of Family History Societies, 1998.

Foster, Janet and Julia Sheppard. *British Archives: A Guide to Archive Resources in the United Kingdom.* 3rd ed. New York: Macmillan Publishers, 1995.

Hawkings, David T. *Criminal Ancestors: A Guide to Historical Criminal Records in England and Wales.* Phoenix Mill, NH: Alan Sutton, 1992.

Humphrey-Smith, Cecil R. and James Bell, ed. *The Phillimore Atlas and Index of Parish Registers.* 3rd ed. Chichester, UK: Phillimore & Co., 1995.

Mellen, Rachael. *A Practical Guide for the Genealogist in England.* Bowie, MD: Heritage Books, 1987.

Moulton, Joy Wade. *Genealogical Resources in English Repositories.* Columbus, OH: Hampton House, 1988.

—. *Supplement to Genealogical Resources in English Repositories.* Columbus, OH: Hampton House, 1992.

Pelling, George and Pauline Litton. *Beginning Your Family History in Great Britain.* 7th ed. Baltimore, MD: Genealogical Publishing Co., 1999.

Pratt, David H. *Researching British Probates, 1354-1858: A Guide to the Microfilm Collection of the Family History Library.* Wilmington, DE: Scholarly Resources, Inc., 1992-.

Preece, Floren Stocks and Phyllis Pastore Preece. *Handy Guide to English Genealogical Records.* Logan, UT: Everton Publishers, 1978.

Rapaport, Diane. *New England Court Records: A Research Guide for Genealogist and Historians.* Burlington, MA: Quill Pen Press, 2006.

Rogers, Colin Darlington. *The Family Tree Detective: Tracing Your Ancestors in England and Wales.* Manchester, ENG: Manchester University Press, 1985.

Steel, D. J., A. E. F. Steel, and Cliff Webb, et. al. *National Index of Parish Registers*. London: Society of Genealogists, 1966-.

Journals:

Ancestors: The Family History Magazine of the Public Record Office
British Heritage
Debrett's Peerage and Baronetage
Family History
Family History News and Digest
Family Tree Magazine
The Genealogists' Magazine
National Genealogical Directory
Publications of the Harleian Society

Estonia:

Beare, Arlene. *A Guide to Jewish Genealogy in Latvia and Estonia.* 2nd ed. London: Jewish Genealogical Society of Great Britain, 2006.

Maldonado, Sigrid Renate. *Estonian Experience and Roots: Ethnic Estonian Genealogy with Historical Perspective, Social Influences and Possible Family History Resources.* Fort Wayne, IN: As Was Publishing, 1996.

Wistinghausen, Henning von. *Quellen zur Geschichte der Rittergüter Estlands im 18. Und 19. Jarhundert: 1772-1889.* Hannover-Döhren: Von Hirschheydt, 1975.

Ethiopia:

Kolmodin, Johannes. *Traditions de Tsazzega et Hassega: Traduction Française.* Upsala: K. W. Appelberg, 1915.

Ludolf, Hiob and Gent J. P. *A New History of Ethiopia, Being a Full and Accurate Description of the Kingdom of Abessinia, Vulgarly, Though Erroneously Called the Empire of Prester John: In Four Books...: Illustrated with Copper Plates.* London: Printed for Samuel Smith, 1682.

Ofcansky, Thomas P. and LaVerle Bennette Berry. *Ethiopia, A Country Study.* 4th ed. Washington, DC: Library of Congress, Federal Research Division, 1993.

Finland:

Christensen, Penelope. *Finding Your Scandinavian Ancestors.* 2nd ed. Toronto, CAN: Heritage Productions, 2001.

Church of Jesus Christ of Latter Day Saints. *Genealogical Word List: Finnish.* Salt Lake City, UT: Family History Library, 1997.

---. *Scandinavia Vital Records Index: Denmark, Finland, Norway, Sweden.* Salt Lake City, UT: Church of Jesus Christ of Latter Day Saints, 2001.

Dickson, Charles. *Scandinavian-American Genealogical Resources.* Westminster, MD: Heritage Books, 2004.

Mattson-Shultz, Virginia. *Far Northern Connections: Researching Your Sami (and other) Ancestors in Northern Norway, Sweden, Finland and Russia.* Pittsburgh, PA: Dorrance Publishing, 2007.

Ropponen, Risto. *Guide to the Military Archives of Finland.* Helsinki, FI: The Military Archives, 1977.

Solsten, Eric and Sandra W. Meditz. *Finland, A Country Study.* Washington, DC: Library of Congress, Federal Research Division, 1990.

Viikki, Raimo and Eljas Orrman. *Guide to the Public Archives of Finland.* Helsinki, FI: National Archives, 1980.

Vincent, Timothy Laitila. *Traveling and Research in Finland.* Salt Lake City, UT: Vincent, 2001.

--- and Rick Tapio. *Finnish Genealogical Research.* New Brighton, MN: Finnish Americana, 1994.

Journals:

Axplock
Findlands Ridderskaps Och Adels Kalender
Genos
Släktbok
Släktforskaren
Sukutieto
Suomen Sukututkijaluettelo=Släktforskarförteckning för Finland
Suomen Sukututkimusseuran Julkaisuja
Suomen Sukututkimusseuran vuosikirja=Genealogiska
    Samgundets i Finland Årsskrift

Uppsatser: Skrifter Utgivna av Helsingfors Släktforskare r.f.
Uusi Sukukirja

France:

Boudreau, Rev. Dennis M. *Beginning Franco-American Genealogy.*
Pawtucket, RI: American-French Genealogical Society, 1993.

Church of Jesus Christ of Latter Day Saints. *Genealogical Word List: French.* 2nd ed. Salt Lake City, UT: Family History Library, 1997.

Church of Jesus Christ of Latter Day Saints. *Letter Writing Guide: French.* Salt Lake City, UT: Family History Library, 1997.

Journals:

Arcadian Genealogy Exchange
Bulletin of the Society for the History of French Protestantism
Bulletin Genealogique D'Information
French Genealogical Review
French Genealogist
Heraldique et Généalogie

Germany:

Anderson, Chris and Ernest Thode. *A Genealogist's Guide to Discovering Your Germanic Ancestors: How to Find and Record Your Unique Heritage.* Cincinnati, OH: Betterway Books, 2000.

Brandt, Edward R., et. al. *Germanic Genealogy: A Guide to Worldwide Sources and Migration Patterns.* 3rd. ed. St. Paul, MN: Germanic Genealogy Society, 2007.

Church of Jesus Christ of Latter Day Saints. *Genealogical Word List, German.* Salt Lake City, UT: Family History Center, 1997.

---. *Letter Writing Guide: German.* Salt Lake City, UT: Family History Library, 1997.

---. *Research Outline: Germany.* Salt Lake City, UT: Family History Library, 1997.

---. *Resource Guide, The Hamburg Passenger Lists, 1850-1934.* Salt Lake City, UT: Family History Library, 1992.

Edlund, Thomas Kent. *Die Ahnenstammkartei des Deutschen Volkes: An Introduction and Register.* St. Paul, MN: Germanic Genealogy Society, 1995.

---. *The German Minority Census of 1939: An Introduction and Register.* Teaneck, NJ: Avotaynu, Inc., 1996.

Ellmann-Krüger, Angelika G. and Edward David Luft. *Library Resources for German-Jewish Genealogy.* Teaneck, NJ: Avotaynu, Inc., 1998.

Jensen, Larry O. *A Genealogical Handbook of German Research.* 3 vols. Pleasant Grove, UT: Jensen Publications, 1980-86.

Johnson, Arta F. *How to Read German Church Records Without Knowing Much German.* Columbus, OH: Copy Shop, 1980.

—. *Origins, Development, and Meanings of German Names.* Columbus, OH: published by the author, 1984.

Riemer, Shirley J. *The German Research Companion.* Rev. ed. Sacramento, CA: Lorelei Press, 2000.

Smith, Clifford Neal and Anna Piszczan-Czaja Smith. *Encyclopedia of German-American Genealogical Research.* New York: R. R. Bowker, 1976.

Journals:

Archiv für Familiengeschichtsforschung = Review for Genealogical Studies
Archiv für Sippenforschung = Archive for Ancestral Research
Blätter für Familienkunde und Familienpflege
Deutsches Familienarchiv = German Families Archive
Donauschwabische Familienkundliche Forschungsblatter
Genealogie: Deutsche Zeitschrift für Familienkunde = Genealogy: German Periodical for Family Studies
German American Genealogy
The German Connection
German Genealogical Digest
Germanic Genealogy Journal
Mitteilungen der Westdeutschen Gesellschaft für Familienkund
The Palatine Immigrant

Ghana:

Berry, La Verle. *Ghana, A Country Study.* Washington, DC: Library of Congress, Federal Research Division, 1995.

Greece:

Broadbent, Molly. *Studies in Greek Genealogy.* Leiden: E.J. Brill, 1968.

Bywater, Lica Catsakis. *Family History Research in Greece.* Salt Lake City, UT: L. H. Catsakis, 2005.

--- and Daniel M. Schlyter. *Greek Genealogical Research.* Salt Lake City. UT: The Section, 1988.

Church of Jesus Christ of Latter-day Saints. *Research Outline:_Greece.* Family History Library, 2001.

Journals:

Deltion Heraldikes Kai Genealogikes Hetairias Hellados

Guyana:

Caribbean Genealogy – Country Resources. www.candoo.com/genresources/index.html#GUYANA

Merrill, Tim. *Guyana, A Country Study.* Washington, DC: Library of Congress, Federal Research Division, 1993.

Smith, Raymond Thomas. *Kinship and Class in the West Indies: A Genealogical Study of Jamaica and Guyana._* Cambridge, UK: Cambridge University Press, 1988.

Haiti:

Baguidy, Joseph D. *Savalou, ou, Les Racines Africaines d'Haïti.* Haiti: Editions des Antilles, 1963-1995.

Church of Jesus Christ of Latter-Day Saints. *Genealogical Word List: French.* 2nd ed. Salt Lake City, UT: Family History Library, 1997.

---. *Letter Writing Guide: French.* Salt Lake City, UT: Family History Library, 1997.

Haggerty, Richard A. *Haiti, A Country Study*. Washington, DC: Library of Congress, Federal Research Division, 1989.

Honduras:

Church of Jesus Christ of Latter Day Saints. *Genealogical Word List: Spanish*. Salt Lake City, UT: Family History Library, 1997.

---. *Research Outline: Latin America*. Salt Lake City, UT: Family History Library, 1992.

Genealogical Society of Utah. *Fuentes Principales de Registros Genealogicos en Honduras*. Salt Lake City, UT: The Society, 1975.

HLAS Online: Handbook of Latin American Studies. 49 volumes. Washington, DC: Library of Congress, 1936-. lcweb2.loc.gov/hlas/mdbquery.html

Merrill, Tim. *Honduras, A Country Study*. Washington, DC: Library of Congress, Federal Research Division, 1995.

Hungary:

Brandt, Edward Reimer. *Contents and Addresses of Hungarian Archives*. 2nd ed. Minneapolis, MN: ER Brandt, 1993.

Burant, Stephen R. *Hungary, A Country Study*. 2nd ed. Washington, DC: Library of Congress, Federal Research Division, 1990.

Nagy, Iván. *Magyarország Családai: Czimerekkel és Nemzékrendi Táblákkal*. 1857. Budapest: Helikon, 1987.

Suess, Jared H. *Handy Guide to Hungarian Genealogical Records*. Logan, UT: Everton Publishers, 1980.

Journals:

Forrás
Magyar Zsidó: Semi Annual Publication of the Greater Hungarian SIG
Régi Magyarország=Old Hungary: the Newsletter of the Sacramentói Magyar/Amerikai Baráti Táraság (Hungarian/American Friendship Society of Sacramento)

Indonesia:

Corfield, Justin J. *Pangkalpinang: A Guide to Cemeteries Bangka Island, South Sumatra, Indonesia.* Rosanna, Voc: Corfield & Co., 1999.

Frederick, William H. and Robert L. Worden. *Indonesia: A Country Study.* 5th ed. Washington, DC: Library of Congress, Federal Research Division, 1993.

Journals:

De Indische Navorscher

Iran:

Curtis, Glenn E., Erick Hooglund, and Helen Chapin Metz. *Iran, A Country Study.* 5th ed. Washington, DC: Library of Congress, Federal Research Division, 2008.

Iraq:

'Amiri, Thamir 'Abd al-Hasan. *Mawsu 'at al- 'Ashair al- 'Iraqiyah.* Baghdad: Dar al-Shuun al Thaqafiyah al- 'Ammah, 1992-1995.

Metz, Helen Chapin. *Iraq, A Country Study.* 4th ed. Washington, DC: Library of Congress, Federal Research Division, 1990.

Rawdan, 'Abd 'Awn. *Mawsu 'at 'ashair al-'Iraq: Tarikh, Ansab, Rijalat, Maathir.* 'Amman: al-Ahliyah, 2003.

Samarrai, Yunus Ibrahim. *al-Qabail wa-al-buyutat al-Hashimiyah fi al-'Iraq.* Baghdad: Y. L. al-Samarrai, 1986-.

Ireland:

Adolph, Anthony. *Tracing Your Irish Family History.* Richmond Hill, ONT: Firefly Books, 2009.

Chater, Kathy. *How to Trace Your Family Tree in England, Ireland, Scotland and Wales: The Complete Practical Handbook for All Detectives of Family History.* London, UK: Southwater, 2006.

Church of Jesus Christ of Latter-Day Saints. *Research Outline: Ireland.* Salt Lake City, UT: Family History Library, 1993.

Helferty, Seamus and Raymond Refaussé, eds. *Directory of Irish Archives*. 4th ed. Blackrock, IR: Irish Academic Press, 2003.

Maxwell, Dr. Ian. *Your Irish Ancestors: A Guide for the Family Historian*. Barnsley, UK: Pen & Sword Family History, 2008.

McCarthy, Tony. *The Irish Roots Guide*. Dublin, UK: Lilliput, 1991.

McKenna, Erin. *A Student's Guide to Irish American Genealogy*. Phoenix, AZ: Oryx Press, 1996.

Mitchell, Brian. *Guide to Irish Parish Registers*. Baltimore, MD: Genealogical Publishing Co., 1988.

—. *Pocket Guide to Irish Genealogy*. 3rd ed. Baltimore, MD: Genealogical Publishing Co., 2008.

Radford, Dwight A. and Kyle J. Betit. *A Genealogist's Guide to Discovering Your Irish Ancestors*. Cincinnati, OH: Betterway Books, 2001.

Ryan, James G. *Irish Church Records: Their History, Availability, and Use in Family and Local History Research*. Dublin, UK: Flyleaf Press, 1992.

—. *Irish Records: Sources for Family and Local History*. Rev. ed. Salt Lake City, UT: Ancestry, 1997.

Journals:

The All-Ireland Heritage
Directory of Irish Family History Research
Éirephile
Familia
The Irish Ancestor
The Irish at Home and Abroad (1993-1999)
Irish Family History
The Irish Genealogical Quarterly
Irish Genealogical Research Society Newsletter
The Irish Genealogist
The Irish Link
Irish Roots
The Journal of the Royal Society of Antiquaries of Ireland
The Septs

Israel:

Metz, Helen Chapin. *Israel, A Country Study.* Washington, DC: Library of Congress, Federal Research Division, 1990.

Sack, Sallyann A. and the Israel Genealogical Society. *A Guide to Jewish Genealogical Research in Israel.* Teaneck, NJ: Avotaynu, 1995.

Segal, Joshua L. *A Field Guide to Visiting a Jewish Cemetery: A Spiritual Journey to the Past, Present, and Future.* Nashua, NH: 2005.

Tagger, Mathilde A. and Yitzchak Kerem. *Guidebook for Sephardic and Oriental Genealogical Sources in Israel.* Bergenfield, NJ: Avotaynu, 2006.

Weiner, Miriam. *Genealogy Research in Eastern Europe and Israel: Ma Bell in Moscow, Tracing Survivors, Jewish Archives, Travel Guides, Census in Russia, Mormon Library, Shtetl Photos, Ghetto Anthology, Memorial Books, Pinkas Ha-Kehillot.* Secaucus, NJ: M. Weiner, 1987.

Journals:

Le-vet Avotam: Mehkarim u-mekorot be-heker ha-mishpahot
Roots: Newsletter of the Society for Jewish Family Heritage
Sharsheret ha-dorot=Sharsheret Hadorot

Italy:

Adams, Suzanne Russo. *Finding Your Italian Ancestors: A Beginner's Guide.* Provo, UT: Ancestry Pub., 2008.

Caratti di Valfrei, Lorenzo. *Guida Alla Ricerca Genealogica.* Bologna: CLUEB, 1998.

Carmack, Sharon DeBartolo. *Italian-American Family History: A Guide to Researching and Writing About Your Heritage.* Baltimore, MD: Genealogical Publishing Co., 1997.

Church of Jesus Christ of Latter-Day Saints. *Genealogical Word List: Italian.* Salt Lake City, UT: Family History Library, 1997.

DeAngelis, Priscilla Grindle. *Italian-American Genealogy: A Source Book.* Rockville, MD: Noteworthy Enterprises Pub., 1994.

Guelfi Camajani, Guelfo. *Genealogy in Italy.* Firenze: Istituto Genealogico Italiano, 1979.

Karcich, Grant. *Finding Your Italian Ancestors*. Toronto, ONT: Heritage Productions, 1999.

Konrad, J. *Italian Family Research*. Rev. ed. Munroe Falls, OH: Summit Publications, 1990.

    Journals:

    Annuario Della Nobiltà Italiana
    Comunes of Italy
    Le Grandi Famiglie Romane
    Italian Genealogical Group: Newsletter
    Italian Genealogist
    L'Aroldo: Almanacco Nobiliare del Napoletano
    Libro d'oro Della Nobiltà Italiana
    POINTers
    Revista del Collegio Araldico

Ivory Coast:

Church of Jesus Christ of Latter-Day Saints. *Genealogical Word List: French*. 2nd ed. Salt Lake City, UT: Family History Library, 1997.

Church of Jesus Christ of Latter-Day Saints. *Letter Writing Guide: French*. Salt Lake City, UT: Family History Library, 1997.

Handloff, Robert Earl and Thomas Duval Roberts. *Cote d'Ivoire, A Country Study*. 3rd ed. Washington, DC: Library of Congress, Federal Research Division, 1991.

Téty Gauze, A. L. and Laurent Gbagbo. *Histoire des Magwe: Contribution à la Connaissance des Peuples de la Côte d'Ivoire Occidentale*. Abidjan: Université Nationale de Côte d'Ivoire, 1982.

Jamaica:

Mitchell, Madeleine E. *Jamaican Ancestry: How to Find Out More*. Bowie, MD: Heritage Books, 1998.

O'Sullivan-Sirjue, Jennifer and Pansey Robinson. *Researching Your Jamaican Family*. Kingston, Jamaica: Arawak, 2007.

Smith, Raymond Thomas. *Kinship and Class in the West Indies: A Genealogical Study of Jamaica and Guyana*._ Cambridge, UK: Cambridge University Press, 1988.

Japan:

Church of Jesus Christ of Latter-Day Saints. *Major Genealogical Record Sources in Japan.* Salt Lake City, UT: Genealogical Society of the Church of Jesus Christ of Latter-Day Saints, 1974.

Dolan, Ronald E. and Robert L. Worden. *Japan, A Country Study.* Washington, DC: Library of Congress, Federal Research Division, 1994.

Maruyama, Koichi. *Kakei no Shirabekata.* Tokoyo: Kinensha, 1983.

Reed, Robert D. and Danek S. Kaus. *How & Where to Research Your Ethnic-American Cultural Heritage: Japanese Americans.* San Jose, CA: R & E Publishers, 1994.

Jordan:

'Akash, Nasim Muhammad. *Al-'Ashair al-Urduniyah Bayna al-madi Wa-al-hadir.* al-Zarqa, al-Urdun: Dar al-'Akash lil Nashr wa-al Tawzi, 1997.

Metz, Helen Chapin. *Jordan, A Country Study.* 4th ed. Washington, DC: Library of Congress, Federal Research Division, 1989.

Kazakstan:

Curtis, Glenn E. *Kazakstan, A Country Study.* Washington, DC: Library of Congress, Federal Research Division, 1996.

Korea:

Chong, Kye-jin. *Pohak Haesol p'Yollam.* Soul T'ukpyolsi: Myongji Ch 'ulp 'ansa, 1989.

Hangugin ui Chokpo P'yonch'an Wiwonhoe. *Kasungbo.* Soul T'ukpyolsi: Ilsingak, 1985.

Savada, Andrea Matles. *North Korea, A Country Study.* 4th ed. Washington, DC: Library of Congress, Federal Research Division, 1994.

— and William Shaw. *South Korea, A Country Study.* 4th ed. Washington, DC: Library of Congress, Federal Research Division, 1992.

Laos:

Savada, Andrea Matles. *Laos, A Country Study.* Washington, DC: Library of Congress, Federal Research Division, 1994.

Latin America:

Platt, Lyman De. *Genealogical Historical Guide to Latin America.* Detroit, MI: Gale Research Co., 1978.

---. *Genealogical Research in Latin America and the Hispanic United States.* St. George, UT: Teguayo Press, 1993.

> *Journals:*
>
> Colección Norberto de Castro
> Estirpe: Revista de Genealogia
> Revista

Latvia:

Beare, Arlene. *A Guide to Jewish Genealogy in Latvia and Estonia.* London: Jewish Genealogical Society of Great Britain, 2001.

Lebanon:

Collelo, Thomas and Harvey Henry Smith. *Lebanon, A Country Study.* 3rd ed. Washington, DC: Library of Congress, Federal Research Division, 1989.

Libya:

Metz, Helen Chapin. *Libya, A Country Study.* 4th ed. Washington, DC: Library of Congress, Federal Research Division, 1989.

Lithuania:

Aaron, Sam. *A Guide to Jewish Genealogy in Lithuania.* London, UK: Jewish Genealogical Society of Great Britain, 2005.

Researching Lithuanian Ancestral Towns. Chicago, IL: Balzekas Museum of Lithuanian Culture, 1995.

Rhode, Harold and Sallyann Amdur. *Jewish Vital Records, Revision Lists, and Other Jewish Records in Lithuanian Archives.* Teaneck, NJ: Avotaynu, Inc., 1996.

Journals:

Proteviai=Forefathers
Lithuanian Genealogical Committee Newsletter

Mauritania:

Handloff, Robert E. and Brian Dean Curran. *Mauritania, A Country Study.* 2nd ed. Washington, DC: Library of Congress, Federal Research Division, 1990.

Mexico:

Church of Jesus Christ of Latter-Day Saints. *Genealogical Word List: Spanish.* 2nd ed. Salt Lake City, UT: Family History Library, 1997.

Church of Jesus Christ of Latter-Day Saints. *Research Outline: Latin America.* Salt Lake City, UT: Family History Library, 1992.

HLAS Online: Handbook of Latin American Studies. 49 volumes. Washington, DC: Library of Congress, 1995.
lcweb2.loc.gov/hlas/mdbquery.html

Konrad, J. *Mexican and Spanish Family Research.* Monroe Falls, OH: Summit Publications, 1987.

Ryskamp, George R. and Peggy Ryskamp. *Finding Your Mexican Ancestors: A Beginner's Guide.* Provo, UT: Ancestry Pub., 2007.

Schmal, John P. and Donna S. Morales. *Mexican-American Genealogical Research: Following the Paper Trail to Mexico.* Bowie, MD: Heritage Press, 2002.

Journals:

Boletín
Memorias de la Academia Mexicana de Genealogía y Heráldica

Mongolia:

Gao, Wende and Zhichun Cai. *Mengu Shi Xi.* Beijing: Zhongguo She Hui Ke Chu Ban She, 1979.

Worden, Robert L. and Andrea Matles Savada. *Mongolia, A Country Study.* Washington, DC: Library of Congress, Federal Research Division, 1991.

Netherlands:

Church of Jesus Christ of Latter-Day Saints. *Genealogical Word List: Dutch.* Salt Lake City, UT: Family History Library, 2001.

---. *Major Genealogical Record Sources in the Netherlands.* Salt Lake City, UT: Genealogical Society, 1968.

Franklin, Charles M. *Dutch Genealogical Research.* Indianapolis, IN: Ye Olde Genealogie Shoppe, 1993.

Okkema, J. C. *Handleiding Voor Genealogisch Onderzoek in Nederland.* 2nd ed. Weesp: Fibula-Van Dishoeck, 1986.

Perry, Esther. *Finding Your Dutch Ancestors* --. 2nd ed. Toronto, CAN: Heritage Productions, 2004.

Vennik, Roelof. *Handleiding voor stamboomonderzoek.* Rotterdam: Wilkerdon, 1987.

Journals:

The Dutch Lion: Journal of the Royal Dutch Society for Genealogy and Heraldry
Genealogie: Kwartaalblad van het Centraal Bureau voor Genealogie
Genealogy: Quarterly of the Centraal Office for Genealogy
Gens Nostra = Ons Geslacht: Maandblad der Nederlandse Genealogische Vereeniging
Jaaboek van het Centraal Bureau voor Genealogie
Nederland's Adelsboek
Nederland's Patriciaat
Our Ancestor: Monthly Journal of the Netherlands Genealogical Society
Sibbe

Nicaragua:

Church of Jesus Christ of Latter-Day Saints. *Genealogical Word List: Spanish.* 2nd ed. Salt Lake City, UT: Family History Library, 1997.

Genealogical Society of Utah. *Fuentes Pricipales de Registros Genealogicos en Nicaragua.* Salt Lake City, UT: The Society, 1975.

HLAS Online: Handbook of Latin American Studies. 49 Volumes. Washington, DC: Library of Congress, 1996. lcweb2.loc.gov/hlas/mdbquery.html

Merrill, Tim. *Nicaragua, A Country Study.* Washington, DC: Library of Congress, Federal Research Division, 1994.

Nigeria:

Metz, Helen Chapin. *Nigeria, A Country Study.* Washington, DC: Library of Congress, Federal Research Division, 1992.

Norway:

Carlberg, Nancy Ellen. *Beginning Norwegian Research.* Anaheim, CA: Carlberg Press, 1991.

Christensen, Penelope. *Finding Your Scandinavian Ancestors.* 2nd ed. Toronto, CAN: Heritage Productions, 2001.

Church of Jesus Christ of Latter-Day Saints. *Genealogical Word List: Norwegian.* 2nd ed. Salt Lake City, UT: Family History Library, 1997.

---. *Major Genealogical Record Sources in Norway.* Salt Lake City, UT: Genealogical Society, 1967.

---. *Research Outline: Norway.* 2nd ed. Salt Lake City, UT: Family History Library, 2000.

Herrick, Linda M. and Wendy K. Uncapher. *Norwegian Research Guide.* Rev. ed. Janesville, WI: Origins, 2001.

Mattson-Schultz, Virginia. *Far Northern Connections: Researching Your Sami (and Other) Ancestors in Northern Norway, Sweden, Finland, and Russia.* Pittsburg, PA: Dorrance Pub., 2007.

Smith, Frank and Finn A. Thomsen. *Genealogical Guidebook & Atlas of Norway.* Logan, UT: Everton, 1970-1979.

Thomsen, Finn A. *The Beginner's Guide to Norwegian Genealogical Research.* Bountiful, UT: Thomsen's Genealogical Center, 1984.

---. *Genealogical Maps & Guide to the Norwegian Parish Registers.* Bountiful, UT: Thomsen's Genealogical Center, 1987.

—. *Scandinavian Genealogical Research Manual.* Bountiful, UT: Thomsen's Genealogical Center, 1993.

Wellauer, Maralyn A. *Tracing Your Norwegian Roots.* Milwaukee, WI: Wellauer, 1979.

Journals:

Avisen
Budstikken
Genealogen
Norsk Slektshistorisk Tidsskrift (Periodical of Norwegian Family History)
Opdalslagets Aarbok=Yearbook

Pakistan:

Blood, Peter. *Pakistan, A Country Study.* Washington, DC: Library of Congress, Federal Research Division, 1995.

Malik, Ghulam Akbar. *Panjab ke Mughal Qabail.* Lahaur: al-'Uqab Pablikeshanz, 1996.

Shahbaz, Anjum Sultan. *Aqvam-I Panjab.* Jihlam: Buk Karnar, 2006.

Panama:

Church of Jesus Christ of Latter-Day Saints. *Genealogical Word List: Spanish.* 2nd ed. Salt Lake City, UT: Family History Library, 1997.

---. *Research Outline: Latin America.* Salt Lake City, UT: Family History Library, 1992.

HLAS Online: Handbook of Latin American Studies. 49 Volumes. Washington, DC: Library of Congress, 1995. lcweb2.loc.gov/hlas/mdbquery.html

Meditz, Sandra W. and Dennis Michael Hanratty. *Panama, A Country Study.* Washington, DC: Library of Congress, Federal Research Division, 1989.

Paraguay:

Church of Jesus Christ of Latter-Day Saints. *Genealogical Word List: Spanish.* 2nd ed. Salt Lake City, UT: Family History Library, 1997.

---. *Research Outline: Latin America.* Salt Lake City, UT: Family History Library, 1992.

Hanratty, Dennis Michael and Sandra W. Meditz. *Paraguay, A Country Study.* Washington, DC: Library of Congress, Federal Research Division, 1990.

HLAS Online: Handbook of Latin American Studies. 49 Volumes. Washington, DC: Library of Congress, 1995. lcweb2.loc.gov/hlas/mdbquery.html

Journals:

El Archivo Nacional

Peru:

Church of Jesus Christ of Latter-Day Saints. *Genealogical Word List: Spanish.* 2nd ed. Salt Lake City, UT: Family History Library, 1997.

---. *Research Outline: Latin America.* Salt Lake City, UT: Family History Library, 1992.

HLAS Online: Handbook of Latin American Studies. 49 Volumes. Washington, DC: Library of Congress, 1995. lcweb2.loc.gov/hlas/mdbquery.html

Hudson, Rex A. *Peru, a Country Study.* Washington, DC: Library of Congress, Federal Research Division, 1993.

Loza Bonifaz, Juan. *Origen y Fundación de los Imperios Incas en el Perú y en el Brasil.* Perú: CONCYTEC, 2002.

Platt, Lyman de. *Peru: General Research Guide.* St. George, UT: Teguayo Press, 1996.

Journals:

Revista del Instituto Peruano de Investigaciones Genealógicas
Apuntes Para el Estudio Genealógico de Familias Limeñas de los Siglos XVII y XVIII

Philippines:

Church of Jesus Christ of Latter-Day Saints. *Research Outline: Philippines.* 2nd ed. Salt Lake City, UT: Family History Library, 2000.

Dolan, Ronald E. *Philippines, a Country Study.* Washington, DC: Library of Congress, Federal Research Division, 1993.

Santiago, Luciano P. R. *The Art of Ancestor Hunting in the Philippines.* Quezon City: New Day Publishers, 1990.

Vance, Lee W. and Violeta C. Canon. *Tracing Your Philippine Ancestors.* Provo, UT: Stevenson's Genealogical Center, 1980.

Poland:

Beider, Alexander. *A Dictionary of Jewish Surnames from the Kingdom of Poland.* Teaneck, NJ: Avotaynu, 1996.

Church of Jesus Christ of Latter-Day Saints. *Genealogical Word List: Polish.* 2nd ed. Salt Lake City, UT: Family History Library, 1997.

Curtis, Glenn E. *Poland, a Country Study.* Washington, DC: Library of Congress, Federal Research Division, 1994.

Frazin, Judith R. *A Translation Guide to 19th Century Polish-Language Civil-Registration Documents: Birth, Marriage and Death Certificates.* 2nd ed. Northbrook, IL: Jewish Genealogical Society of Illinois, 1989.

Gnacinski, Janneyne Longley and Leonard T. Gnacinski. *Polish and Proud: Tracing Your Polish Ancestry.* Rev. Indianapolis, IN: Ye Olde Genealogie Shoppe, 1995.

Hoskins, Janina W. *Polish Genealogy and Heraldry: An Introduction to Research.* New York: Hippocrene Books, 1990.

Ortell, Gerald A. *Polish Parish Records of the Roman Catholic Church.* 3rd rev. Astoria, NY: Gerald A. Ortell, 1989.

Kazmierczak, Wiktor and Edward A. Peckwas. *A Historical Bibliography of Polish Towns, Villages, and Regions.* Chicago, IL: Polish Genealogical Society, 1990.

Konrad, J. *Polish Family Research.* Munroe Falls, OH: Summit Publications, 1977.

Pogonowski, Iwo Cyprian. *Poland: A Historical Atlas.* New York: Hippocrene Books, 1987.

Schlyter, Daniel M. *Essentials in Polish Genealogical Research.* Chicago: Polish Genealogical Society of America, 1993.

Toposki, Jerzy. *An Outline History of Poland.* Warsaw, Poland: Interpress Publishers, 1986.

Weiner, Miriam. *Jewish Roots in Poland.* Secaucus, NJ: Miriam Weiner Routes to Roots Foundation, 1997.

Wellauer, Maralyn A. *Tracing Your Polish Roots.* Rev. and enl. Milwaukee, WI: M. A. Wellauer, 1991.

Wynne, Susan F. *Finding Your Jewish Roots in Galicia: A Resource Guide.* Teaneck, NJ: Avotaynu, Inc., 1998.

Journals:

Bulletin of the Polish Genealogical Society of America
Die Pommerschen Leute
Genealogia: Studia I Materialy Historyczne
Landsmen: Quarterly Publication of the Suwalk-Lomza Interest Group for Jewish Genealogists
Polish Eaglet
Rodziny: the Journal of the Polish Genealogical Society of America
White Eagle: Journal of the Polish Nobility Association Foundation

Portugal:

Church of Jesus Christ of Latter-day Saints. *Genealogical Word List: Portuguese.* 2nd ed. Salt Lake City, UT: Family History Library, 1997.

Faria, António Machado de. *Genealogical Research in Portugal.* Salt Lake City, UT: Genealogical Society of the Church of Jesus Christ of Latter-day Saints, Inc., 1969.

Mello, Cheri. *Finding Your Portuguese Roots.* Torrance, CA: Cheryl L. Mello, 2000.

Reed, Robert D. and Danek S. Kaus. *How & Where to Research Your Ethnic-American Cultural Heritage: Portuguese Americans.* San Jose, CA: R. & E Publishers, 1994.

Solsten, Eric. *Portugal, a Country Study.* 2nd ed. Washington, DC: Library of Congress, Federal Research Division, 1993.

Journals:

>
> Anuário de Nobreza de Portugal
> Armas e Troféus
> Genealogia & Heráldica
> Portuguese Ancestry
> Raízes & Memórias: Orgão Periódico da Associação Portuguesa
> de Genealogia
> Tabardo

Romania:

Bachman, Ronald D. and Eugene K. Keefe. *Romania, a Country Study.* 2nd ed. Washington, DC: Library of Congress, Federal Research Division, 1991.

Herter, Balduin and Maja Philippi. *Siebenbürgische Familien im Sozialen Wandel.* Köln: Böhlau, 1993.

Pascal, Paul. *Romanian Census Records.* Teaneck, NJ: Avotaynu, 1995.

Radulescu, Mihai Sorin. *Genealogia Româneasca: Istoric si Bibliografie.* Braila: Muzel Brailei: Editura Istros, 2000.

Journals:

> Arhiva Genealogica
> Rom Sig News: Jewish Genealogical Special Interest Group for
> Romania
> Siebenbürgische Familienforschung: Mitteilungen der Sektion
> Genealogie im Arbeitskreis für Siebenbürgische Landeskunde

Russia:

Beider, Alexander. *A Dictionary of Jewish Surnames from the Russian Empire.* 2nd ed. Bergenfield, NJ: Avotaynu, 2008.

Bychkova, M. E. *Chto Znachit Imenno Rodnye.* Moskva: Bogorodskii Pechatnik, 2000.

Feldblyum, Boris. *Russian-Jewish Given Names: Their Origins and Variants.* Teaneck, NJ: Avotaynu, Inc., 1998.

Grimsted, Patricia Kennedy. *Archives of Russia: A Directory and Bibliographic Guide to Holdings in Moscow and St. Petersburg.* Armonk, NY: M. E. Sharpe, 2000.

Mattson-Schultz, Virginia. *Far Northern Connections: Researching Your Sami (and Other) Ancestors in Northern Norway, Sweden, Finland, and Russia.* Pittsburg, PA: Dorrance Pub., 2007.

Olenev, Maksim. *Podrobno o Tom, Kak Otyskat' Svoikh Predkov: Genealogicheskie Issledovaniia.* Kaluga: Fridgel'm, 2006.

Shea, Jonathan D. and William F. Hoffman. *In Their Words: A Genealogist's Translation Guide to Polish, German, Latin, and Russian Documents. Volume two, Russian.* New Britain, CT: Language & Lineage Press, 2002.

Weiner, Miriam. *Genealogy Research in Eastern Europe and Israel: Ma Bell in Moscow, Tracing Survivors, Jewish Archives, Travel Guides, Census in Russia, Mormon Library, Shtetl Photos, Ghetto Anthology, Memorial Books, Pinkas Ha-Kehillot.* Secaucus, NJ: M. Weiner, 1987.

Journals:

Genealogicheskii Vestnik
Genealogiia Severnogo Kavkaza
Istoricheskaia Genealogiia
Izvestiia Russkogo Genealogicheskogo Obshchestva
Kuzbasskii Rodoved
Russkii Rodoslovets: Al'Manakh
Severnye Rodosloviia
Ural'skii Rodoved

Saudi Arabia:

Hashimi, Ibrahim ibn Mansur. *Al-Ishraf fi ma 'rifat al-mu 'tanin bi-tadwin Ansab al-ashraf (Ahl al-Hijaz.)* Bayrut: Tawzi', Muassasat al-Rayyan, 2000.

Ibn al-Mibrad, Yusuf ibn Hasan and Muhyi al-Din Mastu. *Kitab al-Shajarah al-Nabawiyah: fi Nasab Khayr al-Bariyah.* Dimashq: Dar al-Kalim al-Tayyib: Dar Ibn Kathir, 1994.

Metz, Helen Chapin. *Saudi Arabia, a Country Study.* 5th ed. Washington, DC: Library of Congress, Federal Research Division, 1993.

Scotland:

Adam, Frank and Sir Thomas Innes. *The Clans, Septs, and Regiments of the Scottish Highlands.* 8th ed. Baltimore, MD: Genealogical Publishing Co., 1970.

Bigwood, Rosemary. *The Scottish Family Tree Detective: Tracing Your Ancestors in Scotland.* Manchester, UK: Manchester University Press, 2006.

Black, George. *The Surnames of Scotland: Their Origin, Meaning and History.* Edinburgh, UK: Birlinn Limited, 1996.

Chater, Kathy. *Tracing Your Family Tree in England, Ireland, Scotland and Wales: Discover Your Roots and Explore Your Family's History.* London, UK: Southwater, 2006.

Church of Jesus Christ of Latter-Day Saints. *Research Outline: Scotland.* Salt Lake City, UT: Family History Library, 1997.

---. *Scotland: A Genealogical Research Guide.* Salt Lake City, UT: Genealogical Library of the Church of Jesus Christ of Latter-Day Saints, 1987.

Cory, Kathleen B. and Leslie Hodgson. *Tracing Your Scottish Ancestry.* 3rd ed. Baltimore, MD: Genealogical Publishing Co., 1990.

Goldie, Douglas Bruce. *In Search of Hamish McBagpipes: A Concise Guide to Scottish Genealogy.* Bowie, MD: Heritage Books, 1992.

Holton, Graham S. and Jack Winch. *Discover Your Scottish Ancestry: Internet and Traditional Resources.* Lanham, MD: Taylor Trade Publications, 2004.

--- and ---. *My Ain Folk: An Easy Guide to Scottish Family History.* East Linton, UK: Tuckwell Press, 1997.

Irvine, Sherry. *Your Scottish Ancestry: Research Methods for Family Historians.* Provo, UT: Ancestry, 2003.

James, Alwyn. *Scottish Roots: A Step-by-Step Guide for Ancestor Hunters.* Gretna, LA: Pelican Publishing Co., 1982.

Jonas, Linda and Paul Milner. *A Genealogist's Guide to Discovering Your Scottish Ancestors.* Cincinnati, OH: Betterway Books, 2002.

Sinclair, Cecil. *Tracing Your Scottish Ancestors: A Guide to Ancestry Research in the National Archives of Scotland.* 3rd ed. Edinburgh, UK: HMSO, 2003.

Stewart, Alan. *Gathering the Clans: Tracing Your Scottish Ancestry on the Internet.* Chichester, UK: 2004.

Journals:

Anglo-Celtic Roots
Scottish-American Genealogist
The Scottish Association of Family History Societies Bulletin
The Scottish Genealogist: The Quarterly Journal of the Scottish Genealogy Society
Scottish Local History

Singapore:

Harfield, A. G. *Early Cemeteries in Singapore.* London, UK: British Association for Cemeteries in South Asia, 1988.

Lepoer, Barbara Leitch. *Singapore, a Country Study.* 2nd ed. Washington, DC: Library of Congress, Federal Research Division, 1991.

Slovenia:

Lapajne, Branka. *Researching Your Slovenian Ancestors.* Willowdale, ONT: BML Publishing Co., 1996.

Somalia:

Abbink, J. *The Total Somali Clan Genealogy: A Preliminary Sketch.* Leiden, the Netherlands: African Studies Centre, 1999.

Metz, Helen Chapin. *Somalia, a Country Study.* 4th ed. Washington, DC: Library of Congress, Federal Research Division, 1993.

Spain:

Church of Jesus Christ of Latter-Day Saints. *Genealogical Word List: Spanish.* 2nd ed. Salt Lake City, UT: Family History Library, 1997.

Konrad, J. *Mexican and Spanish Family Research.* Monroe Falls, OH: Summit Publications, 1987.

Platt, Lyman de. *Spain: Research Guide.* Salt Lake City, UT: Instituto Genealógico e Histórico Latinoamericano, 1990.

Reed, Robert D. and Danek S. Kaus. *How & Where to Research Your Ethnic-American Cultural Heritage: Spanish Americans.* San Jose, CA: R. & E. Publishers, 1994.

Ryskamp, George R. *Tracing Your Hispanic Roots.* Riverside, CA: Hispanic Family History Research, 1984.

Solsten, Eric and Sandra W. Meditz. *Spain, a Country Study.* 2nd ed. Washington, DC: Library of Congress, Federal Research Division, 1990.

Journals:

Estudios Genealógicos y Heráldicos
Genealógia y Heráldica
Hidalguía

Sri Lanka:

Marikar, A. I. L., A. H. Macan Markar, and A. L. M. Lafir. *Genealogical Tables of Sri Lanka Moors, Malays, and Other Muslims.* Colombo: Moors' Islamic Cultural Home, 1981.

Ross, Russell R. and Andrea Matles Savada. *Sri Lanka, a Country Study.* 2nd ed. Washington, DC: Library of Congress, Federal Research Division, 1990.

Sudan:

Bano, Leonzio. *Mezzo Secolo de Storia Sudanese, 1842-1898: Dall'archivio Parrocchiale di Khartum.* Bologna: EMI, 1976.

MacMichael, H. A. *A History of the Arabs in the Sudan and Some Account of the People Who Preceded Them and Of the Tribes Inhabiting Dárfur.* Cambridge, UK: University Press, 1922.

Metz, Helen Chapin. *Sudan, A Country Study.* 4th ed. Washington, DC: Library of Congress, Federal Research Division, 1992.

Qasim, 'Awn al Sharif. *Mawsu 'at al-Qabail Wa-al-ansab Fi al-Sudan Wa-ashhar Asma al-a 'lam Wa-al-Amakin.* Khartoum: 'A.al-Sh. Qasim, 1996.

Sweden:

Carlberg, Nancy Ellen. *Beginning Swedish Research.* Anaheim, CA: Carlberg Press, 2001.

Christensen, Penelope. *Finding Your Scandinavian Ancestors.* 2nd ed. Toronto, CAN: Heritage Productions, 2001.

Clemensson, Per and Kjell Andersson. *Släktforska!, Steg för steg*. 4th rev. Stockholm, SW: LTs förlag, 1993.

--- and ---. *Your Swedish Roots: A Step by Step Handbook*. Provo, UT: Ancestry, 2004.

Dickson, Charles. *Scandinavian-American Genealogical Resources*. Westminster, MD: Heritage Books, 2004.

Erickson, James E. and Nils William Olsson. *Tracing Your Swedish Ancestry*. New York: Swedish Information Service, 2000.

Johansson, Carl-Erik. *Cradled in Sweden*. Rev. ed. Logan, UT: Everton Publishers, 1995.

Mattson-Schultz, Virginia. *Far Northern Connections: Researching Your Sami (and Other) Ancestors in Northern Norway, Sweden, Finland, and Russia*. Pittsburg, PA: Dorrance Pub., 2007.

Minnesota Historical Society. *Swedish Genealogical Resources*. 2nd ed. St. Paul, MN: Swedish Interest Group, 1994.

Saarinen, Jouni and Kerstin Abukhanfusa. *Roots in Sweden: The Genealogist's Guide to the Swedish Archives*. Stockholm, SW: Riksarkivet, 1997.

Thomsen, Finn A. *The Beginner's Guide to Swedish Genealogical Research*. Bountiful, UT: Thomsen's Genealogical Center, 1998.

Thorsell, Elisabeth and Ulf Berggren. *Finn din Släkt!: I Svenska Och Utländska Källor Och På Nätet*. Stockholm, SW: Svenska Förlaget, 2000.

Journals:

Personhistorisk tidskrift (Journal of Personal History)
Släkt och hävd: tidskrift (Family and Tradition)
Släktforskarnas Årsbok
Släkthistoriskt Forum
Svenska Antavlor
Svenska Släktkalendern
Sveriges Ridderskap Och Adels Kalender
Swenson Center News: Publication of the Swenson
    Swedish Immigration Research Center

Switzerland:

Bruckner, Albert. *Archivalische Quellen Für Den Familienforscher.* Basel: Schweizerische Gesellschaft für Familienforschung, 1981.

Church of Jesus Christ of Latter-Day Saints. *Major Genealogical Record Sources in Switzerland.* Salt Lake City, UT: Genealogical Society, 1967.

Moos, Mario von. *Bibliography of Swiss Genealogies.* Camden, ME: Picton Press, 1993.

Rohrbach, Lewis Bunker. *Introductory Guide to Swiss Genealogical Research.* Rockport, ME: Picton Press, 2004.

Suess, Jared H. *Handy Guide to Swiss Genealogical Records.* Logan, UT: Everton Publishers, 1978.

Wellauer, Maralyn A. *Tracing Your Swiss Roots.* Rev. Milwaukee, WI: Wellauer, 1988.

Journals:

Archiv für Familiengeschichtsforschung: AfF = Review for Genealogical Studies
Jahrbuch
Maajan = Die Quelle

Syria:

Collelo, Thomas. *Syria, A Country Study.* 4th ed. Washington, DC: Library of Congress, Federal Research Division, 1988.

Thailand:

LePoer, Barbara Leitch. *Thailand, A Country Study.* 6th ed. Washington, DC: Library of Congress, Federal Research Division, 1989.

Uganda:

Byrnes, Rita M. *Uganda, A Country Study.* 2nd ed. Washington, DC: Library of Congress, Federal Research Division, 1992.

Ukraine:

Geary, Muryl Andrejciw. *Finding Your Ukrainian Ancestors.* Toronto, ONT: Heritage Productions, 2000.

Himka, Paul J. *Sources for Researching Ukrainian Family History.* Edmonton, ALTA: Canadian Institute of Ukrainian Studies, 1984.

Magocsi, Paul Robert. *Galicia: A Historical Survey and Bibliographic Guide.* Toronto, CA: University of Toronto Press, 1983.

Pihach, John D. *Ukrainian Genealogy: A Beginner's Guide.* Edmonton, ALTA: Canadian Institute of Ukrainian Studies Press, 2007.

Weiner, Miriam. *Jewish Roots in Ukraine and Moldova.* New York: YIVO Institute for Jewish Research, 1999.

---. *Routes to Roots in Ukraine, Moldova, Belarus, Latvia and Lithuania.* Secaucus, NJ: M. Weiner, 1995.

Wynne, Susan F. *Finding Your Jewish Roots in Galicia: A Resource Guide.* Teaneck, NJ: Avotaynu, Inc., 1998.

Journals:

Along the Galician Grapevine
The Galitzianer
Galizien German Descendents: Newsletter
Gesher Galicia Family Finder
Henealohichni Zapysky Ukraïns'koko Heral'dychnoho Tovarystva
Hoffnungstal Bessarabia
Wandering Volhynians

Uruguay:

Azarola Gil, Luis Enrique. *Apellidos de la Patria Vieja.* Buenos Aires, ARG: Librería y Editorial "La Facultad," 1942.

Hudson, Rex A. and Sandra W. Meditz. *Uruguay, A Country Study.* 2nd ed. Washington, DC: Library of Congress, Federal Research Division, 1992.

Church of Jesus Christ of Latter-Day Saints. *Research Outline: Latin America.* Salt Lake City, UT: Family History Library, 1992.

Journals:

> Revista del Instituto de Estudios Genealógicos del Uruguay

Venezuela:

Church of Jesus Christ of Latter-Day Saints. *Research Outline: Latin America.* Salt Lake City, UT: Family History Library, 1992.

Haggerty, Richard A. and Howard I. Blutstein. *Venezuela, a Country Study.* 4th ed. Washington, DC: Library of Congress, Federal Research Division, 1993.

Lloréns Casani, Milagro, Sonia Antuña Lloréns, and Astrid Antuña Lloréns. *Genealogía de Familias Venezolanas.* Torreblascopedro, Jaén: M. Lloréns Casani, 2001-.

Sangróniz, José Antonio de. *Familias Coloniales de Venezuela.* Caracas: Editorial Bolívar, 1943-.

Journals:

> Boletín del Instituto Venezolano de Genealogía

Vietnam:

Cima, Ronald J. *Viet Nam, a Country Study.* Washington, DC: Library of Congress, Federal Research Division, 1989.

Nguyen, Đu'c Du. *Gia Pha: Khao Luan Và Thu'c Hành.* Hanoi: Van Hóa, 1992.

---. *Mot Loi Chép Gia Pha That Do'n Gian.* Cà Mau: Nhàa Xuat Ban Mui Cà Mau, 1993.

Nguyen, The Nguyên. *Viet Gia Pha: Suy Nghi Và The Hien.* Hanoi: Nhà Xuat Ban Công an Nhân Dân, 2000.

Yugoslavia:

Curtis, Glenn E. *Yugoslavia, A Country Study.* 3rd ed. Washington, DC: Library of Congress, Federal Research Division, 1992.

Petrie, Hazel. *Handbook for South Slav (Yugoslav) Genealogy, Particularly Pertaining to Central and Lower Dalmatia, Republic of Croatia.* Auckland, N.Z.: The Society, 1992.

Wales:

Hamilton-Edwards, Gerald Kenneth Savery. *In Search of Welsh Ancestry.* Baltimore, MD: Genealogical Publishing Co., 1986.

Istance, Jean and E. E. Cann. *Researching Family History in Wales.* Birmingham, UK: Federation of Family History Societies, 1996.

Lloyd, Annie. *Beginning Welsh Research.* 3rd ed. Culver City, CA: Annie Lloyd, 1998.

Reakes, Janet. *How to Trace Your English Ancestors: (Including Wales, Channel Islands & Isle of Man.)* Sydney, NSW: Hale & Iremonger, 1987.

Rowlands, John, et. al., eds. *Welsh Family History: A Guide to Research.* 2nd ed. Baltimore, MD: Genealogical Publishing Co., 1999.

— and Sheila Rowlands. *Second Stages in Researching Welsh Ancestry.* Baltimore, MD: Genealogical Publishing Co., 1999.

— and — . *The Surnames of Wales: For Family Historians and Others.* Birmingham, UK: Federation of Family History Societies, 1996.

Journals:

Cronicl
South Wales Family History Society Journal
Vital Signs

Zaire:

Meditz, Sandra W. and Tim Merrill. *Zaire, A Country Study.* 4th ed. Washington, DC: Library of Congress, Federal Research Division, 1994.

Legal Resources

Adler, Allan. *Using the Freedom of Information Act: A Step-by-Step Guide.* New York: American Civil Liberties Union, 1997.

> Passed in 1966, and amended in 1974, the Freedom of Information Act (FOIA) is based on the premise argued by James Madison and Alexander Hamilton that openness in government is necessary to assist citizens in making the informed decisions necessary to a democracy. The FOIA creates the vehicle by which any person may obtain records of the agencies of the federal government. This guide will outline the instructions and guidelines for obtaining information needed from government agencies. It contains sample letters for making an effective FOIA request. The three chapters define the FOIA and discuss the Act, exemptions, making a request, access to records and the response time; how to make a effective request, understanding responses and fees; and sample letters, fee waivers, assistance from Congress, working with a court, and working with lawyers. Finally, there is a list of addresses for federal agencies.

Carson, Bryan M. *The Law of Libraries and Archives.* Lanham, MD: The Scarecrow Press, Inc., 2007.

> Carson explains legal concepts pertaining to libraries and archives in layman's terms so that librarians and archivists can more readily understand the legal ramifications of issues dealt with on a daily basis. While providing a basic overview of the law as it affects libraries and archives, he covers such subjects as contracts, copyright and patent law, fair use, copyright exceptions for libraries and the TEACH Act. Also included is trademark law, licensing of databases, information malpractice, professionalism, privacy issues, the PATRIOT Act, employment law, and the basics of starting a nonprofit institution.

Cornish, Graham P. *Copyright: Interpreting the Law for Libraries, Archives and Information Services.* 4th ed. London, UK: Facet Publishing Company, 2004.

> Copyright isn't only an American issue, it is worldwide. In his work, Cornish deals with the copyright laws in Great Britain and the European Union. The book explains the provisions of the UK Copyright Act and supporting legislation. It also explains the EU Copyright Directive and how it is affecting copyright issues around the world. Works covered by copyright include literary, dramatic and musical works; artistic works; sound recordings; films and videos; broadcasts; databases; and computer programs and websites.

Crawford, Tad. *Business and Legal Forms for Authors and Self-Publishers*. 3rd ed. New York: Allworth Press, 2004.

> This book features twenty ready to use forms, negotiation checklists and tear-out forms for use in planning for the publication of your publication whether you choose to publish professionally, or on your own. Crawford provides advice on negotiating winning contracts and profitable deals. This edition also includes information on electronic rights. Each form included in this publication includes and explanatory discussion and step-by-step instructions for filling it out. There is also an introduction to contracts, how to negotiate, advice on standard contractual provisions, and how to contact volunteer lawyers for the arts. Some of the forms in this book include: Contract with a Literary Agent, Privacy Release, Transfer of Copyright, Contract with a Book Distributor, Author's Lecture Contract, Reproduction Rights, and many more.

Crawford, Tad and Kay Murray. *The Writer's Legal Guide: An Authors Guild Desk Reference*. 3rd ed. New York: Allworth Press, 2002.

> Reprinted and revised several times, Crawford and Murray who are both working in the publishing business use real life examples and analysis of potential problems to answer almost every legal question a potential author might have. Coverage includes: business issues , including how to deal with publishers, agents, and collaborators; copyright from protection to fair use and infringement; electronic rights; contracts, including rights, permissions, advances, and royalties; packagers and self-publishing, and many more publishing related legal issues.

Fishman, Stephen. *The Copyright Handbook: How to Protect & Use Written Works*. 9th, ed. Berkeley, CA: Nolo, 2006.

> Fishman's copyright handbooks provide the writer with step-by-step instructions and the legal forms needed to protect creative works. He discusses such issues as registering your copyright, protecting against infringement, and profiting from your work. The book is divided into two sections, part one provides a short overview of copyright law and a how to register guide on copyright notice and registration with the Copyright Office. Part two is a copyright resource, it discusses the important aspects of copyright law, and if this doesn't answer your questions suggests other resources or ultimately suggests a copyright attorney. Other areas also discussed are determining which works can be protected, when and how to use a copyright notice, the rights and duration of

ownership, how long a copyright lasts, transferring ownership, how to use copyrighted works, electronic publishing rights, registration of multimedia works and rights, and protecting creative works on the Internet. Legal forms are also provided.

Neuenschwander, John A. *Oral History and the Law.* 4th ed. Denton, TX: Oral History Association, 2009.

This small book in invaluable as a resource for guiding the oral historian through the ramifications of the legal aspects of utilizing oral history. The guide talks about invasion of privacy, defamation, how to avoid legal problems, sealed interviews, copyright, ownership and transfer, deeds of gift, drafting agreements, contractual agreements, and explaining legal issues to interviewees.

Oral History Association. *Guidelines and Principles of the Oral History Association.* Los Angeles, CA: Oral History Association, 1992.

The Oral History Association has published guidelines for conducting oral history interviews, and in them includes a guide to social, legal, historical and ethical issues involved in the practice of oral history.

Polking, Kirk, ed. *Beginning Writer's Answer Book.* 5th ed. Cincinnati, OH: Writer's Digest Books, 1993.

Garnered from questions regularly asked the staff of *Writer's Digest* magazine and the Writer's Digest School, the *Answer Book* provides the answers to over 900 questions about writing. Organized into specific subject areas, it answers such queries as should I have a specific market in mind when I write an article, or should I write the article first; what is a kill fee and when is it used; what information should my query letter include, and how soon should I follow up if I don't get a response; can I submit my work to more than one publisher at a time; and many other questions. Pointers are given on researching a topic, conducting interviews, generating ideas, and dealing with literary agents.

---, ed. *The Writer's Friendly Legal Guide.* Cincinnati, OH: Writer's Digest Books, 1989.

This guide will help the writer to avoid potential problems by keeping abreast of current changes in the laws governing publication. Polking has gathered counsel from experts in areas such as libel, invasion of privacy, fair use, and freedom of the press. They offer commentary on subsidiary rights, book contracts, taxes, and social security.

Ullmann, John and Jan Colbert. *The Reporter's Handbook: An Investigator's Guide to Documents and Techniques.* 2nd ed. New York: St. Martin's Press, 1991.

Several chapters in this handbook are pertinent to the legalities of oral history, genealogy, and family research. Chapters give information on following a paper trail using things like telephone records, credit card records and other methods; using various state and federal documents, and libraries; the Freedom of Information Act; finding backgrounds on individuals; using tax records; documenting the evidence; tracing land holdings; and other legal issues.

Yow, Valerie R. *Recording Oral History: A Practical Guide for the Humanities and Social Sciences.* Thousand Oaks, CA: Sage Publications, Inc., 2005.

Ethical and legal issues are covered in detail in one of the chapters in Yow's book. She also elaborates on three different types of oral history projects, community studies, biographies, and family histories. In her in-depth study of oral history, Yow shows the oral historian how to select interviewees, phrase questions, build rapport with the interviewee, use the equipment, deal with difficult situations, analyze the tapes and write up the project.

Author's collection: Family buriel site

Writing Your Story

Many of us want to write a book, we think we have something to say, or an idea everyone will love, or maybe we think it's an easy way to make a little money, after all - everyone else seems to be writing successfully.

But what should I write about? It should be something I know, or something I have researched intentionally. Should it be fiction? Fact? A combination of the two? But how do I start, how does one get that first word down on paper, and after the first line, how does one continue?

Two of the most important things in beginning to write are one - to have a topic, and we have one, we're telling our stories, we have researched our genealogy, talked to our living relatives, and found the family papers. Now all we have to do is put it down on paper in narrative form. This leads us to point two - putting it down on paper...which entails finding time to write. The hardest step after finding the topic is finding the time to sit down and actually put the thoughts on paper. Time is something most of us have both in abundance, and not enough of. The idea of writing the story is a good one, but it is also scary. Am I talented enough to write my story? I do not know, but I definitely will not know unless I try. Time is one of those things that gets in the way of the trying.

In order to find the time to write, one must intentionally put aside some time to do so. That is the hardest part of the equation, the part you might never accomplish. If you are at all scared of putting those first few words on paper, you will never find the time. It is easy to find other "more important" things to do with that time. Discipline, yes, that's right, that word you thought never to hear once you'd grown up, *discipline*. Discipline is needed to write. Set a particular time of day, or even week, keep to the schedule if at all possible, if something truly has to be done during your writing time, reschedule, but do not ignore that time, getting off the track can be deadly to your progress.

It is *your* story you are writing, and by this time, you have some things to help you tell that story. You have worked on your genealogy, you have the family tree, you have the oral histories from your family and friends, you have the photographs, and you have the documents you have collected from birth to death for as many members of your family as you could trace...in other words, the research is pretty much complete. I say "pretty much" advisedly here, as once you start writing, you will probably open up some questions you have not yet considered.

You also, have everything well organized, so writing should be a snap, right? You do have it organized? Well, yes, but maybe not in the order you wish it to be for your story. So, you will probably have to reorganize some of your information. For this process, you might want to make some additional copies of some of your documentation rather than rearranging your current filing system (unless, that is, you no longer care if things are logically arranged.) What was organized one way for the family tree research, might not work quite as well for the storyline. But *do not* get bogged down here, this is another one of those traps that may be used to put off the actual writing part.

If you have not already gone the genealogy route with all or most of your research done, there are many books out there, many of them listed in the annotated bibliography part of this work, which suggest questions which may be used to stimulate memories about which you may want to write. Photographs also may be used to jog memories. If you cannot actually put the photo in as part of your project, describe it so the reader knows a little about the photo to which you are referring.

What else do you need to write? A pencil and paper (and eraser) come in handy, even if you are using a computer. With a pencil and paper, not a pen, corrections and changes are easier; you can go back and make changes. If you are not a writer, no, I mean a person with legible handwriting - try a computer. If you can type, you can compute, and computer copy is much easier to change than typewriter copy. Most, if not all word processing programs even tell you when you've misspelled a word! They also do grammar checks, but sometimes this changes the intent of what you were trying to convey, so I would be careful about using the grammar checking in an autobiographical setting. You also do not have to have everything perfectly in order using a computer, you are free to insert information anywhere in the text, if you are footnoting references, and most programs will even update your footnote numbers if you add one after the fact.

Ok, you have the paper, pencil, eraser, or computer; you have your research, your family tree, and your photographs; you have a book of memory stimulating questions; you made a time and a place to work; now you need a catchy beginning. You might want to pick a special event in your family's life, or something memorable in history around which to build your story. For instance, if you come from a large extended family, you might start with what you were all doing September 11, 2001, when the World Trade Centers were bombed, this leads naturally into what the previous generation was doing on December 7, 1941, when Pearl Harbor was bombed. This might not wind up as the beginning of your book when it is completed, but a memorable event will give you a starting point from which to begin your writing. Once you have found a starting point, other events and things will come to you as you proceed either forward or backwards in time from that point.

If you still have close family members around while you are writing, you might consider sharing your progress with them. They may remember something important that you forgot, or did not consider so important, they may also remember it from a different point of view which you might want to incorporate into your text. On the other hand, they might also take exception to something you've written, while you are telling your personal story, also be sensitive to other's feelings. You might not want to change something someone finds offensive, but maybe there is a better way to put it into words.

Once you complete your memoirs, autobiography or family history, you will need to consider how it will be presented. Is it short? Long? Do you just want to make photocopies for a few people, or do you want to get it bound into a book? There are many publishers out there who will do small runs of family histories, and there are also now many web publishers who will do limited runs of bound books…these publishers are easily found on the web, but have vastly varying formats and prices.

Whether you write your family history only for your own enjoyment or for your family or larger audience, it should prove to be a fun and satisfying experience.

Author's collection: Thatched roof cottage, Ring of Kerry, Ireland

Writing, Bookmaking & Publishing Resources

Albert, Susan Wittig. *Writing From Life: Telling Your Soul's Story.*
New York: Putnam Publishing Group, 1996.

Geared towards women, these writing exercises provide a guide to putting your life story on paper. The step-by-step instructions through eight thematic chapters follow through the life cycle to create an autobiography.

My Family.com Inc. *Celebrating the Family: The MyFamily.com Guide to Understanding Your Family History.* New York: Friedman/FairFax, 2002.

While this book crosses over into the photo heritage and preservation fields, it is designed by the experts at MyFamily.com as a guide to producing a primarily visual legacy which may be passed down from generation to generation. Besides creating the scrapbook or heritage book, this guide discusses beginning the reunion tradition, and other ways to bring your family closer together both physically and emotionally. They suggest that the establishment of traditions is one that provides happy and long-lasting memories for both you and your children as many families are already aware.

Appelbaum, Judith. *How to Get Happily Published: A Complete and Candid Guide.* 5th ed. New York: HarperCollins Publishers, Inc., 1998.

The guide provides advice on where to send various types of writing for possible publication and the best methods for presenting the materials. This edition offers advice for working with small publishers, capitalizing on contacts, deciding whether to self-publish, using new electronic media, and making a work sell better.

Baker, Russell and William Zinsser, eds. *Inventing the Truth: The Art and Craft of Memoir.* Boston, MA: Houghton Mifflin Company, 1998.

In this collection, nine famous authors discuss their experiences via anecdote on the subject of writing memoirs. The authors who share their pleasures and problems in memoir writing are Russell Baker, Jill Kerr Conway, Frank McCourt, Eileen Simpson, Henry Louis Gates, Jr., Alfred Kazin, Annie Dillard, Ian Frazier, and Toni Morrison.

Barnes, Donald R. and Richard S. Lackey. *Write it Right: A Manual for Writing Family Histories and Genealogies.* 2nd ed. Ocala, FL: Lyon Press, 1988.

Write it Right was published to provide genealogists with a clear and easily understood guide for writing a family history, genealogy article or book. The authors give advice on how to deal with such issues as adoptees, skeletons, coats of arms, conflicting evidence, and other issues that might arise. They run the prospective author through preparation for writing, the purpose for writing, numbering systems, outlining, drafting the text, refining the final draft, citations, problems encountered, and suggested forms for arrangement.

Barrington, Judith. *Writing the Memoir: From Truth to Art.* Portland, OR: The Eighth Mountain Press, 2002.

Barrington as a memoirist and writing teacher is eminently qualified to offer tips and advice on the writing of memoirs. Advice offered in this work include help with getting started; developing a form; telling the truth, using fictional techniques; expanding language skills; developing sensory detail; writing about living people; and placing your story in a larger context. She also discusses avoiding common pitfalls. Each of the chapters includes writing exercises and the appendix discusses legal issues which affect memoir writing.

Bender, Sheila. *Writing Personal Essays: How to Shape Your Life Experiences for the Page.* Cincinnati, OH: Writer's Digest Books, 1995.

Utilizing essays from her students and professional writers, Bender illustrates how to look inside one's memories and experiences and relate them in a manner that others understand and appreciate. She assists the reader in getting "under the skin" of the memories and discovering what they really meant, how special they were and how to tell them. She shows how to take them and make them clear and evocative on paper. In the last chapter, Bender provides advice on how to publish a personal essay.

Borg, Mary. *Writing Your Life: An Easy-to-Follow Guide to Writing an Autobiography.* 3rd ed. Fort Collins, CO: Cottonwood Press, Inc., 1998.

Writing Your Life presents a guide to assist in the structuring of an autobiography. Included is practical advice for getting started and staying motivated, questions to stimulate memory, activities to help in remembering the past, simple writing tips, and instructions for publishing the completed book for family and friends.

Boyer, Carl. *How to Publish and Market Your Family History.* 4th ed. Santa Clarita, CA: Carl Boyer, 1993.

>Mr. Boyers discusses how to publish and market family histories after you have made the decision that this is your goal. He follows through with researching the relatives, writing the draft, how to approach the publication process, revising the draft, and provides outlines for setting up your own time-table and system.

Campbell-Slan, Joanna. *Scrapbook Storytelling: Save Family Stories and Memories with Photos, Journaling, and Your Own Creativity.* St. Louis, MO: EFG, 1999.

>Most of us have kept scrapbooks or albums at one time or another throughout our lives. Joanna Slan takes this one step farther by showing how to use these as a basis for telling the life story. Sharing writing and journaling secrets, she shows how to preserve your life history. She provides professional tips on how to make writing exciting; journal resources to assist in saying what's in your heart; quotations to help inspire and for your use; ways to say what you want in the space you have; conquering writer's block; questions to assist in communicating about your family; suggestions for involving the family; ways to make writing fun and other steps to make a family history project fun.

Carmack, Sharon DeBartolo. *You Can Write Your Family History.* Cincinnati, OH: Betterway Books, 2003.

>You do not have to be a professional writer to do your family history. Most of them are not great works of art, they are for your personal enjoyment and to pass the stories you have collected on to your family. Your history is made up of vital records, family group sheets, memorabilia, but more than these, your history is made up of names, dates, stories of love and loss, changes, past relatives, future relatives, funny things that happened throughout your life and history itself. Carmack explains how to take these items and turn them into a compelling highly readable true story as she helps you to decide the best type of family history to write: biography, family history, narrative or memoir. She will help you decide on a theme; conduct the appropriate research to flesh out your narrative; and get the words down on paper.

Carson, Dina C. *The Genealogy and Local History Researcher's Self-Publishing Guide: How to Organize, Write, Print, and Sell Your Family or Local History Book.* 2nd ed. Niwot, CO: Iron Gate Pub., 1992.

    Carson has designed a weekly planning calendar for organizing your genealogical writing project. Providing a pace to keep you on track and organized, the guide helps to collect and organize information, how to obtain permission to reprint material, how to add historical detail and write a good story, using a collaborator if necessary, using photographs and illustrations, designing a finished product without breaking your budget, producing camera ready copy, marketing your book, and using publicity. The guide is presented with a few pages of written instructions and then a week's planning calendar to organize your work.

Case, Patricia Ann. *How to Write Your Autobiography: Preserving Your Family Heritage.* 2nd ed. Santa Barbara, CA: Woodbridge Press, 1992.

    While this book is primarily geared toward writing an autobiography, it also presents a good base for the person putting together an interview to do an oral history. Most of the writing tips given make smooth transitions to a spoken format. Especially valuable are the extensive lists of questions which can be tailored easily to an oral history.

Citing Records in the National Archives of the United States. Rev. ed. Washington, DC: National Archives and Records Administration, 2007.

    Much of the information you obtain from the National Archives is considered unpublished. This guide presents formats for documenting these records in bibliographies, as well as formats for other records such as textual records, microform records, electronic records, records in affiliated agencies, digitalized documents and other records. Nontextual records include such items as photographs, posters, motion pictures, tape recordings, maps and architectural drawings.

Craig, Hazel Thompson. *A Priceless Legacy: An Album of Memories for Future Generations.* Sarasota, FL: Banyan Tree Press, 1991.

    Writing the story of how they met at her husband's behest, Craig took that experience and turned it into an instructional guide for others who wish to write the stories of their lives. Condensing her creation, she uses this abridged edition as an example of how to compile a family history. Each chapter is an event within her or your life, following her example should simplify what may seem an overwhelming task at first.

Creating a Book for Your Family in the 21st Century. Salt Lake City, UT: Agreka Books, 2001.

Put together by a family books publisher, this guide discusses how to collect the stories and photos about yourself and your family into a permanent family record. Agreka Books attempts to answer the questions about where to start the project, how far to take it and what to do with it when it is finished. The issues discussed include why it is important to write your family stories; your book idea; where to begin; starting to write; suggested questions; historical events during your life; photos and treasured documents; putting the book together - selling it to others, when to copyright, formatting, etc; Internet searching and webpage design; and many other issues relating to research, writing and designing a publication.

Daniel, Lois. *How to Write Your Own Life Story.* 4th ed. IL: Chicago Review Press, 1997.

Based on the fact that we live in a society where we no longer make a point of passing down oral traditions or usually keep written records of our personal stories, Daniel provides a guide to assist families in preserving their stories for future generations. Her book provides tools to assist in recalling and describing events, lessons, and relationships which played important roles in your life. She suggests topics to write about; foolproof tricks to jog the memory; fun, easy ways to gather the needed facts; guidelines for finding a time and place to write each day; methods for getting the stories down on paper without worrying about how they sound; advice on how to keep from getting bogged down; tips for getting published; help with library research; a chapter on how our grandparents were able to preserve their memories under more difficult circumstances; and other tips to guide in writing your life story.

Diehn, Gwen. *Making Books That Fly, Fold, Wrap, Hide, Pop Up, Twist, and Turn: Books for Kids to Make.* Asheville, NC: Lark Books, 1998.

Designed as a children's book, this book gives ideas for making simple publications of various types. It is a fun book for putting together simple stories, journals, or photo albums for someone who isn't seriously interested in a professional publication. Most of the examples in this book can be made from basic household materials.

Dixon, Janice T. *Family Focused: A Step-by-Step Guide to Writing Your Autobiography and Family History.* Wendover, NV: Mount Olympus Publishing, 1997.

Family Focused explains, with numerous examples, everything one needs to know about writing a diary, autobiography, or a family history. It takes one through the process of research, organizing materials, and incorporating what was found into an interesting narrative presentation. Practical tips on the preservation of photographs and documents, interviewing distant relatives, and finding one's way through church and civil records.

---. and Dora D. Flack. *Preserving Your Past: A Painless Guide to Writing Your Autobiography and Family History.* Garden City, NY: Doubleday & Company, Inc., 1977.

In *Preserving Your Past* Dixon and Flack explain everything one needs to know about writing a diary, autobiography, or a family history. They explain how to research and organize materials, and how to incorporate what was found into an interesting narrative presentation. Practical tips on the maintaining documents, interviewing distant relatives, and finding one's way through church and civil records are offered.

Drake, Paul E. *You Ought to Write All That Down: A Guide to Organizing and Writing Genealogical Narrative.* Rev. ed. Bowie, MD: Heritage Books, 2004.

Drake provides instructions in writing one's genealogical history, the first chapter features organizing the information, defines each element in writing a book, and the correct way for using Roman and Arabic numerals. Further information is given on how to correctly use charts, forms and illustrations; how to test for the soundness of evidence; and how to get more information out of the sources. Sample forms and a list of addresses for state archives are included. There is also a section on wills and estates. This guide is also useful in showing how to search for genealogical materials.

Eardley, Carla Jean. *Your Story: A Writing Guide for Genealogists.* Bowie, MD: Heritage Books, 1994.

Many people never write much beyond a letter, how then does one turn a genealogical project into a story to tell succeeding generations? Eardley illustrates how to turn genealogical research into narrative, filling the gap between genealogical "how-to" books and writing manuals. She combines the art of storytelling with the family history project demonstrating how to discover story potential in the collection of dates and statistics; prewriting and brainstorming to find the central themes in family data; arranging information in coherent form; maximizing interest through key elements - Characters, Conflict, Context and Cohesion; enriching the text with secondary materials; painting pictures which touch the senses and bring ancestors to life; avoiding style and grammar pitfalls; adapting family materials for other subsidiary projects; and producing the final product. This work enhances materials found in basic writing manuals and encourages the family historian to explore sources beyond those of the family data, realia such as clothing, jewelry and other artifacts. She includes a list of aids for putting together the readable family history.

Edel, Leon and Marc Pachter, ed. *Telling Lives: The Biographer's Art*. Washington, DC: New Republic Books, 1979.

This collection of writings discusses the processing and synthesizing data about a biographical subject. Oral history is discussed in the chapter by Theodore Rosengarten.

Elgin, Duane and Coleen LeDrew. *Living Legacies: How to Write, Illustrate, and Share Your Life Stories*. Berkeley, CA: Conari Press, 2001.

Living Legacies draws from personal life stories of friends and family of the authors in illustrating how to chronicle your life stories in an interesting fashion to be read by others. Elgin and LeDrew offer questions and other devices that can be used to draw out memories of experiences that can be used in writing life stories, as well as showing how to illustrate the stories with photos and memorabilia.

Evans, Fanny-Maude. *Changing Memories into Memoirs: A Guide to Writing Your Life Story*. New York: Barnes & Noble Books, 1984.

Everyone has a story to tell...that is the basis of Evans' instructions for *Changing Memories into Memoirs*. And, everyone will be an ancestor one day, remember wondering about yours? Evans shows the reader how to take memories and put them into writing for future generations. She gives tips on talking for a tape recorder, devising a beginning and creating a satisfying ending. Share your story with your family and your future.

Felt, Thomas Edward. *Researching, Writing and Publishing Local History.* 2nd ed. Nashville, TN: American Association for State and Local History, 1981.

> Felt's work takes the writer of history through the three stages critical for a final product, researching, writing, and publishing. Within each section he goes into detail on the various components of the stage of the project. In the chapter on research he covers such issues as beginning questions and planning; taking notes and copying documents; organizing notes; libraries and librarians; interviews and oral history; pictures and picture interpreting; various forms of records and other items of research. In writing he deals with quotations; documentation; footnotes; sources; writing and rewriting; illustrations, editing, and translating among other writing processes. In the final chapter on publishing, Felt discusses design; typeface; paper; illustrations; periodicals and books; choosing a printer; composition; promoting and marketing and other issues concerned with the facets of publication.

Files, Meg. *Write From Life: Turning Your Personal Experiences into Compelling Stories.* Cincinnati, OH: Writer's Digest Books, 2002.

> Your life is a story; you just have to find the way to tell it that makes your family want to read it. Meg Files draws upon her own experience as a writer to help you transform your personal experiences into interesting prose. She suggests ways for tapping into difficult and guarded parts of your life; helps to channel the fear of writing into motivated energy; discusses the best literary form to use; assists in the skill of using realistic and effective dialogue; provides suggestions for telling your story with authority; assists with effective beginnings, middles and ends; discusses the sharing of your work with others and using their reactions; and provides suggestions for editing the final copy. While this book deals a lot with turning real life experiences into fiction, it will also assist the writer of family history in developing skills for turning those experiences into text.

Gouldrup, Lawrence P. *Writing the Family Narrative.* Salt Lake City, UT: Ancestry, 1993.

> Gouldrup provides a clear explanation on the writing of a family history. He shows how to join disjointed facts into a concise narrative that entertains as well as informs. Using examples that both the novice and a professional can understand, he explains how to avoid wordiness and how to focus the narrative. In addition to the guide, there is a *Writing the*

Family Narrative Workbook which takes one step-by-step through the writing process, provides room for collecting data, assists in organizing records and in trying out writing techniques, as well as providing examples of writing techniques from some famous well-known authors. These two books can be purchased separately or as a set.

Greene, Bob and D. G. Fulford. *To Our Children's Children: Preserving Family Histories for Generations to Come.* New York: Doubleday, 1993.

This is a guidebook of questions that makes recording a personal history as easy as writing a letter. After a brief introduction the rest of the book consists of chapters of engaging questions designed to open the doors of memory.

Haga, Enoch. *How to...Prepare Your Genealogy for Publication on Your Home Computer.* Livermore, CA: E. Haga, 2001.

As Mr. Haga notes in his preface, and as we have all see in the last ten to fifteen years, technology is advancing at a pace most of us find difficult to keep up with. The computer gurus all preach, "put it on the computer," but most of us cannot afford the constant upgrades that advice entails. As Haga says, it makes sense to publish your genealogy in book form. What he is providing in this book, is how to use your computer effectively to take your genealogical information, organize it, and put it in a format which you can use to publish your genealogy. He highlights features of word processing which are especially helpful in composing your work, discusses doing the genealogical research and how to organize it, provides sample chapters and charts to be included, tables of contents, gathering and including more data, handling problems that come up, printing and proofreading, and final printing and binding. Throughout the work, he gives samples of what he is discussing in each step of putting the book together. Haga has done his own family genealogy, so is able to provide sound advice on computer genealogical composition.

Hale, Duane K. *Researching and Writing Tribal Histories.* Grand Rapids, MI: Michigan Indian Press, Grand Rapids Inter-Tribal Council, 1991.

Encompassing tribes in both the United States and Canada, this guide illustrates the process necessary for doing genealogical research among the Indian tribes. Information covered includes: library resources for researching Native Americans, a list of Indian periodicals, a bibliography of related genealogical materials, methodology for recording oral histories, and an outline of writing techniques.

Hartley, William G. *Preparing a Personal History.* Salt Lake City: Primer Publications, 1976.

> Hartley offers advice on the reasons for doing a personal history, types of history that can be created, how to file the information gathered, where and how to search for information, how to create a balanced history, what finishing touches you can add to make a difference in the final product and how to update a finished product. He also lists "memory triggers" for those who claim they have nothing to write about.

Hatcher, Patricia L. *Producing a Quality Family History.* Salt Lake City, UT: Ancestry, 1996.

> Hatcher, a professional genealogist, has put together a work on the second most important part of doing genealogy, the end result. Showing how to preserve the record, *Producing a Quality Family History* is a guide to creating and publishing your own family history. She examines the stages of production from organizing the work, writing the narrative, incorporating the photographs and other illustrations to less obvious aspects such as documenting your research, creating a pleasing visual design, and placing your ancestors in context.

--- and John W. Wiley. *Indexing Family Histories: Simple Steps for a Quality Product.* Arlington, VA: National Genealogical Society Special Publications, 1994.

> The index, the "door" as Hatcher and Wiley call it, and good reference librarians swear by it, is the critical spot that most researchers aim for when doing research of any type, and most particularly genealogical research. Hatcher and Wiley provide simple steps to adding a good index to your genealogical history. They describe the basic indexing principles and recommend standards for special consideration in family indexing. Items discussed include arrangement, software, style, content, what to leave out, format, producing drafts, cross-references, usability, and other aspects of producing a usable index.

Hauser, Susan C. *You Can Write a Memoir.* Cincinnati, OH: Reader's Digest Books, 2001.

> Susan Hauser uses samples of her own writing to explain how to write a personal history. She shows how to use details to add color to your story, how to use sensory images to express feelings and beliefs, how to uncover the values and meanings expressed in your

stories, how to find perspective in framing your thoughts and feelings at different stages of life, and how to trust the images and moments as they come to you. She also discusses writing from various aspects of life such as childhood memories, mementos, adolescence and other life changes, adult life and discovering your values. She explains doing research and interviewing as well as the revision and editing of your writing, and publishing your memoir.

Holt, Robert Lawrence. *How to Publish, Promote, and Sell Your Own Book.* New York: St. Martin's Press, 1985.

When we're writing our family's history, we are frequently writing for a limited audience. Because of this our books may not appeal to a commercial publishing house. Holt offers advice in editing, production and marketing basics, including how to work with a printer, creating an attractive cover, pricing and other functions of book production. He also provides information on how to market your book to a major publishing house, discussing how to write a query letter, finding an agent, getting along with an editor, generating reviews and publicity, keeping checklists and other ideas that for most people are common sense solutions.

Johnson, Pauline. *Creative Bookbinding.* 1963. New York: Dover Publications, 1990.

We usually think of hand bound books as great works of art, totally unlike those mass produced by machines. Johnson has compiled and illustrated this guide to hand bookbinding which details the techniques needed to create your own work of art. Following a brief history of the printing and bookbinding craft, Johnson provides an in-depth discussion of book design; the proportion and size of books, the parts of a book, materials, tools, and the equipment needed for book construction. Procedures are clearly defined and illustrated and detail everything from simple folders to more complex, sewn books with cloth and leather bindings. She also includes a chapter on the preservation and repair of irreplaceable and valuable volumes.

Kanin, Ruth. *Write the Story of Your Life.* New York: Hawthorn/Dutton, 1981.

Kanin suggests specific writing exercises to begin the writing process, she says that writing the story of one's life can lead to feeling more positive about one and offer psychological insights. She suggests that using old letters, photos, memoirs documents and diaries are helpful when looking for something to write about.

They stimulate memory and provide something solid to say or discuss. She compares the autobiographical process to self-examination and self-understanding, a form of self-therapy.

Kempthorne, Charley. *For All Time: A Complete Guide to Writing Your Family History*. Portsmouth, NH: Boynton/Cook Publishers, 1996.

Once the interviews are done, and the information gathered, what do you do with it? Kempthorne offers a practical and accessible guide for putting together as much or as little of your information as you wish. He discusses the types of family histories that may be written using various types of documentation, for example, family letters, diaries, and photographs may be utilized to put together short essays, biographies or autobiographies. Family newsletters are also discussed. He explains how to use dialogue and physical detail to make a scene come alive, how to mix summary and anecdotes, and how to use other tools and tricks utilized by professional writers and historians. He also provides a chapter on printing and publishing your family history. Practical writing exercises will provide the future author with a basis for beginning an actual project.

Klein, Reinhard. *Family History Logbook: A Timeline Journal from 1900 - 2000: With Year-by-Year Historical Milestones to Record Your Family's Most Important Experiences*. Cincinnati, OH: Betterway Books, 1996.

Klein has created a readymade journal in which to record family memories. Spanning the years from 1900 to 2000, he provides a two page spread for each year and divides this space into three sections: historical context, family milestones, and a catalog of sources. The historical section has a list of national events and popular culture with such topics as science, government fashion and religion. These events can be used to spark memories for the family milestone section. The catalog of sources section can be used to write down where you obtained information for the milestone section so that you can follow it up later if necessary.

Kozachek, Thomas. *Guidelines for Authors of Compiled Genealogies*. Boston: Newbury Street Press, 1998.

This is a short guide for setting up genealogical research in a publishable format. In assisting researchers in preparing their research for publication, Kozachek provides discussions on formatting, models for organizing genealogical data, and suggestions for manuscript preparation.

Kyvig, David and Myron A. Marty. *Your Family History: A Handbook for Research and Writing.* Arlington Heights, IL: Harlan Davidson, Inc., 1978.

> Every family has a pattern of their own customs and traditions, Kyvig and Marty assist the writer in putting these family patterns down in print for their children and heirs. This guide aids the writer in defining how far back in the past to take the story, how to do the research, what kind of questions to ask and try to get answered, what kind of dangers they might encounter in the gathering process and how much information is enough. Forms for data collecting and organizing the family structure are given at the end.

Larson, Thomas. *The Memoir and the Memoirist: Reading & Writing Personal Narrative.* Athens, OH: Swallow Press, Ohio University Press, 2007.

> Larson provides a guide for the writer of autobiography and memoirs. He discusses the nuances of memory, finding and telling the truth, and disclosing one's deepest self. Using examples of other memoirists, he explores the craft of personal narrative.

Ledoux, Denis. *Turning Memories into Memoirs: A Handbook for Writing Lifestories.* 3rd ed. Lisbon Falls, ME: Soleil Press, 2006.

> Ledoux has taken his writers workshops and turned them into a guide for aspiring writers. This guide will lead the writer step-by-step through writing personal or family history; increase the ability to remember details of stories; provide proven story writing techniques and strategies for success; and will offer skills to gain access to one's inner thoughts. The text is highlighted by exercises to practice with and quotations from other famous and not so famous writers.

McDonnell, Jane Taylor. *Living to Tell the Tale: A Guide to Writing Memoir.* New York: Penguin Books, Inc., 1998.

> Drawing on her own experience as a writer and teacher, Taylor provides techniques and advice on helping a prospective writer discover his or her inner voice, recognize the inner censor, and silence that censor to begin a narrative and develop it with such aids as photographs and documents. She illustrates the ways in which writers can re-create past experiences through memories and imaginatively reshape those memories into the story to be told.

Miller, Patti. *Writing Your Life: A Journey of Discovery: Workshops and Discovery*. Rev. Crows Nest, NSW, Australia: Allen & Unwin, 2001.

> Writing about your life is something anyone can do; you just have to choose what you want to write about. It is just sometimes difficult to figure out how to put it down on paper. Miller helps make the journey to discovering how to put experiences on paper. She makes the writing experience like a journey, showing techniques for getting started, handling point of view, making the parts hang together, and how to bring events to life. She also explores how to deal with selective memory, emotional pain and growth, objections from other family members, how to communicate your philosophic and spiritual truths without cliché and the challenges of deciding what to include.

Mills, Elizabeth S. *Evidence! Citation and Analysis for the Family Historian*. Baltimore: Genealogical Publishing Co., 1997.

> Like most style manuals, *Evidence!* provides the standard for the correct citation style for the family historian. Mills' book also discusses the analysis of the research materials the family researcher has found.

Moffat, Mary Jane. *The Times of Our Lives: A Guide to Writing Autobiography and Memoirs*. 3rd ed. Santa Barbara, CA: John Daniel and Company, 1996.

> Practical advice is given on the special craft of writing about oneself. Based on the premise that we all have a story to tell, Moffat guides the reader through using memories and reflection to create an autobiography. Numerous questions are included to help stimulate memories.

Mungo, Raymond. *Your Autobiography: More Than 300 Questions to Help You Write Your Personal Story*. New York: Macmillan, 1994.

> The 300 questions in Mungo's assist in the compilation of an autobiography or a guideline for creating a family history. These questions cover birth, childhood, school years, college, love, children, friends, work and retirement. Writing tips are also included to assist in looking back on life to create a lasting legacy.

Neubauer, Joan R. *From Memories to Manuscript: The Five-Step Method to Writing Your Life Story.* Salt Lake City, UT: Ancestry, 1994.

> This handbook was designed to help write a quality autobiography that others will want to read. Comprised of five sections, it leads the writer step-by-step through the writing process. Each of the five steps is described in detail. Part one lists possible questions to assist in recreating memories, part two discusses organization, part three talks about the actual writing, part four takes one through the editing process, and part five discusses printing and publishing.

Pengra, Nancy. *Family Histories: An Easy, Step-by-Step Guide to Capturing Your Family's Precious Memories Now, Before They're Lost.* St. Paul, MN: Family Histories, 1995.

> Nancy Pengra developed this book after the death of her grandfather brought the realization that many of her family's stories had been lost with his death. Written with genealogists in mind, she presents an easy to follow guide for getting stories down on paper. She includes hundreds of ideas for jogging memories and triggering stories, ways to add variety to stories, tips for organizing the stories and memorabilia including techniques for writing and publishing, over forty pages of 'trigger' questions and samples of what others have done, a list of historical dates since 1900 on what has been done or invented, and creative ways of sharing the stories.

Polk, Timothy W. *How to Outlive Your Lifetime: Preserving a Place in Your Family's Hearts and History.* Sunnyvale, CA: Family Life International, 1994.

> *How to Outlive Your Lifetime* offers a great variety of ideas on how to preserve your family history. These ideas can be easily translated into preserving any sort of history. From writing projects to organizing photos, there are many suggestions for preserving history and memories. This book is very simple, plainly written and easy to follow. It is divided into sections that can be used together or independently.

Polking, Kirk. *Writing Family Histories and Memoirs.* Cincinnati, OH: Betterway Books, 1995.

> Polking's book is both a research guide and a manual on how to turn your research into a book. In this book he discusses writing styles, how to use memories, how to interview family members, how to find and organize family papers and materials, how to find

records, how to make your writing clear and vivid, and how to choose your publishing options. He includes examples of family writings by others, covers legal issues, and suggests a questionnaire to use to get information from relatives you must contact by mail.

Powell, Kimberly and William G. Hartley. *The Everything Family Tree Book: Research and Preserve Your Family History.* Holbrook, MA: Adams Media Corporation, 2006.

Chapter seven of Powell and Hartley's book describes the process of writing a family biography. Throughout the rest of the book are also scattered suggestions for putting together writing projects. Chapter eight continues the process with a discussion of the publication of your history once it is written.

Poynter, Dan. *Dan Poyntner's Self-Publishing Manual: How to Write, Print, and Sell Your Own Book.* 16th ed. Santa Barbara, CA: Para Publishing, 2007.

Poyntner's guide is a manual designed to show how to break into print and become a published author. As well as providing a step-by-step system for producing a marketable book, he offers tips on starting your own publishing company, printing your book, advertising and promoting your book, determining the worth of your work, and determining the audience. He also discusses publishing technology, electronic books, on-line services, Fax-on-demand and computers. Poyntner has designed this manual to allow the self-publisher all available information on avoiding the middleman.

Roorbach, Bill and Kristen Keckler. *Writing Life Stories: How to Make Memories into Memoirs, Ideas into Essays, and Life into Literature.* 2nd ed. Cincinnati, OH: Writer's Digest Books, 2008.

Turning his writing workshops into a guide book, Roorbach shows the writer how to turn favorite life stories into essays and book-length memoirs with passion and clarity. He guides the writer in bringing back hazy memories from the distant past, interrogating the memory, seeing the people in your life as characters for a story, and other writing techniques for completing your autobiography.

Ross, Tom and Marilyn Heimberg Ross. *The Complete Guide to Self-Publishing.* 4th ed. Cincinnati, OH: Writer's Digest Books, 2002.

The Ross's, professional writing consultants, provide information on desktop writing and publishing systems, databases, printers, and word processing programs; guidance to business matters and production and design basics; marketing contacts; clip art sources; samples of letters, ads, catalog sheets, cover designs, invoices, copyright applications and other forms; and how to get free publicity, advertising, and other innovative ideas. Their book is designed to assist the writer in every stage of the writing process.

Rothman, Seymour. *Your Memoirs: Collecting Them for Fun and Posterity.* Jefferson, NC: McFarland & Company, Inc., Publishers, 1987.

Rothman suggests that memories are best told simply as you would tell them yourself, he recommends not trying to be a professional writer, you are writing for your family, not for strangers. Discussions include where memories come from, what memoirs are, how to unlock your memory, how to put these memories down on paper, deciding who you are and what you want to say, fitting it all together, and wrapping it up. He also offers excerpts of a memoir to provide an example.

Schwarz, Ted. *The Complete Guide to Writing Biographies.* Cincinnati, OH: Writer's Digest Books, 1990.

When writing oral history or genealogical history, you are in essence writing a biography. Schwarz has put together a book of guidelines for doing just that. He discusses why a biography should be written - it's one of the most popular books sold; selecting a subject and planning how to get the information; contacting the people that need to be interviewed and getting them to say yes; researching the subject; library resources that should be used; how to conduct interviews; how much of the information retrieved should be used - those dirty secrets; doing the actual writing and finding a market.

Smith, Nancy. *Write Your Life Story: A Guide to Writing Your Autobiography and Tips on How to Get Published.* Secaucus, NJ: Carol Publishing Group, 1995.

Everyone has a story, you, your family, friends; *Write Your Life Story* is a guide to assist in creating this story either for your own satisfaction, posterity, or publication. Smith offers tips on planning and structuring the story; presenting characters, places and dialogue; how to use fiction techniques such as emotion, conflict or tension; mastering the basics of writing; and how to write for newspapers or magazines. She includes 'memory joggers,' ideas for beginnings and endings, information on finding a market, writing about your whole family, and practical issues such as revision, grammar, titles, copyright and more. She also provides examples and a list of reference books and other useful publications and addresses.

Spence, Linda. *Legacy: A Step-By-Step Guide to Writing Personal History.* Athens, Ohio: University of Ohio Press, 1997.

Through a list of thought-provoking questions, Spence lays the groundwork for creating a personal history. She helps guide the novice historian in cradle to grave interviews to create a family history and memory. Excerpts are given to illustrate what can be done with the information collected.

Stephenson, Lynda Rutledge. *The Complete Idiot's Guide to Writing Your Family History.* Indianapolis, IN: Alpha Books, 2000.

Though primarily a guide to writing your family history, Lynda Stephenson also helps the reader to navigate the basics of genealogy. Genealogy is the beginning of putting together a family history, so having the basics of searching combined with writing the final product puts two valuable resources in one. For writing up your results, Stephenson shows how to determine the difference between family facts and family fictions, how to compile a genealogy chart, how to use journals to jog the memories of both yourself and relatives, how to ask the right questions, how to use the library efficiently, how to determine which form of writing - narrative, memoir, etc. is right for your story, how to use video, journaling and scrapbooking, and finding the missing details.

Stillman, Peter R. *Families Writing.* 2nd ed. Portland, ME: Calendar Islands, 1998.

From his deep belief that families should be recording their recollections, whims, stories of love, pain and laughter, troubling, sad, or silly things that make your family's heritage rich - Stillman details the how and why of recording the words that are the real family treasures. He discusses incorporating letters, poems, journals, anecdotes, family lore, tall tales and incidental jottings of the family and describes various ways of writing that anyone should be able to do. He also includes games and activities for the whole family to do that can assist in stimulating family memories.

Teeters, Peggy and Roseann S. Biederman. *You Can Get Published.* Cincinnati, OH: Writer's Digest Books, 1998.

> Combining clear, informative writing guidelines with seasoned advice, Ms. Teeters gives the would-be writer encouragement to focus on writing creatively. Tips include finding unique story ideas; writing fillers, anecdotes, and light verse; creating an effective writing style; how to capitalize on personal experiences; keys to successful publishing; elements of dialogue, plot and characterization; and other guidelines.

Thomas, Frank P. *How to Write the Story of Your Life.* Cincinnati, OH: Writer's Digest Books, 1989.

> Thomas's book is a compilation of years of teaching people to write, in it he includes the "5 R's of Successful Memoir Writing: Research, Remembering, 'Riting', Reading, and Reproduction; Memory Sparkers: hundreds of ideas to jog your memory and get you started; Organizational Techniques: how to develop your own writing plan and work with photos and documents; Writing Pointers: more than 50 tips for sharpening your writing skills; and Reading References: a writing bibliography and a list of 100 recommended autobiographies."

Turner, Geneva. *How to Plan a Spectacular Family Reunion: Discovering Relationships: From Picnics and Talent Shows to Oral Histories and Family Themes, Genealogy and Family Inve$tment$.* Columbus, GA: Family Projects Publishers/TACF, 1993.

> This manual provides a personal one-stop, resource for creative, fun, easy, and low cost activities that will encourage every family member to participate. Information is provided on obtaining oral and written histories; ideas for a family newsletter; and other ideas; along with easy to follow examples and explanations. Chapter 3 focuses on videotaping and photos, and chapters 8 to 10 and 13 discuss the processes for gathering information and conducting and writing up oral interviews. Included in the appendix are forms for family inventories, personal history, and ancestor charts.

Vanessa-Ann. *Making Scrapbooks: Complete Guide to Preserving Your Treasured Memories.* New York: Sterling Publishing Co., Inc. 1998.

> Vanessa-Ann takes the traditional scrapbook describes ways in which your imagination can create a personable, individual and creative publication to make your memories into a treasure for the

future. Included is a brief chapter on researching your family history and finding historical records, choosing archivally safe materials, and the preservation of photographs.

Walker, Glen. *Create Your Own Life's Story: The Simple Way to Record Your Personal History.* San Leandro, CA: Bristol Publishing Enterprises, Inc., 1992.

This workbook provides questions from life to guide you in writing your own story. A time line is also included at the end of the book to jog your memory of important events that happened during your lifetime.

Wiebe, Katie F. *Good Times With Old Times: How to Write Your Memoirs.* Scottdales, PA: Herald Press, 1979.

Wiebe intends her book for the person who may never have written anything but a letter to family or friends. She discusses the reasons for starting a writing project or writing one's memoirs, examines some of the ways to make the writing more effective, explores areas which might cause problems for amateurs, and considers ways for getting the material into a printed format. Each chapter includes a short piece of the author's own life story or that of one of her family members to illustrate what she is discussing.

Wilson, Richard S. *Publishing Your Family History on the Internet.* La Habra CA: Compuology, 1999.

Wilson answers the questions on how to set up your own website and create your family history online. In addition to setting up your website, he shows how to get Web space for free and advertise your site. Publishing your family history online allows others to find you and add to the information you have already discovered. Several different Web programs are discussed in this book listed in alphabetical order, not order of preference. A glossary is provided to help with unfamiliar terminology.

Author's collection: Book signing

Preservation

Bachman, Konstanze, ed. *Conservation Concerns: A Guide for Collectors and Curators.* Washington, DC: Smithsonian Institution Press, 1992.

This collection of articles on the care and preservation of items which find their way into the collections of private collectors and small museums or historical societies was specifically designed for them. Sometimes the small collector is intimidated by seeking help from a larger entity; this book seeks to reassure the smaller collector that their problems are the same, just on a smaller scale. The articles in this book describe how to take care of and preserve items and include such topics as the control of temperature and humidity; construction materials for storage and exhibition; paper works; signs of the needs for conservation; storage and care of photographs, sound recordings, paintings, fabrics, and other materials; the conservation of furniture and upholstery; and the care of folk art. Also included is a reading list for those who wish more detailed information on any of these topics.

Ball, Kimberly, ed. *The Complete Guide to Creating Heritage Scrapbooks.* Denver, CO: Memory Makers Books, 2002.

One of the Memory Makers series of scrapbooking guides, this workbook gives numerous tips in the construction of a genealogical scrapbook. Utilizing the hundreds of examples of scrapbook pages, you can discover how to use your photos, memorabilia and stories to showcase your heritage. The various chapters in this book highlight ways to display various aspects of life such as military experiences, celebrations, and other unique events; special tips for creating your family tree; hints for researching and obtaining photos and family documentation from other family members; and basic step by step scrapbooking directions. Also included is a 125 year time line with fascinating historical facts.

—, ed. *Memory Makers Scrapbook Journaling Made Simple: Tips for Telling Stories Behind Your Photos.* Denver, CO: Memory Makers Books, 2002.

You bring home the envelope of photos and add them to the box you already have overflowing, or you print your favorites from your digital memory card, and find them in a box a few years later. Do you remember the story that was the reason for taking the picture? Maybe, maybe not. Memory Makers has put together this book of tips for keeping these stories and photos together to make memories that last beyond those few minutes which generated the photo. Included are tips on what to say and how to say it; lists of words and descriptions to add life to your text; clues to overcome the fear of writing and writer's block; interviewing techniques; creative journaling ideas; practical methods for adding journal items to crowded pages; and more.

Best, Laura. *Scrapbooking Your Family History.* New York: Sterling Publishing Co., Inc. 2005.

One of the most popular activities of the late 1990s and early 2000s has been scrapbooking and the creation of memory albums. Laura Best, and expert genealogist and scrapbooker provides advice in creating attractive, yet archivally sound family memories. Using actual family history, photos and memorabilia, she walks the family historian through the supplies necessary and the steps in putting together an album. Each page has tips in the best materials to use and how to use them, as well as tips in gathering the memories from your family and friends.

Braun, Bev Kirschner. *Crafting Your Own Heritage Album: For Genealogists, Scrapbookers, and Family Historians.* Cincinnati, OH: Betterway Books, 2000.

Heritage albums, we used to call the scrapbooks! Computers, easily obtained archival supplies, and a rising interest in preserving our pasts, have all made it easier for the average person to put together a fairly professional looking album. Braun shows how to put together an album to pass on to your descendants for the enjoyment of future generations. She discusses using archivally safe materials to preserve photos and documents; mounting and protecting three-dimensional mementos; organizing and restoring old photographs, incorporating journal entries; using genealogy, family lore and traditions to enhance a family portrait; and how to involve the whole family in this process.

———. *New Ideas for Crafting Heritage Albums: The Latest Tips and Techniques for Preserving Your Family's Memories.* Cincinnati, OH: Betterway Books, 2001.

Picking up where *Crafting Your Own Heritage Album* left off, Braun highlights many new archival products which have been developed and new trends in scrapbooking. She also provides new ideas for preserving and presenting family heirlooms and relics, including video tapes and cassettes, computer software, using scanners, family recipes, and turning scrapbooking into a family activity.

Davis, Nancy. *Handle with Care: Preserving Your Heirlooms.* Rochester, NY: Rochester Museum and Science Center, 1991.

Many people have family treasures which they need to preserve for their children. Many things can be cared for simply, others take more work. Davis's book shows how to do simple and inexpensive preservation for the family archivist. She reviews the primary hazards and remedies of the most damaging threats to old collections with just enough scientific background to answer the "whys" of preservation and suggestions for where to find professional conservators or archival supplies. She also suggests when a professional conservator should be consulted. Advice is given for materials such as family papers, photographs, textiles, furniture, silver, glass and ceramics, and other objects.

Douglas, Althea. *Help! I've Inherited an Attic Full of History, Vol. 1 & 2.* Rev. Toronto, ONT: Ontario Genealogical Society, 2003.

We all, at some time in our lives, inherit heirlooms, antiques and junk from our relatives. Among these valuable family items are papers, photos, furniture, textiles and all sorts of things we never imagined we would have to deal with. Douglas discusses how to archive and assess these items and make decisions on their future - discard or save? Volume one is divided into two parts, the first deals with sorting and making inventory lists. Douglas discusses evaluation and deciding what should be kept and what should be discarded, including deciding who might want what you have and how to locate them. Part two provides information on dating artifacts, photographs, new technologies and postal items. It also, includes a glossary which provides definitions of terms used in the various professions which might be encountered in dealing with your artifacts. A bibliography of further sources for assistance is also provided. Volume two deals more with personal artifacts you find in the home than volume one did, letters, photos, diaries, etc. Douglas discusses basic care techniques and makes recommendations on when the home conservator should seek professional assistance. Discussion includes the use of safety materials such as protective gloves and dust masks; supplies and suppliers; organic materials and acids; newspapers, dangerous copies, and thermal paper copies; other organic materials such as natural fibers, vellum, parchment, leathers, wood, wicker, etc.; non-organic materials such as stones, glass, ceramics, and metal; plastics; polyesters; and many other materials which might be found around the house.

Earnest, Russell D., Corinne P. Earnest and Beverly Repass Hoch. *Grandma's Attic: Making Heirlooms Part of Your Family History.* Albuquerque, NM: Russell D. Earnest Associates, 1991.

> Every family has a collection of family treasures, memorabilia passed from generation to generation, which frequently loses its identity except for the fact that it was handed down with the instruction, "this belonged to your great-grandmother." As each generation collects its special memories to add to the previous generations, there needs to be someone to record the meaning of the mementos. While there might be enough to create a small family museum, it does no good if the treasure has no definitive history attached. Sometimes it is possible to trace collectibles and determine the history of the item itself, thus possibly figuring out what it meant to its owner. Earnest's book gives tips for hunting the provenance of heirlooms and suggestions for the care and providing records of the items you intend to leave for future generations. Heirlooms are also useful when trying to elicit family memories when putting together a family or oral history.

Furgeson, Lael Combe and Stephanie F. Taylor. *Family Scrapbooking: Fun Projects to Do Together.* New York: Sterling Publishing Co., Inc., 2000.

> Scrapbooking has become a major industry and pastime in the last few years. Furgeson and Taylor add their tips on taking, organizing and cropping photographs; using archival papers and supplies; everyday supplies; and ideas for design elements to produce creative, attractive scrapbooks. Other tips take the scrapbooker beyond store-bought supplies and expand the imagination to almost anything you can think of for use with a scrapbook. Tips on removing photos and memorabilia from unsuitable mountings are also included.

Gerbrandt, Michele. *Michele Gerbrandt's Scrapbook Basics: The Complete Guide to Preserving Your Memories.* Denver, CO: Memory Makers Books, 2002.

> Scrapbooking, everyone's doing it, but not everyone does it right! If you wish your precious photos and memories to last a lifetime, you need to learn to use the proper types of materials. Gerbrandt assists the scrapbooker in finding and using "safe" scrapbook products. In addition, she explains scrapbooking terms, discusses the organization of photos and memorabilia, tells what is needed to get started, talks about the page and album making process, how to preserve and display memorabilia, and how to tell the stories behind the photos.

Hart, Cynthia, Lina Morielli and Rynn Williams. *Scrapbook Workshop: A Complete Guide to Preserving Memories in Archival, Heirloom-Quality Books*. New York: Workman Publishing, 1998.

Using more than 30 projects as illustrations, Hart demonstrates both beginning and advanced scrapbooking techniques. This printed workshop covers tools, techniques, tips, and archival guidelines, along with directions for many specific memory book pages and projects. She illustrates how to create book layouts and special pages, the art and craft of collage making, suggests themed designs, patterns and clip art useful for doing memory albums.

Lavédrine, Bertrand, Jean-Paul Gandolfo, and Sibylle Monod. *A Guide to the Preventive Conservation of Photograph Collections*. Los Angeles, CA: The Getty Conservation Institute, 2003.

This book, originally published in France, has been translated and covers recent research in the conservation of the photographic heritage. Recent developments have led to a new understanding of both the fragility of photographs and the means to preserve them. This is intended as a practical handbook for conservators, curators, collection managers, and others interested in the conservation of photographs. Topics covered in this work include: The vulnerability of photographs, standards, protection, exhibition, dissemination and access, and technical and practical information. Both black and white and color photographic issues are addressed.

Levenstein, Mary K. And Cordelia F. Biddle. *Caring for Your Cherished Possessions: The Experts' Guide to Cleaning, Preserving, and Protecting Your China, Silver, Furniture, Clothing, Paintings, and More*. New York: Crown Publishers, Inc., 1989.

We all have those special treasures we wish to keep for our children and future generations of family, but don't really know how to keep them from discoloring, how to store them safely, or we live in areas with high humidity and lots of heat. Levenstein and Biddle share secrets and tips for keeping that keepsake in good condition. Discussing linens, clothing, clothing accessories, handbags, shoes, gloves, jewelry, furs, quilts, rugs, carpets, furniture and wooden objects, paintings/artworks on canvas and paper, books, photographs, metals, ceramics, glass, and other materials, the authors cover storage, preservation and restoration. Each material discussed in a short chapter and the book concludes with a section on sources and services which lists various associations affiliated with different material types, museums, product sources, conservation supply companies and a bibliography of other books with more detailed assistance.

Ling, Evelyn R. *Archives in the Church or Synagogue Library*. 2nd ed. Bryn Mawr, PA: Church and Synagogue Library Association, 1996.

Church and synagogue records are often a valuable resource for family history researchers. In her short work on religious archives, Ling discusses the precedent for congregational archives, getting started in building a congregational archive, selecting materials, processing materials, preserving and storing materials, and using the archives.

Long, Jane S., Richard W. Long and Inge-Lise Eckmann, et. al. *Caring For Your Family Treasures: Heritage Preservation*. New York: Harry N. Abrams, 2000.

The Longs have prepared a concise guide for caring for objects of value, be it sentimental or monetary. They discuss items from photograph albums and home movie collections to holiday ornaments and heirloom quilts. Working with a team of experts in different materials, they provide practical advice and easy-to-use guidelines on maintaining various types of materials without ruining their value. They discuss care and maintenance for daily use as well as preservation of fragile objects and how to store items safely. Archival preservation materials are discussed as well as where to obtain them.

Miller, Ilene Chandler. *Preserving Family Keepsakes*. Yorba Linda, CA: Shumway Family History Services, 1995.

Family mementos and treasures are a big part of compiling a family history. If you intend to pass these on to future generations, however, they need to be taken care of properly. Miller provides a working guide to the preservation of all sorts of family keepsakes including photographs, documents, fabrics and other items of value. In individual chapters on the different types of keepsakes, she discusses what is important in the care of each type of medium. She talks of what to stay away from and what types of materials should be used to get the optimum life from your treasures. Her non-technical approach makes this a resource that can be used by anyone, and also includes information on how to correct mistakes that may have been made in the past storage of your treasured items.

Nerius, Maria G. and Bill Gardner. *Creating Your Family Heritage Scrapbook: From Ancestors to Grandchildren, Your Complete Resource and Idea Book for Creating a Treasured Heirloom.* Roseville, CA: Prima Communications, Inc., 2001.

Step-by-step instructions are given for researching, designing and creating a scrapbook which preserves your family's history and memories. Nerius and Gardner illustrate simple methods for tracing the family lineage; technical tips and shortcuts for building a personal scrapbook, how to utilize and care for family photographs; tips on journaling; and many more helpful hints and resource suggestions. Memory quilts, crafts and family reunions are also discussed.

Rosenbluth, Vera and Susan McDiarmid. *Classic Scrapbooking: The Art and Craft of Creating a Book of Memories.* Pt. Roberts, WA: Hartley & Marks Publishers, Inc., 1998.

Going in and out of style over the generations, scrapbooking is again a popular pastime. Scrapbooking when done properly is an exciting way for most people to keep memories alive and preserve keepsakes. *Classic Scrapbooking* looks at the different types of scrapbooks people keep and why they keep them. Rosenbluth and McDiarmid have interviewed scrapbookers to come up with techniques for taking memorabilia out of shoeboxes and organizing it into a book of memories. The authors provide simple to complicated techniques for designing the perfect scrapbook and also explore how to make book covers, working with the computer, preserving and restoring old scrapbooks, papermaking and flower pressing, the basics of attractive page design, using archival materials, handbinding techniques, scrapboxes, and photography.

Sagraves, Barbara. *A Preservation Guide: Saving the Past and the Present for the Future.* Salt Lake City, UT: Ancestry, 1995.

Sagraves discusses the preservation guidelines for the various types of materials that the average person collects. Specifically in this short guide she talks about paper - letters, newspaper clippings, legal documents, photocopies, and computer printouts; books - printed and manuscript; photographs - color, black and white, negatives, slides, and instant prints; films - Super 8, 16mm, and videotapes; sound recordings - phonograph records, audiotapes and cassettes; computer disks and textiles. Each of these mediums has a chapter dedicated to its care and storage. She also includes a chapter on choosing a conservator for professional assistance and her bibliography lists suppliers of archival materials.

Smith, Demaris C. *Preserving Your Paper Collectibles.* White Hall, VA: Betterway Publications, Inc., 1989.

    Paper collectibles are anything from valuable historical documents to such items as theater tickets, or your children's school papers. Their value varies depending on who is collecting them and why. Popular collectibles often include stamps and first day covers; books and manuscripts; newspapers, comic books, and magazines; sheet music; posters, maps, and photographs; theater playbills and programs; playing cards; and sports cards, particularly baseball. Smith has provided a comprehensive guide to discovering the value of your collection and how to preserve them. She explains what makes the items collectible and identifies those categories that are most likely to appreciate in value. She also discusses the methods used to preserve books and other paper items for the future. The main thrust of this work, however, is to illustrate steps the average person can take to protect the paper items in the home. She talks about the proper handling techniques, and creating the most acid-free environment possible. She describes the materials and supplies necessary for home preservation.

Stephani, Julie. *More Than Memories: The Complete Guide for Preserving Your Family History.* Iola, WI: Krause Publications, 1998.

    More Than Memories instructs on how to organize and protect photos and negatives, how to display photos and memorabilia in unique ways, and how to write captions to tell the story of the photo's history. Called scrapbooking, the process of putting photos in albums is enhanced by adding the stories that tell the history and background of the photo, thereby preserving the memory of the time and family history for future generations. Chapter one discusses the actual process of how to scrapbook correctly and how to find and use the correct supplies. The rest of the chapters discuss the various important events in a person's life that might be chronicled by scrapbooking.

---. *More Than Memories II: Beyond the Basics: Creative Techniques for Preserving Your Family History.* Iola, WI: Krause Publications, 1999.

    Part two of the *More Than Memories* series continues the instruction on the proper way of preserving photographs. It discusses keeping photos in a safe environment, temperature control, humidity, dust, sunlight, "magnetic" albums, and contact with materials of high acidity. The ideas in scrapbooking and journaling in this text will stimulate creativity and help to maintain your favorite photos for your descendents.

---. *More Than Memories III: Mastering the Techniques.* Iola, WI: Krause Publications, 2000.

A continuation of the *More Than Memories* series, this volume continues with techniques for organizing, journaling, creative cutting and using texture, dimension, stickers and paper dolls.

Sturdevant, Katherine Scott. *Organizing and Preserving Your Heirloom Documents.* Cincinnati, OH: Betterway Books, 2002.

Diaries, letters, personal papers, family documents and photos are all things most of us have around the house, and they are all things we find when clearing out closets and homes when we move or go through the estates of family members when they die. Sturdevant discusses the organization of all these materials in this book. She talks about locating missing documents or documents you didn't even know existed; organizing the documents and the time you spend on them; preserving and caring for fragile older paper; transcribing documents; conducting historical research; creating new family histories by interviewing relatives; and suggests organizations that can help you work with documents. She also talks about editing and publishing family documents.

Taylor, Maureen Alice. *Scrapbooking Your Family History.* Cincinnati, OH: Betterway Books, 2003.

We've all done scrapbooks, and we thought they would last forever. We put them away and years later found brittle tape, glue dried, yellowed clippings and pieces of precious memories that were fit only to be trashed. Those memories were priceless at one time and if properly preserved could be priceless to your descendants. They establish a sense of who you were. In this book, Taylor shows how to display these priceless memories in an attractive, well-organized heritage album of important papers, pictures, and memorabilia. She discusses how to begin your family research; tracing your family tree; organizing and caring for your scrapbook materials; creating an archivally sensitive album; finding and identifying family photos; locating and interpreting historical documents about your family; gleaning information from family keepsakes; putting your ancestors into historical perspective; captioning; defining your album theme and layout; organizing the leftovers; and other family research techniques. She also includes skill building exercises and hands-on tutorials.

Tuttle, Craig A. *An Ounce of Preservation: A Guide to the Care of Papers and Photographs.* Highland City, FL: Rainbow Books, 1995.

>Beginning each chapter with a historical overview of the medium he is discussing, Tuttle guide the reader in the preservation techniques to be used with such family treasures as letters, documents, works of art on paper, greeting cards, sports cards, scrapbooks, books, magazines, comic books, stamps, photographs and posters. Issues discussed in their preservation include temperature and humidity control; fungi, insects and rodents; light exposure; pollution and water; framing and lamination; mechanical disfigurement; and fire and theft. Tuttle who is a University Archivist and consultant/lecturer recommends preservation supplies and suppliers, and provides various sources of information with which to plan your preservation projects.

Webb, Martha Ellen. *How to Clean, Repair, Store and Display Your Heirloom Papers and Photographs.* Omaha, NE: Making History, 1999.

>Webb's book assists both novices and experts in preservation. She discusses how to repair damaged memorabilia and artifacts preparing them for storage or display. She also, discusses the care and preservation of paper and photographs and how to safely display them. Various methods of preservation are presented, keeping in mind that many people do not have easy access to professional preservation materials. Lists of preservation resources are also included, as are sources for obtaining these materials.

Author's collection: Preservation materials

"Odds and Ends"

Anderson, Adrienne E. *Fun & Games for Family Gatherings: With a Focus on Reunions.* San Francisco, CA: Reunion Research, 1996.

Anderson provides ideas for entertainment at family reunions which include games for various age levels from young children to young adult with listings and explanations of the games, activities to make reunions exciting for all involved, and ideas for gathering family history from the attendees. Ideas for gathering family history include personalized items, scrapbooks, photo displays, memorabilia displays, and other ideas to stimulate memories.

Anuta, Michael J. *Ships of Our Ancestors.* Menominee, MI: Ships of Our Ancestors, Inc., 1983.

This is not a genealogical sourcebook, but simply a photographical record of the ships that were employed in transporting immigrants to America. Nearly 900 ships are listed in this work in alphabetical order. Each ship is identified by date, shipping line, and source. This provides the researcher with a photograph of the ships in which their ancestors arrived.

Arends, Marthe. *Genealogy Software Guide.* Baltimore, MD: Genealogical Publishing Co., 1998.

Arends reviews all the popular genealogical software programs published prior to 1998. Before reviewing each program, she answers questions regarding why one should use genealogical software, what kind of equipment is needed, how to choose and evaluate a program, what are the different types of software available and where one can purchase the software. Following the discussions on these questions, she lists genealogy database programs, genealogy utilities and research tools, Macintosh and other genealogy software, database comparison charts, software vendors, locating old files, Internet software resources, a list of programs not reviewed, GEDCOM, and computer genealogy publications. The database reviews include basic information about the program and running requirements, program information, reports which may be generated, sources, and comments. Illustrations are also provided introducing the ways in which some of the program screens look and the report formats.

Banister, Manly Miles. *The Craft of Bookbinding.* 1975. New York: Dover Publications, Inc., 1993.

>This republication of the earlier *Bookbinding as a Handcraft* provides a solution for those seeking to extend the life of favorite books that have fallen apart due to age or overuse. Banister's step-by-step guide shows how to restore hardcovers, paperbacks, periodicals and other materials. This book is illustrated with over 250 photos and drawings detailing book sewing as well as the modern practice of perfect binding. He also shows how to make end papers, attach headbands, case in, and cover with book cloth, buckram, artificial leather, and other materials. Adding titles and decoration is also covered. Instructions on buying the appropriate equipment are included as well.

Billingsley, Carolyn Earle and Desmond Walls Allen. *How to Become a Professional Genealogist.* 3rd. ed. Bryant, AR: Research Associates, 1997.

>Billingsley and Allen have developed a guide giving instructions on becoming a professional genealogist. They discuss the standards of the profession and the professional genealogical societies in the country.

Board for Certification of Genealogists. *The BCG Genealogical Standards Manual.* Provo, UT: Ancestry, 2000.

>The Board for Certified Genealogists has developed and published a guide of standards of competence and ethics which have become accepted by professional genealogists. These standards cover collecting information; evaluating evidence and compiling the results. They also, apply to teaching activities such as lecturing, presenting classroom sessions, and preparing written instructional materials. This book is organized into four sections, the first three address standards for researchers, teachers, and ongoing skill development, and the fourth section consists of appendixes that provide information about the Board and example reports and compilations. The board's website is www.bcgcertification.org.

---. *Certification Roster: Researchers, Editors, Instructors, Lecturers, Librarians, and Writers.* Falmouth, VA: BCG, 1998.

>Published in book form, this may also be found online at www.bcgcertification.org. The Board of Certified Genealogists stands for the highest standards in genealogical research and it is to them one may go for assistance in tracing genealogy. They maintain a list of professional genealogists who for a fee will do genealogical

searching. Their website lists such things as the listing of professional genealogists by state, world or areas of specialization. They also list their newsletter, code of ethics and conduct, and information about becoming certified. The website also provides links to the Association of Professional Genealogists, the Federation of Genealogical Societies, GENTECH, the National Genealogical Society and the New England Historic Genealogical Society.

Bock, Gordon. *Caring for Your Historic House.* New York: Harry N. Abrams, 1998.

Gaining importance as Americans are beginning to realize the value of having a heritage is the care and preservation of major properties such as houses and other historic properties. Towns, major cities and governments, are beginning to look at their more historic areas and starting to encourage their preservation. Grants are being given to renovate properties and community leaders are beginning to see the value of these properties within their communities. *Caring for Your Historic House* discusses not only the restoration of historic properties, but the preventive maintenance which can be done that makes the restoration easier or unnecessary. Contained in this work are chapters which deal with getting to know your house, establishing a maintenance program, structural integrity, roofs, masonry, woodwork, windows, paints and finishes, plaster, wallpapers, flooring and floor finishes, heating/cooling systems, kitchens and bathrooms, lighting and electric, landscaping, fire protection and appraisals, insurance and other legal matters. Included are suggested preservation resources and further reading materials on any of the above listed subjects.

Bonsey, Lynn and Lorna Healey. *It's All Relative: How to Create Your Own Personal Family History Trivia Game.* Bowie, MD: Heritage Books, 1988.

Once you've accomplished your family history research, or needing a place to start, this concept of creating a family history trivia game can provide both fun and information for future research. This book could also provide material for putting together an oral history interview session. Bonsey and Healey provide a means of brainstorming using a timeline to connect national and world events with family events, using genealogical records and other studies of your family's past to create questions which will raise even more questions and make finding out your family history more fun and exciting.

Bonsib, Sandy. *Quilting More Memories: Creating Projects With Image Transfers*. Bothell, WA: Martingale & Company, 2001.

This quilting manual illustrates how to make memory quilts by transferring photo images onto fabric. Bonsib has provided ten quilt patterns using the transfer method. She also suggests other ideas such as using children's drawings, wedding invitations, leaves, old postcards, and other items of memorabilia. Illustrations provide examples of works completed, and suggestions are made about fabrics.

Burden, Ernest E. *Illustrated Dictionary of Architectural Preservation: Restoration, Renovation, Rehabilitation, Reuse*. New York: McGraw-Hill, 2004.

While most of us remain at the paper and artifact stages of preservation, there are those of us who advance to the stage where we're restoring historic houses or become active in associations restoring historic properties. This illustrated dictionary provides images and information for practical solutions in preservation. The dictionary defines materials, components, building systems and codes, photos, and illustrations of historic properties. Users will find information and examples on adaptive reuse, the creation of designated historic districts, structural restoration of landmark buildings, and cleaning and preserving of great works of architecture by leading historic preservation firms.

Clifford, Karen. *Becoming an Accredited Genealogist: Plus 100 Tips to Ensure Your Success*. Salt Lake City, UT: Ancestry, 1998.

Accreditation for becoming an accredited genealogist comes through the Family History Library in Salt Lake City. In this text, Clifford outlines the benefits of becoming an accredited genealogist; describes the knowledge and basic research skills expected of a professional; examines the experiences, testing procedures, and application processes required to apply for accreditation; and focuses on preparing for accreditation with self-assessment tests and personal insights. Based on her history of genealogy research, she also, provides over 100 'Tips for Success.' The book is full of practical information on researching, writing research guides and research assignments for sharpening your skills.

Clunies, Sandra MacLean. *A Family Affair: How to Plan and Direct the Best Family Reunion Ever.* Nashville, TN: Rutledge Hill Press, 2003.

Big family/little family, family reunions are a great place to get together to share those memories and to make new ones. Getting together with relatives you haven't seen in years will sometimes open the floodgates of memories; all you need to know is how to tap into them and how to record them when they begin. Clunies provides step-by step direction in setting up a family reunion. Suggestions for making it a success include: enlisting the help of other family members; selecting the best date and location; establishing a budget and identifying sources of income; locating faraway relatives; organizing mailings and responses; planning meals and activities; and creating special mementos for the participants. Other resources include checklists, sample forms, web sites to topics of interest, and tips from others who have held successful reunions.

Cogswell, Robert Elzy. *Copyright Law for Unpublished Manuscripts and Archival Collections.* Dobbs Ferry, NY: Glanville Publishers, Inc., 1992.

In searching both archives and family collections for materials to use in publishing not only family histories, but articles of interest to archivists and the general public, one needs to be aware of copyright issues. Cogswell's book deals with these issues and uses illustrative case law to show what rights archivists and researchers have in publishing archival materials. Within his work he provides information on statutory backgrounds, common law right to first publication, the significance of publication, fair use, right to privacy, records produced during employment or duties, copying in libraries and archives, forms and policies for archives, and new technologies.

Crichton, Jennifer. *Family Reunion: Everything You Need to Know to Plan Unforgettable Get-Togethers.* New York: Workman Publishing, 1998.

Crichton has provided a guide for every phase of planning a family reunion from the 'back yard' cookout for a small group up to 60 participants, to a 'weekend classic' for up to 300 participants. Chapters discuss the reasons for having family reunions, the type of reunions, structuring the reunions, planning and selecting locations, family stories, family trees, the food, games and entertainment for all ages, family dynamics, photography, oral history, and post reunion activities.

Dewey, Barbara I., ed. *Raising Money for Academic and Research Libraries: A How-to-Do-It Manual for Librarians.* New York: Neal-Schuman Publishers, Inc., 1991.

This "how-to" manual provides practical advice for all types of academic and research libraries embarking on development programs. The authors provide information on various aspects of fundraising.

Drake, Paul E. *What Did They Mean By That? A Dictionary of Historical & Genealogical Terms for Old & New.* Bowie, MD: Heritage Books, 1998, 2000.

This is a dictionary of virtually every term that might be found in records pertaining to genealogical research. There is a list of common abbreviations listed at the beginning of the dictionary, and a Saxon alphabet translation. There are also, some sample records throughout to show how some of these terms were used in context.

---. *What Did They Mean By That? A Dictionary of Historical Terms for Genealogists, Some More Words.* Volume 2. Bowie, MD: Heritage Books, Inc., 1998.

Old records such as estate records, old books, letters, ledgers and courts' records contain many old, obsolete words that have never entered the main stream of the English language as common usage. In volume two, Drake has added another 1500 words not found in his original volume *What Did They Mean by That?*

Duncan, Ed E. *The Complete Guide to Planning Your Family Reunion.* Cleveland, OH: Cleve-Coast Enterprises, 1993.

Ed Duncan has provided a basic step-by-step guide to planning everything from a no-frills affair to a formal family reunion. He discusses organizing planning committees; deciding on the type of reunion to hold; locating and contacting family members; choosing accommodations, food, and activities; and deciding on the budget. This is a short no-frills book, itself, for those who prefer not to take the time to get into the extensive planning guides.

Evans, Barbara J. *A to Zax: A Comprehensive Dictionary for Genealogists and Historians.* 3rd. ed. Alexandria, VA: Hearthside Press, 1995.

There are numerous terms, abbreviations and names listed throughout genealogical sources that are either totally unfamiliar to the amateur genealogist, or are not familiar in the context in which they are being used. This book lists thousands of little-used or old-fashioned words and abbreviations that might be encountered in the course of genealogical research. Terminology covered includes: colloquial, ethnic, foreign, geographical, historical, household, legal, medical, monetary, occupational, relational, and religious. The dictionary also includes a list of nicknames and Dutch given names.

Floyd, Elaine. *Creating Family Newsletters: 123 Ideas for Sharing Memorable Movements with Family and Friends.* Cincinnati, OH: Writer's Digest Books, 1998.

Elaine Floyd presents hints and ideas for creating hand-crafted to computer-generated newsletters. Her 123 ideas illustrate possibilities for sharing memorable family moments such as weddings, births, holidays, reunions and other special events. She shows how to create a newsletter without writing a word, creating poetry newsletters, scrapbook newsletters, organizing and collecting stories, genealogy newsletters, how to find free templates and clip art online, and many other ideas and techniques for reaching family and friends and gathering information.

Gawne, Jonathan. *Finding Your Father's War: A Practical Guide to Researching and Understanding Service in the World War II US Army.* Philadelphia, PA: Casemate, 2006.

Gawne, a military historian, has created an accessible handbook on doing military research for people seeking information on a relative's service during World War II. The book introduces military units, researching individual and organizational records, discovering records in the archives and finding tangible evidence of a soldier's service. He has included over 470 photos, charts and insights into wartime service.

Howells, Cyndi. *Planting Your Family Tree Online: How to Create Your Own Family History Web Site.* Nashville, TN: Rutledge Hill Press, 2003.

Cyndi Howells of Cyndislist fame utilizes her expertise in web site creation to instruct family researchers in putting their family trees online. Her step-by-step process takes one from research to completed site design, avoiding the technicalities that scare off those who are not computer gurus. Subjects include why a family history web site will enhance research and bring families closer together; finding the right hosting service; planning, creating and personalizing your site; evaluating, testing and maintaining the site; and publicizing the site. One major advantage to having a web site is that relatives you might not be aware of may find you and answer some questions for which you have been unable to find answers.

Hoyer, Frederick Charles, Jr. and John D. McCann. *Find Them Fast, Find Them Now! The Handbook for Finding Missing Persons.* Secaucus, NJ: Citadel Press, 1988.

No one can truly vanish without a trace. Hoyer and McCann suggest places to go and people to see, listed in a detailed checklist. Background questionnaires and genealogical forms are given, as well as the best sources of investigative and missing person resource materials. As this is already a 23 year-old resource, some of the addresses given may no longer be current, though the ideas of search spots are good. The authors say in the introduction that some of their ideas are illegal in some parts of the country, so you may want to double check some ideas before actually using them.

Jerger, Jeanette L. *A Medical Miscellany for Genealogists.* Bowie, MD: Heritage Books, Inc., 1995.

Jerger's *Medical Miscellany* provides genealogist's with a medical dictionary that identifies illnesses and medical terms which may no longer be in a person's daily vocabulary. Words like lumbago, chirurgery, croup, are no longer part of most people's medical lexicon. Many old family records will have the contemporary usage of their day used for identifying illnesses and medical conditions. Jerger has also included terms from myth and magic which a researcher may encounter as they relate to healing through the ages. The book is formatted as a dictionary and incorporates not only English medical terminology, but also terms from Europe, Asia Africa and Native American medical lore.

Kirkham, E. Kay. *The Handwriting of American Records for a Period of 300 Years.* Logan, UT: The Everton Publishers, Inc., 1973.

E. Kay Kirkham has made an extensive study of American handwriting styles. These styles are variable and are not always good for determining the age of records as the education of the writer frequently determines the spelling and type of handwriting.

Kirk man attempts to bring the mystery of handwriting to a point where it is helpful to genealogists attempting to determine the age of a record.

—. *How to Read the Handwriting and Records of Early America.* Rev. ed. Salt Lake City, UT: Kay Publishing Co., 1965.

Many of the early genealogical and census records were hand written. Kirkham's book offers tips and assistance in interpreting the handwriting to make the reading and use of these records easier.

Lawrence, Priscilla O'Reilly. *Before Disaster Strikes: Prevention, Planning, and Recovery - Caring for Your Personal Collections in the Event of Disaster.* New Orleans, LA: The Historic New Orleans Collection, 1992.

Disaster's strike usually when you are the least prepared. While it's best to remember that no possession is as valuable as your life, there are some sensible precautions you can take while you have the time to do so. Family heirlooms are your treasures and are always irreplaceable; this guide discusses various means of preventing them from becoming total losses in the event of simple environmental damage, fire, hurricane or other calamity. Advance planning, while it doesn't always mean damage might not be done, can potentially lead to the recovery of precious keepsakes. This simple guide walks the reader through ideas for prevention of damage, planning for disasters, and the recovery of your possessions after disaster strikes. Included are suggestions for taking care of paintings, paper and books, photographs, textiles, furniture and wooden objects, metal objects, and glass and ceramics. A chapter on where to find conservation resources and information is also included.

Martin, Mary, ed. *Local and Regional Government Information: How to Find It, How to Use It.* Westport, CT: Greenwood Press, 2005.

Genealogists and family historians frequently need to consult records compiled or held by government agencies. Martin's book on locating local and regional information from government agencies provides not only information on the type of materials available, but tips on how to access the information. Topics covered in this collection include court records; public health records; school records; municipal, county, and regional government archives; local publications; guides and directories; land records; probate records; census records; local government resources on genealogy; and many other record types. The various contributors' also discuss potential barriers to accessing government records; freedom of information and privacy laws and how to obtain government records from various levels of the government.

Matthews, Tony. *Paper Trees: Genealogical Clip-Art.* Baltimore, MD: Genealogical Publishing Co., 1999.

This is a collection of hand-drawn family trees and charts which you can photocopy fill in and color yourself. They are original designs which can be used as clip-art for cards, announcements, book covers, section dividers, reunion T-Shirts, mugs, newspaper designs, research aids or any number of things.

Meshenberg, Michael J. *Documents of Our Ancestors: A Selection of Reproducible Genealogy Forms and Tips for Using Them.* Teaneck, NJ: Avotaynu, 1996.

Much information on ancestors is easy to find if you know the proper ways to go about it. Meshenberg provides tips on finding information on post-1880 American immigrant ancestors, family members caught up in the Holocaust, or other ancestors that seem difficult to track down. In this volume, he has included forms needed to request documents from various archives and organizations, and forms on which to record the results. Among the document record forms included are U.S. government census records, passenger records, draft registrations, naturalization petitions, and declarations of intention to register, requests for veteran's records and Social Security forms. Request forms include requests for vital records and census information, forms for the International Red Cross, International Tracing Service, Hamburg lists, Polish vital records, the Family History Library, and many others.

Ninkovich, Tom and Barbara E. Brown. *Family Reunion Handbook: A Complete Guide for Reunion Planners.* 2nd ed. San Francisco, CA: Reunion Research, 1998.

Put together from interviews, surveys, reunion attendance and personal experiences in planning reunions, this book provides ideas and tips from people who have had successful family reunions. The author discusses the decision making process - type of reunion, how often to have one, where to have one, how to choose facilities; getting organized - committees, meetings, seed money, ideas; money and finances - budgeting, estimating expenses, setting rates, raising money, gifts, tickets, bank accounts, and keeping a financial history; keeping records - types of information, filing systems, using computers; family communications - mailings, contents of newsletters, family surveys; mailing - postage, labels, return addresses; getting ready - help from the commercial community, hosting, registration, identification, decorations, music, activities, program, emergencies; feeding the family - cooking, catering, potluck, serving and clean-up, banquet checklist; showing the kids a good time - continuing traditions, mixing games, site selection, involving kids in family history, indoor activities, family games, creating your own games; making history - interviewing, genealogical research, producing family history, family directories, photography, videos; distinctive destinations - resorts, shipboard, searching for roots, outdoors, ecotourism, adventures; family associations - creating a family association, surname associations, sources for information; finding people - using resources for searching, media, database searches, telephone directories; techniques for graphics and design - letterheads, originals, formatting, desktop publishing; and many other ideas and steps toward a successful reunion. The chapters on Making History, Family Associations, and Finding People are particularly relevant for those people looking for tips on doing family history research. Numerous tips are given on interviewing skills and on how to draw the family history from those attending the reunion.

Owen, Carol. *Crafting Personal Shrines: Using Photos, Mementos & Treasures to Create Artful Displays.* New York: Lark Books, 2004.

A shrine is often thought of as a place of religious devotion. However, it is also a display of items of personal importance frequently dedicated to a person who was important in your life. Carol Owen shows how to build a personal shrine from the artifacts of your life, photos, mementos, and treasures that you have gathered which bring back important memories. A personal shrine can be used to tell the story of the important people and events of your life.

Porter, Pamela Boyer. *APG Directory of Professional Genealogists, 2001-2002.* Denver, CO: APG, 2001.

This directory lists professional genealogists around the country. These genealogists are for hire for specialized information, or to do complete family research. They are listed in alphabetical order by name, with as much information as the Association had available to them, including contact information and any specialties if they have them. There are also, cross-reference lists so that you may look them up by specialty or geographical location.

Reminiscing: The Game for People Over Thirty and the Younger People They Let Play. The Millennium Edition. Itasca, IL: TDC Games, Inc., 1989.

A game of memories, the time period is from the 1940s to 1990s. Made up of four player books and one Reminiscing book, fill-in-the blank flashback questions are asked along with a corresponding set of clues. When required, a person must tell a story from their own personal past related to one of the subjects. As the point of this game is to stimulate memories, the questions may be easily adapted to an oral interview format, particularly useful for generating memories of the social times of the interviewees' life.

Rickards, Maurice, Michael Twyman, Sally De Beaumont, and Amoret Tanner. *Encyclopedia of Ephemera: A Guide to the Fragmentary Documents of Everyday Life for the Collector, Curator, and Historian.* New York: Routledge, 2000.

We all have ephemera, that collection of souvenirs, collectibles, and odds and ends we simply cannot bring ourselves to discard. This "stuff" of life often holds sentimental memories and reminders of times past as it chronicles our social history. Sometimes they contain valuable antiques. This encyclopedia is a sourcebook of over 400 entries covering all aspects of everyday documents and artifacts, from bookmarks to birth certificates and beyond. This book defines and describes the purpose and origins of much of what man has collected throughout his life.

Saldana, Richard H. *A Practical Guide to the "Misteaks" Made in Census Indexes.* Salt Lake City, UT: R. H. Saldana & Co., 1987.

Indexing requires a great deal of precision and involves a great deal of tedium. It is further complicated by the fact that many census records are poorly filmed, had poor handwriting, had errors made by the original census taker, were done by census takers who could not spell, were sometimes done by census takers who were drunk or otherwise incapacitated, different transcribers interpreted handwriting differently, and many other problems. Saldana has created a book that explains how to recognize many of these mistakes and how to work around them. Chapters explain differences between Accelerated Indexing Systems International and Index Publishing; how records are indexed; and common types of mistakes found.

Schultz, Arthur W. and Huntington T. Block. *Caring for Your Collections.* New York: Abrams, 1992.

> We all have collections! For that matter, though we see museums full of collections, most are still in the hands of private collectors. This guide is a comprehensive care manual written for the average person, by expert conservators. Each chapter covers a specific art form such as paintings, paper, books, photographs, furniture, textiles ceramics, glass, metal, stone, musical instruments, and other objects. While the authors stress preventive maintenance, they also provide the dos and don'ts of routine care. Recommendations on what to do if damage has occurred are also a part of this text. Before and after photos are also utilized to show what can be done in various situations. Besides care, the authors also discuss environmental guidelines, hiring a professional conservator, security, appraisal and authentication of collectibles. A list of resource organizations is also provided along with a section featuring brief biographies of cited authorities in the collectibles field.

Setnik, Linda. *Victorian Costume for Ladies, 1860-1900.* Atglen, PA: Schiffer Publishing, Ltd., 2000.

> Over 350 nineteenth-century photographs provide documentation of American women's fashion from 1860 to 1900. Chapters describe the various forms of clothing from underwear to sports clothes, common dress, laundry and clothing manufactures. Information about jewelry and hairstyles also is included making this a good resource for dating vintage photographs.

Shea, Jonathan D. and William F. Hoffman. *Following the Paper Trail: A Multilingual Translation Guide.* Teaneck, NJ: Avotaynu, 1994.

> Shea and Hoffman have prepared a guide for translating vital statistic records and other genealogy-related records in 13 languages, Czech, French, German, Hungarian, Italian, Latin, Lithuanian, Polish, Portuguese, Romanian, Russian, Spanish and Swedish. Sections show the alphabet of each language, sample records and their translation, and a list of words commonly encountered.

Smith, Lorna D. *Genealogy is More Than Charts.* Ellicott City, MD: Lifetimes, 1991.

> This book is an addendum for the genealogist. It provides over 100 activities for using the genealogical information gleaned from the search. Chapters include information on celebrating life, food ideas, words and pictures, displaying heirlooms, writing the history, asking questions about the past, and many other ideas.

Sperry, Kip. *Reading Early American Handwriting*. Baltimore, MD: Genealogical Publishing Co., 1998.

> If you have ever tried to read a census record or an ancestor's letter from many years ago, you will have discovered that handwriting has changed over the years. Sperry's book is designed to assist in deciphering the handwriting on early American documents. It provides samples of alphabets and letter forms, and defines terms and abbreviations commonly used for early American documents such as wills, deeds, and church records. He also, provides samples of early American documents so that the reader can see how to interpret the handwriting. He illustrates his work with approximately 100 documents in varying degrees of difficulty. Numbers and Roman numerals are also discussed, as well as the change from the Julian Calendar to the Gregorian Calendar, and date abbreviations commonly found in American records. He also includes a section on the Internet and compact discs, and an annotated bibliography of books and articles of particular interest to genealogists and historians.

Strangstad, Lynette. *A Graveyard Preservation Primer*. Walnut Creek, CA: AltaMira Press, 1995.

> Though not directly a genealogical studies book, the preservation of graveyards is important to genealogists looking for information on their family histories. This guide acquaints those interested in maintaining the quality of a graveyard and tombstones with the most effective way for caring for the surviving stones. Some of the information in this book will also be helpful to the genealogist. There is discussion on stone rubbing, documenting the stone, and graveyards as an educational site. Photos also show some of the classic old designs and figures show how to chart a graveyard.

---. *Preservation of Historic Burial Grounds*. Washington, DC: National Trust for Historic Preservation, 1992, 2003.

> Number 76 in the National Trust's Information Series, this leaflet is a guide to the significance of historical burial grounds. It identifies common threats to gravestones and graveyards. Appropriate methods for conservation and topics such as project organization, planning, setting priorities, continuing maintenance, and protection are discussed.

Stryker-Rodda, Harriet. *Understanding Colonial Handwriting.* Rev. ed. Baltimore, MD: Genealogical Publishing Co., 2007.

The deciphering of handwriting is no longer as necessary in genealogy as it once was. Since the middle of the twentieth century, many genealogical and historical primary materials have been transcribed, translated, typed, copied, microfilmed, printed and reprinted. Some of these have not been well done however, and frequently the need still exists to refer back to the original handwritten document. To analyze the original document, one must understand its history, purpose, and its scribe and manner of writing. Stryker-Rodda discusses the different types of documents available and the different handwriting styles that may be found and how to read them. She also, gives examples of different handwriting styles from the Colonial age.

Thornton, Tamara Plakins. *Handwriting in America: A Cultural History.* New Haven, CT: Yale University Press, 1996.

In her work, Thornton has traced the development of handwriting in American from colonial times to the present. She has investigated the shifting functions and meanings of handwriting and shows its links to identity. Trends in handwriting can be used in dating documents to their time periods, so learning how to analyze styles and stylistic changes over time can be of great value to the genealogist needing to date family papers.

Thoyts, Emma E. *The Key to the Family Deed Chest: How to Decipher and Study Old Documents: Being a Guide to the Reading of Ancient Manuscripts.* London, UK: Elliot Stock, 1903, 1974.

Mrs. Cope discusses the deciphering of handwriting and document language in her book on family deeds. She also, discusses ink, paper, paper marks and seals, which are valuable when trying to date materials. She gives hints to the beginning researcher; tells how to judge character by handwriting styles; discusses Saxon, Norman-French, and Law Latin; old deeds; law technicalities; manor and court rolls; monastic charters; parish registers; parish officers and their account books; and old letters. She also, provides a list of abbreviations. This book was reprinted in 1972 under the title *How to Read Old Documents* by E. E. Thoyts.

Trinkle, Dennis A. and Scott A. Merriman. *The History Highway: A 21st Century Guide to Internet Resources.* Rev. Armonk, NY: M. E. Sharpe, 2006.

Trinkle and Merriman have compiled an Internet directory which gives the historian a directory to over 3000 websites available for historic research. Coverage includes US and world history sites, and all sub-fields. Ten new chapters include: futurism, environmental history, immigration history, and Mediterranean and Middle Eastern history. Included is a CD of the entire contents with links to the internet sites.

Author's Collection: Mother - Muriel (bottom center), and her sisters, l-r: Marcella, Mildred and Marion.

Journals:

Oral History

Bios: Zeitschrift für Biographieforschung und Oral History (Germany)
Bulletin de Liaison du Laboratoire Universitaire de la Tradition Orale (France)
Catálogo - Programa de Historia Oral (Mexico)
Historia Antropologia y Fuentes Orales (Spain)
História Oral: Revista da Associação Brasileira de História Oral (Brazil)
Historia y Fuente Oral (Spain)
International Journal of Oral History
Journal of American History
Journal of the Brazil Oral History Association
Ljóri (Iceland)
On Tape (Australia)
Oral History
Oral History Association of Australia Journal
Oral History in New Zealand
Oral History Review
Oral History Association Newsletter
Oral History Forum
Oral History in New Zealand
Oral History Association of Australia Journal
Voces Recobradas: Revista de Historia Oral (Argentina)
Words and Silences

Archive, Family History & Preservation

Amate: Organo Bimestral de Communicación del Sistema Red de Información en Materia de Conservación de Documentos (Mexico)
Creating Keepsakes
Family Trails
Kiroku to Shiryo=Records & Archives: Journal of the Japan Society of Archives Institutions
LifeStory Magazine
NPO Journal (British)
Preservation & Access International Newsletter
Reminisce: The Magazine That Brings Back the Good Times
Reunions Magazine
Revista de Archivos, Bibliotecas y Museos (Spain)
Revista de Conservación del Papel del la Biblioteca del Congreso de la

Nación (Argentina)
Revista de la Sociedad de Geografía e Historia de Honduras (Honduras)
Snapshot Memories
Trudy Moskovskogo Gosudarstvennogo Istoriko-Arkhivnogo Instituta (Russia)
Van Thu' Lu' u Tru' (Vietnam)

Genealogy

The American Cemetery
The American Genealogist
American Visions Magazine
Ancestry Daily News (electronic)
Ancestry Magazine
Ancestry Genealogical Computing
Ancestry Quarterly Bulletin
Ansearching News
Appalachian Families
Apple Seeds
Avotaynu: The International Review of Jewish Genealogy
Association of Professional Genealogists Quarterly
Canadian Federation of Genealogical & Family History Societies: Newsletter
Caribbean Historical and Genealogical Journal
Computers in Genealogy
De Nederlandsche Leeuw Maandblad van het Koninklijk Nederlandsch
Genootschap voor Geslacht- en Wapenkunde (Netherlands)
Discovering Family and Local History
Eastman's Online Genealogy Newsletter (electronic)
Everton's Genealogical Helper
Family Chronicle, The Magazine for Families Researching Their Roots
Family History Monthly
Family History News: The Newsletter for Genealogical and Historical
Researchers (Canada)
Family History News and Digest
Family Records Today
The Family Tree
Family Tree Finders (online)
Family Tree Magazine Update (online)
Family Tree (New Zealand)
Flower of the Forest Black Genealogical Journal
Forum
Genealogical Computing
Genealogical Computing Newsletter
The Genealogical Helper

Genealogical Journal
The Genealogist
Genealogy: A Journal of American Ancestry
Genealogy & History Devoted to American Family and Local History, and Allied Interests
German Genealogical Society of America Bulletin
Heritage Quest Magazine
Heritage Scrapbook Ideas
Heritage Writer: Official Publication of Family History Services
International Review of Jewish Genealogy
International Society for British Genealogy and Family History, Newsletter
Irish Family History
The Irish Genealogist
Irish Heritage Links (Northern Ireland)
The Irish Link: the Irish Family History Magazine
Irish Roots
Journal of Negro History
Journal of Online Genealogy
Journal of the Afro-American Historical and Genealogical Society
Journal of the American Institute for Conservation
Journal of the Association of Gravestone Studies
Markers I: The Journal of the Association for Gravestone Studies
Markers II: The Journal of the Association for Gravestone Studies
NEXUS, The Newsmagazine of the New England Historic Genealogical Society
NGS Newsletter
NGS Quarterly
NGS/SIG Digest
NGS/SIG Newsletter
National Genealogical Society Quarterly
Negro History Bulletin
New England Ancestors
New England Historical and Genealogical Register
New York Genealogical and Biographical Record
North Carolina Genealogical Society Journal
North Irish Roots: Journal of the North of Ireland Family History Society
Pamietnik Sandomierski (Poland)
Paperkuts Scrapbook Magazine
Pebbles in My Pocket
Photographic Conservation
Practical Family History
Quaker Connections: Magazine of the Quaker Family History Society
Quarterly Journal of the National Genealogical Society

Reunions Magazine
Scribbles 'n Scraps
Topics in Photographic Preservation
UGA News
USCT Civil War Digest (Afro-American)
Views: The Newsletter of the Aural and Graphic Records Section of the Society of American Archivists

From the author's collection: John and Muriel (parents -- 1940's)

*Archival, Genealogical & Oral History Organizations**

ARMA International
(Association of Records Managers and Administrators, Inc.)
11880 College Boulevard, Suite 450
Overland Park, KS 66210
913-341-3808
800-422-2762
Fax: 913-341-3742
www.arma.org

AfriGeneas~African Ancestored Genealogy
4725 Walton Xing, #1129
Atlanta, GA 30331
404-344-7177
webmaster@afrigeneas.com
www.afrigeneas.com

African-American Family History Association (AAFHA)
c/o Robert W. Woodruff Library, Atlanta Univ. Center
111 James P Brawley Drive, SW
Atlanta, GA 30314
404-978-2052
archives@auctr.edu
www.auctr.edu/FindingAWay/AAFHA.asp

Afro-American Historical and Genealogical Society, Inc. (AAHGS)
P O Box 73067
Washington, DC 20056-3067
info@aahgs.org
www.aahgs.org

Allen County Public Library
900 Library Plaza
Fort Wayne, IN 46802
260-421-1200
FAX: 260-421-1386
ask@acpl.info
www.acpl.lib.in.us/genealogy

*Some organizations change addresses when Presidents
and/or membership secretaries change,
please check websites prior to mailing written correspondence

American Antiquarian Society
185 Salisbury Street
Worcester, MA 01609-1634
508-755-5221
FAX: 508-753-3311
library@americanantiquarian.org
www.americanantiquarian.org

American Association for State and Local History
1717 Church Street
Nashville, TN 37203-2991
615-320-3202
Fax: 615-327-9013
membership@aaslh.org
www.aaslh.org

American Association of Handwriting Analysts (AAHA)
AAHAemail@aol.com
www.handwriting.org/aaha/aahamain.html

American Baptist Historical Society
3001 Mercer University Drive
Atlanta, GA 30341
678-547-6680
www.abhsarchives.org

American-Canadian Genealogical Society (ACGS)
PO Box 6478
Manchester, NH 03108-6478
603-622-1554
ACGS@acgs.org
www.acgs.org

American Catholic History Research Center and University Archives
Catholic University of America
620 Michigan Avenue, NE
101 Aquinas Hall
Washington, DC 20064
202-319-5065
FAX: 202-319-6554
archives@mail.lib.cua.edu
archives.lib.cua.edu

American Folklore Society
Mershon Center, Ohio State University
1501 Neil Avenue
Columbus, OH 43201-2602
614-292-4715
Fax: 614-292-2407
afsnet.org

American-French Genealogical Society
PO Box 830
78 Earle Street
Woonsocket, RI 02895-0870
401-765-6141
Fax: 401-597-6290
www.afgs.org

American Historical Association
400 A Street, SE
Washington, DC 20003-3889
202-544-2422
Fax: 202-544-8307
info@historians.org
www.historians.org

American Irish Historical Society Library
991 Fifth Avenue
New York, NY 10028
212-288-2263
FAX: 212-628-7927
aihs@aihs.org
www.aihs.org

American Italian Historical Association
c/o The John D. Calandra Italian American Institute
Queens College/CUNY
25 West 43rd, 17th Floor
New York, NY 10036
www.aihaweb.org

Archdiocese for the Military Services
PO Box 4469
1025 Michigan Avenue, NE
Washington, DC 20017-0469
202-719-3600
Fax: 202-269-9022
milarch.org

Archives of the Brethren in Christ Church
Messiah College
PO Box 3002
One College Avenue
Grantham, PA 17027-0901
717-691-6048
Fax: 717-691-6042
archives@bic-church.org
www.bic-church.org

Archives of the Greek Orthodox
Archdiocese of North America
8 East 79th Street
New York, NY 10075-0106
212-570-3517
Fax: 212-570-3562
archives@goarch.org
www.archives.goarch.org

Association of Personal Historians
Regional Associations/see website
www.personalhistorians.org

Association of Professional Genealogists
Kathleen Hinckley, Executive Director
PO Box 350998
Westminster, CO 80035-0998
303-465-6980
FAX: 303-456-8825
admin@apg.org
www.apgen.org

Association of Sons of Poland
333 Hackensack Street
Carlstadt, NJ 07072
201-935-2807
Fax: 201-935-2752
sonsofpoland@yahoo.com
www.sonsofpoland.org

Board for Certification of Genealogists
PO Box 14291
Washington, DC 20044
office@bcgcertification.org
www.bcgcertification.org

Bureau of Land Management (US)
(Information Resources Management)
1849 C Street, NW, Room 5665
Washington, DC 20240
202-208-3801
Fax: 202-208-5242
www.blm.gov/nhp/index.htm

Chicano Research Collection
Department of Archives and Manuscripts
Hayden Library, Arizona State University
Box 871006
Tempe, AZ 85287-1006
480-965-4932
Fax: 480-965-0776
www.asu.edu/lib/archives/chicano.htm

Chinese Historical Society of America
965 Clay Street
San Francisco, CA 94108
415-391-1188
info@chsa.org
www.chsa.org

Church of the Brethren
Brethren Historical Library and Archives
1451 Dundee Avenue
Elgin, IL 60120
847-742-5100, ext. 294
Fax: 847-742-6103
kshaffer_gb@brethren.org
www.cob-net.org/genhis.htm

Clayton Library, Houston Public Library
Center for Genealogical Research
5300 Caroline
Houston, TX 77004-6896
832-393-2600
www.hpl.tx/clayton/family_histories.html

Cleveland Public Library
325 Superior Avenue NE
Cleveland, OH 44114-1271
216-623-2818
Special.Collections@cpl.org
www.cpl.org

Colonial Dames of America, National Society of the
2715 Que Street, NW
Washington, DC 20007-3071
202-337-2288
Fax: 202-337-0348
info@dumbartonhouse.org
www.dumbartonhouse.org

Concordia Historical Institute
(Lutheran Church-Missouri Synod)
804 Seminary Place
St. Louis, MO 63105-3014
314-505-7900
Fax: 314-505-7901
chi@chi.lcms.org
chi.lcms.org

Congregational Christian Historical Society
14 Beacon Street
Boston, MA 02108
617-523-0470
Fax: 617-523-0491
www.14beacon.org

Creole-American Genealogical Society, Inc.
PO Box 3215
Church Street Station
New York, NY 10008

Dallas Public Library
J. Erik Jonsson Library
1515 Young Street
Dallas, TX 75201
214-670-1433
genealogy@dallaslibrary.org
www.dallaslibrary2.org

Daughters of American Colonists, National Society
2205 Massachusetts Avenue, NW
Washington, DC 20008-2813
202-667-3076
cc@nsdac.org
www.nsdac.org

Daughters of the American Revolution, National Society
1776 D Street, NW
Washington, DC 20006-5303
202-628-1776
www.dar.org

Daughters of Union Veterans of the Civil War (DUV)
National Headquarters, DUV Registrar's Office
PO Box 211
503 South Walnut Street
Springfield, IL 62705-0211
217-544-0616
duvcw@sbcglobal.net
www.duvcw.org

David Library of the American Revolution
PO Box 748
1201 River Road
Washington Crossing, PA 18977
215-493-6776
Fax: 215-493-9276
www.dlar.org

Denver Public Library
Western History and Genealogy Division
10 West Parkway 14th Avenue Parkway
Denver, CO 80204-2731
720-865-1821
Fax: 720-865-1880
TTY: 720-865-1825
history.denverlibrary.org

Descendants of the Signers of the Constitution, Society of
www.dsdi1776.com

Disciples of Christ Historical Society
Library Archives
1101 Nineteenth Avenue, S
Nashville, TN 37212-2196
866-834-7563
615-327-1444
mail@discipleshistory.org
www.discipleshistory.org

Ellis Island Foundation, Inc.
The Statue of Liberty-Ellis Island Foundation, Inc.
17 Battery Place #120
New York, NY 10004-3507
212-561-4588
historycenter@ellisisland.org
www.ellisisland.org

Enoch Pratt Free Library
400 Cathedral Street
Baltimore, MD 21201-4484
410-396-5430
Fax: 410-396-1441
TTY: 410-396-3761
www.prattlibrary.org

Ephemera Society of America, Inc
PO Box 95
Cazenovia, NY 13035-0095
315-655-9139
Fax: 315-655-9139
info@ephemerasociety.org
www.ephemerasociety.org

Evangelical & Reformed Historical Society
555 West James Street
Lancaster, PA 17603
717-290-8734
Fax: 717-394-4254
erhs@lancasterseminary.edu
www.erhs.info

Evangelical Congregational Historical Society
Evangelical Theological Seminary
121 South College Street
Myerstown, PA 17077
717-866-5775
Fax: 717-866-4667
theisey@evangelical.edu
www.eccenter.com/226234.ihtml

Evangelical Covenant Church Archives
North Park University
F. M. Johnson Archives and Special Collections
3225 West Foster Avenue, Box 38
Chicago, IL 60625-4895
773-244-6224
www2.northpark.edu/Brandel-Library/Archives

Evangelical Lutheran Church in America Archives
321 Bonnie Lane
Elk Grove Village, IL 60007
847-690-9410
archives@ELCA.org
archive.elca.org/archives

Family History Library of
The Church of Jesus Christ of the Latter-day Saints
35 Northwest Temple Street, Room 344
Salt Lake City, UT 84150-3440
866-406-1830
801-240-2584
Fax: 801-240-1794
fhl@familysearch.org
www.familysearch.org

Federation of East European Family History Societies
PO Box 510898
Salt Lake City, UT 84151-0898
info@feefhs.org
www.feefhs.org

Federation of Genealogical Societies
PO Box 200940
Austin, TX 78720-0940
888-347-1500
Fax: 888-347-1350
office@fgs.org
www.fgs.org

Filipino-American National Historical Society
National Pinoy Archives
810 18th Avenue, Suite 100
Seattle, WA 98122
206-322-0203
fanhsnational@earthlink.net
www.fanhs.net

Finnish-American Heritage Center & Historical Archive
Finlandia University
601 Quincy Street
Hancock, MI 49930
906-487-7347
Fax: 906-487-7557
archives@finlandia.edu
www.finlandia.edu/fueled/Department/FAHC/fahc.html

First Church of Christ, Scientist
Archives and Library of the Mother Church
Mary Baker Eddy Library
200 Massachusetts Avenue
Boston, MA 02115
888-222-3711
research@marybakereddylibrary.org
www.marybakereddy.org

GENTECH/National Genealogical Society
3108 Columbia Pike, Suite 300
Arlington, VA 22204-4370
703-525-0050
800-473-0060
Fax: 703-525-0052
ngs@ngsgenealogy.org
www.ngsgenealogy.org/cs/ngs_gentech/

Genealogical Society of Mayflower Descendants
PO Box 3297
Plymouth, MA 02361
508-746-3188
www.themayflowersociety.com

Genealogical Speakers Guild
PO Box 38314
Olmsted Falls, OH 44138-0314
www.genealogicalspeakersguild.org/index.php

General Commission on Archives and History, GCAH
The United Methodist Church
Drew University
PO Box 127
36 Madison Avenue
Madison, NJ 07940
973-408-3189
gcah@gcah.org
www.gcah.org

General Society of the War of 1812
See website for state organization information
www.societyofthewarof1812.org

Grand Army of the Republic Wary Museum/Ruan House Library
4278 Griscom Street
Philadelphia, PA 19124-3954
215-289-6484
garmuslib@verizon.net
garmuslib.org

Heirlines Family History and Genealogy
800-570-4049
www.heirlines.com/

Hispanic Genealogical Society
PO Box 231271
Houston, TX 77223-1271
Fax: 281-449-4020
www.hispanicgs.com

Historical Society of Pennsylvania
1300 Locust Street
Philadelphia, PA 19107
215-732-6200
Fax: 215-732-2680
library@hsp.org
www.hsp.org

Holland Society of New York
20 West 44th Street, 5th floor
New York, NY 10036
212-758-1675
Fax: 212-758-2232
info@hollandsociety.org
www.hollandsociety.org

Huguenot Society of America/Library
20 West 44th Street, Suite 510
New York, NY 10036
Tel: 212-755-0592
Fax: 212-317-0676
hugsoc@verizon.net
huguenotsocietyofamerica.org/?page=library

Immigrant Genealogical Society
PO Box 7369
1310-B West Magnolia Boulevard
Burbank, CA 91510-7369
818-848-3122
Fax: 818-716-6300
www.immigrantgensoc.org

Immigration History Research Center
University of Minnesota
311 Elmer L. Andersen Library
222-21st Avenue South
Minneapolis, MN 55455
612-625-4800
Fax: 612-626-0018
ihrc@umn.edu
www.ihrc.umn.edu

Institute of Genealogy and History for Latin America
2191 South 2200 East
Mt. Springs, UT 84757
435-652-1710
Fax: 435-674-5787
lplatt@infowest.com
www.genealogy.com/00000140.html

International Commission for the Accreditation of Professional
Genealogists
PO Box 4464
Salt Lake City, UT 84110-4464
866-813-6729
information@icapgen.org
www.icapgen.org

International Council on Archives
60 Rue des Francs - Bourgeois
75003 Paris, France
+33 (0) 1 40 27 63 06
Fax: +33 (0) 1 42 72 20 65
ica@ica.org
www.ica.org

International Oral History Association
c/o Institut für Geschichte und Biographie
Fernuniverstät Hagen, Liebigst., 11
D-58511 Ludenscheid
Germany
almut.leh@FernUni-Hagen.de
iohanet.org

International Society of Family History Writers and Editors
PO Box 38314
Olmstead Falls, OH 44138-0314
isfhwe.org

International Society of Sons and Daughters of Slave Ancestry (ISDSA)
PO Box 436937
Chicago, IL 60643-6937
www.rootsweb.ancestry.com/~ilissdsa

The Irish Ancestral Research Association (TIARA)
Dept. W
2120 Commonwealth Avenue
Auburndale, MA 02466-1909
President2@tiara.ie
tiara.ie

Irish Genealogical Society, Intl. (IGSI)
1185 Concord Street, Suite 218
South St. Paul, MN 55075
research@IrishGenealogical.org
www.irishgenealogical.org

Italian Genealogical Group, Inc.
PO Box 626
Bethpage, New York 11714-0626
www.italiangen.org

The Italian Genealogical Society of America
PO Box 3572
Peabody, MA 10961-3572
www.italianroots.org

Japanese American History Archives
1840 Sutter Street
San Francisco, CA 94115
415-776-0661
www.amacord.com/fillmore/museum/jt/jaha/jaha.html

Jewish Genealogical Society, Inc.
15 West 16th Street
New York, NY 10011
info@jgsny.org
www.jgsny.org

JewishGen, Inc.
Museum of Jewish Heritage
Edmund J. Safra Plaza
36 Battery Place
New York, NY 10280
646-437-4326
www.jewishgen.org

La Société des Cajuns
PO Box 433
Larose, LA 70373
la_societe@vienici.com
www.vienici.com/lasociete

Leo Baeck Institute
Center for Jewish History
15 West 16th Street
New York, NY 10011
212-744-6400
Fax: 212-988-1305
lbaeck@lbi.cjh.org
www.lbi.org

Library of Congress
Local History and Genealogy Room
Thomas Jefferson Building, LJ G42
101 Independence Avenue, SE
Washington, DC 20540-4660
202-707-5537
Fax: 202-707-1957
www.loc.gov/rr/genealogy

Los Angeles Public Library
History and Genealogy Department
630 West Fifth Street
Los Angeles, CA 90071
213-228-7400
Fax: 213-228-7409
www.lapl.org/central/history.html

Lutheran Historical Conference
c/o Marvin Huggins, Membership Secretary
5732 White Pine Drive
St. Louis, MO 63129-2936
314-505-7921
Fax: 314-505-7901
luthhist@luthhist.org
www.luthhist.org

Mennonite Heritage Center
565 Yoder Road
Harleysville, PA 19438-1020
215-256-3020
info@mhep.org
www.mhep.org

Mid-Continent Public Library
Genealogy & Local History Research
317 West 24 Highway
Independence, MO 64050-2747
816-252-7228
ge@mymcpl.org
www.mymcpl.org

Morman History Association
10 West 100 South, Suite 610
Salt Lake City, UT 84101
801-521-6565
888-642-3678
Fax: 801-521-8686
www.mhahome.org

National Archives and Records Administration
8601 Adelphi Road
College Park, MD 20740-6001
866-272-6272
Fax: 301-837-0483
TDD: 301-837-0482
www.archives.gov/genealogy/index.html

National Association of Tribal Historic Preservation Officers
PO Box 19189
1625 K Street, NW, 11th Floor
Washington, DC 20036-9189
Phone: 202-628-8476
Fax: 202-628-2241
info@nathpo.org
www.nathpo.org

National Genealogical Society/Library
3108 Columbia Pike, Suite 300
Arlington, VA 22204-4370
800-473-0060
703-525-0050
Fax: 703-525-0052
ngs@ngsgenealogy.org
www.ngsgenealogy.org

National Huguenot Society
7340 Blanco Road, Suite 104
San Antonio, TX 78216-4970
210-366-9995
Fax: 210-341-5337
www.huguenot.netnation.com/general

National Institute on Genealogical Research
P O Box 118
Greenbelt, MD 20768-118
NatInsGen@juno.com
www.rootsweb.ancestry.com/~natgenin

National Italian American Foundation
1860 19th Street, NW
Washington, DC 20009
202-387-0600
Fax: 202-387-0800
information@niaf.org
www.niaf.org

National Maritime Historical Society
PO Box 68
5 John Walsh Boulevard
Peekskill, NY 10566
914-737-7878
800-221-6647
Fax: 914-737-7816
nmhs@seahistory.org
www.seahistory.org

National Railway Historical Society
100 North 20th Street, Suite 400
Philadelphia, PA 19103-1462
215-557-6606
Fax: 215-963-9785
www.nrhs.com

National Society for Graphology
250 West 57th Street, Suite 1228A
New York, NY 10107-0001
212-265-1148
www.handwriting.org/nsg/nsgmain.html

New England Historical and Genealogical Society
99-101 Newbury Street
Boston, MA 02116
617-536-5740
888-296-3447
Fax: 617-536-7307
research@nehgs.org
www.NewEnglandAncestors.org

New York Institute of Photography
211 East 43rd Street, Suite 2402
New York, NY 10017
800-445-7279
212-867-8260
Fax: 800-822-0023 or 212-867-8122
info@nyip.com
www.nyip.com

New York Public Library
The Irma and Paul Milstein Division of U.S. History,
Local History and Genealogy Division
Fifth Avenue and Forty-second Street, Room 121
New York, NY 10018-2788
histref@nypl.org
www.nypl.org/locations/schwarzman/milstein-division-us-history-local-history-genealogy

Newberry Library
60 West Walton Street
Chicago, IL 60610-7324
312-255-3512
312-255-3506
genealogy@newberry.org
reference@newberry.orf
www.newberry.org

North Carolina Baptist Historical Collection
Z. Smith Reynolds Library
PO Box 7777
Wake Forest University
Winston-Salem, NC 27109
336-758-3978
Fax: 336-758-5605
zsr.wfu.edu/collections/special/baptist

Norwegian-American Historical Association (NAHA)
Saint Olaf College
Rolvaag Memorial Library
1510 Saint Olaf Avenue
Northfield, MN 55057-1097
507-786-3221
Fax: 507-786-3734
naha@stolaf.edu or naha-archivists@stolaf.edu
www.naha.stolaf.edu

Oral History Association (USA)
Dickinson College
PO Box 1773
Carlisle, PA 17013-2896
717-245-1036
Fax: 717-245-1046
oha@dickinson.edu
www.oralhistory.org

Order of Descendants of Ancient Planters
www.ancientplanters.org

Oregon-California Trails Association
PO Box 1019
534 South Osage Street
Independence, MO 64051-0519
888-811-6282
816-252-2276
Fax: 816-836-0989
octa@octa-trails.org
www.octa-trails.org

Organization of American Historians
112 North Bryan Avenue
Bloomington, IN 474084141
812-855-7311
Fax: 812-855-0696
questions@oah.org
www.oah.org

Palatines to America (Pal-Am)
PO 141260
Columbus, OH 43214
614-267-4700
palam.org

Pilgrim Society
Pilgrim Hall Museum
75 Court Street
Plymouth, MA 02360
508-746-1620
director@pilgrimhall.org
www.pilgrimhall.org

Polish Genealogical Society of America
Polish Museum of America Archives and Library
984 North Milwaukee Avenue
Chicago, IL 60642-4101
PGSAmerica@pgsa.org
www.pgsa.org

Polish National Alliance of the United States of North America
6100 North Cicero Avenue
Chicago, IL 60646
773-286-0500
800-621-3723
www.pna-znp.org

Polynesian Voyaging Society
10 Sand Island Parkway
Honolulu, HI 96819
808-842-1101
Fax: 808-842-1112
pvshawaii@hawaiiantel.net
pvs.kcc.hawaii.edu

Presbyterian Historical Society
425 Lombard Street
Philadelphia, PA 19147-1516
215-627-1852
Fax: 215-627-0509
refdesk@history.pcusa.org
www.history.pcusa.org

Russian Baltic Information Center - BLITZ
907 Mission Avenue
San Rafael, CA 94901-2910
415-453-3579
Fax: 415-453-0343
E-mail: enute@igc.org
www.feefhs.org/members/blitz/frgblitz.html

St. Louis Public Library
History and Genealogy Department
1301 Olive Street
St. Louis, MO 63103
314-241-2288
Fax: 314-359-0393
TDD: 314-539-0364
www.slpl.org

Samford University Library-Special Collections
800 Lakeshore Drive
Birmingham, AL 35229
205-726-2748
library.samford.edu/sc/treasure/Homewoodcampus.html

Seattle Public Library
1000 Fourth Avenue
Seattle, WA 98104-1109
206-386-4636
www.spl.lib.wa.us

Seventh-day Adventists
General Conference of Seventh-day Adventists
Office of Archives and Statistics
12501 Old Columbia Pike
Silver Springs, MD 20904-6600
www.adventistarchives.org/DocArchives.asp

Seventh Day Baptist Historical Society Library
PO Box 1678
3120 Kennedy Road
Janesville, WI 53547
608-752-5055
Fax: 608-752-7711
sdbhist@seventhdaybaptist.org
www.sdbhistory.org

Smithsonian Institution Libraries
PO Box 37012
SI Building, Room 153, MRC 010
Washington, DC 20013-7012
202-633-1000
TTY: 202-633-5285
info@si.edu
www.si.edu

Society of American Archivists
17 North State Street, Suite 1425
Chicago, IL 60602-3315
312-606-0722
866-722-7858
Fax: 312-606-0728
info@archivists.org
www2.archivists.org

Sons of Confederate Veterans
PO Box 59
Columbia, TN 38402
800-380-1896
Fax: 931-381-6712
exedir@scv.org
scv.org

Sons of the American Revolution, National Society
1000 South Fourth Street
Louisville, KY 40203-3208
502-589-1776
Fax: 502-589-1671
www.sar.org

Sons of Union Veterans of the Civil War National Headquarters
PO Box 1865
Harrisburg, PA 17105
717-232-7000
www.suvcw.org

Southern Oral History Program
Center for the Study of the American South
CB#9127, UNC-CH
410 East Franklin Street
Chapel Hill, NC 27599-9127
919-962-5665
Fax: 919-962-4433
csas@unc.edu
www.sohp.org

State Historical Society of Wisconsin
816 State Street
Madison, WI 53706
608-264-6460
www.wisconsinhistory.org

Story Circle Network
PO Box 500127
Austin, TX 78750-0127
512-454-9833
storycircle@storycircle.org
www.storycircle.org

Sutro Library – Genealogy and Family History
480 Winston Drive
San Francisco, CA 94132
415-731-4477
Fax: 415-557-9325
sutro@library.ca.gov
www.library.ca.gov

Swedish-American Historical Society
3225 West Foster Avenue, Box 48
Chicago, IL 60625
773-583-5722
773 244 6224 (archives)
info@swedishamericanhist.org or archives@northpark.edu
www.swedishamericanhist.org

Swenson Swedish Immigration Research Center
Augustana College
639 38th Street
Rock Island, IL 61201-2296
309-794-7204
Fax: 309-794-7443
sag@augustana.edu
www.augustana.edu/swenson

United Daughters of the Confederacy
UDC Memorial Building
328 North Boulevard
Richmond, VA 23220-4009
804-355-1636
Fax: 804-355-1396
hqudc@rcn.com
www.hqudc.org

United States Catholic Historical Society
201 Seminary Avenue
Yonkers, NY 10704
914-337-8381
Fax: 914-337-6379
execdirector@uschs.com
www.uschs.com

United States Citizenship and Immigration Services
www.uscis.gov/portal/site/uscis

United States Civil War Center
Hill Memorial Library
Louisiana State University
Baton Rouge, LA 70803-3300
225-578-6568
Fax: 225-578-9425
www.cwc.lsu.edu

United States Holocaust Memorial Museum
100 Rauol Wallenberg Place, Southwest
Washington, DC 20024-2126
202-488-0400
TTY: 202-488-0406
www.ushmm.org

Vesterheim Norwegian-American Museum
PO Box 379
523 West Water Street
Decorah, IA 52101
563-382-9681
Fax: 563-382-8828
info@vesterheim.org
vesterheim.org

Western Historical Association
152C University Center
One University Blvd.
St. Louis, MO 63121
314-516-7282
Fax: 314-516-7272
wha@umsl.edu
www.westernhistoryassociation.org

Western Reserve Historical Society
10825 East Boulevard
Cleveland, OH 44106
216-721-5722
reference@wrhs.org
www.wrhs.org

Archival, Family History, and Genealogical Publishers

Ancestry.com
The Generations Network
360 West 4800 North
Provo, UT 84604
801-705-7000
Fax: 801-705-7001
800-262-3787
support@ancestry.com
www.ancestry.com

Anundsen Publishing Co.
108 Washington Street, Box 230
Decorah, IA 52101
563-382-4295
888-382-4291
Fax: 563-382-6532
mail@anundsen.publ.com
www.anundsenpubl.com

Betterway Books
F & W Media, Inc.
4700 East Galbraith Road
Cincinnati, OH 45236
Fax: 513-531-2690
www.fwpublications.com/genealogy.asp

Clearfield Company
3600 Clipper Mill Road, Suite 200
Baltimore, MD 21211
800-296-6687
Fax: 410-752-8492
Fax: 800-599-9561
info@genealogical.com
www.genealogical.com

Closson Press
257 Delilah Street
Apollo, PA 15613-1933
724-337-4482
Fax: 724-337-9484
clossonpress@comcast.net
www.clossonpress.com

Everton Publishers, Inc.
PO Box 442
Garden City, UT 84028
800-443-6325
cs@everton.com
www.everton.com

Family Chronicle
PO Box 194
Niagara Falls, NY 14304

or

505 Consumers Road, #312
Toronto, ON M2J 4V8
888-326-2476
416-491-3699
Fax: 416-491-3996
magazine@familychronicle.com
www.familychronicle.com

Family History Publishers
801-295-7490
sales@familyhistorypublisher.com
www.familyhistorypublisher.com

Genealogical Publishing Company
3600 Clipper Mill Road, Suite 200
Baltimore, MD 21211
410-837-8271
800-296-6687
Fax: 410-752-8492
Fax: 800-599-9561
info@genealogical.com
www.genealogical.com

Heritage Books, Inc.
100 Railroad Avenue, Suite 104
Westminster, MD 21157
800-876-6103
Fax: 410-558-6574
Info@HeritageBooks.com
www.heritagebooks.com

Higginson Book Company
148 Washington Street
Salem, MA 01970
978-745-7170
Fax: 978-745-8025
www.higginsonbooks.com

Jonathan Sheppard Books
PO Box 2020
Plaza Station
Albany, NY 12220
Fax: 518-766-9181
Sales@jonathansheppardbooks.com
www.jonathansheppardbooks.com

Masthof Bookstore and Press (Mennonite Family History)
219 Mill Road
Morgantown, PA 19543
610-286-0258
Fax: 610-286-6860
mast@masthof.com
www.masthof.com

Newbury Street Press
101 Newbury Street
Boston, MA 02116
888-296-3447
617-536-5740
Fax: 617-536-7307
NPS@nehgs.org
www.newenglandancestors.org/publications/
newbury_street_press.asp

Picton Press
PO Box 1347
Rockland, ME 04841
207-596-7766
Fax: 207-596-7767
sales@pictonpress.com
www.pictonpress.com

Primary Source Media
12 Lunar Drive
Woodbridge CT 06525-2398
800-444-0799
gale.sales@cengage.com
www.gale.com/psm

Proquest Information and Learning
789 East Eisenhower Parkway
PO Box 1346
Ann Arbor, MI 48106-1346
734-761-4700
www.proquest.com/en-us

S-K Publications
PO Box 8173
Wichita, KS 67208-0173
316-685-3201
Fax: 316-685-6650
genie@skpub.com
www.skpub.com/genie/

Southern Historical Press
PO Box 1267
375 West Broad Street
Greenville, SC 29601
800-233-0152
Fax: 864-233-2349
www.southernhistoricalpress.com

U.S. Government Bookstore
732 North Capitol Street, NW
Washington, DC 20401
866-512-1800
202-512-1800
Fax: 202-512-2104
ContactCenter@gpo.gov
bookstore.gpo.gov

Archival & Genealogical Supply Sources

These companies either sell or specialize in archival supplies including boxes, folders, acid-free papers, protective photographic items, and library and archival storage equipment; i.e. shelving units and display cases.

American Institute for Conservation of Historic & Artistic Works (AIC)
1156 15th Street NW, Suite 320
Washington, DC 20005-1714
202-452-9545
Fax: 202-452-9328
info@conservation-us.org
aic.stanford.edu

Ancestry Incorporated
360 West 4800 North
Provo, UT 84604
801-705-7000
Fax: 801-705-7001
support@ancestry.com
www.ancestry.com

Archival Products, Inc.
PO Box 1413
Des Moines, IA 50306-1413
800-526-5640
Fax: 888-220-2397
info@archival.com
www.archival.com

Clear File (USA) Inc.
407-703-1905
800-423-0274
Fax: 407-886-0008
www.clearfile.com

Conservation Center for Art & Historic Artifacts
264 South 23rd Street
Philadelphia, PA 19103
215-545-0613
Fax: 215-735-9313
ccaha@ccaha.org
www.ccaha.org

Conservation Resources International, LLC.
US - 5532 Port Royal Road
Springfield, VA 22151
703-321-7730
800-634-6932
Fax: 703-321-0629
sales@conservationresources.com
www.conservationresources.com

or

UK – Unit 2, Ashville Way
Off Watlington Road
Cowley, Oxford OX4 6TU
England
+44 (0) 1865 747755
Fax: +44 (0) 1865 747035
ConservArts@aol.com
www.conservationresources.com

DEMCO, Inc.
Box 7488
Madison, WI 53707-7488
800-962-4463
Fax: 800-245-1329
custserv@demco.com
www.demco.com

Everton Publishers
PO Box 442
Garden City, UT 84028
cs@everton.com
www.everton.com

Gaylord Bros.
P O Box 4901
Syracuse, NY
13221-4901
800-962-9580
Fax: 800-272-3412
www.gaylord.com

Genealogical Publishing Company, Inc.
3600 Clipper Mill Road, Suite 260
Baltimore, MD 21211
800-296-6687
410-837-8271
Fax: 800-599-9561
Fax: 410-752-8492
info@genealogical.com
www.genealogical.com

Heritage Books, Inc.
100 Railroad Avenue, Suite 104
Westminster, MD 21157-4286
800-876-6103
Fax: 410-588-6574
info@heritagebooks.com
www.heritagebooks.com

Highsmith Library and Audiovisual Equipment and Supplies
P O Box 5210
401 South Wright Road
Janesville, WI 53547-5210
800-558-2110
920-563-9571
Fax: 800-835-2329
service@highsmith.com
www.highsmith.com

Hollinger Metal Edge
9401 Northeast Drive
Fredericksburg, VA 22408
800-634-0491
Fax: 800-947-8814
hollingercorp@earthlink.net
www.hollingercorp.com

or

6340 Bandini Boulevard
Commerce, CA 90040
800-862-2228
Fax: 888-822-6937
hollingercorp@earthlink.net
www.hollingercorp.com

Northeast Document Conservation Center (NEDCC)
100 Brickstone Square
Andover, MA 01810-1494
978-470-1010
Fax: 978-475-6021
E-mail: see staff list on site
www.nedcc.org

The Paige Company
400 Kelby Street
Fort Lee, NJ 07024
201-461-7800
800-662-6937
Fax: 201-461-2677
www.paigecompany.com

University Products, Inc.
PO Box 101
517 Main Street
Holyoke MA 01401-0101
800-628-1912
Fax: 800-532-9281
custserv@universityproducts.com
www.universityproducts.com

Author's collection: part of certificate awarded at
Grace Lutheran Church, Lakeland, FL, 1937

Photograph Copying and Restoration Services*

Brant Photographers
2400 130th Place, NE
Bellevue, WA 98004
425-454-7676
Fax: 425-454-7782
info@brantphotographers.com
www.brantphotographers.com

Crystal Image Photography
Rt. 1, Box 59BB
Pamplin, VA 23958
434-610-8917
www.crystalimagephoto.com/comments.htm

Hansen Studio Inc.
PO Box 738
Cheshire, MA 01225
413-743-4918
rolf708@aol.com
www.rolfhansen.com

Just Black & White
PO Box 4628
Portland, ME 04112
207-233-3055
www.justblackandwhite.com

Winpenny Photography, The Studio
3 Wesley Street
Otley, West Yorkshire LS21 1AZ
+44 (0) 1943-462597
Fax: +44 (0) 1943-850861
info@winpennyphoto.co.uk
www.winpennyphoto.co.uk

*There are numerous copying and photo-restoration services available throughout the country, check your local yellow pages or the Internet for more resources.

Scrapbooking Resources

The Archival Company/University Products
517 Main Street
Holyoke, MA 01040
800-628-1912
413-532-3372
Fax: 413-532-9281
info@universityproducts.com
www.archivalsuppliers.com

Avery Dennison Consumer Service Center
50 Pointe Drive
Brea, CA 92821
800-462-8379
Fax: 800-831-2496
www.avery.com

Chatterbox, Inc.
6049 Slauson Avenue
City of Commerce, CA 90040
877-749-7797
Fax: 323-325-9605
info@chatterboxinc.com
www.chatterboxinc.com

Creative Memories
PO Box 1839
3001 Clearwater Road
St. Cloud, MN 56302-1839
800-468-9335
Fax: 800-605-2454
www.creativememories.com

EK Success Ltd.
www.eksuccess.com

Exposures
PO Box 3615
1 Memory Lane
Oshkosh, WI 54903-3615
800-222-4947
Fax: 800-699-6993
TDD: 920-231-5506
csr@exposuresonline.com
www.exposuresonline.com

Fiskars Brands, Inc.
School, Office and Craft
2537 Daniels Street
Madison, WI 53718
866-348-5661
socconsumeraffairs@fiskars.com
www.fiskars.com

Provo Craft
151 East 3450 North
Spanish Fork, UT 84660
800-937-7686
Fax: 801-794-9006
www.coluzzle.com

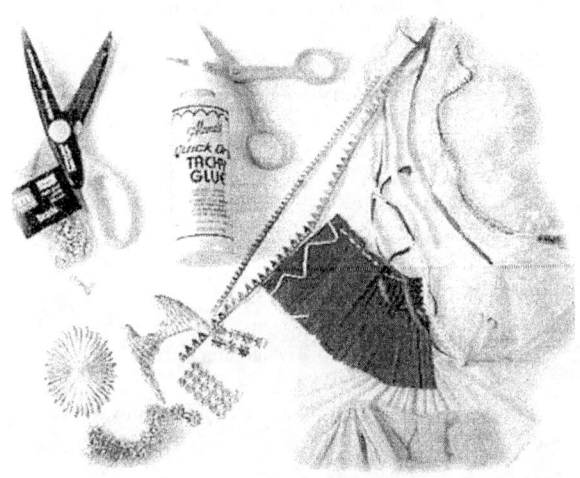

From: www.dropshipstrategy.com/google images

Archives, Genealogical Societies, Libraries, and Vital Records

State Agencies:

Alabama

> Alabama Department of Archives & History
> PO Box 300100
> 624 Washington Avenue
> Montgomery, AL 36130-0100
> 334-242-4435
> www.archives.state.al.us

> Alabama Genealogical Society, Inc.
> Samford University Library
> AGS Depository and Headquarters
> PO Box 2296
> 800 Lakeshore Drive
> Birmingham, AL 35229-0001
> algensoc.org

> Alabama Historical Association
> PO Box 300100
> Montgomery, AL 36130
> www.archives.state.al.us/aha/aha.html

> Alabama Historical Commission
> 468 South Perry Street
> Montgomery, AL 36104
> 334-242-3184
> www.preserveala.org

> Alabama Public Library Service
> 6030 Monticello Drive
> Montgomery, AL 36130
> 334-213-3900
> Fax: 800-392-5671(Alabama only)
> Fax: 334-213-3993
> statelibrary.alabama.gov/content/index.aspx

Alabama State Vital Records Office
  Center for Health Statistics
  PO Box 30317
  Suite 1150
  201 Monroe Street, RSA Tower
  Montgomery, AL 36103-3017
  334-206-5300
  800-252-1818
  www.adph.org/vitalrecords

Archdiocese of Mobile Archives
  15 South Franklin Street
  Mobile, AL 36602
  251-415-3850
  www.mobilearchdiocese.org

Birmingham Public Library
  2100 Park Place
  Birmingham, AL 35203
  205-226-3600
  www.bham.lib.al.us

Birmingham Southern College Library Archives
  900 Arkadelphia Road
  Birmingham, AL 35254
  800-523-5793
  205-226-4752
  Library.bsc.edu/tools/special_collection

Draughon Library, Special Collections & Archives
  Auburn University
  Auburn, AL 36849-5606
  334-844-1732
  800-446-0387
  Fax: 334-844-1704
  www.lib.auburn.edu/sca

Huntsville-Madison County Public Library
  915 Monroe Street
  Huntsville, AL 35801
  256-532-5969
  hhrdept@hmcpl.org
  hmcpl.org/hhr

Samford University
    Harwell Goodwin Davis Library
    (Baptist Church Records)
    800 Lakeshore Drive
    Birmingham, AL 35229
    205-726-2749
    library.samford.edu

Alaska

    Alaska Bureau of Land Management Office
        Anchorage Federal Office Building
        222 West Seventh Avenue, #13
        Anchorage, AK 99513-7504
        907-271-5960
        Fax: 907-271-3684
        AK_AKSO_Public_Room@blm.gov
        www.blm.gov/ak/st/en.html

    Alaska Historical Society
        PO Box 100299
        Anchorage, AK 99510-0299
        907-276-1596
        members@alaskahistoricalsociety.org
        www.alaskahistoricalsociety.org

    Alaska State Archives
        PO Box 110525
        141 Willoughby Avenue
        Juneau, AK 99801-0525
        907-465-2270
        Fax: 907-465-2465
        archives@alaska.gov
        www.archives.state.ak.us

    Alaska State Library and Historical Collections
        PO Box 110571
        333 Willoughby Avenue, 8th Floor
        Juneau, AK 99811-0571
        907-465-2921
        Fax: 907-465-2990 (Historical Collection)
        asl@alaska.gov or asl.historical@alaska.gov
        www.library.state.ak.us

Alaska State Vital Records Office
PO Box 110675
Bureau of Vital Statistics
5441 Commercial Boulevard
Juneau, AK 99801
907-465-3391
Fax: 907-465-3618
BVSOFFICE@health.state.ak.us
health.hss.state.ak.us/dph/bvs
(Check website for offices in Fairbanks and Anchorage)

Anchorage Genealogical Society
PO Box 242294
Anchorage, AK 99524-2294
AGS@ak.net
www.rootsweb.ancestry.com/~akags

National Archives and Records Administration – Pacific Alaska Region, Anchorage
654 West Third Avenue
Anchorage, AK 99501-2145
907-261-7820
Fax: 907-261-7813
alaska.archives@nara.gov
www.archives.gov/pacific-alaska/anchorage

Elmer E. Rasmuson Library
University of Alaska, Fairbanks
PO Box 756808
310 Tanana Loop
Fairbanks, AK 99775-6800
907-474-2791
fyapr@uaf.edu
library.uaf.edu/apr

Arizona

Arizona Bureau of Land Management
One North Central Avenue, Suite 800
Phoenix, AZ 85004-4427
602-417-9200
ASOWEB_AZ@blm.gov
www.blm.gov/az/st/en.html
(see website for district information)

Arizona Historical Foundation
    Hayden Library
    Arizona State University
    Box 871006
    Tempe, AZ 85287-1006
    480-965-3283
    Fax: 480-965-5744
    contact@ahfweb.org
    www.ahfweb.org

Arizona Historical Society
    Museum at Papago Park
    1300 North College Avenue
    Tempe, AZ 85281
    480-929-9499
    Fax: 480-967-5450
    AHSTempe@azhs.gov
    www.arizonahistoricalsociety.org

Arizona Historical Society
    Northern Division
    2340 North Fort Valley Road
    Flagstaff, AZ 86001
    928-774-6272
    Fax: 928-774-1596
    AHSFlagstaff@ashs.gov
    www.arizonahistoricalsociety.org

Arizona Historical Society
    Sanguinetti House Museum and Garden
    240 S. Madison Avenue
    Yuma, AZ 85364
    928-782-1841
    Fax: 928-783-0680
    AHSYuma@azhs.gov
    www.arizonahistoricalsociety.org

Arizona Historical Society
    Southern Division
    949 East Second Street
    Tucson, AZ 85719
    520-628-5774
    Fax: 520-629-8966
    AHSTucson@azhs.gov
    www.arizonahistoricalsociety.org

Arizona State Library, Archives, and Public Records
1901 West Madison
Phoenix, AZ 85009
602-926-3720
Fax: 602-256-7982
www.lib.az.us/archives

Arizona State Office of Vital Records
PO Box 3887
1818 West Adams Street
Phoenix, AZ 85030
602-364-1300
888-816-5907
webovr@azdhs.gov
www.azdhs.gov/vitalrcd

Mesa Arizona Regional Family History Center
41 South Hobson
Mesa, AZ 85204
480-964-1200
Fax: (480) 964-7137
www.mesarfhc.org

Arkansas

Arkansas Genealogical Society
PO Box 26374
Little Rock, AR 72221-6374
AskAGS@agsgenealogy.org
www.agsgenealogy.org

Arkansas Historical Association
416 Old Main, University of Arkansas
Fayetteville, AR 72701
479-575-5884
Fax: 479-575-2775
dludlow@uark.edu
www.arkansashistoricalassociation.org

Arkansas State Library
900 West Capitol, Suite 100
Little Rock, AR 72201
501-682-2053
Fax: 501-682-1529
www.asl.lib.ar.us

Arkansas History Commission
   One Capitol Mall
   Little Rock, AR 72201
   501-682-6900
   state.archives@arkansas.gov
   www.ark-ives.com

Arkansas State Vital Records Office
   Vital Records, Slot 44
   4815 West Markham Street, Slot 44
   Little Rock, AR 72205
   501-661-2336
   800-637-9314
   Fax: 501-661-2717
   www.healthyarkansas.com

Hendrix College Library
   Olin C. Bailey Library
   1600 Washington Avenue
   Conway, AR 72032
   501-450-1303
   Fax: 501-450-3800
   murphyb@hendrix.edu
   www.hendrix.edu/baileylibrary

Texarkana Public Library
   600 West 3rd Street
   Texarkana, AR 75501-5054
   903-794-2149
   Fax: 903-794-2139
   txarkpublib@txar-publib.org
   www.txar-publib.org

University of Arkansas Archives
   Special Collections
   365 North McIlroy Avenue
   Fayetteville, AR 72701-4002
   866-818-8115
   479-575-4104
   Fax: 479-575-6656
   specoll@uark.edu
   libinfo.uark.edu/specialcollections

California

Bancroft Library
University of California
Berkeley, CA 94720-6000
510-642-6481
Fax: 510-642-7589
bancref@library.berkeley.edu
bancroft.berkeley.edu/collections

California Bureau of Land Management
2800 Cottage Way, Suite W-1834
Sacramento, CA 95825-1886
916-978-4400
Fax: 916-978-4416
TDD: 916-978-4419
www.blm.gov/ca/st/en.html

California Department of Public Health
Office of Vital Records-MS 5103
PO Box 997410
1501 Capitol Avenue
Sacramento, CA 95899-7410
916-445-2684
ovrmail@cdph.ca.gov
www.cdph.ca.gov/certlic/birthdeathmar/Pages/default.aspx

California Genealogical Society and Library
2201 Broadway, Suite LL2
Oakland, CA 94612-3031
510-663-1358
Fax: 510-663-1596
Contact@CaliforniaAncestors.org
Californiaancestors.org

California Historical Society
678 Mission Street
San Francisco, CA 94105
415-357-1848
Fax: 415-357-1850
reference@calhist.org
www.californiahistoricalsociety.org

California State Archives
  1020 'O' Street
  Sacramento, CA 95814
  916-653-2246 (reference)
  Fax: 916-653-7363
  www.sos.ca.gov/archives

California State Library
  Library and Courts Building II
  PO Box 942837
  900 N Street
  Sacramento, CA 94237-0001
  916-654-0261
  Fax: 916-376-5310
  cslinfo@library.ca.gov
  www.library.ca.gov

California State Library - Sutro Branch
  480 Winston Drive
  San Francisco, CA 94132
  415-731-4477
  Fax: 415-557-9325
  sutro@library.ca.gov
  www.library.ca.gov

Los Angeles Public Library
  History and Genealogy Department
  630 West Fifth Street
  Los Angeles, CA 90071
  213-228-7400
  Fax: 213-228-7409
  www.lapl.org/central/history.html

Los Angeles Family History Library
  10741 Santa Monica Boulevard
  West Los Angeles, CA 90025
  310-474-9990
  lafamhist@lafh.org
  www.larfhc.org

National Archives and Records Administration - Pacific Southwest Region
24000 Avila Road, Suite 3513
Laguna Niguel, CA 92677-3497
949-448-4922
laguna.workshops@nara.gov
www.archives.gov/pacific/laguna/index.html

National Archives and Records Administration – Riverside
NARA
Caller Service 8305
23133 CAjalco Road
Perris, CA 92572
951-956-2000
951-956-2029
riverside.center@nara.gov
www.archives.gov/pacific/riverside

National Archives and Records Administration – San Francisco
Leo J. Ryan Memorial Federal Building
1000 Commodore Dr.
San Bruno, CA 94066-2350
650-238-3501
Fax: 650-238-3510
sanbruno.archives@nara.gov
www.archives.gov/pacific/san-francisco/index.html

San Diego Family History Center
4195 Camino del Rio South
San Diego, CA 91208
619-584-7668

San Diego Genealogical Society
7343 Ronson Road, Suite O
San Diego, CA 92111-1430
858-279-7347
SDGSinfo@yahoo.com
www.rootsweb.ancestry.com/~casdgs

San Diego Historical Society
1649 El Prado, Suite 3
San Diego, CA 92101
619-232-6203
Fax: 619-232-6297
www.sandiegohistory.org

Santa Barbara Trust for Historic Preservation
123 East Canon Perdido Street
Santa Barbara, CA 93101
805-965-0093
Fax: 805-568-1999
www.sbthp.org

Southern California Genealogical Society and Family Research Library
417 Irving Drive
Burbank, CA 91504
818-843-7247
Fax: 818-843-7262
scgs@scgsgenealogy.com
www.scgsgenealogy.com

Sutro Library – Genealogy and Family History
480 Winston Drive
San Francisco, CA 94132
415-731-4477
Fax: 415-557-9325
sutro@library.ca.gov
www.library.ca.gov

Colorado

Colorado Bureau of Land Management
2850 Youngfield Street
Lakewood, CO 80215-7093
303-239-3600
Fax: 303-239-3933
www.blm.gov/co/st/en.html

Colorado Council of Genealogical Societies
PO Box 40270
Denver, CO 80204-0270
cocouncilweb@gmail.com
www.rootsweb.ancestry.com/~coccgs

Colorado Genealogical Society
PO Box 9218
Denver, CO 80209-0218
303-866-3682
info@cogensoc.us
www.cogensoc.us/

Colorado Historical Society
1560 Broadway, Suite 400
Denver, CO 80203
303-866-3682
information@chs.state.co.us
www.coloradohistory.org
(check website for other site location addresses)

Colorado State Archives
1313 Sherman Street, Room 1B20
Denver, CO 80203
303-866-2358
Fax: 303-866-2257
www.colorado.gov/dpa/doit/archives

Colorado State Library
201 E. ColFax Ave., Room 309
Denver, CO 80203-1799
303-866-6900
Fax: 303-866-6940
www.cde.state.co.us/cdelib/

Denver Public Library
10 W. Fourteenth Avenue Parkway
Denver, CO 80204
720-865-1821
denverlibrary.org
(see website for branch information)

National Archives and Records Administration - Rocky Mountain Region
PO Box 25307
West 6th Avenue and Kipling Street
Denver Federal Center
Buildings 46 & 48
Denver, CO 80225-0307
303-407-5740 (archives)
303-407-5751 (genealogy)
Fax: 303-407-5753
denver.archives@nara.gov
www.archives.gov/rocky-mountain/index.html

University of Colorado, Library Archives
184 UCB
1720 Pleasant Street
Boulder, CO 80309-0184
303-492-7242
Fax: 303-492-3960
arv@colorado.edu
ucblibraries.colorado.edu/archives/index.htm

Vital Records Office
Colorado Department of Public Health and Environment
4300 Cherry Creek Dr. S
HSVRD-VR-A1
Denver, CO 80246-1530
303-692-2200
800-886-7689 (Colorado only)
TTD: 303-691-7700
www.cdphe.state.co.us/certs/index.html

Connecticut

Connecticut Ancestry Society
PO Box 249
Stamford, CT 06904-0249
www.connecticutancestry.org

Connecticut Department of Public Health
State Office of Vital Records
PO Box 340308
410 Capitol Ave., MS#11 VRS
Hartford, CT 06134-0308
860-509-7700
Fax: 860-509-7964
www.ct.gov/dph/site/default.asp

Connecticut Historical Society
1 Elizabeth Street
Hartford, CT 06105
860-236-5621
Fax: 860-236-2664
Research_center@chs.org
www.chs.org

Connecticut League of History Organizations
940 Whitney Ave.
Hamden, CT 06517-4002
203-624-9186
Fax: 203-773-0107
info@clho.org
www.clho.org

Connecticut Society of Genealogists
PO Box 435
Glastonbury, CT 06033-0435
175 Maple St.
East Hartford, CT 06118
860-569-0002
Fax: 860-569-0339
www.csginc.org

Connecticut State Archives
Connecticut State Library
231 Capitol Ave.
Hartford, CT 06106
860-757-6511
Fax: 860-757-6542
www.cslib.org/archives.htm

Connecticut State Library
231 Capitol Ave.
Hartford, CT 06106
860-757-6500
Fax: 860-757-6677
866-886-4478
isref@cslib.org
www.cslib.org

Connecticut Trust for Historic Preservation
940 Whitney Ave.
Hamden, CT 06517-4002
203-562-6312
Fax: 203-773-0107
contact@cttrust.org
www.cttrust.org

New Haven Colony Historical Society
114 Whitney Avenue
New Haven, CT 06510
203-562-4183
Fax: 203-562-2002
www.newhavenmuseum.org

Sterling Memorial Library, Yale University
PO Box 208240
128 Wall Street
New Haven, CT, 06520-8240
203-432-1735
Fax: 203-432-7441
www.library.yale.edu/mssa

United Methodist Archives Center
Drew University Library
PO Box 127
36 Madison Ave.
Madison, NJ 07940
973-408-3189
gcah@gcah.org
www.gcah.org/

Delaware

Delaware Genealogical Society
505 North Market St.
Wilmington, DE 19801-3091
delgensoc.org

Delaware Public Archives
Hall of Records
121 Duke of York Street
Dover, DE 19901
archives.delaware.gov

Historical Society of Delaware
505 North Market St.
Wilmington, DE 19801
302-655-7161
Fax: 302-655-7844
deinfo@dehistory.org
www.hsd.org

Hugh M. Morris Library
   University of Delaware Library
   181 South College Avenue
   Newark, DE 19717-5267
   302-831-2229
   www.lib.udel.edu

Vital Records Office
   Division of Public Health
   (Check website for office locations and contact information)
   www.dhss.delaware.gov/dph/ss/vitalstats.html

District of Columbia

   Daughters of the American Revolution Library
      1776 D. Street NW
      Washington, DC 20006-5303
      202-628-1776
      www.dar.org/library/default.cfm

   District of Columbia Department of Health
      825 N. Capitol Street, NE - 2nd Floor
      Washington, DC 20002
      202-442-5955
      Fax: 202-442-4795
      doh@dc.gov
      dchealth.dc.gov/doh/site/default.asp

   District of Columbia Public Library
      901 "G" St. NW
      Washington, DC 20001
      202-727-0321
      TTY: 202-727-2255
      dclibrary.org

   Historical Society of Washington, DC
      801 K Street, NW
      at Mount Vernon Square
      Washington, DC 20001
      202-383-1850
      info@HistoryDC.org
      www.historydc.org

Library of Congress
> Humanities and Social Sciences Division
> Thomas Jefferson Building
> Room LJ 100
> 101 Independence Ave., SE
> Washington, DC 20540-4660
> 202-707-3399
> Fax: 202-707-1957
> www.loc.gov/rr/main

National Archives and Records Administration – Archives I
> 700 Pennsylvania Avenue, NW
> Washington, DC 20408-0001
> 202-357-5400
> 866-272-6272
> www.archives.gov/dc-metro

National Archives and Records Administration - Archives II
> 8601 Adelphi Road
> College Park, MD 20740-6001
> 866-272-6272
> Fax: 301-837-0483
> TDD: 301-837-0482
> www.archives.gov/dc-metro/college-park

The White House Historical Association
> 1450 Pennsylvania Avenue, NW
> PO Box 27624
> Washington, DC 20038-7624
> 202-737-8292
> Fax: 202-789-0440
> webmaster@whha.org
> www.whitehousehistory.org

Florida

The Alma Clyde Field Library of Florida History
> 435 Brevard Ave.
> Cocoa, FL 32922
> 321-690-1971
> archivist@myfloridahistory.org
> www.myfloridahistory.org

Florida Baptist Historical Society
    5400 College Drive
    Graceville, FL 32440
    800-328-2660, ext. 480
    info@floridabaptisthistory.org
    www.floridabaptisthistory.org

Florida State Genealogical Society
    PO Box 10249
    Tallahassee, FL 32302-2249
    www.rootsweb.ancestry.com/~flsgs

Florida State Library and Archives
    R.A. Gray Building
    500 S. Bronough St.
    Tallahassee 32399-0250
    850-245-6700
    Fax: 850-488-4894
    TDD: 850-245-6096
    info@dos.state.fl.us
    dlis.dos.state.fl.us/index_researchers.cfm

Indian River County Public Library
    1600 Twenty-first St.
    Vero Beach, FL 32960
    772-770-5060
    Fax: 772-770-5066
    genealogy@irclibrary.org
    www.irclibrary.org

Largo Public Library
    120 Central Park Drive
    Largo, FL 33771-2110
    727-586-7410
    Fax: 727-587-7353
    genealogy@largo.com
    www.largo.com/department/?fDD=11-0

Orlando Public Library
    101 E. Central Blvd.
    Orlando, FL 32801
    407-835-7323
    www.ocls.lib.fl.us
    (see website for branch information)

PK Yonge Library of Florida History
    University of Florida George A. Smathers Libraries
    PO Box 117007
    Gainesville, FL 32611-7001
    352-273-2778
    www.uflib.ufl.edu/spec/pkyonge/

Pace Library, University of West Florida
    Building 32
    11000 University Parkway
    Pensacola, FL 32514
    850-474-2213
    library.uwf.edu/

Polk County Historical and Genealogical Library
    100 E. Main Street
    Bartow, FL 33830-4269
    863-534-4380
    Fax: 863-534-4382
    library.mypclc.org/historical

St. Augustine Historical Society
    271 Charlotte Street
    St. Augustine, FL 32084
    904-824-2872
    Fax: 904-824-2569
    sahsdirector@bellsouth.net
    www.staugustinehistoricalsociety.org

Society of Florida Archivists
    PO Box 2746
    Lakeland, FL 33806-2746
    www.florida-archivists.org

University of Miami, Otto G. Richter Library
    PO Box 248214
    1300 Memorial Drive
    Coral Gables, FL 33124-0320
    305-284-3233
    Fax: 305-284-4027
    www.library.miami.edu

Vital Records Office
Department of Health
PO Box 210
1217 Pearl St.
Jacksonville, FL 32231-0042
904-359-6900
Fax: 904-359-6931
VitalStats@doh.state.fl.us
www.doh.state.fl.us/planning_eval/vital_statistics/index.html

Georgia

African-American Family Historical Association
Robert W. Woodruff Library
Atlanta University Center
111 James P. Brawley Drive
Atlanta, GA 30314
404-978-2052
archives@auctr.edu
www.auctr.edu/FindingAWay/AAFHA.asp

Coweta County Genealogical Society
PO Box 427
5 West Broad Street
Grantville, GA 30220
info@ccgsinc.org
www.ccgsinc.org/

Georgia Department of Archives
5800 Jonesboro Road
Morrow, GA 30260
678-364-3700
sos.georgia.gov/archives/

Georgia Genealogical Society
PO Box 550247
Atlanta, GA 30355-2747
www.gagensociety.org

Georgia Historical Society
501 Whittaker Street
Savannah, GA 31401
912-651-2128
877-424-4789
Fax: 912-651-2831
www.georgiahistory.com

or

Atlanta Office
260 14th Street, NW, Suite A-148
Atlanta, GA 30318
404-671-8570
www.georgiahistory.com

Georgia Public Library Service
1800 Century Pl. NE, Ste. 150
Atlanta, GA 30345-4304
404-235-7200
www.georgialibraries.org/

The Georgia Trust
1516 Peachtree St. NW
Atlanta, GA 30309
404-881-9980
Fax: 404-875-2205
www.georgiatrust.org

Hargrett Library Rare Books & Manuscript Library, Rare Map Collection
Main Library
University of Georgia
320 S. Jackson St.
Athens, GA 30602-1641
706-542-7123
Fax: 706-542-0672
www.libs.uga.edu/darchive/hargrett/maps/maps.html

National Archives and Records Administration, Southeast Region
5780 Jonesboro Road
Morrow, GA 30260
770-968-2100
Fax: 770-968-2547
atlanta.archives@nara.gov
www.archives.gov/southeast/index.html

and

Atlanta Records Center
4712 Southpark Boulevard
Ellenwood, GA 30294
404-736-2820
Fax: 404-736-2931
atlanta.archives@nara.gov
www.archives.gov/southeast/index.html
University of Georgia Libraries

University of Georgia
Athens, GA 30602-1641
706-542-3251
www.libs.uga/edu

Vital Records Service
Georgia Department of Human Resources
2600 Skyland Drive NE
Atlanta, GA 30319
404-679-4702
phvitalrecords@gdph.state.ga.us
health.state.ga.us/programs/vitalrecords

Hawaii

Hawaiian Historical Society
560 Kawaiaho`a Street
Honolulu, HI 96813
808-537-6271
Fax: 808-537-6271
hhsbarb@lava.net
www.hawaiianhistory.org

Hawaii State Archives
Department of Accounting and General Services
Kekāuluohi Building, 'Iolani Palace Grounds
364 S. King Street
Honolulu, HI 96813
808-586-0329
Fax: 808-586-0330
archives@hawaii.gov
hawaii.gov/dags/archives

Hawaii State Department of Health/Vital Records
1250 Punchbowl Street
Honolulu, HI 96813
808-586-4533
Vr-info@doh.hawaii.gov
hawaii.gov/health/vital-records/vital-records

Hawaii State Public Library System
Hawaii State Library
478 S. King St.
Honolulu, HI 96813-2901
808-586-3621
www.librarieshawaii.org
(see website for other libraries in the system)

National Memorial Cemetery of the Pacific
2177 Puowaina Dr.
Honolulu, HI 96813-1729
808-566-3720
Fax: 808-532-3756
www.cem.va.gov/CEMs/nchp/nmcp.asp

Idaho

David O. McKay Library
Brigham Young University-Idaho
Rexburg, ID 83460
208-496-2386
familyhistory@byui.edu
abish.byui.edu/specialcollections/famhist/index.cfm

Idaho Bureau of Land Management
1387 S. Vinnell Way
Boise, ID 83709-1657
208-373-4000
Fax: 208-373-3899
id_so_information@blm.gov
www.id.blm.gov

Idaho Commission for Libraries
325 W. State St.
Boise, ID 83702
208-334-2150
800-458-3271 (in state)
Fax: 208-334-4016
www.lili.org

Idaho Genealogical Society, Inc.
PO Box 1854
Boise, ID 83701-1854
208-384-0542
idahogenealogy@hotmail.com
www.idahogenealogy.org

Idaho State Historical Society and Library
2205 Old Penitentiary Road
Boise, ID 83712
208-334-2682
Fax: 208-334-2774
idahohistory.net

Idaho State Vital Records Office
Bureau of Vital Records and Health Statistics
450 W. State St.
Boise, ID 83720
208-334-5988
Fax: 208-389-9096
www.vitalrec.com/id.html

University of Idaho Library
Special Collections and Archives
PO Box 442351
Rayburn Street
Moscow, ID 8344-2351
208-885-7951
Fax: 208-885-6817
libspec@uidaho.edu
www.lib.uidaho.edu/special-collections/sc-desc.htm

Illinois

Brethren Historical Library and Archives
1451 Dundee Ave.
Elgin, IL 60120
800-323-8039 ext. 294
Fax: 847-742-6103
Kshaffer_gb@brethren.org
www.brethren.org/site/PageServer?pagename=office_
    general_secretary_brethren_historical_library_
    archives

Evangelical Lutheran Church in America Archives
321 Bonnie Lane
Elk Grove Village, IL 60007
847-690-9410
archives@elca.org
www.elca.org/archives

Evangelical Lutheran Church in America Library
8765 W. Higgins Rd.
Chicago, IL 60631
800-638-3522 ext. 2811
www.elca.org/Who-Are/Our-Three-
    Expressions/Churchwide-Organization/Office
    -of-the-Secretary/Library.aspx

Illinois Heritage Association
602 ½ E. Green St.
Champaign, IL 61820
217-359-5600
plmxiha@prairienet.org
illinoisheritage.prairienet.org

Illinois Historic Preservation Agency
Abraham Lincoln Presidential Library
112 North Sixth Street
Springfield, IL 62701507
217-558-8844
Fax: 217-785-6250
HPA.info@illinois.gov
www.state.il.us/hpa/lib

Illinois Mennonite Historical and Genealogical Society
675 State Rte. 116
Metamora, IL 61548-7732
309-367-2551
info@imhgs.org or imhc@mtco.com
www.imhgs.org

Illinois State Archives
Margaret Cross Norton Building
Capitol Complex
Springfield, IL 62756
217-782-4682
Fax: 217-524-3930
www.sos.state.il.us/departments/archives/archives.html

Illinois State Genealogical Society
PO Box 10195
Springfield, IL 62791-0195
217-789-1968
isgs.secy@sbcglobal.net
www.rootsweb.ancestry.com/~ilsgs

Illinois State Historical Society
PO Box 1800
210 ½ South Sixth Street, Suite 200
Springfield, IL 62705-1800
217-525-2781
Fax: 217-525-2783
wfurry@historyillinois.org
www.historyillinois.org

Illinois State Library
Gwendolyn Brooks Building
300 South Second Street
Springfield, IL 62701-1796
217-785-5600
800-665-5576 (in state only)
TDD: 888-261-2709
www.cyberdriveillinois.com/departments/library/

National Archives Records Administration, Great Lakes Branch
7358 South Pulaski Rd.
Chicago, IL 60629-5898
773-948-9001
Fax: 773-948-9050
chicago.archives@nara.gov
www.archives.gov/great-lakes

Newberry Library
60 West Walton St.
Chicago, IL 60610-3305
312-255-3506
reference@newberry.org
www.newberry.org/

Polish Genealogical Society and Museum of America
984 N. Milwaukee Ave.
Chicago, IL 60642-4101
773-384-3352
PGSAmerica@pgsa.org
www.pgsa.org

Swedish American Historical Society, Inc.
Box 48
3225 W. Foster Ave.
Chicago, IL 60625
773-583-5722
773-244-6224 (archives)
info@swedishamericanhist.org
www.swedishamericanhist.org

Swenson Swedish Immigration Research Center
%Augustana College
639 - 38th Street
Rock Island, IL 61201-2296
309-794-7204
Fax: 309-794-7443
sag@augustana.edu
www.augustana.edu/swenson

University of Illinois Library
1408 West Gregory Drive, MC-522
Urbana, IL 61801
217-333-2290
www.library.uiuc.edu

Vital Records Office
605 W. Jefferson Street
Springfield, IL 62702-5097
217-782-6553
Fax: 217-785-3209
TTY 800-547-0466
vitalrecords@idph.state.il.us
www.idph.state.il.us/vitalrecords/index.htm

Indiana

Allen County Public Library
900 Library Plaza
Fort Wayne, IN 46802
260-421-1252
Fax: 260-421-1386
www.acpl.lib.in.us

Indiana Genealogical Society
PO Box 10507
Fort Wayne, IN 46582
www.indgensoc.org

Indiana Historical Society
    William Henry Smith Memorial Library
    450 West Ohio Street
    Indianapolis, IN 46202-3269
    317-232-1882
    800-447-1830
    reference@indianahistory.org
    www.indianahistory.org

Indiana State Archives
    6440 E. Thirtieth St.
    Indianapolis, IN 46219-1007
    317-591-5222
    Fax: 317-591-5324
    www.in.gov/icpr

Indiana State Library
    315 West Ohio Street
    Indianapolis, IN 46204-2296
    317-232-3689
    866-683-0008
    www.in.gov/library

Indiana State Vital Records Department
    Indiana State Department of Health
    2 North Meridian Street
    Indianapolis, IN 46204
    www.in.gov/isdh/23574.htm

Mennonite Church USA Historical Committee and Archives
    1700 S. Main St.
    Goshen, IN 46526-4794
    574-535-7477
    Fax: 574-535-7756
    Archives@MennoniteUSA.org
    www.mcusa-archives.org

Mennonite Historical Library
    Goshen College
    1700 S. Main St.
    Goshen, IN 46526
    574-535-7418
    Fax: 574-535-7438
    mhl@goshen.edu
    www.goshen.edu/mhl

Iowa

Danish American Heritage Society
4105 Stone Brooke Rd.
Ames, IA 50010
515-232-7479 or 480-816-8725
iversenji@qwest.net
www.danishamericanheritagesociety.org/

Danish Immigrant Museum
PO Box 470
2212 Washington St.
Elk Horn, IA 51531-0470
712-764-7001
800-759-9192
Fax: 712-764-7002
www.dkmuseum.org

Danish Immigrant Museum
Family History and Genealogical Center
4210 Main Street
PO Box 429
Elk Horn, IA 51531-0249
712-764-7008
877-764-7008
Fax: 712-764-7010
librarian@danishmuseum.org
www.danishmuseum.org

German American Heritage Center
712 W. Second St.
Davenport, IA 52802-1410
563-322-8844
gahc.org/

Iowa Department of Public Health
Bureau of Health Statistics
Lucas State Office Building, First Floor
321 East 12th Street
Des Moines, IA 50319-0075
515-281-4944
idph.state.ia.us/apl/health_statistics.asp

Iowa Genealogical Society
    628 E. Grand Ave.
    Des Moines, IA 50309-1924
    515-276-0287
    Fax: 515-727-1824
    igs@iowagenealogy.org
    www.iowagenealogy.org

State Historical Society of Iowa
    State of Iowa Historical Building
    600 East Locust
    Des Moines, IA 50319-0290
    515-281-5111
    Fax: 515-242-6498 or 515-282-0502
    dmlibrary@iowa.gov
    www.iowahistory.org

        or

State Historical Society of Iowa
    Centennial Building
    402 Iowa Ave.
    Iowa City, IA 52240-1806
    319-335-3916
    Fax: 319-335-3935
    libstu@blue.weeg.uiowa.edu
    www.iowahistory.org

State Library of Iowa
    Ola Babcock Miller Building
    1112 E. Grand Ave.
    Des Moines, IA 50319-0233
    515-281-4105
    800-248-4483
    Fax: 515-281-6191
    www.statelibraryofiowa.org

Vesterheim Norwegian American Museum
    PO Box 379
    523 West Water Street
    Decorah, IA 52101
    563-382-9681
    info@vesterheim.org
    vesterheim.org/index.php

Kansas

Kansas Council of Genealogical Societies
PO Box 3858
Topeka, KS 66604-6858
kscouncilgensoc@juno.com
skyways.lib.ks.us/genweb/kcgs

Kansas Genealogical Society Library
Village Square Mall
PO Box 103
2601 Central Avenue
Dodge City, KS 67801-0103
620-225-1951
ks-genlibrary@hotmail.com
www.dodgecity.net/kgs

Kansas State Historical Society
Kansas History Center
6425 SW Sixth Ave.
Topeka, KS 66615
785-272-8681
Fax: 785-272-8682
TTY: 785-272-8683
reference@kshs.org
www.kshs.org

Kansas State Library
300 SW Tenth Ave., Room 343-N
Topeka, KS 66612-1593
785-296-3296
800-432-3919 (KS only)
Fax: 785-368-7291
infodesk@kslib.info
skyways.lib.ks.us/kansas/KSL

Kenneth Spencer Research Library
Kansas Collections, University of Kansas
1450 Poplar Lane
Lawrence KS 66045-7616
785-864-4334
Fax: 785-864-5803
spencer.lib.ku.edu/kc

Mennonite Library and Archives
%Bethel College
300 E. Twenty-seventh St.
North Newton, KS 67117-0531
316-284-5304
Fax: 316-284-5843
mla@bethelks.edu
www.bethelks.edu/mla

Midwest Historical and Genealogical Society
PO Box 1121
1203 North Main
Wichita, KS 67201-1121
316-264-3611
mhgs1121@aol.com
skyways.lib.ks.us/genweb/mhgs/index.html

Office of Vital Statistics
Kansas State Department of Health and Environment
1000 SW Jackson Street
Topeka, KS 66612-2221
785-296-1400
Vital.Records@kdheks.gov
www.kdhe.state.ks.us/vital

Riley County Genealogical Society Library
2005 Claflin
Manhattan, KS 66502
785-565-6495
www.rileycgs.com

Kentucky

Cabinet for Health and Family Services
Office of Vital Statistics
275 E. Main St.
Frankfort, KY 40621
502-564-4212
chfs.ky.gov/dph/vital

Filson Historical Society
  1310 S. Third St.
  Louisville, KY 40208
  502-636-5083
  Fax: 502-635-5086
  www.filsonhistorical.org

Kentucky Department for Libraries and Archives
  300 Coffee Tree Rd.
  Frankfort, KY 40601
  502-564-8300
  800-928-7000
  kdla.archives@ky.gov
  www.kdla.ky.gov/

Kentucky Genealogical Society
  PO Box 153
  Frankfort, KY 40602
  Kygs@fewpb.net
  www.kygs.org

Kentucky Historical Society
  100 West Broadway
  Frankfort, KY 4060
  502-564-1792
  history.ky.gov

Kentucky Library
  Western Kentucky University
  1906 College Heights Blvd. #11067
  Bowling Green, KY 42101-1067
  270-745-6125
  Fax: 270-745-6422
  Library.web@wku.edu
  www.wku.edu/library/tip/genealogy.html

Margaret I. King Library
  Special Collections and Archives
  University of Kentucky
  179 Funkhouser Drive
  Lexington, KY 40506-0039
  859-257-8611
  Fax: 859-257-6311
  www.uky.edu/Libraries/lib.php?lib_id=13

National Society Sons of the American Revolution
1000 S. Fourth St.
Louisville, KY 40203
502-589-1776
www.sar.org

Louisiana

East Baton Rouge Parish Library
7711 Goodwood Boulevard
Baton Rouge, LA 70806
225-231-3750
www.ebr.lib.la.us

Howard-Tilton Memorial Library
Special Collections
Tulane University
7001 Freret Street
New Orleans, LA 70118
504-865-5605
specialcollections.tulane.edu

Jackson Barracks Military Library
Office of Adjutant General
Jackson Barracks, Area A, Building 53
New Orleans, LA 70146-0330
504-278-8241
jbmuseum@la-arng.ngb.army.mil
www.la.ngb.army.mil/dmh

Louisiana Division, City Archives and Special Collections
New Orleans Public Library
219 Loyola Ave.
New Orleans, LA 70112
504-596-2610
nutrias.org/spec/speclist.htm

Louisiana Office of Historic Preservation
Captiol Annex Building
PO Box 44247
1051 North Third Street
Baton Rouge, LA 70802
225-342-8160
Fax: 225-219-0765
hp@crt.state.la.us
www.crt.state.la.us/hp

Louisiana Genealogical and Historical Society
PO Box 82060
Baton Rouge, LA 70884-2060
bstahr@bellsouth.net
www.rootsweb.ancestry.com/~la-lghs

Louisiana Historical Association
Dupré Library, Room 321
PO Box 42808
302 East St. Mary Boulevard
Lafayette, LA 70504-2808
337-482-6350
Fax: 337-482-6028
lha@louisiana.edu
cls.louisiana.edu/lha/index.shtml

Louisiana Historical Society
1401 Foucher Street
New Orleans, LA 70115
504-897-8090
sakr@cox.net
www.louisianahistoricalsociety.org

Louisiana State Archives
PO Box 94125
3851 Essen Lane
Baton Rouge, LA 70809-2137
225-922-1000
Fax: 225-922-0433
library@sos.louisiana.gov
www.sos.louisiana.gov/tabid/53/Default.aspx

Louisiana State Library
Po Box 131
701 North 4th Street
Baton Rouge, LA 70821
225-342-4923
Fax: 225-219-4804
www.state.lib.la.us

Office of Public Health, Vital Records Registry
New Orleans State Office Building
PO Box 60630
New Orleans, LA 70160
504-219-4500
800-454-9570
Fax: 504-219-4478
dhh-vitalweb@la.gov
www.dhh.louisiana.gov/offices/?ID=252
(See website for various Parish offices)

La Societe Des Cajuns
PO Box 433
Larose, LA 70373
la_societe@vienici.com
www.vienici.com/lasociete

Maine

Folger Library
University of Maine
5729 Folger Library
Orono, ME 04469-5729
207-581-1661
Fax: 207-581-1653
www.library.umaine.edu/resources.htm

Maine Department of Health and Human Services
Office of Vital Statistics
11 State House Station
244 Water Street
Augusta, ME 04333-0011
207-287-3181
888-664-9491
www.maine.gov/dhhs/vitalrecords.htm

Maine Genealogical Society
PO Box 221
Farmington, ME 04938-0221
mainegenealogical@yahoo.com
www.rootsweb.ancestry.com/~megs

Maine Historical Society
489 Congress St.
Portland, ME 04101
207-774-1822
Fax: 207-775-4301
info@mainehistory.org
www.mainehistory.org

Maine State Archives
84 State House Station
State House Complex/Cultural Building
Augusta, ME 04333-0084
207-287-5790
Fax: 207-287-5739
www.state.me.us/sos/arc/

Maine State Library
64 State House Station
230 State Street
Augusta, ME 04333-0064
207-287-5600
Fax: 207-287-5615
TTY: 888-577-6690
reference.desk@maine.gov
www.state.me.us/msl

Maryland

American Latvian Association, Inc.
400 Hurley Ave.
Rockville, MD 20850-3121
301-340-1914
Fax: 301-340-8732
alainfo@alausa.org
www.alausa.org

Division of Health Statistics
Maryland Department of Health and Mental Hygiene
6550 Reisterstown Road
Reisterstown Road Plaza
Baltimore, MD 21215
410-764-3038
800-832-3277
DESmith@dhmh.state.md.us
vsa.maryland.gov

or

Vital Statistics Data for Research Purposes:
Metro Executive Building
4201 Patterson, MD 21215
410-764-3514

Enoch Pratt Free Library
    Maryland Department
    400 Cathedral Street
    Baltimore, MD 21201
    410-396-5430
    TTY 410-396-3761
    SLRC@prattlibrary.org
    www.prattlibrary.org

Maryland Genealogical Society
    201 West Monument St.
    Baltimore, MD 21201
    www.mdgensoc.org

Maryland Historical Society Library
    201 West Monument St.
    Baltimore, MD 21201-4674
    410-685-3750
    Fax: 410-385-2105
    library_dept@mdhs.org
    www.mdhs.org

Maryland State Archives
    Dr. Edward C. Papenfuse State Archives Building
    350 Rowe Boulevard
    Annapolis, MD 21401
    800-235-4045
    410-260-6400
    archives@mdsa.net
    www.msa.md.gov

Maryland State Law Library
  Robert C. Murphy Courts of Appeal Building
  361 Rowe Blvd.
  Annapolis, MD 21401
  410-260-1430
  888-216-8156
  Fax: 410-260-1572
  lawlibrary@mdcourts.gov
  www.lawlib.state.md.us

National Archives and Records Administration
  8601 Adelphi Rd.
  College Park, MD 20740-6001
  301-837-2000
  866-272-6272
  www.archives.gov/dc-metro/college-park/index.html

United Methodist Historical Society
  %Lovely Lane Museum Library
  2200 St. Paul St.
  Baltimore, MD 21218-5897
  410-889-4458
  www.loc.gov/rr/main/religion/umhs.html

Massachusetts

American Antiquarian Society Library
  185 Salisbury Street
  Worcester, MA 01609-1634
  508-755-5221
  Fax: 508-753-3311
  library@americanantiquarian.org
  www.americanantiquarian.org/genealogy.htm

American Jewish Historical Society
  160 Herrick Rd.
  Newton Centre, MA 02459
  617-226-1245
  Fax: 617-226-1248
  www.ajhsboston.org

American-Portuguese Genealogical and Historical Society, Inc.
  PO Box 644
  Taunton, MA 02780-0644
  www.apghs.com/index.html

Association for Gravestone Studies
    Greenfield Corporate Center
    101 Munson Street – Suite 108
    Greenfield, MA 01301
    413-772-0836
    info@gravestonestudies.org
    www.gravestonestudies.org

Boston Public Library
    Copley Square
    700 Boylston St.
    Boston, MA 02116
    617-536-5400
    ask@bpl.org
    www.bpl.org

Haverhill Public Library
    99 Main Street
    Haverhill, MA 01830
    978-373-1586
    Fax: 978-373-8466
    www.haverhillpl.org/Departments/special.html

The Irish Ancestral Research Association
    Dept. W.
    2120 Commonwealth Avenue
    Auburndale, MA 02466-1909
    president@tiara.ie
    tiara.ie

Italian Genealogical Society of America
    PO Box 3572
    Peabody, MA 01961-3572
    www.italianroots.org

Massachusetts Archives
    Secretary of the Commonwealth
    220 Morrissey Blvd.
    Boston, MA 02125
    617-727-2816
    Fax: 617-288-8429
    archives@sec.state.ma.us
    www.sec.state.ma.us/ARC/arcidx.htm

Massachusetts Genealogical Council
PO Box 5393
Cochituate, MA 01778-5393
archives@massgencouncil.com
www.massgencouncil.com

Massachusetts Historical Society
1154 Boyleston Street
Boston, MA 02215-3695
617-536-1608
Fax: 617-859-0074
www.masshist.org/welcome

Massachusetts Society of Genealogists, Inc.
PO Box 215
Ashland, MA 01721-0215
president@massachusettssocietyofgenealogists.org
massachusettssocietyofgenealogists.org/

Massachusetts State Vital Records Office
Registry of Vital Records and Statistics
150 Mount Vernon Street, 1st Floor
Dorchester, MA 02125-3105
617-740-2600
Fax: 617-825-7755
vital.recordsrequest@state.ma.us
www.mass.gov/dph/rvrs

National Archives - New England Region
Frederick C. Murphy Federal Center
380 Trapelo Road
Waltham, MA 02452-6399
781-663-0130
Fax: 781-663-0154
waltham.archives@nara.gov
www.archives.gov/northeast/boston

National Archives – Pittsfield Region
Silvio O. Conte National Records Center
10 Conte Drive
Pittsfield, MA 01201-8230
413-236-3600
Fax: 413-236-3609
pittsfield.archives@nara.gov
www.archives.gov/northeast/pittsfield

New England Historic Genealogical Society
99-101 Newbury St.
Boston, MA 02116
617-536-5740
888-296-3447
Fax: 617-536-7307
research@nehgs.org
www.newenglandancestors.org

State Library of Massachusetts
State House, Room 341
24 Beacon St.
Boston, MA 02133
617-727-2590
Fax: 617-727-9730
www.state.ma.us/lib

Swedish Ancestry Research Association
PO Box 70603
Worcester, MA 01607-0603
info@sarassociation.org
sarassociation.tripod.com/sara/SARA_Home_Page.htm

Michigan

Archives of Michigan
Michigan Library and History Center
702 W. Kalamazoo St.
Lansing, MI 48913
517-373-1481
archives@michigan.gov
www.michigan.gov/dnr/0,1607,7-153-4463_19313--,00.html

Bentley Historical Library
University of Michigan
1150 Beal Avenue
Ann Arbor, MI 48109-2113
734-764-3482
Fax: 734-936-1333
bentley.ref@umich.edu
bentley.umich.edu/

Detroit Public Library
  Burton Historical Collection
  5201 Woodward Avenue
  Detroit, MI 48202
  313-833-1480
  www.detroit.lib.mi.us/burton/burton_index.htm

French-Canadian Heritage Society, Michigan
  PO Box 1900
  Royal Oak, MI 48068-1900
  FCHSM-email@Habitant.org
  fchsm.habitant.org/

Genealogical Society of Flemish Americans
  18740 Thirteen Mile Rd.
  Roseville, MI 48066
  www.rootsweb.ancestry.com/~gsfa

Historical Society of Michigan
  1305 Abbott Rd.
  East Lansing, MI 48823
  517-324-1828
  Fax: 517-324-4370
  hsm@hsmichigan.org
  www.hsofmich.org

Library of Michigan
  PO Box 30007
  702 West Kalamazoo St.
  Lansing, MI 48909-7507
  517-373-1300
  Fax: 517-373-4800
  librarian@michigan.gov
  www.michigan.gov/libraryofmichigan

Michigan Department of Community Health
  Capitol View Building
  201 Townsend Street
  Lansing, MI 48913
  517-373-3740
  VRCustomerService@michigan.gov
  www.michigan.gov/mdch/0,1607,7-132-4645- - -,00.html

Michigan Genealogical Council
PO Box 80953
Lansing, MI 48908-0953
migencouncil@att.net
www.mimgc.org

Minnesota

American Swedish Institute
2600 Park Ave.
Minneapolis, MN 55407
612-871-4907
Fax: 612-871-8682
info@americanswedishinst.org
www.americanswedishinst.org/ASI/Home.html

Czechoslovak Genealogical Society International
PO Box 16225
St. Paul, MN 55116-0225
651-450-2322
research@cgsi.org
www.cgsi.org

Danish American Center
3030 West River Parkway South
Minneapolis, MN 55406
612-729-3800
dainfo@dac.mn
www.dac.mn

German-Bohemian Heritage Society
PO Box 822
1200 South Broadway (rear entrance)
New Ulm, MN 56073-0822
507-359-2121
www.rootsweb.ancestry.com/~gbhs

Germanic Genealogy Society
PO Box 16312
St. Paul, MN 55116-0312
ggsmn.org

Irish Genealogical Society, Int'l
1185 Concord Street N., Suite 218
South St. Paul, MN 55075
Research@IrishGenealogical.org
www.irishgenealogical.org

Minnesota Genealogical Society
    1185 Concord Street N., Suite 218
    South St. Paul, MN 55075-1150
    651-445-9057
    mngs.org

Minnesota State Historical Society and Archives
    345 Kellogg Blvd. W.
    St. Paul, MN 55102-1906
    651-259-3300
    800-657-3773
    reference@mnhs.org
    www.mnhs.org

Minnesota State Vital Records Office
    Minnesota Department of Health
    Birth and Death Records
    PO Box 64499
    St. Paul, MN 55164-0499
    612-676-5121
    www.health.state.mn.us
    (See website for regional office information.)

Norwegian-American Historical Assocation
    1510 St. Olaf Avenue
    Northfield, MN 55057-1097
    507-786-3229
    Fax: 507-786-3734
    naha@stolaf.edu or naha-archivists@stolaf.edu
    www.naha.stolaf.edu

Southern Minnesota Historical Center
    University Archives
    Minnesota State University – Mankato
    PO Box 8419
    Mankato, MN 56001-8419
    507-389-1029
    Fax: 507-389-5155
    archives@mnsu.edu
    www.lib.mnsu.edu/lib/archives/archives.html

University of Minnesota
Immigration History Research Center
Elmer L. Andersen Library, Suite 311
222 - 21st Avenue S.
Minneapolis, MN 55455
612-625-4800
Fax: 612-626-0018
irhc@umn.edu
www.ihrc.umn.edu

Mississippi

Evans Memorial Library
105 North Long Street
Aberdeen, MS
622-369-4601
Fax: 622-369-2971
eml@tombigbee.lib.ms.us
www.tombigbee.lib.ms.us/evans

Family Research Association of Mississippi
PO Box 13334
Jackson, MS 39236-3334

Mississippi Archives and Library
William F. Winters Archives and History Building
PO Box 571
200 North St.
Jackson, MS 39205-0571
601-576-6876
Fax: 601-576-6964
webadmin@mdah.state.ms.us
mdah.state.ms.us

Mississippi Historical Society
PO Box 571
Jackson, MS 39205-0571
mhs@mdah.state.ms.us
mdah.state.ms.us/admin/mhistsoc.html

Mississippi Library Commission
3881 Eastwood Dr.
Jackson, MS 39211
800-647-7542
Fax: 601-432-4486
mlcref@mcl.lib.ms.us
www.mlc.lib.ms.us

Mitchell Memorial Library
Special Collections
Mississippi State University
PO Box 5408
395 Hardy Road
Mississippi State, MS 39762-5408
662-325-7679
sp_coll@library.msstate.edu
library.msstate.edu/specialcollections

State Department of Health
Mississippi Vital Records
Underwood Building
571 Stadium Drive
Jackson, MS 39216-4511
601-576-7981
Fax: 601-576-7505
VRInfo@msdh.state.ms.us
www.msdh.state.ms.us/msdhsite/_static/31,0,109.html

Missouri

Afro-American Historical & Genealogical Society, Inc.
PO Box 73067
Washington, DC 20056-3067
info@aahgs.org
www.aahgs.org

Kansas City Public Library
Missouri Valley Special Collections
14 West 10th Street
Kansas City, MO 64105
816-701-3427
Fax: 816-701-3401
TTY: 816-701-3403
History@kclibrary.org
www.kclibrary.org

Mid-Continent Library
    Midwest Genealogy Center
    3440 S. Lee's Summit Road
    Independence, MO 64055-1923
    816-252-7228
    www.mcpl.lib.mo.us

Missouri Department of Health
    Bureau of Vital Records
    PO Box 570
    Jefferson City, MO 65102-0570
    573-751-6387
    VitalRecordsInfo@dhss.mo.gov
    www.dhss.mo.gov/BirthAndDeathRecords

Missouri Historical Society and Museum
    PO Box 11940
    5700 Lindell Boulevard
    St. Louis, MO 63112
    314-361-7395
    Fax: 314-454-3162
        Library
        225 South Skinker Boulevard
        314-746-4500
    library@mohistory.org
    www.mohistory.org

Missouri State Archives
    State Information Center
    PO Box 1747
    600 W. Main St.
    Jefferson City, MO 65102
    573-751-3280
    Fax: 573-526-7333
    archref@sos.mo.gov
    www.sos.mo.gov/archives

Missouri State Genealogical Association
    PO Box 833
    Columbia, MO 65205-0833
    mosga@mosga.org
    www.mosga.org

Missouri State Library
> State Information Center
> PO Box 387
> 600 W. Main Street
> Jefferson City, MO 65101
> 573-751-3615
> Fax: 573-526-1142
> libref@sos.mo.gov
> www.sos.mo.gov/library

National Archives and Records Administration - Central Plains Region
> 400 West Pershing Road
> Kansas, MO 64108
> 816-268-8000
> Fax: 816-268-8038
> kansascity.archives@nara.gov
> www.archives.gov/central-plains/kansas-city/ index.html

National Archives and Records Administration – Central Plains Region, Lee's Summit
> 200 Space Center Drive
> Lee's Summit, Missouri 64064-1182
> 816-268-8100
> Fax: 816-268-8159
> leessummit.reference@nara.gov
> www.archives.gov/central-plains/lees-summit

St. Louis County Library
> 1640 So. Lindbergh Boulevard
> St. Louis, MO 63131
> 314-994-3300
> reference@slcl.org
> www.slcl.org/branches/hq/sc/sc-genpg.htm

St. Louis Public Library
> 1301 Olive St.
> St. Louis, MO 63103
> 314-241-2288
> Fax: 314-539-0393
> TDD: 314-539-0364
> webref@slpl.org
> www.slpl.org/index.asp

State Historical Society of Missouri
1020 Lowry Street
Columbia, MO 65201-7298
573-882-1187
800-747-6366
shsofmo@umsystem.edu
shs.umsystem.edu/index.shtml

Montana

Bureau of Land Management, Montana State Office
5001 Southgate Dr.
Billings, MT 59101
406-896-5000
Fax: 406-896-5299
MT_SO_Information@blm.gov
www.mt.blm.gov

Bureau of Records and Statistics
State Department of Health and Environmental Science
Helena, MT 59620
406-444-2614
www.bowercommunity.com/homestead/info-Montana.htm

Montana Historical Society
PO Box 201201
225 North Roberts
Helena, MT 5960-1201
406-444-2694
mhslibrary@mt.gov
montanahistoricalsociety.org

Montana State Genealogical Society
c/o Lewis & Clark Library
PO Box 5313
Helena, MT 59604
www.rootsweb.ancestry.com/~mtmsgs/index.htm

Montana State Library
PO Box 201800
1515 E. Sixth Ave.
Helena, MT 59620-1800
406-444-3115
Fax: 406-444-0204
MSLReference@mt.gov
msl.state.mt.us

Montana State University Library
Special Collections
PO Box 173320
Bozeman, MT 59717-3320
406-994-4242
Fax: 406-994-2851
spcoll@www.lib.montana.edu
www.lib.montana.edu/archives

Montana State Vital Records Office
PO Box 4210
111 N. Sanders, Room 201
Helena, MT 59604-4210
406-444-4228
montanagenealogy.com/vital.htm

University of Montana –Maureen and Mike Mansfield Library
Special Collections
32 Campus Drive
Missoula, MT 59812-9936
406-243-2053
Fax: 406-243-4067
library.archives@umontana.edu
www.lib.umt.edu/asc

Nebraska

American Historical Society of Germans from Russia
631 D. St.
Lincoln, NE 68502-1199
402-474-3363
Fax: 402-474-7229
ahsgr@ahsgr.org
ahsgr.org

Danish Immigrant Archives
Dana College
PO Box 7
2848 College Dr.
Blair, NE 68008
402-250-6691
daaljill@gmail.com
www.danishamericanarchive.org

Love Memorial Library
    Archives & Special Collections
    PO Box 844100
    29 Love Library
    City Campus
    University of Nebraska
    Lincoln, NE 68588-4100
    402-472-2531
    Fax: 402-472-5181
    libraries.unl.edu/spec

Nebraska Department of Health and Human Services
    Vital Records
    PO Box 95065
    1033 "O" Street, Suite 130
    Golds Galleria, 1st Floor
    Lincoln, NE 68509-5065
    402-471-2871
    DHHS.VitalRecords@nebraska.gov
    www.hhs.state.ne.us/vital_records.htm

Nebraska Library Commission
    The Atrium
    1200 North St., Ste. 120
    Lincoln, NE 68508-2023
    800-307-2665 (Nebraska only)
    402-471-2045
    Fax: 402-471-2083
    www.nlc.state.ne.us

Nebraska State Genealogical Society
    PO Box 5608
    Lincoln, NE 68505-0608
    402-471-4771
    nesgs@nesgs.org
    www.nesgs.org

Book collection @ Beatrice Public Library
    100 North 16th St.
    Beatrice, NE 68310
    402-223-3584

Nebraska State Historical Society and Nebraska State Archives
PO Box 82554
1500 "R" Street
Lincoln, NE 68501
402-471-4751
Fax: 402-471-3100
Nshs.libarch@nebraska.gov
www.nebraskahistory.org/lib-arch/index.htm

Omaha Public Library
215 S. 15th Street
Omaha, NE 68102
402-444-4826
www.omahapubliclibrary.org

North Platte Public Library
120 W 4th Street
North Platte, NE 69101
308-535-8036
Fax: 308-535-8296
library@ci.north-platte.ne.us
www.ci.north-platte.ne.us/library

Nevada

Nevada Bureau of Land Management
PO Box 12000
1340 Financial Boulevard
Reno, NV 89502
775-861-6500
Fax: 775-861-6606
nviac@blm.gov
www.blm.gov/nv/st/en.html

Nevada Historical Society
1650 N. Virginia St.
Reno, NV 89503
775-688-1190
Fax: 775-688-2917
www.museums.nevadaculture.org/index.php?option=
com-content&view=article&id=446&Itemid=122

Nevada State Genealogical Society
PO Box 20666
Reno, NV 89515-0666
www.rootsweb.ancestry.com/~nvsgs

Nevada State Library and Archives
100 N. Stewart St.
Carson City, NV 89701-4285
775-684-3360
800-922-2880 (Nevada only)
Fax: 775-684-3311
nsla.nevadaculture.org

Nevada State Museum and Historical Society
708 North Curry Street
Las Vegas, NV 89703
775-687-4340
Fax: 775-687-4333
museums.nevadaculture.org

Office of Vital Records
4150 Technology Way, Suite 104
Carson City, NV 89706
775-684-4242
Fax: 775-684-4156
vitalrecords@health.nv.gov
health.nv.gov/VS.htm

New Hampshire

American-Canadian Genealogical Society
PO Box 6478
Manchester, NH 03108-6478
603-622-1554
research@acgs.org
www.acgs.org

New Hampshire Department of State
Division of Vital Records Administration
71 South Fruit Street
Concord, NH 03301-2410
vitalrecords@sos.state.nh.us
www.sos.nh.gov/vitalrecords

New Hampshire Division of Archives and Records Management
71 S. Fruit St.
Concord, NH 03301
603-271-2236
Fax: 603-271-2272
archives@sos.state.nh.us
www.sos.nh.gov/archives

New Hampshire Historical Society, NHHS Tuck Library
30 Park St.
Concord, NH 03301-6384
603-228-6688
Fax: 603-224-0463
www.nhhistory.org

New Hampshire Old Graveyard Association
PO Box 1016
Goshen, NH 03752
www.rootsweb.ancestry.com/~nhoga

New Hampshire Society of Genealogists
PO Box 2316
Concord, NH 03302-2316
www.nhsog.org

New Hampshire State Library
20 Park St.
Concord, NH 03301
603-271-6823
www.state.nh.us/nhsl

New Jersey

Archibald S. Alexander Library
Special Collections and Archives
Rutgers University
169 College Avenue
New Brunswick, NJ 08901-1163
732-932-7006
Fax: 732-932-7021
www.libraries.rutgers.edu/rul/libs/scua/scua.shtml

The Genealogical Society of New Jersey
PO Box 1476
Trenton, NJ 08607-1476
www.gsnj.org

General Commission on Archives and History - GCAH
　　　The Archives and History Center of the United
　　　　　Methodist Church
　　　PO Box 127
　　　36 Madison Avenue
　　　Madison, NJ 07940-0127
　　　973-408-3189
　　　gcah@gcah.org
　　　www.gcah.org

Harvey S. Firestone Library, Princeton University
　　　Rare Books and Special Collections
　　　One Washington Road
　　　Princeton, NJ 08544
　　　609-258-3184
　　　Fax: 609-258-2324
　　　rbsc@princeton.edu
　　　www.princeton.edu/rbsc/index.shtml

New Jersey Department of Health and Senior Services
　　　Bureau of Vital Statistics and Registration
　　　PO Box 370
　　　140 East Front Street
　　　Trenton, NJ 08625-0370
　　　609-292-4087
　　　866-649-8726
　　　www.state.nj.us/health/vital/vital.shtml

The New Jersey Historical Society
　　　52 Park Pl.
　　　Newark, NJ 07102
　　　973-596-8500
　　　Fax: 973-596-6957
　　　contactNJHS@jerseyhistory.org
　　　www.jerseyhistory.org

New Jersey State Archives
　　　Department of State Building
　　　PO Box 307
　　　225 West State Street
　　　Trenton, NJ 08625-0307
　　　609-292-6260
　　　Fax: 609-292-9105
　　　archives.reference@sos.state.nj.us
　　　www.state.nj.us/state/darm/links/archives.html

New Jersey State Library
PO Box 520
185 West State St.
Trenton, NJ 08625-0520
609-278-2640
Fax: 609-278-2645
www.njstatelib.org

New Mexico

Albuquerque-Bernalillo County Library System
Special Collections Library
423 Central Avenue NE
Albuquerque, NM 87102
505-768-5141
specialcollections@cabq.gov
www.cabq.gov/library/specol.html

Center for Southwest Research and Special Collections
University of New Mexico
UNM Zimmerman Library, CSWR
1900 Roma NE
MSC 05 3020
1 University of New Mexico
Albuquerque, NM 87131-0001
505-277-6451
Fax: 505-277-0397
cswrref@unm.edu
elibrary.unm.edu/cswr

Historical Society of New Mexico
PO Box 1912
Santa Fe, NM 87504
hsnminfo@ptd.net
www.hsnm.org

Angélico Chávez History Library/Museum of New Mexico
Palace of the Governors
120 Washington Avenue
Santa Fe, NM 87501
505-476-5090
Fax: 505-476-5104
historylibrary@state.nm.us
www.palaceofthegovernors.org/library.html

New Mexico Bureau of Land Management
PO Box 27115
301 Dinosaur Trail
Santa Fe, NM 87502-0115
505-954-2000
nm_comments@nm.blm.gov
www.blm.gov/nm/st/en.html

New Mexico Genealogical Society
PO Box 27559
Albuquerque, NM 87125-7559
www.nmgs.org

New Mexico State Records and Archives
1205 Camino Carlos Rey
Santa Fe, NM 87507
505-476-7908
Fax: 505-476-7909
archives@state.nm.us
www.nmcpr.state.nm.us

New Mexico State Library
1209 Camino Carlos Rey
Santa Fe, NM 87505-5166
505-476-9702
reference@state.nm.us
www.nmstatelibrary.org

Vital Statistics
New Mexico Health Services Division
PO Box 26110
1105 St. Francis Drive
Santa Fe, NM 87502
505-827-0121
866-534-0051
dohewbs2.health.state.nm.us/

New York

National Archives – New York City
201 Varick Street, 12th Floor
New York, NY 10014-4811
212-401-1620
866-840-1752
Fax: 212-401-1638
newyork.archives@nara.gov
www.archives.gov/northeast

New York Genealogical and Biographical Society Library
36 West 44th Street, 7th Floor
New York, NY 10036-8105
212-775-8532
Fax: 212-754-4218
www.newyorkfamilyhistory.org/modules.php?name
=Content&pa=showpage&pid=10

New York Historical Society Library
170 Central Park West
New York, NY 10024
212-873-3400
webmaster.nyhistory.org
www.nyhistory.org/web/default.php?section=library

New York Public Library
5th Avenue and 42nd Street
New York City, NY 10018-2788
212-275-6975
www.nypl.org

New York State Archives
New York State Education Department
Cultural Education Center
Albany, NY 12230
518-474-8955
archref@mail.nysed.gov
www.archives.nysed.gov/aindex.shtml

New York State Department of Public Health
Vital Records
800 North Pearl Street
2nd Floor - Room 200
Menards, NY 12204
vr@health.state.ny.us
www.health.state.ny.us/nysdoh/consumer/vr.htm

New York State Library
Cultural Education Center
222 Madison Avenue
Albany, NY 12230
518-474-5355
518-474-5161 (genealogy)
Fax: 518-474-5786
www.nysl.nysed.gov

Daniel A. Reed Library
Archives and Special Collections
SUNY Fredonia
Fredonia, NY 14063
716-673-3183
FAX: 716-673-3185
special.collections@fredonia.edu
www.fredonia.edu/library/special_collections

Schomburg Center for Research in Black Culture/NYPL
515 Malcolm X Boulevard
New York, NY 10037-1801
212-491-2200
www.nypl.org/research/sc/sc.html

North Carolina

Carolinas Genealogical Society
The Heritage Room, Old Union County Courthouse
First Floor
PO Box 397
Monroe, NC 28111
Fax: 704-283-3782
www.rootsweb.ancestry.com/~ncunion/
Genealogical_society.htm

Moravian Archives (Southern Province)
    457 S. Church St.
    Winston-Salem, NC 27101
    336-722-1742
    moravianarchives@mcsp.org
    www.moravianarchives.org

North Carolina Department of Health and Human Services
    Vital Records
    Cooper Memorial Health Building
    1903 Mail Service Center (mail requests)
    225 N. McDowell Street
    Raleigh, NC 27699-1903
    919-733-3000
    Fax: 919-733-1571
    vitalrecords@dhhs.nc.gov
    vitalrecords.nc.gov/vitalrecords

North Carolina Genealogical Society, Inc.
    PO Box 30815
    Raleigh, NC 27622-0815
    www.ncgenealogy.org

North Carolina Office of Archives and History:
    4610 Mail Service Center (mail)
    109 E. James St.
    Raleigh, NC 27699-4610
    919-807-7280
    Fax: 919-733-8807
    ahweb@ncdcr.gov
    www.ah.dcr.state.nc.us

North Carolina State Archives
    4614 Mail Service Station (mail)
    109 E. Jones St.
    Raleigh, NC 27699-4614
    919-807-7310
    Fax: 919-733-1354
    archives@ncdcr.gov
    www.ah.dcr.state.nc.us/archives

North Carolina State Library
    Archives and History/State Library Building
    109 E. Jones St.
    Raleigh, NC 27699
    919-807-7450
    Fax: 919-733-5679
    slnc.reference@ncdcr.gov
    statelibrary.ncdcr.gov

William R. Perkins Library
    Rare Book, Manuscript, and Special Collections
    Duke University
    103 Perkins Library
    Durham, NC 27708-0185
    919-660-5822
    Fax: 919-660-5934
    special-collections@duke.edu
    library.duke.edu/specialcollections

Rowan Public Library
    201 W. Fisher Street
    Salisbury, NC 28144
    704-216-8253
    www.rowancountync.gov/GOVERNMENT/
        DepartmentRowanPublicLibrary/HistoryRoom/
        tabid/454/Default.aspx

Society of North Carolina Archivists
    PO Box 20448
    Raleigh, NC 27619
    info@ncarchivists.ort
    www.ncarchivists.org

North Dakota

    Division of Vital Records
        State Capitol
        600 E. Boulevard Avenue
        Bismarck, ND 58505-0200
        701-328-2360
        Fax: 701-328-1850
        vitalrec@nd.gov
        www.ndhealth.gov/vital

Germans from Russia Heritage Society
    1125 W. Turnpike Ave.
    Bismarck, ND 58501
    701-223-6167
    Fax: 701-223-4421
    grhs@grhs.org
    www.grhs.org

Institute for Regional Studies & University Archives
    North Dakota State University Libraries
    NDSU Dept. #2080
    PO Box 6050
    Skills & Technology Training Center, Room 117
    1305 19th Avenue North
    Fargo, ND 58108-6050
    701-231-8914
    Fax: 701-231-5632
    NDSU.Library.Archives@ndsu.edu
    library.ndsu.edu/archives/collections-institute

North Dakota Genealogical Society
    www.rootsweb.ancestry.com/~ndsgs

North Dakota State Archives and Historical Research Library
    612 East Boulevard Avenue
    Bismarck, ND 58505
    701-328-2091
    701-328-3710
    archives@nd.gov
    history.nd.gov/archives/index.html

North Dakota State Library
    604 E. Boulevard Avenue, Dept. 250
    Bismarck, ND 58505-0800
    701-328-4622
    800-472-2104
    Fax: 701-328-2040
    statelib@nd.gov
    www.library.nd.gov/

State Historical Society of North Dakota
North Dakota Heritage Center
612 East Boulevard Avenue
Bismarck, ND 58505-0830
701-328-2666
Fax: 701-328-3710
histsoc@state.nd.us
history.nd.gov/archives/index.html

Ohio

American Jewish Archives
3101 Clifton Ave.
Cincinnati, OH 45220
513-221-1875
Fax: 513-221-7812
www.americanjewisharchives.org

Bureau of Vital Statistics
Ohio Department of Health
Vital Statistics - Revenue Room
PO Box 15098
225 Neilston Street
Columbus, OH 43215-0098
614-466-2531
VitalStat@odh.ohio.gov
www.odh.ohio.gov/vitalstatistics/vitalstats.aspx

Mennonite Historical Collection
Bluffton College
Musselman Library
1 University Drive
Bluffton, OH 45817-2104
419-358-3275
www.bluffton.edu/library/coll/asc

National Archives and Records Administration – Great Lakes Region, Dayton
3150 Springboro Road
Dayton, OH 45439-1883
937-425-0600
Fax: 937-425-0640
dayton.reference@nara.gov
www.archives.gov/great-lakes

Ohio Genealogical Society
    611 State Route 97 West
    Bellville, OH 44813-8813
    419-886-1903
    Fax: 419-886-0092
    ogs@ogs.org
    www.ogs.org

Ohio Historical Society
    Archives/Library
    1982 Velma Ave.
    Columbus, OH 43211
    614-297-2300
    800-686-6124
    reference@ohiohistory.org
    www.ohiohistory.org

Ohio State Library
    274 East First Avenue, Suite 100
    Columbus, OH 43201
    614-644-7051
    Fax: 614-644-7004
    www.library.ohio.gov/

Public Library of Cincinnati and Hamilton County
    800 Vine St.
    Cincinnati, OH 45202-2009
    513-369-6905
    TDD/TTY: 513-665-3384
    www.cincinnatilibrary.org

Western Reserve Historical Society
    10825 East Blvd.
    Cleveland, OH 44106
    216-721-5722
    reference@wrhs.org
    www.wrhs.org

Oklahoma

American Indian Institute, University of Oklahoma
1639 Cross Center Drive
Norman, OK 730719-2219
800-522-0772, ext. 4127
405-325-4127
Fax: 405-325-7757
aii@ou.edu
aii.outreach.ou.edu

Bizzell Memorial Library, Western History Collection
University of Oklahoma Libraries
Monnet Hall
630 Parrington Oval
Norman, OK 73019
405-325-3641
Fax: 325-6069
libraries.ou.edu/locations/?id=22

Five Civilized Tribes Museum
1101 Honor Heights Drive
Muskogee, OK 74401
918-683-1701
Fax: 918-683-3070
5tribesdirector@sbcglobal.net
www.fivetribes.org

Lawton Public Library
110 SW 4th Street
Lawton, OK 73501
580-581-3450
www.cityof.lawton.ok.us/library/genealogy.htm

Oklahoma Department of Libraries
Allen Wright Memorial Library Building
200 Northeast 18th St.
Oklahoma City, OK 73105
800-522-8116
405-521-2502
Fax: 405-525-7804
www.odl.state.ok.us

Oklahoma Genealogical Society
PO Box 12986
4509 Classen Boulevard, #102
Oklahoma City, OK 73157-2986
405-637-1907
president@okgensoc.org
www.okgensoc.org

Oklahoma Historical Society
Oklahoma History Center
800 Nazih Zuhdi Drive
Oklahoma City, OK 73105
405-521-2491
research@okhistory.org
www.okhistory.org

Oklahoma State Historic Preservation Office
Oklahoma Historical Society/Oklahoma History Center
800 Nazih Zuhdi Drive
Oklahoma City, OK 73105
405-521-6249
Fax: 405-522-0816
research@okhistory.org
www.okhistory.org/shpo/shpom.htm

Vital Records Service
Oklahoma State Department of Health
1000 NE Tenth Street
Oklahoma City, OK 73117
405-271-4040
AskVR@health.ok.gov
www.ok.gov/health/Birth_and_Death_Certificates/index.html

Oregon

Genealogical Forum of Oregon
PO Box 42567
1505 SE Gideon
Portland, OR 97242-0567
503-963-1932
Fax: 503-963-1932
gfoinfo@hotmail.com
www.gfo.org

Knight Library
    University of Oregon
    1501 Kincaid Street
    Eugene, OR 97403-1299
    541-346-3053
    Fax: 541-346-3485
    libref@uoregon.edu
    libweb.uoregon.edu/knight/index.html

Multnomah County Library
    801 S. W. 10th Avenue
    Portland, OR 97205
    503-988-5234
    www.multcolib.org/ref/gene.html

Oregon Bureau of Land Management
    PO Box 2965
    333 S. W. 1st Avenue
    Portland, OR 97208
    503-808-6001
    Fax: 503-808-6308
    ORwaland@blm.gov
    www.blm.gov/or/st/en.html

Oregon Genealogical Society and Research Library
    PO Box 10306
    955 Oak Alley
    Eugene, OR 97440-2306
    541-345-0399
    www.oregongenealogicalsociety.org

Oregon Historical Society
    1200 SW Park Avenue
    Portland, OR 97205-2483
    503-222-1741
    Fax: 503-221-2035
    orhist@ohs.org
    www.ohs.org

Oregon Public Health Division
    Center for Health Statistics
    PO Box 14050
    800 NE Oregon St., Suite 205
    Portland, OR 97293-0050
    971-673-1190
    Fax: 971-673-1201
    oregon.gov/DHS/ph/chs/order/index.shtml

Oregon State Archives
    800 Summer Street, NE
    Salem, OR 97310
    503-373-0701
    Fax: 503-378-4118
    reference.archives@state.or.us
    arcweb.sos.state.or.us

Oregon State Library
    250 Winter Street, NE
    Salem, OR 97310-3950
    503-378-4243
    Fax: 503-585-8059
    reference@library.state.or.us
    oregon.gov/OSL

Scandinavian Heritage Foundation
    8800 SW Oleson Road
    Portland, OR. 97223
    Phone: 503-977-0275
    Fax: 503-977-0177
    shf@mindspring.com
    www.scanheritage.org/

Pennsylvania

    American Swedish Historical Museum
        1900 Pattison Ave.
        Philadelphia, PA 19145
        215-389-1776
        Fax: 215-389-7701
        info@americanswedish.org
        www.americanswedish.org

Bureau of the State Library of Pennsylvania
333 Market St.
Harrisburg, PA 17126-1745
717-783-5968
www.statelibrary.state.pa.us

Evangelical and Reformed Historical Society
555 W. James St.
Lancaster, PA 17603
717-290-8734
Fax: 717-393-4254
erhs@lancasterseminary.edu
www.erhs.info

Genealogical Society of Pennsylvania
2207 Chestnut Street
Philadelphia, PA 19103-3010
215-545-0391
Fax: 215-545-0936
ExecDir@GenPa.org
www.genpa.org

Germantown Historical Society
5501 Germantown Avenue
Philadelphia PA 19144-2225
215-844-1683
Fax: 215-844-2831
info@germantownhistory.org
www.germantownhistory.org/library.html

The Historical Society of Pennsylvania
1300 Locust Street
Philadelphia, PA 19107
215-732-6200
Fax: 215-732-2680
library@hsp.org
www.hsp.org

Lancaster Mennonite Historical Society
2215 Millstream Road
Lancaster, PA 17602-1499
717-393-9745
Fax: 717-393-8751
lmhs@lmhs.org
www.lmhs.org

Moravian Archives - North Province
41 West Locust Street
Bethlehem, PA 18018
610-866-3255
Fax: 610-866-9210
info@moravianchurcharchives.org
www.moravianchurcharchives.org

National Archives, Mid-Atlantic Region (Philadelphia)
900 Market Street (main entrance on Chestnut Street)
Philadelphia, PA 19107-4292
215-606-0100
Fax: 215-606-0116
philadelphia.archives@nara.gov
www.archives.gov/midatlantic

Pennsylvania Heritage Society
Commonwealth Keystone Building
400 North St.
Harrisburg, PA 17120-0024
717-787-2407
866-823-6539
Fax: 717-346-9099
RA-paheritagesociety@state.pa.us
www.paheritage.org

Pennsylvania Historical & Museum Commission
350 North St.
Harrisburg, PA 17120-0090
717-783-3362
Fax: 717-783-9924
ra-statearchives@state.pa.us
www.portal.state.pa.us/portal/server.pt
/community/state_archives/2887

State Department of Health
Division of Vital Records
PO Box 1528
101 South Mercer Street, Room 410
New Castle, PA 16103
724-656-3100
www.dsf.health.state.pa.us/health/site/default.asp

Rhode Island

American-French Genealogical Society
PO Box 830
78 Earle St.
Woonsocket, RI 02895-0870
401-765-6141
Fax: 401-597-6290
contact@afgs.org
www.afgs.org

Newport Historical Society
82 Touro Street
Newport, RI 02840
401-846-0813
Fax: 401-846-1853
info@newporthistorical.org
www.newporthistorical.org

Office of Vital Records
Rhode Island Department of Health
Cannon Building, Room 101
3 Capitol Hill
Providence, RI 02908-5097
401-222-5960
800-942-7434 (in-state)
Fax: 401-222-6548
www.health.state.ri.us/chic/vital/index.php

Rhode Island Genealogical Society
PO Box 211
Hope, RI 02831
www.rigensoc.org

Rhode Island Historical Society Library
110 Benevolent Street
Providence, RI 02906
401-331-8575
Fax: 401-351-0127
reference@rihs.org
www.rihs.org

Rhode Island State Archives and Public Records Administration
337 Westminster St.
Providence, RI 02903
401-222-2353
Fax: 401-222-3199
statearchives@sos.ri.gov
sos.gov/Archives

Rhode Island State Library
State House Room 208
Providence, RI 02903
401-222-2473
401-222-3034
statelibrary@sec.state.ri.us
sos.ri.gov/library

University of Rhode Island Library
15 Lippitt Road
Kingston, RI 02881-2011
401-874-2594
Fax: 401-874-4608
archives@etal.uri.edu
www.uri.edu/library/special_collections

South Carolina

Division of Vital Records
South Carolina Department of Health and
Environmental Control
2600 Bull Street
Columbia, SC 29201
803-898-3630
Fax: 803-898-3761
www.scdhec.net/administration/vr

South Carolina Department of Archives and History
8301 Parklane Road
Columbia, SC 29223
803-896-6104
Fax: 803-896-6198
scdah.sc.gov

South Carolina Genealogical Society
SCGS Treasurer
PO Box 24526
Columbia, SC 29224-4526
www.scgen.org

South Carolina Historical Society
100 Meeting St.
Charleston, SC 29401
843-723-3225
Fax: 843-723-8584
www.southcarolinahistoricalsociety.org/

South Carolina State Library
PO Box 11469
1500 Senate St.
Columbia, SC 29211
803-734-8026
Fax: 803-734-4757
reference@statelibrary.sc.gov
www.statelibrary.sc.gov

South Caroliniana Library
University of South Carolina
910 Sumter Street
Columbia, SC 29208
803-777-5158
Fax: 803-777-5747
sclref@mailbox.sc.edu
sc.edu/library/socar/index.html

Sumter County Genealogical Society
PO Box 2543
219 West Liberty Street
Sumter, SC 29151-2543
803-774-3901
sumtergensoc@aol.com
www.sumter.scgen.org/

South Dakota

> Alexander Mitchell Public Library
> 519 South Kline Street
> Aberdeen, SD 57401
> 605-626-7097
> Fax: 605-626-3506
> history@aberdeen.sd.us
> ampl.sdln.net
>
> North American Baptist Heritage Commission
> 2100 South Summit Avenue
> Sioux Falls, SD 57105-2729
> 605-274-2731
> Fax: 605-335-9090
> nabarchives@sfseminary.edu
> www.nabarchives.org
>
> South Dakota Genealogical Society
> PO Box 1101
> Pierre, SD 57501-1101
> pierregen@pie.midco.net
> www.rootsweb.ancestry.com/~sdgs/
>
> South Dakota State Archives
> 900 Governors Dr.
> Pierre, SD 57501-2217
> 605-773-3804
> Fax: 605-773-6041
> archref@state.sd.us
> history.sd.gov/archives
>
> South Dakota State Historical Society
> 900 Governors Dr.
> Pierre, SD 57501-2217
> 605-773-3458
> Fax: 605-773-6041
> sdshswebmaster@state.sd.us
> www.sdhistory.org

South Dakota State Library
Mercedes McKay Building
800 Governors Drive
Pierre, SD 57501-2294
800-423-6665
605-773-3131
Fax: 605-773-6962
library@state.sd.us
library.sd.gov

Vital Records
South Dakota Department of Health
207 E. Missouri, Suite 1-A
Pierre, SD 57501
605-773-4961
doh.sd.gov/VitalRecords/default.aspx

I. D. Weeks Library,
University of South Dakota
414 E. Clark St.
Vermillion, SD 57069
605-677-5450
Fax: 605-677-5488
speccoll@usd.edu
www.usd.edu/library/archives-and-special collections.cfm

Tennessee

Disciples of Christ Historical Society
1101 Nineteenth Ave. S.
Nashville, TN 37212
866 834 7563
mail@discipleshistory.org
www.discipleshistory.org

Southern Baptist Historical Library and Archives
901 Commerce, Suite 400
Nashville, TN 37203-3630
615-224-0344
Fax: 615-782-4821
www.sbhla.org

Tennessee Genealogical Society and Library
    PO Box 1824
    7779 Poplar Pike
    Germantown, TN 38183-1824
    901-757-8480
    tngs@tngs.org
    www.tngs.org

Tennessee State Library and Archives:
    State Library Building
    403 Seventh Ave. N
    Nashville, TN 37243-0312
    615-741-2764
    Fax: 615-532-2472
    reference.tsla@tn.gov
    www.tn.gov/tsla

Tennessee Vital Records
    Central Services Building
    421 Fifth Ave. N., First Floor
    Nashville, TN 37243
    615-741-1763
    tn.health@tn.gov
    health.state.tn.us/Vr/index.htm

University of Tennessee Library
    1015 Volunteer Boulevard
    Knoxville, TN 37996-1000
    865-974-4480
    special@utk.edu
    www.lib.utk.edu/special/archives

Texas

Baylor University Institute for Oral History
    Carroll Library, Suite 304
    One Bear Place #97271 (Mail)
    1429 South Fifth Street
    Waco, TX 76798-7271
    254-710-3437
    Fax: 254-710-4679
    BUIOH@baylor.edu
    www.baylor.edu/oral_history

Clayton Library Center for Genealogical Research
5300 Caroline
Houston, TX 77004-6896
832-393-2600
www.hpl.lib.tx.us/clayton

Dallas Public Library
1515 Young Street
Dallas, TX 75201-5415
214-670-1433
genealogy@dallaslibrary.org
dallaslibrary.org

Dolph Briscoe Center for American History
University of Texas
Sid Richardson Hall 2.101 (Mail)
1 University Station D1100
Unit 2
512-495-4532
Fax: 512-495-4542
Austin, TX 78712-0335
www.cah.utexas.edu

Federation of Genealogical Societies Business Office
PO Box 200940
Austin, TX 78720-0940
888-347-1500
Fax: 866-347-1350
office@fgs.org
www.fgs.org

National Archives and Records Administration – Southwest Region - Fort Worth
PO Box 6216
501 W. Felix St., Building 1 (microfilm)
Fort Worth, TX 76115-3405
817-831-5620
Fax: 817-551-2034
ftworth.archives@nara.gov
www.archives.gov/southwest

and

National Archives and Records Administration – Southwest Region, Fort Worth
    1400 John Burgess Drive (Textual & mail)
    Fort Worth, TX 76104
    817-551-2051
    Fax: 817-551-2034
    Ftworth.archives@nara.gov
    www.archives.gov/southwest

Texas Bureau of Vital Statistics
    PO Box 12040
    1100 West 49th St.
    Austin, TX 78711-2040
    888-963-7111
    Fax: 512-458-7711 or 458-7670
    registrar@dshs.state.tx.us
    www.dshs.state.tx.us/vs

Texas General Land Office
    Archives and Records Division
    Stephen F. Austin State Office Building
    1700 North Congress Avenue, Suite 130
    Austin, TX 78701-1495
    archives@glo.state.tx.us
    www.glo.state.tx.us/archives/service.html

Texas State Genealogical Society
    PO Box 7308
    Tyler, TX 75711-7308
    www.rootsweb.ancestry.com/~txsgs

Texas State Library and Archives Commission
    PO Box 12927
    1201 Brazos
    Austin, TX 78711-2927
    512-463-5480 (Archives)
    archinfo@tsl.state.tx.us
    512-463-5463 (Genealogy)
    geninfo@tsl.state.tx.us
    www.tsl.state.tx.us

Utah

    Bureau of Land Management
    Utah State Office
    PO Box 45155
    440 West 200 South, Suite 500
    Salt Lake City, UT 84145-0155
    801-539-4001
    Fax: 801-539-4013
    TDD: 801-539-4133
    utsomail@blm.gov
    www.blm.gov/ut/st/en.html

    Church of Jesus Christ of Latter-day Saints
    Church History Library and Archives
    Church Office Building
    15 East North Temple Street
    Salt Lake City, UT 84150
    801-240-2745
    Fax: 801-240-2804
    www.lds.org/churchhistory/library

    Family Search Center
    Joseph Smith Memorial Building
    15 East South Temple Street
    Salt Lake City, UT 84150
    801-240-4085
    familysearch@ldschurch.org
    www.familysearch.org/Eng/Library/FHL/
        frameset_library.asp?PAGE=library_JSMB.asp

    Genealogical Society of Utah
    50 East North Temple
    Salt Lake City, UT 84150
    801-538-2978
    Fax: 801-240-1448
    www.gensocietyofutah.org

    Harold B. Lee Library
    Brigham Young University
    Family History & Genealogy Resources
    PO Box 26800
    Provo, UT 46602-6800
    801-422-2927
    www.lib.byu.edu/sites/familyhistory

Icelandic Association of Utah
PO Box 874
Spanish Fork, UT 84660
utahicelanders.com

Institute of Genealogy and History for Latin America
2191 South 2200 East
Mt. Springs, UT 84757
435-652-1710
Fax: 435-674-5787
www.genealogy.com/00000140.html

International Society-Daughters of Utah Pioneers
Pioneer Memorial Museum
300 N. Main Street
Salt Lake City, UT 84103-1699
801-532-6479
Fax: 801-532-4436
info@dupinternational.org
www.dupinternational.org

Office of Vital Records and Statistics
Utah Department of Health
Martha Hughes Cannon Health Building
PO Box 141012
288 North 1460 West
Salt Lake City, UT 84114-1012
801-538-6105
vrequest@utah.gov
health.utah.gov/vitalrecords

Salt Lake City Public Library
Main Building
210 East 400 South
Salt Lake City, UT 84111
801-524-8200
www.slcpl.lib.ut.us

University of Utah
J. Willard Marriott Library
295 South 1500 East
Salt Lake City, UT 84112-0860
801-581-8558
Fax: 801-585-3464
www.lib.utah.edu/portal/site/marriottlibrary

Utah Genealogical Association
PO Box 1144
Salt Lake City, UT 84110
888-463-6842
info@infouga.org
www.infouga.org

Utah Heritage Foundation
Memorial House in Memory Grove Park
PO Box 28
485 North Canyon Rd.
Salt Lake City, UT 84110-0028
801-533-0858
Fax: 801-537-1245
www.utahheritagefoundation.com

Utah State Archives and Records Service
State Capitol, Archives Building
300 South Rio Grande Street
Salt Lake City, UT 84101
801-533-3535
Fax: 801-533-3504
www.archives.state.ut.us

Utah State Historical Society
300 South Rio Grande Street
Salt Lake City, UT 84101
801-533-3535
Fax: 801-533-3504
TDD: 801-533-3502
history.utah.gov

Utah State Library Division
250 North 1950 West, Suite A
Salt Lake City, UT 84116-7901
801-715-6777
800-662-9150 (Utah only)
Fax: 801-715-6767
library.utah.gov

Vermont

Bailey-Howe Memorial Library/Special Collections
University of Vermont
538 Main Street
Burlington, VT 05405-0036
802-656-2138
Fax: 802-656-3048
uvmsc@uvm.edu
library.uvm.edu/sc

Genealogical Society of Vermont
PO Box 14
Randolph, VT 05060-0014
www.genealogyvermont.org/index.html

Vermont Department of Health
Vital Records
108 Cherry St.
Burlington, VT 05402-0070
800-464-4343 (Vermont only)
802-863-7200
802-865-7754
healthvermont.gov/research/records/vital_records.aspx

Vermont Department of Libraries
109 State St.
Montpelier, VT 05609
802-828-3268
Fax: 802-828-1481
libraries.vermont.gov

Vermont Historical Society
60 Washington Street
Barre, VT 05641-4209
802-479-8500
Fax: 802-479-8510
vhs-info@state.vt.us
www.vermonthistory.org

Vermont State Archives & Records Administration
Secretary of State Office
1078 Route 2, Middlesex
Montpelier, VT 05633-7701
802-828-3700
Fax: 802-828-3710
archives@sec.state.vt.us
vermont-archives.org

Virginia

Alderman Library
University of Virginia
PO Box 400113
Charlottesville, VA 22904-4113
434-924-3021
Fax: 434-924-1431
library@virginia.edu
www.lib.virginia.edu

Genealogical Research Institute of Virginia
PO Box 29178
Richmond, VA 23242-0178
mail@griva.org
www.griva.org

The Library of Virginia (includes State Archives)
800 East Broad St.
Richmond, VA 23219-8000
804-692-3500
TTY/TDD: 804-692-3976
www.lva.lib.va.us

National Genealogical Society
3108 Columbia Pike, Suite 300
Arlington, VA 22204-4370
800-473-0060
703-525-0050
Fax: 703-525-0052
ngs@ngsgenealogy.org
www.ngsgenealogy.org

Presbyterian Church Archives, Union Theological Seminary
3401 Brook Rd.
Richmond, VA 23227
804-278-4336
Fax: 804-278-4375
www.loc.gov/rr/main/religion/uts.html

VDH, Office of Vital Records
PO Box 1000
The Shops at Willow Lawn
1601 Willow Lawn Dr., Suite 275
Richmond, VA 23218-1000
804-662-6200
VitalRec.Questions@vdh.virginia.gov
www.vdh.virginia.gov/vital_records/

Virginia Genealogical Society
1900 Byrd Avenue, Suite 104
Richmond, VA 23230-3033
804-285-8954
mail@vgs.org
www.vgs.org

Virginia Historical Society and Library
PO Box 7311
428 North Boulevard
Richmond, VA 23211-0311
804-342-9649
804-355-2399
www.vahistorical.org/research/main.htm

Washington

Department of Health
Center for Health Statistics
PO Box 9709
101 Israel Road SE
Olympia, WA 98507-9709
360-236-4313
Fax: 360-352-2586
contactchs@doh.wa.gov
www.doh.wa.gov/ehsphl/chs/cert.htm

National Archives – Pacific Alaska Region, Seattle
    6125 Sand Point Way NE
    Seattle, WA 98115-7999
    206-336-5115
    Fax: 206-336-5112
    seattle.archives@nara.gov
    www.archives.gov/pacific-alaska/seattle

Seattle Public Library
    Genealogy Collection
    1000 Fourth Ave.
    Seattle, WA 98104-1109
    206-386-4636
    www.spl.org/default.asp?pageID=collection

Washington State Archives
    PO Box 40238
    1129 Washington St. SE
    Olympia, WA 98504-0238
    360-586-1492
    archives@sos.wa.gov
    www.sos.wa.gov/archives/default.aspx

Washington State Genealogical Society
    1901 S. 12th Avenue
    Union Gap, WA 98903-1256
    www.rootsweb.ancestry.com/~wasgs

Washington State Historical Society and Museum
    1911 Pacific Ave.
    Tacoma, WA 98402
    888 238 4373
    253-272-3500
    Fax: 253-272-9518
    www.wshs.org

Washington State Library
    PO Box 42460
    Olympia, WA 98504-2460
    Point Plaza East
    6880 Capitol Blvd. S.
    Tumwater, WA
    360-704-5221
    askalibrarian@sos.wa.gov
    www.sos.wa.gov/library/Default.asp

West Virginia

    Vital Registration
        350 Capitol Street, Room 165
        Charleston, WV 25301-3701
        304-558-2931
        Fax: 304-558-1051
        dhhvitalreg@wv.gov
        www.wvdhhr.org/bph/hsc/vital/

    West Virginia State Archives
        Archives and History Library/The Cultural Center
        1900 Kanawha Boulevard East
        Charleston, WV 25305-0300
        304-558-0230, ext. 168
        Fax: 304-558-2779
        TDD: 304-558-3562
        www.wvculture.org/history/wvsamenu.html

    West Virginia Genealogical Society
        PO Box 249
        Elkview WV 25071
        304-965-1179 (cannot return long distance calls)
        www.rootsweb.ancestry.com/~wvgs

    West Virginia Library Commission
        Cultural Center, Bldg. 9
        1900 Kanawha Blvd. E.
        Charleston, WV 25305
        800-642-9021(in state)
        304-558-2041
        Fax: 304-558-2044
        web_one@wvlc.lib.wv.us
        librarycommission.lib.wv.us

    West Virginia University Library
        West Virginia and Regional History Collection
        PO Box 6069
        1549 University Avenue
        Morgantown, WV 26506-6069
        304-293-3536
        Fax: 304-293-3981
        ask_a_librarian@mail.wva.edu
        www.libraries.wvu.edu/wvcollection

Wisconsin

    Golda Meir Library/Archives
        University of Wisconsin
        PO Box 604
        2311 East Hartford Avenue
        Room W250
        Milwaukee, WI 53201-0604
        414-229-6979
        Fax: 414-229-3605
        www.uwm.edu/Libraries/arch/

    Milwaukee Public Library
        814 W. Wisconsin Ave.
        Milwaukee, WI 53233
        414-286-3000
        www.mpl.org/file/branch_central.htm

    Wisconsin Evangelical Lutheran Synod
        Department of Archives and History
        2929 North Mayfair Rd.
        Milwaukee, WI 53222
        414-256-3888
        www.wels.net/cgi-bin/site.pl

    Wisconsin Historical Society, Archives
        816 State Street
        Madison, WI 53706-1417
        608-264-6460
        www.wisconsinhistory.org/libraryarchives

    Wisconsin State Genealogical Society, Inc.
        PO Box 5106
        Madison, WI 53705-0106
        wsgs@wsgs.org
        wsgs.wetpaint.com

    Vital Records
        1 West Wilson St., Room 158
        PO Box 309
        Madison, WI 53701-0309
        608-266-1373
        DHSVitalRecords@wisconsin.gov
        dhs.wisconsin.gov/VitalRecords/index.htm

Wyoming

> Laramie County Library
> 2200 Pioneer Avenue
> Cheyenne, WY 82001
> 307-773-7232
> www.lclsonline.org/specialcollections/specialcollection
>
> Vital Records Services
> Wyoming Department of Health
> Hathaway Building
> 2300 Capitol Avenue
> Cheyenne, WY 82002
> 307-777-7591
> Fax: 307-777-2483
> wdh.state.wy.us/rfhd/vital_records/index.html
>
> Wyoming Bureau of Land Management
> PO Box 1828
> 5353 Yellowstone Road
> Cheyenne, WY 82003
> 307-775-6256
> Fax: 307-775-6129
> www.blm.gov/wy/st/en.html
>
> Wyoming State Archives
> Barrett Building
> 2301 Central Ave.
> Cheyenne, WY 82002
> 307-777-7826
> Fax: 307-777-7044
> wyoarchives.state.wy.us
>
> Wyoming State Historical Society
> Located at the University of Wyoming
> 1000 E. University Avenue
> Laramie, Wyoming 82071
> Membership: PMB #184
> 1740H Dell Range Blvd.
> Cheyenne, WY 82009-4946
> wyshs.org

Wyoming State Library
2800 Central Avenue
Cheyenne, WY 82002
307-777-6333
Fax: 307-777-6289
will.state.wy.us

International:

Albania

　　Direction Generale des Archives de la Republique D'Albanie
　　Rruga Jordan Misja
　　Tirana
　　Albania
　　355 4 22 79 59
　　Fax: 355 4 22 79 59
　　dpa@albarchive.gov.al
　　www.albarchive.gov.al

Algeria

　　Archives Nationales
　　Rue Hassane Benaamane, 16330
　　Birkhadem
　　Mail - B.P. 61
　　Algiers-Gare, Algeria
　　213 2 542 160
　　Fax: 213 2 541 616
　　www.archives-dgan.gov.dz (site in Arabic)

Andorra

　　Arxius Nacionals D'Andorra
　　Edifici Prada Casdet
　　C/. Prada Casadet 8-12
　　Andorra La Vella
　　Andorra (Principat)
　　00 376 802 288 or 00 376-802-287
　　Fax: 00 376 868 645
　　ana.gov@andorra.ad
　　www.arxius.ad

Angola

    Arquivo Histórico Nacional, Centro National de Documentação
    e Investigação
       PO Box: Caixa Postal n° 2468
       Rua Pedro Félix Machado, No. 49 R/CH
       Luanda, Angola
       244 2 333512
       Fax: 244 2 334410

Antigua & Barbuda

    Antigua & Barbuda National Archives
       Rappaport Centre, Victoria Park
       Factory Road
       St. John's
       Antigua & Barbuda
       1 268 462 3946/7

Argentina

    Archives General de la Nacion
       Av. Paseo Colón 1093 – C1063ACK
       Buenos Aires, Argentina
       54 11 4339 0800
       Fax: 54 11 4334 0065
       archivo@mininterior.gov.ar
       www.mininterior.gov.ar

Aruba

    Archivo Nacional Aruba
       Sabana Banco 60
       Dakota
       Oranjstad
       Aruba
       297 583 4880
       Fax: 297 583 9275
       arna@setarnet.aw

Australia

> Australian Institute of Genealogical Studies, Inc.
> 41 Railway Road
> Blackburn, Victoria, 3130
> Australia
> +61 3 9877-3789
> info@aigs.org.au
> www.aigs.org.au
>
> National Archives of Australia
> PO Box 7425
> Queen Victoria Terrace
> Parkes ACT 2600
> Canberra, BC
> ACT 2610
> 61 2 6212 3900
> Fax: 61 2 6212 3999
> archives@naa.gov.au
> www.naa.gov.au
> (There are also archival locations in each state capitol and Darwin.)
>
> Oral History Association of Australia
> c/o Oral History Program
> State Library of New South Wales
> Macquarie Street
> Sydney NSW 2000
> Australia
> +61-02-9273-1697
> www.nla.gov.au/oh/ohaa.html
> (Locations may also be found in South Australia, Tasmania, Queensland, Victoria, and Western Australia.)

Austria

> Austrian State Archives/Österreichisches Staatsarchiv
> Nottendorfer Gasse 2
> A-1030 Wien
> Austria
> +43 1 79540 0
> gdpost@oesta.gv.at
> www.oesta.gv.at

Azerbaijan

    Central Directorate of Archives at the Cabinet of Ministers of Azerbaijan
    3 Ziya M. Bunyatov Propect
    Baku
    Azerbaijan 370106
    99 412 629 431/775
    Fax: 99 412 629 447

Bahamas

    Bahamas National Archives
    Mackey and Shirley Streets
    PO Box SS-6341
    Nassau, NP
    Bahamas
    1 242 393 2175
    Fax: 1 242 393 2855
    archives@batelnet.bs
    www.bahamasnationalarchives.bs

Bangladesh

    National Archives and Library of Bangladesh
    32 Justice S.M. Murshed Sarani
    Agargaon Sher-e-Bangla Nagar
    Dhaka-1207, Bangladesh
    0088 02 9129992
    Fax: 0088 02 9118704
    nanldirector@gmail.com
    www.nanl.gov.bd

Barbados

    Barbados National Archives
    Black Rock
    St. James, Barbados
    1-246-425-1380
    Fax: 1-246-425-5911
    archives@sunbeach.net
    www.gov.bb/portal/page/portal/BIG_Department_of_Archives

Belarus

> National Archives of the Republic of Belarus
> Prospect Nezavisimosti
> 116, Minsk 220114
> Republic of Belarus
> Phone/Fax +375 (17) 237 67 78
> narb@narb.by
> narb.by

Belgium

> State Archives in Belgium
> Ruisbroekstraat, 2
> Bruxelles
> Région de Bruxelles-1000
> (+32) 02/513.76.80
> Fax: (+32) 02/513.76.81
> Algemeen.Rijksarchief@arch.be
> arch.arch.be

Belize

> Belize Archives and Records Service
> 26/28 Unity Boulevard
> Belmopan City
> Belize, C.A.
> 501 822 2097, or 2247
> Fax: 501 822 3140
> www.belizearchives.gov.bz

Benin

> Direction des Archives Nationales du Bénin
> Ouando
> Face à l'Ecole Régionale de la Magistrature
> Porto Novo, Benin
> 229 21-30-79
> anbenin@intnet.bj
> www.anbenin.bj

Bermuda

    Bermuda Archives
        Government Administration Building
        30 Parliament Street
        Hamilton, HM 12, Bermuda
        441.295.5151
        Fax: 441.295.8751

Bhutan

    National Library and Archives of Bhutan
        Ministry of Home and Cultural Affairs
        GPO PO Box 185
        Kawangjangtsa
        Thimphu
        Bhutan
        975 2 322693
        Fax: 975 2 322693
        library.bhutan@gmail.com or nlb@library.gov.bt
        www.library.gov.bt/index.html

Bolivia

    Archivo y Biblioteca Nacionales de Bolivia
        Mail: Casilla 793
        Calle Espana 43
        Sucre, Bolivia
        011 591 64 21481
        Fax: 011 591 64 61208
        abnb@mara.scr.entelnet.bo
        www.h-net.org~latam/archives/project3

Bosnia-Herzegovina

    State Archives
        Reisa Džemaludina Čauševića 6
        Sarajevo
        Bosnia-Herzegovina
        Tel/Fax: 387-33-206-492
        info@arhivbih.gov.ba
        www.arhivbih.gov.ba/eng/starteng.htm

Botswana

> Botswana National Archives and Records Services
> PO Box 239
> Garbarone, Botswana
> 267 3911 820
> Fax: 267 3908 545

Brazil

> Arquivo Nacional
> Praça da República, 173
> Rio De Janeiro, RJ
> Brazil 20211-350
> 55 21 2179 1273
> www.arquivonacional.gov.br/cgi/cgilua.
> exe/sys/start.htm

Brunei (negara Darussalam)

> Brunei Museums
> Main Office, National Archives Building
> Jalan Menteri Besar BB 3910
> Brunei (Negara Darussalam)
> 673 2 381 691/672
> Fax: 673 2 384 371/381 686
> www.museums.gov.bn

Bulgaria

> Bulgarian National Archives
> 5, Moskovska Str.
> Sofia, Bulgaria 1000
> 359 2 940 0101
> Fax: 359 2 980 1443
> daa@archives.government.bg
> www.archives.government.bg

Burkina Faso

> Centre National des Archives
> PO Box 03 B.P. 7030
> Ouagadougou, Burkina Faso
> 226 50 33 61 96
> Fax: 226 50 31 49 26

Burundi

> Archives Nationales du Burundi
> PO Box: B. P. 1095
> Boulevard Rohero I, Avenue du 1er Novembre
> Bujumbura, Burundi
> 257 22 5051
> Fax: 257 22 6231 or 257 21 9295

Cabo Verdi

> Instituto do Arquivo Historico Nacional da República de Cabo Verdi
> PO Box Caixa Postal 321
> Praia, Cabo Verdi
> 238 261 3962
> Fax: 238 61 39 64

Cambodia

> National Archives of Cambodia
> PO Box 1109
> Phnom-Penh, Cambodia
> 855 23 430 582
> archives.cambodia@camnet.com.kh
> www.camnet.com.kh/archives.cambodia

Cameroon

> Archives Nationales du Cameroun
> BP 14617
> Yaoundé, Cameroon
> 237 22 22 47 48
> Fax: 237 22 22 47 85

Canada

> Alberta Family Histories Society
> 712-16 Ave. NW
> Calgary, Alberta T2M 0J8
> 403-214-1447
> www.afhs.ab.ca

Alberta Genealogical Society
    162, 14315-118 Avenue
    Edmonton, AB T5L 4S6
    780-424-4429
    Fax: 780-423-8980
    abgensoc@interbaun.com
    abgensoc.ca

Archives of Manitoba
    130-200 Vaughan Street
    Winnipeg, MB R3C 1T5
    204-945-3971
    800-617-3588 (Manitoba only)
    Fax: 204-948-2008
    archives@gov.mb.ca
    www.gov.mb.ca/chc/archives

Archives of Ontario
    134 Ian Macdonald Boulevard
    Toronto, ON M7A 2C5
    416-327-1600
    800-668-9933 (Ontario only)
    Fax: 416-327-1999
    reference@ontario.ca
    www.archives.gov.on.ca

British Columbia Genealogical Society
    PO Box 88054
    Lansdowne Mall
    Richmond, BC V6X 3T6
    604-502-9119
    Fax: 604-502-9119
    bcgs@bcgs.ca
    www.bcgs.ca

British Columbia Vital Statistics Agency
    PO Box 9657 Stn. Prov. Govt.
    818 Fort Street
    Victoria, BC V8W 9P3
    250-952-2681
    888-876-1633 (British Columbia only)
    www.vs.gov.bc.ca

Canadian Oral History Association
    University of Winnipeg
    515 Portage Avenue
    Winnipeg, MB R3B 2E9
    www.canoha.ca

Centre d'Archives de Québec
    Pavillon Louis-Jacques-Casault
    Campus de l'Université Laval
    1055, avenue du Séminaire
    CP 10450
    Sainte Foy, Québec G1V 4N1
    418-643-8904
    Fax: 418-646-0868
    anq.quebec@banq.qc.ca
    www.banq.qc.ca/portal/dt/accueil.jsp?bnq_resolution=mode_1024

Genealogical Association of Nova Scotia Scotia
    3045 Robie Street, Suite 222
    HaliFax, NS B3K 4P6
    902-454-0322
    gans@chebucto.ns.ca
    www.chebucto.ns.ca/Recreation/GANS

Library and Archives Canada
    395 Wellington St.
    Ottawa, ON K1A 0N4
    613-996-5115 (Reference)
    613-996-7458 (Genealogy)
    866-578-7777
    Fax: 613-995-6274
    TTY: 613-992-6969
    TTY: 866-299-1699 (Canada only)
    www.collectionscanada.ca/index-e.html

Manitoba Genealogical Society
    Unit E - 1045 St. James St.
    Winnipeg, Manitoba R3H 1B1
    204-783-9139
    contact@mbgenealogy.com
    www.mbgenealogy.com

Manitoba Historical Society
61 Carlton Street
Winnipeg, Manitoba R3C 1N7
204-947-0559
Fax: 204-943-2565
info@mhs.mb.ca
www.mhs.mb.ca

Manitoba Vital Statistics Agency
254 Portage Avenue
Winnipeg, MB RC3 0B6
204-945-3701
866-949-9296
Fax: 204-948-3128
vitalstats@gov.mb.ca
vitalstats.gov.mb.ca/index.html

New Brunswick Genealogical Society, Inc.
PO Box 3235
Station B
Fredericton, NB E3A 5G9
www.nbgs.ca

New Brunswick Vital Statistics
432 Queen Street
PO Box 1998
Fredericton, NB E3B 1B6
506-453-2834
Fax: 506-444-4253
snb@snb.ca
www.snb.ca/e/1000/1000-01/e/index-e.asp

Newfoundland and Labrador
Vital Statistics Division
Department of Government Services
PO Box 8700
5 Mews Place
St. John's, NF A1B 4J6
709-729-3308
Fax: 709-729-0946
vstats@gov.nl.ca
www.gs.gov.nl.ca/faq/vital_stats.html
(For records prior to 1892 contact the Provincial Archives
of Newfoundland and Labrador)

Northwest Territories Registrar-General of Vital Statistics
    Department of Health and Social Services
    Government of Northwest Territories
    Bag 9
    107 MacKenzie Road/IDC Building, 2nd Floor
    Inuvik, NT X0E 0T0
    867-777-7400
    Fax: 867-777-3197
    hsa@gov.nt.ca
    www.hlthss.gov.nt.ca/english/services/vital_statistics/default.htm

Nova Scotia Archives and Records Management
    Public Archives Building
    6016 University Ave.
    HaliFax, NS B3H 1W4
    902-424-6060
    Fax: 902-424-0628
    nsarm@gov.ns.ca
    www.gov.ns.ca/nsarm

Nova Scotia Vital Statistics
    Service Nova Scotia and Municipal Relations
    PO Box 157
    1690 Hollis St.
    Joseph Howe Building, Ground Floor
    HaliFax, NS B3J 2M9
    902-424-4381
    1-877-848-2578 (Nova Scotia only)
    Fax: 902-424-0678
    vstat@gov.ns.ca
    www.gov.ns.ca/snsmr/vstat

Nunavut Archives Program
    Department of Culture, Language, Elders and Youth
    Box 1000, Stn. 800
    Iqaluit, Nunavut X0A 0H0
    866-934-2035
    867-975-5500
    Fax: 867-975-5504
    cley@gov.nu.ca
    www.gov.nu.ca/cley/english/archives.html

OCFA: Ontario Cemetery Finding Aid
Metchosin Central
Box 48058
3575 Douglas St.
Victoria, BC V8Z 7H5
rsd@islandnet.com
www.islandnet.com/ocfa

Ontario Genealogical Society
Suite 102
40 Orchard View Boulevard
Toronto, ON M4R 1B9
416-489-0734
Fax: 416-489-9803
research@ogs.on.ca
www.ogs.on.ca

Ontario Office of the Registrar General
PO Box 4600
189 Red River Road
In person: College Park
Thunder Bay, ON P7B 6L8
777 Bay Street
416-325-8305 (Toronto)
Toronto, ON M5G 2C8
800-461-2156
Fax: 807-343-7459
infoMGS@ontario.ca
www.ontario.ca/en/residents/119274

Prince Edward Island
Vital Statistics
Department of Health
126 Douses Road
Montague, PE C0A 1R0
902-838-0880
877-320-1253
Fax: 902-838-0883
www.gov.pe.ca/health/index.php3?number=
1020358&lang=E

Prince of Wales Northern Heritage Centre
Box 1320
4750 48th Street
Yellowknife, NT X1A 2L9
867-873-7551
Fax: 867-873-0205
www.pwnhc.ca

Provincial Archives
655 Belleville Street
Victoria, BC V8W 9W2
250-387-1952
Fax: 250-387-2072
access@bcarchives.bc.ca
www.bcarchives.bc.ca/bcarchives/default.aspx

Provincial Archives of New Brunswick
University of New Brunswick
Bonar Law - Bennett Building
PO Box 6000
23 Dineen Drive
Fredericton, NB E3B 5H1
506-453-2122
Fax: 506-453-3288
Reception.Marysville@gnb.ca
archives.gnb.ca/Archives/Default.aspx?culture =en-CA

Provincial Archives of Newfoundland and Labrador &
Newfoundland and Labrador Genealogical Society "The Rooms"
PO Box 1800, Station C
9 Bonaventure Avenue
St. John's, NL A1C 5P9
709-757-8030
Fax: 709-757-8031
archives@therooms.ca
www.therooms.ca/archives

Public Archives and Records Office of Prince Edward Island
Hon. George Coles Building
PO Box 1000
175 Richmond Street
Charlottetown, PE C1A 7M4
902-368-4290
Fax: 902-368-6327
archives@edu.pe.ca
www.gov.pe.ca/archives

Québec Family History Society
    PO Box 1026
    173 Cartier Avenue, Suite 102
    Pointe Claire, PQ H9S 4H9
    514-695-1502
    Fax: 514-695-3508
    admin@qfhs.ca
    www.qfhs.ca

Québec Vital Statistics
    Quebec City
    Directeur de l'état civil service centres
    2535, boulevard Laurier, RC
    Québec (Québec) G1V 5C5
    418-643-3900
    (Place-des-Arts metro station)
    800-567-3900 (elsewhere in Québec)
    etatcivil@dec.gouv.qc.ca
    www.etatcivil.gouv.qc.ca

        or

    Montréal
    Le Directeur de l'état civil
    2050, rue de Bleury, ground floor
    Montréal QC H3A 2J5
    514-864-3900
    800-567-3900 (elsewhere in Québec)
    Fax: 514-864-4563
    etatcivil@dec.gouv.qc.ca
    www.etatcivil.gouv.qc.ca

Saskatchewan Genealogical Society
    PO Box 1894
    110-1514 - 11th Avenue
    Regina SK S4P 3E1
    306-780-9207
    Fax: 306-780-3615
    saskgenealogy@sasktel.com
    www.saskgenealogy.com

Saskatchewan Vital Statistics
Saskatchewan Health
1301 1st Avenue
Regina, SK S4R 8H2
306-798-0641
866-275-4721
Fax: 306-798-6839
ask@isc.ca
www.health.gov.sk.ca/vital-statistics

Service Alberta
Alberta Registries, Vital Statistics
PO Box 2023
Edmonton, AB T5J 4W7
780-427-7013
vs@gov.ab.ca
www.servicealberta.gov.ab.ca/VitalStatistics.cfm

Yukon Vital Statistics
Government of Yukon
PO Box 2703
4th Floor, 204 Lambert St.
Whitehorse YK Y1A 2C6
867-667-5207
800-661-0408, ext. 5207 (Within Yukon)
Fax: 867-393-6486
Vital.Statistics@gov.yk.ca
www.hss.gov.yk.ca/programs/vitalstats

Caribbean

Généalogie et Histoire de la Caraïbe
Pavillion 23
12 Avenue Charles de Gaulle
28230 Le Pecq
France
GHCaraibe@noos.fr
www.ghcaraibe.org
(Mostly in French)

Cayman Islands

> The Cayman Islands National Archive
> Government Administration Building
> 37 Archive Lane
> George Town, Grand Cayman KY1-9000
> 345-949-9809
> Fax: 345-949-9727
> CINA@gov.ky
> www.cina.gov.ky/portal/page?_pageid=1748,1&_dad=portal&_schema=PORTAL

Central Africa

> Archives Nationales
> PO Box: BP 881
> Bangui
> Central African R.
> 236 61 3871
> Fax: 236 61 0633

Chad

> Direction des Archives Nationales et de la Documentation
> PO Box: BP 5394
> Ndjamena
> Chad
> 235 52 33 75/28 20 56
> Fax: 235 52 55 38

Channel Islands

> States of Guernsey Island
> Information Centre
> North Esplanade
> St. Peter Port
> Guernsey, GY1 2LQ
> 01481 713888
> www.gov.gg

Chile

    Archivo Nacional de Chile
    Correo Central
    PO Box: Clasificador 1400
    Miraflores N° 50
    Santiago de Chile
    Chile
    56 2 360 5250
    archivo.nacional@dibam.cl
    www.dibam.cl/archivo_nacional

China

    State Archives Administration of China
    21 Feng Sheng Hutong
    Beijing
    China
    86 10 661 76325
    Fax: 86 10 661 75532
    www.saac.gov.cn

Colombia

    National Library of Columbia/Biblioteca Luis Angel Arango
    Calle 24 N°5-60
    Bogata, Colombia
    571 381 6464
    Fax: 571 381 6449
    bnc@mincultura.gov.co
    www.bibliotecancional.gov.co

Comoros

    Centre National de Documentation et Recherche Scientifique
    PO Box: BP 169
    Moroni
    Comoros
    972 9 238 4456
    Fax: 972 9 238 7982

Congo

> Archives Nationales de la Republique Democratique du Congo (ANC)
> PO Box: B.P. 11.122
> 42/A avenue de la Justice
> Commune de la Gombe
> Kinshasa
> Congo (D. R. of)
> 243 815 172327/243 892 3624
> Fax: 243 801 905 0662

Congo (R. of)

> Centre National Des Archives et de la Documentation
> PO Box: BP 1489
> Brazzaville
> Congo (R. of)
> 242 663 1259
> Fax: 242 81 50 09

Costa Rica

> Archivo Nacional de Costa Rica
> Apdo. 41-2020
> Zapote
> Del Centro Comercial Plaza del Sol
> San Jose, Costa Rica
> 506 2283-1400
> Fax: 506 2234 7312
> ancost@ice.co.cr
> www.archivonacional.go.cr

Croatia

> Croatian State Archives
> Marulic´ev trg 21
> 10 000 Zagreb
> Croatia
> 385 1 4801 921
> Fax: 385 1 4829 000
> hda@arhiv.hr
> www.arhiv.hr

Cuba

> Archivo Nacional de la Repúbica de Cuba
> Calle Compostela N° 906 esq. San Isadro
> Habana Vieja
> LaHabana, Cuba 10100
> 537 862 9436
> Fax: 537 866 8089
> www.arnac.cu

Cypress

> State Archives of Cypress
> Nicosia
> Cypress 1461
> 357 22 302664
> Fax: 357 22 667680

Czech Republic

> Czech Republic State Archives/Archivni Sprava Ceske Republiky
> Ministerstva vnitra CR
> Archivni 4/2257
> Praha 4
> Chodovec 149 01
> Czech Republic
> 420 233 326 755
> na@nacr.cz
> www.nacr.cz/eindex.htm

Denmark

> Danish Emigration Archives
> Arkivstræde 1
> Box 1353
> 9100 Aalborg
> Denmark
> 45 99 31 42 20
> Fax: 45 98 10 22 48
> emiarch@emiarch.dk
> www.emiarch.dk

State Archives
Rigsarkivet
Rigsdagsgården 9
1218 København K
Denmark
45 33 92 33 10
mailbox@ra.sa.dk
www.sa.dk

Djibouti

Direction Nationale Des Archives
PO Box: B. P. 387
Djibouti, Djibouti
253 35 02 01
Fax: 253 35 85 38

Dominica Commonwealth

National Documentation Centre Library and Information
Services of Dominica
Kennedy Avenue
Roseau, Dominica Commonwealth
767 448 2401, ext. 3341
Fax: 767 448 7928

Dominican Republic

Archivo General de la Nacion
c/Modesto Diaz N° 2
Santo Domingo
Dominican Republic 2870
809 362 1111
Fax: 809 362 1110
www.agn.gov.do/

East Timor

Arquivo Nacional de Timor Leste
Codigo Postal 343
Estrada de Caicoli
Dili, Timor Leste
670 0333 954
arquivotimor@yahoo.com.au
www.estatal.gov.tl/English/Directorates

Ecuador

>Archivo Nacional
>Casilla 17-12-878
>Av. 10 de Agosto N11-539 y Santa Prisca
>Quito, Ecuador
>593-2-228-0431
>Fax: 593 2 228 0431
>www.ane.gov.ec

Egypt

>National Library and Archives
>PO Box N° 8 - Sabttiya
>Corniche El-Nil
>Ramlat Boulaq
>Cairo, Egypt 11638
>202 575 1078/0886
>Fax: 202 576 5634
>info@darelkotab.org
>www.darelkotob.org

Eritrea

>Research and Documentation Center
>PO Box 897
>Asmara, Eritrea
>291 1 122808
>Fax: 291 1 122902
>rdc@eol.com.er
>www.eritreanarchives.org/

Estonia

>National Archives of Estonia
>J. Liivi 4
>Tartu, 50409
>Estonia
>372 738 7500
>Fax: 372 738 7510
>rahvusarhiiv@ra.ee
>www.ra.ee

Ethiopia

>   Ethiopian National Archives and Library Agency
>   PO Box 717
>   Addis Ababa
>   Ethiopia
>   251 11 5516532
>   Fax: 251 11 5526411
>   nale@ethionet.et
>   www.nale.gov.et

Faroe Islands

>   Faroese National Archives
>   V. U. Hammershaimbsgota 24
>   FO-100 Torshavn
>   Faroe Islands 100
>   298 3166 77
>   Fax: 298 3186 77
>   fararch@lss.fo
>   www.lss.fo

Fiji

>   National Archives of Fiji
>   PO Box 2125
>   Government Buildings
>   Suva, Fiji
>   679 3304144
>   Fax: 679 3307 006
>   archives@govnet.gov.fj
>   www.info.gov.fj/archives.html

Finland

>   Genealogical Society of Finland
>   Liisankatu 16 A
>   00170 Helsinki, Finland
>   358 10 387 7900
>   kirjasto@genealogia.fi
>   www.genealogia.fi

Institute of Migration - Siirtolaisuusinstituutti
Eerikinkatu 34
20100 Turku, Finland
358-2-2840-440
Fax: 358-2-2333-460
www.migrationinstitute.fi/index_e.php

National Archives of Finland
PO Box 258
Rauhankatu 17
00171 Helsinki, Finland
011-358-9-228 521
Fax: 011-358-9-176 302
kansallisarkisto@narc.fi
www.narc.fi/Arkistolaitos/eng

France

Direction des Archives de France
56 rue des Francs-Bourgeois
75141 Paris cedex 03
France
33 1 40 27 6000
Fax: 33 1 40 27 6606
www.archivesdefrance.culture.gouv.fr

Bibliothèque Nationale/Richelieu Library
5, rue Vivienne
75002 Paris, France
33 (0) 1 53 79 59 59
www.bnf.fr

Fryom (formerly Yugoslav Republic of Macedonia)

Arhiv na Makedonija
Gligor Prlichev 3
Skopje 1000
Fryom
389 2 3115 783
Fax: 389 2 3165 944

Gabon

> Archives Nationales
> B. P. 1188
> Libreville, Gabon
> 241 73 62 35/73 02 39
> Fax: 241 73 28 71

Gambia

> National Records Service (PMO)
> Personnel Management Office
> The Quadrangle
> Banjul, Gambia
> 220 4223251/9935780/7935780
> Fax: 220 4202086/4223813

Georgia

> National Archives of Georgia
> Vazha - Pshavela av. #1
> 0160 Tbilisi, Georgia
> 995 32 37 28 01
> Fax: 995 32 94 25 32
> info@archives.gov.ge
> archives.gov.ge

Germany

> National Archives of the Federal Republic of Germany (since 1945)
> Bundesarchiv
> Potsdamer Str. 1
> 56075 Koblenz, Germany
> 0261/505-0
> Fax: 0261/505-226
> koblenz@bundesarchiv.de
> www.bundesarchiv.de
> (other city locations as well)

Ghana

Public Records and Archives Administration Department
PO Box 3056
Accra, Ghana
233 21 22 12 34
Fax: 233 21 22 00 14
archives@4u.com.gh
www.praad.gov.gh

Great Britain

British Library, Department of Western Manuscripts
St. Pancras
96 Euston Road
London NW1 2DB
44 (0) 20 7412 7676
www.bl.uk/

British Library, Newspaper Library
Colindale Ave.
London, NW9 5HE
44 (0) 20 7412 7353
www.bl.uk/reshelp/inrrooms/blnewspapers/newsrr.html

National Archives
Kew, Richmond
Surrey, TW9 4DU
44 (0) 20 8876 3444
www.nationalarchives.gov.uk

Oral History Society (UK)
PO Box 464
Berkhamsted, Hertfordshire
United Kingdom HP4 2UR
01442 879097
Fax: 01442 872279
oralhistory@webscribe.co.uk
www.oralhistory.org.uk

Society of Genealogists - UK
14 Charterhouse Buildings
Goswell Road
London EC1M 7BA
44 0 20 7251 8799
Fax: 44 0 20-7250-1800
genealogy@sog.org.uk
www.sog.org.uk

Greece

General State Archives
61 Dafnis Street
154 52, Psychiko
Greece
30 210 6782200
Fax: 30 210 6782215
archives@gak.gr
www.gak.gr

Guinea

Direction Nationale des Archives de Guinee
Boite Postale 1005
Conakry, Guinea
224 41 42 97
Fax: 224 41 42 19

Guinea Bissau

Institut National D'etudes et de Recherches (Iner)-Archives
Historiques
B.P. 112
Complexo Escolar 14 de Novembro
Bairro Cobornel
Bissau, Guinea Bissau
245 251867
Fax: 245 251125

Guyana

> National Archives of Guyana
> Homestretch Avenue
> D'urban Park
> Georgetown, Guyana
> 592 22 77687
> narchivesguyana@yahoo.com
> www.mcys.gov.gy/na_about.html

Haiti

> Archives Nationales d'Haiti
> Boite Postale 1299
> 22 Angle Rues Borgella & Geffrard
> Port-au-Prince, Haiti
> 509 2221-0292
> Fax: 509 222 6280/221 2125
> www.anhhaiti.org

Hungary

> National Archives of Hungary
> PO Box 3
> H-1250 Budapest
> 2-4 Square Kapu Bécsi tér 2-4
> Budapest, H-1014
> 36 (1) 225 2843
> Fax: 36 1 225 2817
> info@mol.gov.hu
> www.mol.gov.hu

Iceland

> National Archives of Iceland
> PO Box R5-5390
> Laugavegur 162
> 105 Reykjavik
> Iceland
> 354 590 3300
> Fax: 354 590 3301
> upplysingar@skjalasafn.is
> www.archives.is

National and University of Library of Iceland
Arngrímsgata 3
107 Reykjavik
Iceland
354 5255600
Fax: 354 5255615
upplys@bok.hi.is
www.bok.hi.is

India

National Archives of India
Janpath
New Delhi, India 110001
91 11 230 73462
Fax: 91 11 233 84127
archives@nic.in
nationalarchives.nic.in

Indonesia

Arsip Nasional Republik Indonesia
Jl. Ampera Raya No. 7
Jankarta 12560
Indonesia
62 21 7805851
Fax: 62 21 7810280/7805812
info@anri.go.id
www.anri.go.id

Iran

National Library and Archives of Iran
Local Access Road
Mirdamad Underground Station
Shahid Haqani Highway
Tehran, Iran 44072
98 21 886 44080-81
Fax: 98 21 886 44082
nli@nlai.ir
www.nlai.ir

Iraq

> Iraqi National Library and Archive
> M.B.: Iraq-baghdad-bab almuadam-14340
> Baghdad, Iraq
> 4141303-4141314
> Fax: 4141810
> info.nla@iraqnla.org
> www.iraqnla.org/

Ireland

> General Register Office
> Government Offices
> Convent Road
> Roscommon, Ireland
> +353 (0) 90 6632900
> Local: 1890 252 076
> Fax: +353 (0) 90 663 2999
> www.groireland.ie

> General Register Office (Northern Ireland)
> Oxford House
> 49-55 Chichester St.
> Belfast BT1 4HL
> Northern Ireland
> +44 (0) 28 9151 3101
> Fax: +44 (028) 9025 2120
> GRO_NISRA@dfpni.gov.uk
> www.groni.gov.uk
> (see website for local District offices)

> Linen Hall Library
> 17 Donegall Square North
> Belfast BT1 5GD
> Northern Ireland
> +44 (0) 28 9032 1707
> Fax: +44 (0) 28 9043 8586
> info@linenhall.com
> www.linenhall.com

National Archives of Ireland
Bishop Street
Dublin 8, Ireland
353 (0)1 407-2300
Local: 353 1809 252424
Fax: 353 (0)1 407-2333
mail@nationalarchives.ie
www.nationalarchives.ie

National Library of Ireland
Kildare St.
Dublin 2, Ireland
+353 (0)1 603-0200
Fax: +353 (0)1 661-2523
info@nli.ie
www.nli.ie/en/homepage.aspx

Public Records Office, Northern Ireland (PRONI)
2 Titanic Boulevard
Belfast, BT3 9HQ
Northern Ireland
(+44) 028 9025 5900
Fax: (+44) 028 9053 4900
proni@dcalni.gov.uk
www.proni.gov.uk

Israel

The Central Archives for the History of the Jewish People
P.O.B. 39077
Giv'at Ram Campus, Hebrew University
Jerusalem 91390
Israel
972-2-6586249
Fax: 972-2-6535426
archives@vms.huji.ac.il
sites.huji.ac.il/cahjp

Leo Baeck Institute Jerusalem
Bustenai St. 33
Jerusalem, Israel
+972-02-563 37 90
Fax: +972-02-566 95 05
leobaeck@netvision.net.il
www.leobaeck.org/

National Library of Israel
Hebrew University
Edmond Safra campus, Givat Ram
POB 39105
Jerusalem 91390
Israel
972-2-6585027
Fax: 972-2-6586315
jnul.huji.ac.il

Italy

Ministero peri i Beni e le Attività Culturali - Direzione Generale
per gli Archivi
Via Gaeta 8/A
Roma, Italy I-00185
39 06 49 225 1
Fax: 39 06 446 4912
dg-a@beniculturali.it
www.archivi.beniculturali.it/dipab.html

Ivory Coast/Cote D'Ivoire

Direction des Archives Nationales et de la Documentation
PO Box: BP V 126
1 rue van Vollenhoven
Abidjan, Cote D'Ivoire
225 20 21 74 20
Fax: 225 20 21 75 78

Jamaica

Jamaica Archives and Records Department
Corner of King and Manchester Streets
Spanish Town
St. Catherine, Jamaica
876 984 5001
Fax: 876 984 8254
jarchives@jard.gov.jm
www.jard.gov.jm

Japan

> National Archives of Japan
> 3-2 Kitanomaru Koen
> Chiyoda-ku, Tokyo 102-0091
> 81 3 3214-0641
> www.archives.go.jp

Jordan

> Royal Hashemite Documentation Center
> PO Box 961508
> Amman, Jordan
> 962 6 4626211/201/799
> Fax: 962 6 4626899
> www.rhdc.gov.jo

Kazakhstan

> Committee on Management of Archives and Documentation
> 30, ave. Abaia
> Almaty, Kazakhstan
> 3272 626044
> Fax: 3272 629182/696358

Kenya

> Kenya National Archives
> PO Box 49210
> Moi Avenue
> Nairobi 0010
> Kenya
> 254 20 2228959
> Fax: 254 20 2228020
> info@kenyarchives.go.ke
> www.kenyarchives.go.ke

Kiribati, Republic of

> National Archives and Library of Kiribati
> PO Box 6
> Bairiki, Tarawa
> Republic of Kiribati
> 686 21338
> Fax: 686 21337

Korea (P. D. R. of)

    State Bureau of Archives, DPR of Korea
    Jyngsungdong
    Central District
    Pyongyang, Korea (P. D. R. of)
    850 2 18111/8084
    Fax: 850 2 3814410

Kuwait

    Historical Documents and Emiri Court Library
    PO Box 799
    Seif Palace
    Al-Diwan, Al-Amiri
    Safat, Kuwait 13008
    965 2456921
    Fax: 965 2411 099

Kyrgyzstan

    State Archival Agency of the Kyrgyz Republic
    Ul. Toktogul 105
    Bishkek, Kyrgyzstan 720 040
    996 312 663 368/624 889
    Fax: 996 312 663 368
    www.archive.kg/index_en.htm

Latvia

    State Archives of Latvia
    Bezedelīgu Street 1
    Riga, LV-1048
    Latvia
    371 67412819
    www.lvarhivs.gov.lv/indexe.php?id=41

Lebanon

    Centrë des Archives Nationales
    PO Box 113
    Rue Hamra – Imm. Picadelly 6eme et 7eme etage
    6378 Beirut, Lebanon
    961-1-365783 / 344941 / 345854
    www.can.gov.lb/

Lesotho

>National Archives of Lesotho
>P.O. Box 52
>Maseru, Lesotho
>226 223 12047
>Fax: 266 223 10194

Liberia

>Center for National Documents and Records Agency
>12th Street Sinkor
>Monrovia, Liberia
>231 273 12000/12003/778 43265

Liechtenstein

>Liechtensteinisches Landesarchiv
>Postfach 684
>9490 Vaduz, Liechtenstein
>423 236 63 40
>Fax: 423 236 63 59
>www.la.llv.li

Lithuania

>Lithuanian Archives Department
>Algirdo 31
>LT-03219
>Vilnius, Lithuania
>370 5 265 1137
>Fax: 370 5 265 2314
>arch.dep@archyvai.lt
>www.archyvai.lt

Luxembourg

>Archives Nationales de Luxembourg
>Boite Postale 6
>Plateau du Saint Esprit
>L-2010 Luxembourg
>Grand-Duché de Luxembourg
>352 2478 6660/6661
>Fax: 352 47 4692
>archives.nationales@an.etat.lu
>www.anlux.lu

Madagascar

> Direction des Archives Nationales de Madagascar
> PO Box 3384
> 23 Karije Street Tsaralalana
> Anatananarivo, Madagascar 101
> 261 20 22 235 34/33110 8062
> www.archivesnationales.gov.mg/

Malawi

> National Archives of Malawi
> PO Box 62
> Mkulichi Road
> Zomba, Malawi
> Tel/Fax: 265 1 525 240
> Fax: 265 1 525 362
> archives@sdnp.org.mw
> chambo.sdnp.org.mw/ruleoflaw/archives/index.htm

Malaysia

> National Archives of Malaysia
> Jalan Duta
> 50568 Kuala Lumpur, Malaysia
> 60 03 6201 0688
> Fax: 60 03 6201 5679
> www.arkib.gov.my

Mali

> Archives Nationales du Mali
> Boite Postale159
> Koulouba, Bamako, Mali
> 223 222 58 44/223 0393
> Fax: 223 229 9403

Malta

> National Archives of Malta
> Santo Spirito
> Hospital Street
> Rabat, RBT 1043, Malta
> 356 214 59 863
> Fax: 356 21 450 078
> customercare.archives@gov.mt
> www.archives.gov.mt

Man (Isle of)

    Manx National Heritage
    Manx Museum
    Douglas, Man (Isle of) IM1 3Ly
    44 0 1624 648000
    Fax: 44 0 1624 648001
    enquiries@mnh.gov.im
    www.gov.im/mnh/heritage/library/national
        library.xml

Mariana Islands

    Northern Mariana College Archives
    PO Box 501250
    As Terlaje Campus
    Saipan, MP 96950
    Mariana Islands
    670 234 5498
    Fax 670 234 1270
    www.nmcnet.edu/content.php?id=3&cat=20

Mauritius

    National Archives
    Development Bank of Mauritius Complex
    Coromandel, Mauritius
    (230) 233 2791/2170
    Fax: (230) 233 4299
    arc@mail.gov.mu
    www.gov.mu/portal/site/mac/menuitem.adf
        2c4b1c2d8d5aca6597adaa0208a0c

Mexico

    Archivo General de Nacion
    Eduardo Molina y Albaniles
    Col. Penitenciaria Ampliacion, Delegacion
    Venustiano Carranza
    CP 15350, Mexico, D. F.
    52 55 51339903
    Fax: 52 55 57895296
    www.agn.gob.mx

Micronesia (Federal States of)

    Yap State Archives
    PO Box 1070
    Colonia, Yap
    Micronesia (Federal States of)
    691 350 3684

Moldova

    Central State Archives/Service des Archives de l'etat de la Republique de Moldavie
    Strada Gheorghe Asachi 67-B
    Chisinau 2028
    Moldova
    373 2 72 97 93
    Fax: 373 2 73 58 36

Mongolia (P. R. of)

    National Archival Administration of Mongolia
    A. Amarii Gudamj-2
    Sukhbaatar Duureg
    Ulaanbaatar, Mongolia (p. R. of)
    976 1 32 39
    Fax: 976 1 324 533

Montenegro

    State Archives of Montenegro
    Novice Cerovica 2
    Cetinje, Montenegro 81250
    381 86 230 225
    Fax: 381 86 230 226

Morocco

    Bibliothèque Générale et Archives
    BP 1003
    5, avenue Ibn Batouta
    Rabat, Morocco
    212 376 70461
    Fax: 212 377 76062

Mozambique

    Arquivo Histórico de Moçámbìque
    C. P. 2033
    Travessa do Varietá n° 58,
    Maputo, Mozambique
    258 21 32 11 78
    www.ahm.uem.mz

Myanmar (Burma)

    National Archives Department
    114 Pyidaungsu Yeiktha Road
    Dagon Township
    Yangon, Myanmar (Burma)
    951 272 708
    Fax: 951 254011
    nad@mptmail.net.mm
    www.mnped.gov.mm/nationalchives.asp

Namibia

    National Library and Archives of Namibia
    Private Bag 13349
    1-7 Eugene Marais Street
    Windhoek, Namibia
    (264) 61 293 5300
    Fax: (264) 61 293 5321
    natlib@mec.gov.na
    www.nln.gov.na/

Nepal

    National Archives
    Ramshahpath
    5/16 Jhochhe Layakusal
    Kathmandu, Nepal
    977 1 426 4353
    mail@nationalarchives.gov.np
    www.nationalarchives.gov.np

Netherlands

    Central Bureau for Genealogy (Centraal Bureau voor Genealogie)
        Postbus 11755
        Prins Willem-Alexanderhof 22
        NL-2502 AT Den Haag
        The Netherlands
        31-70-3150570
        31-70-3478394
        info@cbg.nl
        www.cbg.nl

    Dutch Genealogical Society (Nederlandse Genealogische Vereniging)
        Postbus 26
        1380 AA Weesp
        Physical: Papelaan 6
        1382 RM Weesp
        The Netherlands
        0294-413301
        www.ngv.nl

    National Archives (Algemeen Rijksrchief)
        Postbus 90520
        Prins Willem-Alexanderhof 20
        2509 LM The Hague
        The Netherlands
        31 70 331 5400
        Fax: 31 70 331 5540
        info@nationaalarchief.nl
        www.nationaalarchief.nl

    The Royal Dutch Society for Genealogy and Heraldry
        (Koninklijk Nederlands Genootschap voor Geslacht-en Wapenkunde)
        Prins Willem-Alexanderhof 24
        Postbus 85630
        2508 CH Den Haag
        The Netherlands
        01 80 661 973
        www.knggw.nl

New Zealand

> Archives New Zealand
> Head Office, Wellington
> PO Box 12-050
> 10 Musgrave Street
> Thorndon, Wellington 6011
> New Zealand
> 64-4 499 5595
> Fax: 64-4 495 6210
> reference@archives.govt.nz
> www.archives.govt.nz
>
> National Oral History Association of New Zealand
> PO Box 3819
> Te Kete Kōrero-a-Waha p Te Motu
> Wellington, New Zealand
> www.oralhistory.org.nz

Niger

> Directon des Archives Nationales du Niger
> BP 550
> Niamey, Niger
> 227 72 26 82
> Fax: (227) 72 36 54

Nigeria

> National Archives of Nigeria
> Department of National Archives of Nigeria
> Radio House, Garki
> Abuja, Nigeria
> 234-9-2344105

Niue (Island)

> Niue National Archives
> PO Box 77
> Alofi, Niue (Island)
> 683-4634
> Fax: 683-4391

Norway

> National Archival Services of Norway
> Postboks 4013
> Folke Bernadottes vei 21
> Ullevål stadion
> N–0806 Oslo, Norway
> 47 22 02 26 00
> Fax: 47 22 23 74 89
> riksarkivet@arkivverket.no
> www.arkivverket.no
>
> Norwegian Emigration Center
> Strandkain 31
> 4005 Stavanger,
> Norway
> +47 5153-8860
> Fax: +47 5153-8863
> www.emigrationcenter.com
>
> Norwegian Historical Data Centre
> The Faculty of Social Sciences
> University of Tromsø
> N–9037 Tromsø, Norway
> +47 77 64 41 80
> Fax: +47 77 64 41 82
> rhd-web@sv.uit.no
> www.rhd.uit.no

Oman (Sultanate of)

> National Records and Archives Authority
> PO Box 483
> Al Azaiba
> Muscat
> Oman (Sultanate of) 130
> 968 244 92835/1793
> Fax: 968 244 95933

Pakistan

>National Archives of Pakistan
>Pakistan Secretariat
>Block N, Islamabad
>Pakistan 44000
>92 51 9202044
>Fax: 92 51 9203545
>info@nap.gov.pk
>www.nap.gov.pk

Palau

>Division of Palau National Archives
>PO Box 100
>Koror, Palau 96940
>680 488 4720/6778
>archives@palaunet.com
>www.palaugov.net/PalauGov/Executive
>/Ministries/MCCA/Archive.htm

Palestinian National Authority

>National Authority
>PO Box 66353
>Beitunia Street
>Al-taher Bld.
>Ramallah, Palestinian National Authority
>970 2 290 4121/2
>Fax: 972 2 290 4124

Panama

>Registro Publico de Panama
>Avenida Peru, entre Calle 31 y 32
>Panama 0830-1596
>507 501-6150
>Fax: 507 501-6152
>www.registro-publico.gob.pa

Papua New Guinea

>National Archives
>PO Box 1089
>Boroko, Papua New Guinea
>675 325 0687/4332
>Fax: 675 325 4251

Philippines

>National Archives of the Philippines
>TNL Building, T. M. Kalaw Street
>Ermita, Manila
>Philippines 1000
>632 525 1407/521 6830
>Fax: 632 525 6830/525 1828
>phinatarch@yahoo.com
>www.nationalarchives.gov.ph

Poland

>State Archives of Poland/Naczelna Dyrekcja
>Archiwów Państwowych
>>Archiwum Główne Akt (Ancient Documents)
>>ul. Rakowiecka 2 D
>>02-517 Warszawa
>>Polska (Poland)
>>+48 22 565-46-00
>>Fax: +48 22 565-46-14
>>ndap@archiwa.gov.pl
>>www.archiwa.gov.pl

Portugal

>Arquivo Nacional da Torre do Tombo
>Alameda da Universidade
>1649-010 Lisboa, Portugal
>315 217811500
>Fax: 315 217937230
>mail@dgarq.gov
>antt.dgarq.gov.pt

Puerto Rico

>Arquivo Nacional de Puerto Rico
>PO Box: Apartado 9024184
>San Juan, Puerto Rico
>1 787 724 0700
>Fax: 1 787 724 8393

Romania

> National Archives of Romania/Arhivele Nationale
> Bd. Regina Elisabeta nr.49
> Sector 5
> Bucureşti, Romania C-050013
> 21 303 70 80
> Fax: 021 312 58 41/021 313 18 38
> secretariat.an@mai.gov.ro
> www.arhivelenationale.ro

Russia, Federation of

> Committee on Archives by the Government of Udmurt Republic
> ul. Borodina 21
> 426057 IZEVSK
> Russia (Federation of)
> 7 3412 754296/12 69
> Fax: 7 3412 754497
> www.gasur.narod.ru
>
> General Archival Department Under the Cabinet of Ministers of the Republic of Tatarstan
> Kremlin Str. 2/6
> 420111 Kazan
> Russia (Federation of)
> 7 8432 928794
> Fax: 7 8432 923760
>
> Russian Federal Archival Agency
> Ilyinka 12
> 103132 Moscow
> Russia (Federation of)
> 7 495-606 3531
> Fax: 7 495 606 5587
> support@archives.ru
> www.rusarchives.ru
>
> Russia State Historical Archives
> Zanevski Prospect 36
> 195112 Saint-Petersburg
> Russia (Federation of)
> 8 812 438 552 0
> Fax: 8 812 438 55 94
> fgurgia@mail.ru
> rusarchives.ru/federal/rgia

State Archives of the Russian Federation
Bolchaïa Pirogovskaya ul., 17
119817 Moscow
Russia (Federation of)
7 495 245 1287
Fax: 7 495 245 1287
garf@online.ru
garf.ru/

Rwanda

Archives Nationales
BP 1044
Kigali, Rwanda
250 5835 25
Fax: 250 5835 18

Saint Lucia

Saint Lucia National Archives
P.O. Box 3060
Clarke Avenue Vigie
Castries, Saint Lucia
1758 452 1654
Fax: 1758 453 1405

San Marino

Archivio Pubblico Dello Stato
Contrada Omerelli 13
47890 San Marino RSM
San Marino
0549 882486
Fax: 0549 882481
archivio@pa.sm
www.archiviodistato.sm

São Tomé e Príncipe

Arquivo Histórico de São Tomé e Príncipe
Boîte Postale 87
Av. Marginal 12 de Julho
São Tomé e Príncipe
239 12 21630
Fax: 239 12 24201

Saudi Arabia

    National Center for Documents and Archives
    Ministerial Court
    P.O. Box 150 486
    Riyadh
    Saudi Arabia
    966 148 82348
    Fax: 966 144 13905

Scotland

    National Archives of Scotland
    H M General Register House
    2 Princes Street
    Edinburgh, EH1 3YY
    +44 (0) 131 535 1314
    Fax: +44 (0) 131 535 1328
    enquires@nas.gov.uk
    www.nas.gov.uk

    or

    West Register House
    17a Charlotte Street
    Edinburgh, EH2 4DJ
    +44 (0) 131 535 1400
    Fax: +44 (0) 131 535 1411
    wsr@nas.gov.uk
    www.nas.gov.uk

    National Library of Scotland
    George IV Bridge
    Edinburgh, EH1 1EW
    +44 (0) 131-623 3700
    Fax: +44 (0) 131-623 3701
    enquires@nls.uk
    www.nls.uk

    The Registrar
    General Search Unit
    3 West Register Street
    New Register House
    Edinburgh EH1 3YT
    +44 0131 334 0380
    www.gro-scotland.gov.uk

Scottish Genealogy Society
15 Victoria Terrace
Edinburgh EH1 2JL
Tel: +44 (0)131 220 3677
enquiries@scotsgenealogy.com
www.scotsgenealogy.com

Sénégal

Archives du Sénégal
Immeuble Administratif
Avenue Léopold Sédar
Senghor, Dakar
221 823 50 72
Fax: 221 822 51 26
pmarchi@primature.sn
www.archivesdusenegal.gouv.sn

Serbia

The Archives of Serbia
Karnegijeva br. 2
11000 Beograd
Serbia
381 11 3370 072
Fax: 381 11 33-70-246
office@archives.org.rs
www.archives.org.rs

Seychelles

National Archives of Seychelles
P. O. Box 720
5th June Avenue
Victoria
Mahe, Seychelles
248-321-333
Fax: 248-322-481
archives@seychelles.net
www.sna.gov.sc/

Singapore

> National Archives of Singapore
> 1 Canning Rise
> Singapore 179868
> 65 6 332 7909
> Fax: 65 6 339 3583
> nhb_nasreg@nhb.gov.sg
> www.nhb.gov.sg/NAS

Slovakia

> Slovak National Archives/Slovenský Národný Archív
> Drotárska cesta 42
> 817 01 Bratislava
> 421 2 672 981 11
> Fax: 421 2 628 012 47
> archiv@sna.vs.sk
> www.civil.gov.sk/snarchiv

Slovenia

> Archives of the Republic of Slovenia
> PO Box 21, Slovenia
> Zvezdarska 1
> SI-1127 Ljubljana
> +386 12414200
> Fax: +386 12414269
> ars@gov.si
> www.arhiv.gov.si

Solomon Islands

> National Archives
> PO Box 781
> Honiara, Solomon Islands
> 677 24897

South Africa

>National Archives of South Africa
>Private Bag X236
>24 Hamilton Street
>Arcadia, Pretoria 0001
>(012) 441 3200
>Fax: (012) 323 5287
>Archives@dac.gov.za
>www.national.archives.gov.za

Spain

>Subdirección General de los Archivos Estatales
>Plaza del Rey 1
>28004 Madrid
>902 55 55 00
>www.mcu.es/archivos/index.html

Sri Lanka

>Department of National Archives
>PO Box 1414
>No. 7, PhilipGunawardena Mawatha (Reid Avenue)
>Colombo 7
>Sri Lanka
>94 11 269 4523
>Fax: 94 11 269 44 19
>narchive@slt.lk
>www.archives.gov.lk/

St. Kitts and Nevis

>National Archives St. Kitts and Nevis
>Government Headquarters
>Church Street
>Basseterre, St. Kitts and Nevis
>869 465 2521, ext. 1208
>Fax: 869 465 1001
>nationalarchives@gov.kn or
>stkitts.archives@gmail.com
>www.nationalarchives.gov.kn/

St. Vincent & Grenadines

    Department of Libraries, Archives and Documentation Services
    Lower Middle Street
    Kingstown
    St. Vincent & Grenadines
    1 784 457 2022
    Fax: 1 784 485 6454

Sudan

    National Archives
    P.O. Box 1914
    Khartoum, Sudan
    249 11 784 135/255
    Fax: 249 11 778 603

Swaziland

    Swaziland National Archives
    PO Box 946
    Mbabane, Swaziland
    9268-416 1196
    Fax: 9268- 416 1241/404 1719
    www.gov.sz

Sweden

    Federation of Swedish Genealogical Societies
    Post Sveriges Släktforskarförbund
    SE-171 54 Solna
    Anderstorpsvägen 16, Solna
    Sweden
    46 8 440 75 50
    Fax: 46 8- 695 08 24
    redaktor@genealogi.se
    www.genealogi.se/roots

    National Archives (Riksarkivet) in Marieberg
    Box 125 41
    Fyrverkarbacken 13
    SE-102 29 Stockholm
    Sweden
    46(0)10-476 71 00
    Fax: 46(0)10-476 71 20
    riksarkivet@riksarkivet.ra.se
    www.riksarkivet.se

National Archives in Arninge, Stockholm
Mätslingan 17
SE-187 66 Täby
Sweden
+46(0)10-476 72 00
Fax: +46(0)10-476 72 20

Switzerland

Swiss Federal Archives
Archivstrasse 24
CH-3003 Berne
Switzerland
+41 31 322 89 89
Fax: +41 31 322 78 23
bundesarchiv@bar.admin.ch
www.bar.admin.ch

Swiss Genealogical Society
c/o Dr. Heinz Ochsner
Grabenweg 1
CH-4414 Füllinsdorf
Switzerland
h.oschsner@dplanet.ch
www.eye.ch/swissgen/SGFF.html

Syria

Historical Document Center
Sarojah
Damas, Syria
963 112 313283/4
Fax: 963 112 313279

Tajikistan

Direction Generale des Archives Pres le Conseil des Ministres
Rep. Tadjikistan
(Glavarkhiv)
Douchanbe
Tajikistan

Tanzania

>National Archives
>PO Box 2006
>Vijibweni Street – off Magore Road
>Dar es Salaam, Tanzania
>255 22 215 2875
>Fax: 255 22 215 1279

Thailand

>National Archives of Thailand
>Office of the National Culture Commission
>Samsen Road
>Dusit, Bangkok
>Thailand
>662 281 6947
>Fax: 662 281 5341 or 628 5172
>www.culture.go.th

Togo

>Bibliotheque et Archives Nationales du Togo
>POB B.P. 1002
>41 Avenue Sarakauva
>Lomé, Togo
>228 221 63 67
>Fax: 228 222 07 83 / 221 57 06

Tonga

>Tonga Traditions Committee
>PO Box 6
>Nuku' Alofa, Tonga
>676 25 063
>Fax: 676 24 102

Trinidad and Tobago

> National Archives Trinidad and Tobago
> PO Box 763
> 105 St. Vincent Street
> Port-of-Spain
> Trinidad and Tobago, West Indies
> 868-623-2874
> Fax: 868-625-2689
> nattenquiries@moi.gov.tt
> natt.gov.tt/

Tunisia, Republic of

> National Archives of Tunisia / Archives Nationales Tunisiennes
> 122, Boulevard 9 avril 1938
> 1030 Tunis, Tunisia
> 216 71 576 800 or 71 576 500
> Fax: 216 71 569 175
> archives.nationales@email.ati.tn
> www.archives.nat.tn

Turkey

> T. C. Basbakanlik Devlet Arsivleri Genel Müdürürlügü
> Ivedik Caddesi Nº 59
> Ankara, Turkey
> 06180 Yenimahalle
> 90 312 344 5909
> Fax: 90 312 315 1000
> dagm@devletarsivleri.gov.tr
> www.devletarsivleri.gov.tr

Turkmenistan

> Archives Administration within the Cabinet of Ministers of Turkmenistan
> Makhtumkuly Avenue 88
> Ashgabat
> Turkmenistan 744000
> 993 1 2253609
> Fax: 993 1 2253609

Tuvalu

    National Library and Archives, Tuvalu
    PO Box 67
    Funafuti
    Tuvalu
    688 20711
    Fax: 688 20405 / 20113

Ukraine

    Central State Committee on Archives of Ukraine
    vul. Solom'ianska 24
    Kiev, Ukraine 03110
    380 44 275 2777
    Fax: 380 44 275 3655
    mail@archives.gov.ua
    www.archives.gov.ua

United Arab Emirates

    National Archives, Cultural Foundation
    PO Box 2380
    Abu Dhabi
    United Arab Emirates
    9712 4445100
    Fax: 9712 44456400

United Kingdom

    National Archives
    Kew, Richmond TW9 4DU
    Surrey, United Kingdom
    +44 (0) 20 8876 3444
    Minicom: +44 (0) 20 8392 9198
    www.nationalarchives.gov.uk

Uruguay

    Archivo General de la Nacion
    Convencion 1474
    11.100 Montevideo
    Uruguay
    059 8 2900 7232
    Fax: 059 8 2908 1330
    Direccion@agn.gub.uy
    www.agn.gub.uy

Vanuatu

    Department of Culture, Religion, Women's Affairs and National Archives
    PMB 0091
    Port-Vila
    Vanuatu
    678 22498
    Fax: 678 26353

Vatican

    Vatican Secret Archives/Archives Secretes Vaticanes
    00120 Cite du Vatican
    39 06 698 83314
    Fax: 39 06 698 85574
    asv@asv.va
    asv.vatican.va/en/arch/1_past.htm

Vietnam

    State Records and Archives Department of Vietnam
    12 Dao Tan Street
    Ba Dinh District
    Hanoi, Vietnam (S. R. of)
    84 4 37660370
    Fax: 84 4 37665165
    tinhoc@archives.gov.vn
    www.luutruvn.gov.vn

Wales

    Association of Family History Societies of Wales
    AFHSW Secretary
    National Library of Wales
    Aberystwyth SY23 3BU
    secretary@fhwales.info
    www.fhswales.org.uk

    Llyfrgell Genedlaethol Cymru/The National Library of Wales
    Aberystwyth, Ceredigion
    Wales SY23 3BU
    +44 (0) 1970 632800
    Fax: +44 (0) 1970 615709
    holi@llgc.org.uk
    www.llgc.org.uk/cac

Western Samoa

>National Archives of Western Samoa
>PO Box 1869
>APIA
>Western Samoa
>685 21911 ext. 769
>Fax: 685 21917

Yemen

>National Center for Archives
>Al Zubairi Street
>PO Box 846
>SANAA
>Yemen
>967 127 6818
>Fax: 967 128 8161

Zambia

>National Archives of Zambia
>POB 500 10
>Government Road
>Lusaka
>Zambia
>260 1-250-446
>Fax: 260 1-254-080
>www.zambiarchives.org

Zimbabwe

>National Archives of Zimbabwe
>Private Bag 7729
>Borrowdale Road, Gunhill
>Causeway, Harare
>00-263-4-792741
>Fax: 00-263-4-792398
>nat.archives@gta.gov.zw
>www.gta.gov.zw/index.php?option=com_content&vie
>w=article&id=82&itemid=147

Archives - *General interest:*

UNESCO Archives Portal
www.unesco-ci.org/cgi-bin/portals/archives/page.cgi

Genealogy/Oral History Web Sites:

Acadian Genealogy Homepage
3-304 Stone Road West, Suite 311
Guelph, Ontario, Canada N1G 4W4
cajun@acadian.org
www.acadian.org

African-American Cemeteries Online
support@africanamericancemeteries.com
africanamericancemeteries.com

Afrigeneas - African Ancestored Genealogy
4725 Walton Xing #1129
Atlanta, GA 30331
404-344-7177
www.afrigeneas.com

American Battle Monuments Commission
Courthouse Plaza II, Suite 500
2300 Clarendon Boulevard
Arlington, VA 22201
703-696-6900
info@abmc.gov
www.abmc.gov

American Civil War Home Page
sunsite.utk.edu/civil-war

American Civil War Research Database
Historical Data Systems, Inc.
PO Box 35
Duxbury, MA 02331
800-244-3446
781-934-1353
civilwardata@sprynet.com
www.civilwardata.com

Ancestors - the companion site to the PBS family history and genealogy television series.
www.byub.org/ancestors

Ancestry.com
360 West 4800 North
Provo, UT 84604
801-705-7000
801-705-7001
www.ancestry.com

Archives: Search & Discover
www.archives.com

Arkansas Land Records Interactive Search
searches.rootsweb.ancestry.com/cgi-bin/arkland/arkland.pl

Australian Family History Compendium
www.cohsoft.com.au/afhc

Avotaynu, Inc.: Publisher of Works on Jewish Genealogy
155 N. Washington Avenue
Bergenfield, NJ 07621
201-387-7200
www.avotaynu.com

Belgian Genealogy Homepages
members.tripod.com/~therresa/glinks.html

Board for Certification of Genealogists
PO Box 14291
Washington, DC 20044
office@bcgcertification.org
www.bcgcertification.org

Bureau of Reclamation Photography and Engineering Drawing Collections
Land Resources Office
PO Box 25007 (84-53000)
Denver Federal Center, Building 67
6th and Kipling
Denver, CO 80225-0007
303-445-2072
Fax: 303-445-6303
Library@usbr.gov
www.usbr.gov/history/photos.htm

Canadian Genealogy: Canadian Genealogy Resources
www.canadiangenealogy.net

Cemeteries from the U.S. Civil War Center
www.civilwarhome.com/hist.htm#cemeteries

Cemetery Iconography
www.ancestry.com/learn/library/article.aspx?article=868

Cemetery Junction Directory
www.daddezio.com/cemetery

Cemetery Records Online
interment.net

Channel Islands Genealogy
www.rootsweb.ancestry.com/~ukchanis

Christine's Genealogy Website
Focuses on African- and Native-American Genealogies
ccharity.com

Civil War Archive
www.civilwararchive.com

Civil War Soldiers and Sailors System
www.itd.nps.gov/cwss

CivilWar.com
www.civilwar.com

Cornell University Library/Making of America
digital.library.cornell.edu/m/moa/index.html

Cyndi's List of Genealogy Sites on the Internet
Cyndi@Cyndislist.com
www.cyndislist.com

CousinConnect
www.cousinconnect.com

Digital Archive of American Architecture
www.bc.edu/bc_org/avp/cas/fnart/fa267

Directory of Irish Genealogy
　　　Carraig, Cliff Road
　　　Windgates, Bray, Co Wicklow
　　　Ireland
　　　Sjbmurphy@eircom.net
　　　homepage.eircom.net/~seanjmurphy/dir

Family Search: Church of Jesus Christ of Latter-Day Saints
　　　www.familysearch.org

Family Tree Maker®2010
　　　familytreemaker.com

FamilyHistory.com
　　　www.familyhistory.com

Federation of Genealogical Societies
　　　PO Box 200940
　　　Austin, TX 78720-0940
　　　888-347-1500
　　　Fax: 888-380-1350
　　　office@fgs.org
　　　www.fgs.org

50 Family History Interview Questions
　　　www.scrapbookscrapbook.com/familytree
　　　　questions.html

Find A Grave
　　　www.findagrave.com

FrancoGene: French Genealogy of North America
　　　www.francogene.com/genealogy

GEN-UKI: UK & Ireland Genealogy
　　　www.genuki.org.uk

Genealogy.org
　　　Genealogy Search Online
　　　genealogy.org

GeneaSearch Cemetery Records Online
　　　www.geneasearch.com/cemeteries.htm

GenCircles
　　　www.gencircles.com

Gengateway
www.gengateway.com

Historic USGS Maps of New England & New York
docs.unh.edu/nhtopos/nhtopos.htm

Historical Maps of Illinois and the Northwest Territory
images.library.uiuc.edu/projects/maps

HyperHistory
www.hyperhistory.com/online_n2/History_n2/a.html

Illinois Public Domain Land Tract Sales
www.cyberdriveillinois.com/departments/archives/data_lan.html

Indiana Land Records
www.in.gov/icpr/2580.htm

Irish Roots
www.irelandroots.com

ItalianGenealogy.com
italiangenealogy.tardio.com/

JewishGen: The Home of Jewish Genealogy
Edmond J. Safra Plaza
36 Battery Place
New York, NY 10280
646-437-4326
info@jewishgen.org
www.jewishgen.org

Land Office Patents and Grants, Library of Virginia
ajax.lva.lib.va.us/F/?func=file&file_name=find-b-clas30&local_base=CLAS30

Louisiana Land Records Interactive Search
searches.rootsweb.ancestry.com/cgi-bin/laland/laland.pl

Lusaweb: Portuguese-American Community
www.lusaweb.com

Master Index of Army Records
    Addresses vary by service dates
    www.army.mil/CMH/reference/records.htm

Military History Maps (U.S. Military Academy)
    digital-library.usma.edu/collections/maps/

National Archives Research Online Ordering
    8601 Adelphi Road
    College Park, MD 20740-6001
    866-272-6272
    Fax: 301-837-0483
    TDD: 301-837-0482
    www.archives.gov/research/order

National Genealogical Society
    3108 Columbia Pike, Suite 300
    Arlington, VA 22204-4370
    703-525-0050
    800- 473-0060
    Fax: 703-525-0052
    ngs@ngsgenealogy.org
    www.ngsgenealogy.org

National Obituary Archive
    PO Box 16522
    3615 South Stadium
    Jonesboro, AR 72403
    noa@continentalcomputers.com
    www.arrangeonline.com

Native American Genealogy
    www.accessgenealogy.com/native

NativeWeb - Resources for Indigenous Cultures around the World
    www.nativeweb.org

North Dakota Land Records
    www.land-records.com/land-records/north-dakota-land-records.htm

Olive Tree Genealogy
    Canadian and American Genealogical Research
    olivetreegenealogy.com

POW-MIA Korean War Casualties
   www.Koreanwar.org/html/Korean_war_databases.html

The Quaker Corner
   www.rootsweb.ancestry.com/~quakers

Revolutionary War Bounty Warrants
   ajax.lva.lib.va.us/F/?func=file&file_name=find-b-clas39&local_base=CLAS39

RootsWeb.com: The oldest and largest free genealogy site.
   www.rootsweb.ancestry.com

Scottish and Irish Clans & Families
   www.electricscotland.com/webclans

Scottish and LDS Genealogical Reference Information
   www.ktb.net/~dwills/scotref/13300-scottish reference.htm

Social Security Death Index (SSDI)
   ssdi.genealogy.rootsweb.ancestry.com

The Statue of Liberty-Ellis Island Foundation, Inc.
   Attention: History Center
   17 Battery Place #210
   New York, NY 10004-3507
   212-561-4588
   www.ellisisland.org

Swiss Genealogy on the Internet
   www.eye.ch/swissgen

Tombstone Meanings
   homepages.rootsweb.ancestry.com/~maggieoh/tomb.html

The Tombstone Transcription Project
   usgwtombstones.org/

Tracing Your Scottish Ancestry
   www.geo.ed.ac.uk/home/scotland/genealogy.html

The United States Civil War Center
        Hill Memorial Library/LSU
        Baton Rouge, LA 70803
        225-578-6568
        Fax: 225-578-9425
        www.cwc.lsu.edu/

United States Vital Records Information
        vitalrec.com

USGenWeb Digital Library (Archives)
        www.usgenweb.com

Valley Forge Muster Roll Database
        www.ushistory.org/valleyforge/served/index.html

Vitalchek Network, Inc.: Ordering vital records electronically - U.S.
        www.vitalchek.com

Wisconsin Land Records Interactive Search
        searches.rootsweb.ancestry.com/cgi-in/wisconsin/
        wisconsin.pl

World War I Draft Registration Cards
        www.genealogybranches.com/worldwaronedraft
        cards.html

WWW Virtual Library - American Indians
        www.hanksville.org/NAresources

*Author's collection: John & Muriel (parents),
Don & Ernie, uncles; at the cabin in Emily, Minnesota*

Preservation, Family Albums and Scrapbooking:

Advisory Council on Historic Preservation
1100 Pennsylvania Avenue, NW, Suite 803
Old Post Office Building
Washington, DC 20004
202-606-8503
achp@achp.gov
www.achp.gov

American Family: Journey of Dreams
www.pbs.org/americanfamily/your_album.html

American Institute for Conservation of Historic and Artistic Works
1156 15th Street NW, Suite. 320
Washington, DC 20005
202-452-9545
Fax: 202-452-9328
info@conservation-us.org
aic.stanford.edu

Care, Handling and Storage of Photographs
www.loc.gov/preserv/care/photolea.html

Computer Scrapbooking
www.computerscrapbooking.com

CoOl: Conservation On-Line, Resources for Conservation Professionals
Cool.conservation-us.org

Creative Memories
PO Box 1839
3001 Clearwater Road
St. Cloud, MN 56302-1839
800-341-5275
www.creativememories.com

The Cropping Corner Scrapbook Supplies
800-608-2467
www.croppingcorner.com

dMarie Scrapbook Place
www.dmarie.com

Gift of Heritage (film documentary)
    Mary Lou Productions
    Fax: 612-727-2705
    800-224-8511
    marylou@giftofheritage.com
    www.giftofheritage.com

Heritage Preservation
    1012 14th Street, NW
    Suite 1200
    Washington, DC 20005
    202-233-0800
    Fax: 202-233-0807
    www.heritagepreservation.org

Kodak: Preserving Family Albums
    www.kodak.com/US/en/corp/membersGallery/
    archiving/caringForAlbums.shtml

Lifejournal
    Chronicles Software Company
    PO Box 220
    Sarasota, FL 34230-0220
    www.lifejournal.com

Lots of Layouts
    328 North State Street
    Ukiah, CA 95482
    www.lolsb.com

National Trust for Historic Preservation
    1785 Massachusetts Avenue NW
    Washington, DC 20036-2117
    202-588-6000
    800-944-6847
    Fax: 202-588-6038
    www.preservationnation.org

Research and Marketing Resources for Historic Preservation
    7017 N. Alma Avenue
    Portland, OR 97203
    503-223-4939
    preservationdirectory@comcast.net
    www.preservationdirectory.com

Scrapbooking
scrapbooking.about.com

Scrapbooking 101.net
www.scrapbooking101.net

Scrapbooking Links
www.scraplink.com

Scrapbooking.com Magazine
scrapbooking.com

Scrapjazz: The Scrapbooking Megasite
www.scrapjazz.com

Genealogical Software:

AllCensus
comments@allcensus.com
www.allcensus.com

Ancestral Quest 2002
Incline Software, LC
PO Box 95543
South Jordan, UT 84095-0543
800-825-8864
801-280-4434
Fax: 801-254-1147
ancquest@ancquest.com
www.ancquest.com

Ancestry.com
360 West 4800 North
Provo, UT 84604
801-705-7000
Fax: 801-705-7001
www.ancestry.com

Barnette's Family Tree Book Co.
barnettesbooks.com

Brother's Keeper
    John Steed
    6907 Childsdale Avenue
    Rockford, MI 49341
    Brothers_Keeper@msn.com
    www.bkwin.org

Census Tools
    www.censustools.com

Clooz
    Ancestor Detective
    PO Box 6386
    Plymouth, MI 48170-8486
    734-354-6449
    www.clooz.com

DoroTree Technologies, Ltd.
    Manachat Technology Park
    Building 1 / 22, Third Floor
    IL-96951 Jerusalem
    Israel
    +972 2 679 7490
    Fax: +972 2 679 7470
    www.dorotree.com

Everton Publishers, Inc.
    PO Box 442
    Garden City, UT 84028
    800-443-6325
    cs@everton.com
    www.everton.com

Family Matters
    MatterWare
    381 Garnet Court
    Fort Mill, SC 29708
    803-396-2011
    ray@matterware.com
    www.matterware.com

Family Origins
    800-766-8762
    www.formalsoft.com

Family Tree Legends
Pearl Street Software
www.familytreelegends.com

GEDitCOM (for Macs)
www.geditcom.com

Genealogical Publishing Company
3600 Clipper Mill Road, Suite 260
Baltimore, MD 21211
800-296-6687
410-837-8271
Fax: 800-599-9561 or 410-752-8492
info@genealogical.com
www.genealogical.com

Heritage Books, Inc.
100 Railroad Avenue, Suite 104
Westminster, MD 21157-5026
800-876-6103
231-537-4021
Fax: 401-558-6574
Info@heritagebooks.com
www.heritagebooks.com

Legacy Family Tree 4.0
Millennia Corporation
PO Box 9410
Surprise, AZ 85374
800-753-3453
623-444-8918
Fax: 425-940-1610
Info@LegacyFamilyTree.com
www.legacyfamilytree.com

Millisecond Publishing Company, Inc.
Family Forest Department
PO Box 6168
Kamuela, HI 96743
P/F: 808-883-8060
familyforest@hawaii.rr.com
www.familyforest.com

Reunion (for Macs)
    Leister Productions
    PO Box 289
    Mechanicsburg, PA 17055
    717-697-1378
    sales@leisterpro.com
    www.leisterpro.com

RootsMagic, Inc.
    PO Box 495
    Springville, UT 84663
    800-766-8762
    www.rootsmagic.com

S-K Publications
    PO Box 8173
    Wichita, KS 67208-0173
    316-685-3201
    Fax: 316-685-6650
    genie@skpub.com
    www.skpub.com/genie

U.S. Genealogy Data Publisher
    1623 West 3640 South
    St. George, UT 84790
    435-674-7516
    globalcd@infowest.com
    www.gencd.com

Wholly Genes Software
    5114 Flowertuft Court
    Columbia, MD 21044
    877-864-3264
    410-715-2260
    Fax: 410-730-9734
    support@whollygenes.com
    www.whollygenes.com

Microforms & Miscellaneous Information Sources:

Federal Records:

    National Archives Census Microfilm Rental Program
        National Archives and Records Administration
        700 Pennsylvania Avenue, NW
        Washington, DC 20408-0001
        202-357-5400
        www.archives.gov/research/order/renting-microfilm.html

        order address: National Archives Trust Fund
        Cashier (NAT)
        Form 72 Order
        8601 Adelphi Road
        College Park, MD 20740-6001

    Federal Population Census: Catalogs of Microfilm Copies
        8601 Adelphi Road
        College Park, MD 20740-6001
        (301) 837-0470
        www.archives.gov/research/census

Passports prior to 1926-mail orders

    National Archives and Records Service
        Attn: Archives I Research Support Branch (NWCC1)
        700 Pennsylvania Avenue, NW
        Washington, DC 20408-0001
        202-357-5400
        www.archives.gov/researc/passport/index.html

    Passport Applications 1925 to Present
        Department of State
        Research & Liaison Branch
        1111 19th Street NW, Suite 200
        Washington, DC 20522-1705

Court Records:

> *Federal Court Records, a Select Catalog of NARA Microfilm Publications.* 1987. Washington, DC: National Archives, 1991.
> 8601 Adelphi Road
> College Park, MD 20740-6001
> 866-272-6272
> Fax: 301-837-0483
> www.archives.gov/publications/microfilm-catalogs/fed-courts/index.html

Immigration and Naturalization Service:

> National Archives
> Immigration and Passenger Arrivals
> 700 Pennsylvania Avenue, NW
> Washington, DC 20408-0001
> 202-357-5400
> www.archives.gov/research/immigration/index.html

Military Records:

> *American Civil War Biographical Bibliographies*
> U.S. Army Heritage and Education Center
> 950 Soldiers Drive
> Carlisle, PA 17013-5021
> 717-245-3971
> www.carlisle.army.mil/ahec/index.htm
>
> National Archives and Records Administration (military records)
> 700 Pennsylvania Avenue, NW
> Washington, DC 20408-0001
> 202-357-5400
> inquire@nara.gov (request forms)
> www.archives.gov/research/military/index.html
>
> Civil War Records
> National Archives
> 700 Pennsylvania Avenue, NW
> Washington, DC 20408-0001
> 202-357-5400
> www.archives.gov/research/military/civil-war/index.html

Confederate Pension Records.
National Archives
700 Pennsylvania Avenue, NW
Washington, DC 20408-0001
202-357-5400
www.archives.gov/research/military/civil-war-
  genealogy-esources/confederate/pension.html
(see list for state locations)

Military Service Records, a Select Catalog of NARA Microfilm Publications
Obtaining copies of records:
700 Pennsylvania Avenue, NW
Washington, DC 20408-0001
202-357-5400
www.archives.gov/publications/microfilm-catalogs
  .html
(catalogs of other research areas as well)

State-Level Lists of Casualities from the Korean War (1951-1957) and Vietnam Conflict (1956-)
Reference Services
Electronic and Special Media Records Services
  Division (NWME)
8601 Adelphi Road
College Park, MD 20740-6001
(301) 837-0470
cer@nara.gov
www.archives.gov/research/military/vietnam-
  war/casualty-lists/index.html

Native Americans

American Indians: A Select Catalog of NARA Microfilm Publications.
The National Archives and Records Administration
700 Pennsylvania Avenue, NW
Washington, DC 20408-0001
202-357-5400
8601 Adelphi Road (mail)
College Park, MD 207-6001
1-866-272-6272
301-837-0483
www.archives.gov/research/alic/reference/native-
  americans.html

Naturalization Records

>The National Archives and Records Administration
>700 Pennsylvania Avenue, NW
>Washington, DC 20408-0001
>202-357-5400
>www.archives.gov/research/naturalization/index.html

>The Reunion Network
>5688 Washington Street
>Hollywood, FL 33023
>800-225-5044
>954-983-7077
>Fax: 954-983-7078
>info@reunionfriendly.com
>Reunionfriendly.com

>Social Security Administration
>OEO FOIA Workgroup
>300 North Green Street
>PO Box 33022
>Baltimore, MD 21290-3022
>800-772-1213
>TTY: 800-325-0778
>www.ssa.gov/foia/html/foia_guide.htm

Genealogical Services:

>Association of Professional Genealogists
>Kathleen Hinckley, Exec. Dir.
>PO Box 350998
>Westminster, CO 80035-0998
>303-465-6980
>Fax: 303-456-8825
>admin@apg.org
>www.apgen.org

>Board for Certification of Genealogists
>P O Box 14291
>Washington, DC 20044
>office@bcgcertification.org
>www.bcgcertification.org

Leo Baeck Institute
15 West 16th Street
New York, NY 10011
212-744-6400
Fax: 212-988-1305
lbaeck@lbi.cjh.org
www.lbi.org

YIVO Institute for Jewish Research
Center for Jewish History
15 West 16th Street
New York, NY 10011
212-246-6080
Fax: 212-292-1892
yivomail@yivo.cjh.org
www.yivoinstitute.org

Form Services:

Bailey's Free Genealogy Forms
www.cs.williams.edu/~bailey/genealogy

Family Tree Magazine
www.familytreemagazine.com/info/basicforms

Archives & Genealogy Listservs:

Adoption GEN
Send message to:
ADOPTION-GEN-L-request@rootsweb.com

With message: Subscribe

Archives Listserv –
Archives@forums.archivists.org

Visit: www.archivsts.org/listservs/arch_listserv_terms.asp

Login via your SAA profile if you don't already have a profile, click on the link "Find/Create a SAA Profile"

City Directory Listserv -
    Send message to:
        CITY-DIRECTORIES-L-request@rootsweb.com

    With message: Subscribe

Oral History Listserv -
        H-ORALHIST@H-NET.MSU.EDU

    Visit: www.h-net.org/~oralhist

Vintage Photos -
    RootsWeb send message to:
        VINTAGE-PHOTOS-L-request@rootsweb.com

    With message: Subscribe

Writing Life Stories and Family History -
    RootsWeb send message to:
        WRITING-LIFESTORIES-AND-FAMILY-HISTORY-L-request@rootsweb.com

    With message: Subscribe

There are many other listservs available by simply going to www.rootsweb.com and clicking on "Mailing Lists" and then typing in your keyword in the search box.

*web sites are frequently changed, if you can't get in with a given URL, try searching for the site through a search engine such as Google.

ABOUT THE AUTHOR

MARY FLEKKE recently retired from her job as a Senior Instructional Services Librarian at Florida Southern College in Lakeland, Florida. In addition to her work in Reference and Bibliographic Instruction at the college, Mary developed an interest in oral history and family research. In 1995, she was appointed Archivist of the Florida-Bahamas Synod of the Evangelical Lutheran Church in America and as part of this position has done several lectures on oral history and genealogy for the Congregational Heritage Workshop at Lutheran Theological Southern Seminary and for the Florida-Bahamas Synod Assembly and other groups in Lakeland, as well as for the Association of Christian Librarians.

Mary is a member of multiple professional and community organizations in which she has served in a variety of offices. These include the Florida Library Association, the former Polk County Library Association, the Society of Florida Archivists, a Trustee of the Board of the James R. Crumley, Jr. Archives of Region 9, ELCA, Thrivent Financial for Lutherans Chapter Board, the Lakeland Choral Society, and is an active member of Grace Evangelical Lutheran in Lakeland — serving as Congregational President, Bell Choir Director and a member of the Praise Band. Mary is also an avid photographer.

Mary is author of *Grace Evangelical Lutheran Church History, 1909–2009: Incorporating Previous Church Histories*, these by B. P. Reinsch and Elizabeth Eicher; co-author of two books, *Lakeland* and *Cypress Gardens*; and has chapters in *Survival Handbook for the New Chemistry Instructor* ed. by Diane M. Bunce and Cinzia M. Muzzi; and *Lake Hollingsworth: Reflections and Studies on a Florida Landmark* (also photographs) ed. by John R. Haldeman and Bernard W. Quetchenbach. She also had an article on oral history in *The Christian Librarian*, an article on the reading habits of children in *Church and Synagogue Libraries* and a H-Net book review. She is currently working on a couple of other writing projects.

www.ingramcontent.com/pod-product-compliance
Lightning Source LLC
Chambersburg PA
CBHW060909300426
44112CB00011B/1398